LINUX
IN A
WINDOWS
WORLD

Roderick W. Smith

O'REILLY®

Beijing · Cambridge · Farnham · Köln · Paris · Sebastopol · Taipei · Tokyo

Linux in a Windows World
by Roderick W. Smith

Copyright © 2005 O'Reilly Media, Inc. All rights reserved.
Printed in the United States of America.

Published by O'Reilly Media, Inc., 1005 Gravenstein Highway North, Sebastopol, CA 95472.

O'Reilly books may be purchased for educational, business, or sales promotional use. Online editions are also available for most titles (*safari.oreilly.com*). For more information, contact our corporate/institutional sales department: (800) 998-9938 or *corporate@oreilly.com*.

Editor:	David Brickner
Production Editor:	Mary Anne Weeks Mayo
Cover Designer:	Emma Colby
Interior Designer:	David Futato

Printing History:

February 2005:	First Edition.

RepKover™ This book uses RepKover™, a durable and flexible lay-flat binding.

ISBN: 0-596-00758-2
[M]

QA76.76
.B63S58
2005

copy 1

This book is for Theo.
May his Apatosaurs, Dilophosaurs, and
Gigantosaurs forever be his friends.

Table of Contents

Preface

Hardly a day goes by when Linux doesn't make the news. Judging by the buzz, you might think that Linux is poised for world domination—the stated goal for Linux in a now-famous quip by its creator, Linus Torvalds. In truth, Linux still faces numerous challenges before it can dominate the computing world, much less the world at large. One of these challenges is the huge installed base of Microsoft Windows systems. As a practical matter, Linux must coexist with these systems. Indeed, the challenge of coexisting with Windows can be viewed as an opportunity: Linux can be integrated into a Windows network, providing a reliable and low-cost platform on which to run vital services for Windows systems, or even serving as a workstation on an otherwise Windows-dominated network.

This book is dedicated to describing this opportunity for Linux. If you're reading this Preface, chances are you work with a Windows-dominated network but know something about Linux and wonder how you can best use Linux to improve your Windows network. In broad strokes, you can replace Windows servers, supplement Windows servers with Linux servers, use Linux to implement new services you don't currently run, deploy Linux-based thin clients, or migrate some or all of your Windows desktop systems to Linux. This book provides guidance about how to accomplish these tasks, with an emphasis on Linux in the role of network server operating system (OS).

This book will help you reduce costs and improve reliability by describing how several common Linux programs and protocols—Samba, OpenLDAP, VNC, BIND, and so on—can be integrated into a Windows network. This book provides enough information to get any of these programs up and running, provided you've already got a working Linux system. Of course, a book of this size can't cover every detail; if you need to do very complex things, you'll need to consult other books or documentation. The relevant chapters provide pointers.

Audience

I've written this book with an administrator of a Windows network in mind, but with the assumption that you know the basics of Linux system administration. You might be uncertain of the details as to where Linux might fit into your network or how to get started configuring particular Linux server programs. That's where this book can help: it introduces the most cost-effective ways to add Linux to your network and describes the basics of how to get started configuring specific servers.

If you're not already familiar with basic Linux system administration, you should consult a book on the topic, such as *Running Linux* (O'Reilly) or *Linux System Administration* (Sybex). Such books will help you with tasks ranging from installing Linux to recompiling your kernel.

You should be familiar with networking basics. Although I sometimes provide brief overviews of important prerequisite knowledge, this book doesn't dwell on the details of the TCP/IP stack or how best to lay out a network. Likewise, knowledge of your own network is vital; you shouldn't start adding servers to a network you don't understand. Perhaps you have little idea of how you want to deploy Linux, or perhaps you've got specific plans. If the former, reading the first couple of chapters of this book will give you a better idea of how Linux can be used. If you have well-formed plans, you can skip ahead to more relevant chapters, although reading the first couple of chapters may help you verify (or *not* verify) that your plans are reasonable.

Contents of This Book

This book is organized in five parts, plus two appendixes. If you want a good general grounding in how Linux can be deployed on a network, you can read this book cover to cover; however, most chapters are self-contained enough to be useful on their own. There are a few exceptions to this rule, though. As already noted, if you're not sure how to deploy Linux, you should read Part I for some basic tips. Chapter 4 (on Samba share definitions) depends on Chapter 3, so you should probably read those two sequentially. Likewise, the remaining chapters in Part II depend on Chapter 3. If you intend to use a remote authentication database from Linux rather than deploy Linux solely as the repository for such a database, you should read Appendix A with any of the chapters of Part III. Kerberos depends on all the systems having matching clocks, so you should read the NTP section of Chapter 15 in conjunction with Chapter 9. Some backup strategies described in Chapter 14 depend on Samba information, particularly as described in Chapters 3 and 4. These interdependencies are pointed out in the chapters themselves.

Part I, *Linux's Place in a Windows Network*
> This part of the book provides an overview of how Linux can be used to improve an otherwise Windows-dominated network. It consists of two chapters that

describe Linux's features and provide an overview of strategies for deploying Linux. This material is targeted at readers who have the least experience with Linux or who aren't sure precisely how Linux can help them.

Part II, *Sharing Files and Printers*

This part of the book describes Samba, a file- and printer-sharing server package that is arguably the most important Windows integration tool available for Linux. Samba implements the Server Message Block/Common Internet File System protocol, which has long been the backbone of file and printer sharing in the Windows world. A Linux system running the Samba suite can fit right in, delivering files or making printers accessible to Windows systems. This part's four chapters describe basic Samba configuration, creating file and printer shares, using Samba as a domain controller, and using Linux's SMB/CIFS client features.

Part III, *Centralized Authentication Tools*

Many networks employ centralized authentication tools that enable you to maintain a single account database for all the clients and servers on your network. If you wish to use Linux on a network that already runs such a system, you should know how to get Linux working with it. You can also use Linux to manage accounts for Windows systems. This part of the book describes three such systems: Windows NT domains, the Lightweight Directory Access Protocol, and Kerberos.

Part IV, *Remote Login Tools*

One of Linux's strengths has always been its support for remote login protocols—the ability to use Linux from remote locations. This support is handy both for system administration (simplifying your life should a server need support while you're not physically present) and for regular users who remotely access Linux or wish to use Linux to remotely access other systems. This part of the book includes three chapters that describe text-mode remote access protocols, GUI remote-access protocols, and use of Linux in a thin-client configuration (that is, using a minimal OS on a simple computer to run programs on a more powerful central login computer).

Part V, *Additional Server Programs*

This part of the book describes several miscellaneous server programs. Chapter 13 describes mail server programs that enable Linux to function as a network's primary mail server or as a supplementary system to filter mail or retrieve mail from outside sites and forward it to another computer. Chapter 14 describes network backups. Linux can be a good platform for this task because its backup software packages are inexpensive (most are free), and some of Linux's other tools (such as Samba) provide several opportunities for backing up Windows systems. Chapter 15 describes three other protocols and their servers: the Dynamic Host Configuration Protocol for remotely configuring client computer's network stacks, the Domain Name System for managing hostname-to-IP-address mappings, and the Network Time Protocol for keeping clocks synchronized.

Appendixes

Two appendixes describe some additional miscellaneous topics. Appendix A covers the Pluggable Authentication Module approach to Linux authentication. Knowing how to modify a PAM configuration is vital if Linux is to coexist with a network's centralized authentication tools, as covered in Part III of the book. Appendix B covers the basics of deploying Linux on the desktop. If you decide to replace Windows desktop systems with Linux systems, Appendix B provides help to get this job done.

Conventions Used in This Book

The following typographical conventions are used in this book:

Plain text
Indicates menu titles, menu options, menu buttons, and keyboard accelerators (such as Alt and Ctrl).

Italic
Indicates new terms, URLs, email addresses, filenames, file extensions, pathnames, directories, and Unix utilities.

`Constant width`
Indicates commands, options, switches, variables, attributes, keys, functions, types, classes, namespaces, methods, modules, properties, parameters, values, objects, macros, the contents of files, or the output from commands.

`Constant width bold`
Indicates commands or other text that should be typed literally by the user.

`Constant width italic`
Indicates text that should be replaced with user-supplied values.

 This icon signifies a tip, suggestion, or general note.

 This icon indicates a warning or caution.

Using Code Examples

This book is here to help you get your job done. In general, you may use the code in this book in your programs and documentation. You don't need to contact us for permission unless you're reproducing a significant portion of the code. For example, writing a program that uses several chunks of code from this book does not require permission. Selling or distributing a CD-ROM of examples from O'Reilly books does require permission. Answering a question by citing this book and quoting example code does not require permission. Incorporating a significant amount of example code from this book into your product's documentation does require permission.

We appreciate, but do not require, attribution. An attribution usually includes the title, author, publisher, and ISBN. For example: *"Linux in a Windows World* by Roderick W. Smith. Copyright 2005 O'Reilly Media, Inc., 0-596-00758-2."

If you feel your use of code examples falls outside fair use or the permission given above, feel free to contact us at *permissions@oreilly.com*.

Comments and Questions

Please address comments and questions concerning this book to the publisher:

O'Reilly Media, Inc.
1005 Gravenstein Highway North
Sebastopol, CA 95472
(800) 998-9938 (in the United States or Canada)
(707) 829-0515 (international or local)
(707) 829-0104 (fax)

There's a web page for this book that lists errata, examples, and any additional information. You can access this page at:

http://www.oreilly.com/catalog/linuxwinworld

To comment or ask technical questions about this book, send email to:

bookquestions@oreilly.com

For more information about books, conferences, Resource Centers, and the O'Reilly Network, see the O'Reilly web site at:

http://www.oreilly.com

Safari Enabled

 When you see a Safari® Enabled icon on the cover of your favorite technology book, it means the book is available online through the O'Reilly Network Safari Bookshelf.

Safari offers a solution that's better than e-books. It's a virtual library that lets you easily search thousands of top tech books, cut and paste code samples, download chapters, and find quick answers when you need the most accurate, current information. Try it for free at *http://safari.oreilly.com*.

Acknowledgments

Published books aren't the creation of just one person; they're collaborative efforts, although the person identified as the author is the most visible of this team. For this book, I'd like to thank O'Reilly editors Andy Oram, who got the ball rolling, and David Brickner, who saw the project through to the end. Technical reviewers for this book were Gerald Carter, Steve Suehring, Alan Schwartz, and Curtis Preston; these people kept me from making technical blunders—but if any remain, they're my own. Mary Anne Weeks Mayo provided copy editing, to keep my prose not just technically accurate, but readable. The book's proofreader, Marlowe Shaeffer, guarded against typos and similar problems. Finally, I'd like to thank Neil Salkind and others at Studio-B, who helped get things started and provided the occasional necessary prod to keep them moving.

## PART I

Linux's Place in a Windows Network

The fact that you're reading this book suggests that you want to use Linux on a Windows-dominated network. Most of this book is devoted to specific ways in which you can accomplish this goal—configuring a Samba server, using a Linux backup server, or migrating desktop systems to Linux, for instance. To begin, though, this book provides some context. Chapter 1 covers Linux's features—where you can use it in a network, what types of hardware and software you need, and how it compares to Windows. Chapter 2 continues this examination by looking at some broad strategies you can adopt when introducing Linux on an existing Windows network.

Linux's Features

Linux can be an effective addition to a Windows network for several reasons, most of which boil down to cost. Windows has achieved dominance, in part, by being less expensive than competitors from the 1990s, but today Linux can be less expensive to own and operate. This is particularly true if you're running Windows NT 4.0, which has reached end-of-life and is no longer supported. (Windows 2000 will soon fall into this category, as well.) For these old versions of Windows, you're faced with the prospect of paying to upgrade to a newer version of Windows or switch to another operating system. Linux can be that other OS, but you should know something about Linux's features and capabilities before you deploy it.

Effectively deploying Linux requires understanding the OS's capabilities and where it makes the most sense to use. This chapter begins with a look at the Linux roles that this book describes in subsequent chapters. The bulk of this chapter is devoted to an overview of Linux's capabilities and requirements when used as a server or as a desktop system. Because you may be considering replacing Windows systems with Linux, this chapter concludes with a comparison of Linux to Windows in these two roles.

Where Linux Fits in a Network

Most operating systems—and Linux is no exception to this rule— can be used in a variety of ways. You can run Linux (or Windows, or Mac OS, or most other common general-purposes OSs) on personal productivity desktop systems, on mail server computers, on routers, and so on. This book doesn't cover every possible use of Linux; instead, it focuses on how Linux interacts with Windows systems on a local area network (LAN) or how Linux can take over traditional Windows duties. This book will further focus on areas in which you can get the most "bang for the buck" by deploying Linux, either in addition to or instead of Windows systems. Chapter 2 covers Linux deployment strategies in greater detail, but, for now, consider Figure 1-1, which depicts a typical office network. Linux's mascot is a penguin (known as *Tux*), so Figure 1-1 uses penguin images to mark the areas of Linux deployment covered in this book.

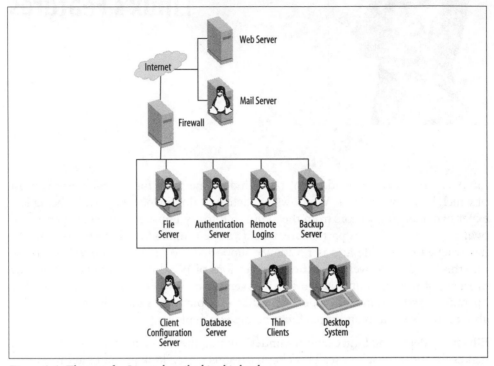

Figure 1-1. The uses for Linux described in this book

Of course, Linux can be used in roles not shown in Figure 1-1. In fact, Linux can be an excellent choice for an OS for such roles as a web server; however, because such uses aren't LAN-centric or don't tie closely to Windows, this book doesn't cover them. You might want to begin with just one or two functions for Linux on your network, such as a file server or a Dynamic Host Configuration Protocol (DHCP) server. Some systems, such as backend database servers, may be so vital and data-intensive that replacing them with Linux systems, although possible, is a major undertaking that can't be adequately covered here.

Linux as a Server

Traditionally, Linux's strength has been as a server OS. Many businesses rely upon Linux to handle email, share files and printers, assign IP addresses, and so on. Linux provides a plethora of open source programs to handle each of these server tasks, and many more. Before you attempt to deploy a Linux server, though, you should understand Linux's strengths and weaknesses in this role, what type of hardware you're likely to need, and what types of software you'll need.

Linux Server Capabilities

As seen in Figure 1-1, Linux can be deployed in many different ways. Indeed, Figure 1-1 presents an incomplete picture because it focuses on only those roles described in this book. Linux firewalls, web servers, databases, and more are all available. Still, Linux has certain strengths and weaknesses as a server that you should understand as you plan where to use it. Linux's greatest strengths as a server include the following:

Reliability

Linux has earned a reputation as a very reliable OS, which, of course, is a critically important characteristic for servers.

Cost

You can download Linux from the Internet at no cost (aside from connect charges), which can be important in keeping costs down. Of course, the up-front purchase price (or lack of it) is only part of the equation; support costs, hardware costs, and other factors can be much more important. Linux's total cost of ownership (TCO) is a matter of some debate, but most studies give Linux high marks in this area.

License issues

The Linux kernel is licensed under the GNU General Public License (GPL), and much of the rest of Linux uses the same license. Most other Linux programs use other open source licenses. The result is that you're not bound by restrictive commercial license terms; as a user or administrator, you can do anything with Linux that you can do with a commercial OS, and then some. If you want to redistribute *changes* to a program, though, some open source licenses impose restrictions, so you should check the license to see how you're permitted to distribute the changes. (Of course, most commercial OSs don't even let you *see* the source code!)

Security issues

Linux isn't vulnerable to the worms and viruses that plague the Internet today; almost all of these pests target Windows systems. Of course, a Linux server can still be inconvenienced by worms and viruses because it may need to process them in some way; a Linux mail server may still need to accept email with worms and perhaps then identify and delete the worm. Linux won't be infected by the worm, though—at least, not by any worm that's known to be spreading as I write.

Server software selection

As a Unix-like OS, Linux has inherited many popular Unix servers, such as sendmail and Samba. In fact, some of these, including Samba, were written using Linux as a primary target OS.

Remote administration

Linux provides several remote administration methods, ranging from remote logins using text-mode tools such as Secure Shell (SSH) or Telnet to tools designed for remote administration via web browsers, such as Webmin (*http://www.webmin.com*). Of course, remote administration isn't unique to Linux, but Linux presents more options than do most non-Unix OSs.

Resource use

With Linux, you have fine control over what programs you run, which enables you to trim a system of unnecessary items to help get the most out of your hardware. For instance, most servers don't need to run a local GUI, so Linux enables you to run a system without one, and even to omit the X files and programs from the hard disk.

Customization

In addition to customizing the system to minimize resource use, you can modify Linux to achieve other ends. For instance, you can recompile the kernel to add or omit features that help the system operate as a router, or you can alter the startup sequence to accommodate special needs. Taken to the extreme, these features help those who run Linux on specialized embedded devices, but such uses are well beyond the scope of this book.

Hardware flexibility

Linux is available on a variety of hardware, ranging from specialized embedded versions of Linux to supercomputers. This book is designed to help those running Linux on fairly traditional small- to mid-sized servers and desktop systems using conventional Intel Architecture 32 (IA-32; a.k.a. x86) hardware or other hardware of comparable power. Even in this realm, Linux is very flexible; you can run it on AMD64, PowerPC (PPC), Alpha, and other CPUs, which lets you standardize your OS even if you happen to have different hardware platforms.

 Most of these advantages are advantages of Unix-like OSs generally, and so apply to other OSs, such as Solaris and FreeBSD. Compared to such OSs, Linux's greatest strengths are its hardware flexibility, open source licensing, and low cost (although several other low-cost and open-source Unix-like OSs exist).

Of course, no good thing is without its problems, and Linux is no exception to this rule. Fortunately, Linux's problems are minor, particularly when the OS is used on a server:

Administrative expertise requirements

Linux requires more in the way of administrative expertise than do some alternatives. For most organizations, this factor ultimately boils down to one of the variables in TCO calculations: Linux administrators are likely to demand higher salaries than Windows administrators do. On the other hand, Linux's reliability, scalability, and other factors frequently more than compensate for this problem in the TCO equation.

Security issues

Although immunity to infection by common Windows worms and viruses is a Linux advantage, Linux has its own security drawbacks. *Crackers* frequently attempt to break into Linux servers, and they sometimes succeed. In theory, this should be difficult to do with a well-administered system, but neglecting a single package upgrade or making some other minor mistake can leave you vulnerable. Of course, Linux isn't alone in this drawback, but it's one to which you should be alert at all times.

 The term *hacker* is used by the popular media to refer to computer miscreants—those who break into computers and otherwise wreak havoc. This term has an older and honorable meaning as referring to skilled and enthusiastic computer experts, and particularly programmers. Many of the people who wrote the Linux kernel and the software that runs on it consider themselves hackers in this positive sense. For this reason, I use an alternative term, *cracker*, to refer to computer criminals.

Overall, Linux's strengths as a server far outweigh its weaknesses. The OS's robustness and the number of server programs it runs are powerful arguments in its favor. Indeed, those are the reasons commercial Unix variants have traditionally run many important network services. Linux has been slowly eroding the commercial Unix market share, and its advantages can help you fill the gaps in a Windows-dominated network or even replace existing Windows servers.

Typical Linux Server Hardware

As noted earlier, one of Linux's strengths is that it runs on a very wide range of hardware. Of course, this isn't to say that you can use any hardware for any particular role; Linux won't turn a 10-year-old 80486 system with a 1-GB hard disk into a powerhouse capable of delivering files to thousands of users.

Linux most commonly runs on IA-32 hardware, and much Linux documentation, including this book, frequently presents IA-32 examples. IA-32 hardware is inexpensive, and it's the original and best-supported hardware platform for Linux. Still, other options are available, and some of these are well worth considering for a Linux server.

One of the problems with IA-32 is that it's a 32-bit platform. Among other things, this means that IA-32 CPUs are limited to addressing 2^{32} bytes, or 4 GB, of RAM. (Intel Xeon processors provide a workaround that involves *page swapping*, or hiding parts of memory to keep the total available to the CPU at just 4 GB.) Although a 4-GB memory limit isn't a serious problem for many purposes, some high-powered servers—particularly those that support many user logins—need more RAM. For them, using a 64-bit CPU is desirable. Such CPUs can address 2^{64}, or 1.8×10^{19}, bytes of RAM, at least in theory. (In practice, many impose lower limits at the moment, but those limits are still usually in the terabyte range.

Several 64-bit CPUs are available, including the DEC (now Compaq) Alpha, several AMD and Intel CPUs that use the AMD64 architecture, Intel's IA-64 Itanium, the IBM Power64 (the first of which is the PowerPC G5), and the SPARC-64. Of these, the Power64 and AMD64 platforms are likely to become more common in the next few years. With AMD and Intel both producing AMD64 CPUs, they are likely to take over the market dominated by IA-32 CPUs through most of the 1990s and early 2000s. Apple is rapidly shifting its Macintosh line to the Power64, and IBM and a few others are producing Power64-based servers. Of course, if you already have another type of 64-bit system, or you have an opportunity to get one at a good price, you can run Linux on it quite well. Linux support for the AMD64 and Power64 platforms is likely to be more mature than for other 64-bit platforms, though.

Of course, not all servers need 64-bit CPUs. For them, IA-32 CPUs, such as Intel's Pentium 4 or AMD's Athlon, are perfectly adequate. In fact, many systems can make do with much weaker CPUs. A DHCP server can run quite well on an old 80386, for instance. Just how much CPU power you need depends on the function of the server. Functions such as handling thin-client or other remote logins, converting PostScript into non-PostScript printer formats (particularly for multiple heavily used printers), and handling hundreds or thousands of clients, are likely to require lots of CPU power. Lighter duties, such as running a DHCP server, a local Domain Name System (DNS) server, or even a remote login server for a network with a dozen or so computers, requires much less in the way of CPU power. For such purposes, you can probably run Linux on a spare or retired computer. Even a system that's too weak to run a modern version of Windows can make a good small server.

Disk space requirements also vary with the server's intended role. Most obviously, a file server is likely to require lots of disk space. Precisely what "lots" is, though, depends on how many users you have and what types of files they store. Disk-intensive servers frequently use Small Computer Systems Interface (SCSI) hard disks rather than Advanced Technology Attachment (ATA) disks, because SCSI disks scale better in multidisk setups and because disk manufacturers often offer higher-performance disks in SCSI form only. SCSI disks cost more than do ATA disks, though. You'll have to judge for yourself whether your budget permits the use of SCSI disks. Recently, Serial ATA (SATA) disks have started to emerge as an alternative to traditional parallel ATA disks and SCSI. Depending on the drivers, SATA disks may *appear* to be SCSI disks in Linux, but they aren't.

Although servers can vary greatly in their major hardware components and needs, network connectivity is a common factor. All servers require good network links. On a LAN, this most commonly means 100- or 1000-Mbps (1-Gbps, or gigabit)

Ethernet. Linux ships with excellent Ethernet support; chances are any Ethernet adapter will work. Modern motherboards frequently come with built-in Ethernet, too. Of course, not all Ethernet adapters are created equal: some are more stable, produce better throughput, or consume less CPU time. As a general rule, Ethernet adapters from major manufacturers, such as Intel, 3Com, and Linksys, are likely to perform best. No-name bargain-basement Ethernet cards will almost certainly work, but they may give more problems or perform less well under heavy network loads.

Most servers have similar video display capabilities. In this case, though, servers' needs are unusually light; because a server's primary duty is to deliver data over a network, a high-end graphics card is not a requirement. You might want something that's at least minimally supported by Linux (or by a Linux X server, to be precise) so you can administer the computer at the console using GUI administration tools; however, this isn't a requirement.

Typical Linux Server Software

When deciding how to deploy Linux on a LAN, you must consider what hardware and software to use. Linux isn't a monolithic beast you can decide to install and be done with; you must make choices about your Linux installation. These choices begin with your decision about a Linux *distribution*—a collection of software and configuration files that's bundled together with an installation program. Some distributions are better suited than others to use on a server, although with enough extra effort, you can use just about any Linux distribution on a server computer. Beyond the distribution, you must pick individual server programs. These choices are very specific for the purpose of the computer. For instance, if you run a mail server computer, you need to decide which mail server program to run, and this decision can have important consequences for everything else you do on the computer. Such a decision is likely to be relatively unimportant on other types of server computers.

 The term *server* can have multiple meanings; it can refer to either an individual program that delivers network services or to the computer on which that program runs. (A similar dual meaning applies to the word *client* on the other end of the connection.) In most cases, the meaning is obvious from the context, but when necessary, I clarify by explicitly specifying a server computer or program. Some people use the term *service* to refer to server programs or to the features that they provide.

Picking a distribution for server use

Your choice of distribution depends partly on your choice of hardware platform. Some distributions, such as Debian GNU/Linux, are available on a wide range of CPU architectures, whereas others, such as Slackware Linux, are available for just one CPU. If you're already familiar with a distribution, and you want to use it for your server, you may want to plan your hardware purchases around this fact. If you already have the hardware, though, or if you're constrained to use a particular platform for policy or budget reasons, you may need to narrow the range of your hardware choices. Broadly speaking, the IA-32 platform has the most choices for distributions, although a few distributions run only on other platforms. The most popular Linux distributions used on servers include the following:

CentOS

> This distribution, headquartered at *http://freshmeat.net/projects/centos/*, is a community-based fork of Red Hat's Enterprise Linux. As such, it's technically very similar to Red Hat, but support details are quite different.

Debian

> This distribution is one of the few completely noncommercial distributions; it's maintained entirely by volunteers. It uses the Debian package format and is well-respected for its stable main ("stable") branch. This branch is on a very long release cycle, though, so it sometimes lags when major new versions of component packages are released. (Bug-fix and security updates are prompt, however.) Debian's "unstable" branch is much more up to date, but it's not as well-tested as the reliable main "stable" branch. Keeping up to date is fairly simple because of Debian's Advanced Package Tools (APT) package, which enables software updates over the Internet by typing a couple of commands. Because Debian doesn't sell official packages with support, obtaining outside support requires you to hire an independent consultant. To configure Debian, you normally edit text-mode configuration files in a text editor rather than use a GUI configuration tool. Overall, Debian is a good choice for servers, which usually must be stable above all else. Debian is available for an unusually wide range of CPUs, including IA-32, SPARC, PowerPC, Alpha, IA-64, and several other platforms. To learn more, check Debian's web site, *http://www.debian.org*.

Fedora Core

> This distribution is the freely redistributable version of Red Hat. Its development cycle is faster than that of the official Red Hat releases, and part of Fedora's purpose is to serve as a test bed for new packages that will eventually work their way into Red Hat. Fedora can be a good choice if you like Red Hat, don't have a lot of money to spend on a commercial distribution, and don't mind doing without the official Red Hat support. Fedora Core is available for IA-32 and AMD64 CPUs; you can find it at *http://fedora.redhat.com*.

Gentoo

> Like Debian, Gentoo is maintained by volunteers. This distribution emphasizes building packages from source code; its package manager, known as *portage*, enables you to type a one-line command that downloads the source code and patches, compiles the software, and installs it. (This system is similar to the *ports* system of FreeBSD.) Portage can be a good way to tweak compiler settings for your CPU, installed libraries, and so on, but the time spent compiling packages

can be a drawback. Also, if you maintain many systems with differing hardware, you may have trouble cloning a system, because the optimizations used on your original system may not work on other systems. One advantage of Gentoo is that it's easy to keep up to date with the latest packages, but you can make your system unstable if the latest version of an important package breaks other programs. Like Debian, Gentoo eschews GUI configuration tools in favor of raw text-mode configuration file editing. Gentoo is available for IA-32, AMD64, SPARC, and PowerPC CPUs. You can learn more at *http://www.gentoo.org*.

Red Hat

Red Hat is probably the most popular distribution in North America, particularly if you include its Fedora variant. This distribution originated the RPM Package Manager (RPM) package format. Even many programs that don't ship with Red Hat are available in IA-32 and source RPM packages, which makes software installation easy. Many third-party programs are released with Red Hat in mind, making Red Hat a safe bet for running such programs. With the release of Fedora 1, Red Hat has been focused its main product line (Red Hat Enterprise) on the business market, especially servers, although it can certainly be used on desktops. The main selling point of Red Hat Enterprise is its support, including system updates and maintenance via the Red Hat Network. These include GUI update tools that can grab updates over the Internet. Red Hat ships with a number of Red Hat-specific GUI configuration tools, but they're often limited enough that you'll need to bypass them and edit configuration files by hand. IA-32 is the primary Red Hat platform, although some versions are available for AMD64, Itanium, and certain IBM servers. Some older versions ran on SPARC and Alpha CPUs, but these versions are very outdated. The official Red Hat web site is *http://www.redhat.com*.

Slackware

Slackware is the oldest of the common Linux distributions. It uses tarballs as its package distribution format and eschews GUI configuration tools. Slackware ships with fewer packages than most Linux distributions; to install more exotic programs, you may need to compile them from source. Slackware may be a good choice if you're used to "old-style" Unix system administration, but if you're relatively new to Linux, you may want to pick something else. Slackware is available only on the IA-32 platform. You can learn more at *http://www.slackware.com*.

SuSE

This distribution is RPM-based but isn't derived from Red Hat directly. It's a good choice for both server and desktop use, and it includes a GUI administration tool called *YaST*. You can update packages over the Internet with this tool, as well as administer the local system. SuSE is primarily an IA-32 and AMD64 distribution, although an older PowerPC release is also available. Check *http://www.suse.com* for more information. SuSE was originally an independent German company, but it was purchased by Novell in early 2004.

Ultimately, any of these distributions (or various other less popular ones) can be configured to work equally well, assuming you're using IA-32 hardware. You may be better able to get along with a particular distribution depending on your system administration style and particular needs, though. If you like to tweak your system to get the very best possible performance, Gentoo's local-build approach may be appealing. If you like GUI configuration tools for handling the simple tasks, Red Hat or SuSE should work well. For an extremely stable system, Debian is hard to beat. If your hardware is old, consider Debian or Slackware, which tend to install less extraneous software than the others. If you want to use the most popular distribution, look at Red Hat. If the package management tool is important, pick a distribution that uses the tool you like.

Although the Linux kernel and most Linux tools are open source, some distributions include small amounts of proprietary software. This inclusion makes redistribution of the OS illegal. For this reason, you should check license terms before doing so or before installing it on many systems. Most distributions are freely redistributable, although most of them are available for sale. Buying a full package helps provide financial support to the distributions, which helps to advance future development. (Debian and Gentoo are exceptions; no commercial packages of these distributions are available, although you can buy them on cut-rate CDs that provide little or no profit to the actual developers. CentOS and Fedora have no for-sale versions, either, unless you count Red Hat in that role.)

Distribution choice is a highly personal matter. What works well for one administrator may be a poor choice for another. You may also run into policy issues at your workplace; for instance, you may need to buy a package from a vendor that offers certain support terms, which might rule out some distributions. If you haven't used Linux extensively in the past, you should study the options, focusing on distributions that provide GUI configuration tools you can use to get the basics up and running quickly. For more experienced administrators, I recommend whatever you've used in the past, provided you found it satisfactory. If you've used other Unix-like OSs but not Linux, try to find a Linux distribution with an administrative style similar to what you've used before. You should also try to minimize the number of Linux distributions you use, ideally to just one; this helps simplify system administration because you'll have just one set of distribution-specific tools and packages to learn, and you can retrieve package updates from just one source.

Picking individual server programs

Once you've picked and installed a Linux distribution, you'll need to decide what server programs to use. For most major server classes, most distributions provide a single default choice, such as the sendmail mail server. It's usually easiest to stick with the default, but if the server in question is the primary function of the computer, and if the default choice isn't what you'd like to use, you can change it.

Sometimes the alternative programs work with the same protocol as the default; for instance, the Postfix, Exim, and qmail servers are all popular alternatives to sendmail. All are implementations of the Simple Mail Transfer Protocol (SMTP), and you can replace one package with another without changing the server computer's interactions with other computers. (You usually need to implement minor or major changes to the server system's local configuration, though, and perhaps replace some support programs.) Other protocols for which multiple server program implementations are available in Linux include pull email using the Post Office Protocol (POP) or Internet Message Access Protocol (IMAP), the File Transfer Protocol (FTP), Hypertext Transfer Protocol (HTTP; a.k.a. web server protocol), the Kerberos authentication protocol, the Remote Frame Buffer (RFB) remote GUI login protocol, and the DNS protocol. This book covers many, but not all, of these protocols. In some cases, alternative servers are configured in similar ways, but sometimes configuration is very different for the various server programs.

Other times, you may need to choose between two incompatible protocols that accomplish similar tasks. For instance, POP and IMAP are two different ways to deliver email received by an SMTP server to client systems (that is, users running mail programs such as Outlook Express or KMail). Other examples include RFB and X11R6 for remote GUI access; Telnet and SSH for remote text-mode access; the Server Message Block/Common Internet File System (SMB/CIFS), Network File System (NFS), and AppleShare for remote file-sharing protocols; SMB/CIFS, AppleShare, Line Printer Daemon (LPD), and Common Unix Printing System (CUPS) for printer sharing; SSH and FTP for remote file transfers; and NetBIOS domain logins, Lightweight Directory Access Protocol (LDAP), Kerberos, and Network Information Services (NIS) for remote authentication. In all these cases, the competing protocols have their own advantages and disadvantages. For instance, SSH provides encryption whereas FTP and Telnet do not. Some protocols are closely associated with particular OSs; for instance, SMB/CIFS and NetBIOS most commonly are used on Windows-dominated networks, whereas NFS is used in Unix-to-Unix file sharing and AppleShare is used most often with Mac OS systems. This book covers many of these protocols, but it focuses on those that are used most commonly on Windows-dominated networks, or at least that have potential to enhance such networks.

Chapter 2 describes in greater detail when you're likely to deploy each server covered in this book, and subsequent chapters describe the protocols and servers themselves.

Linux on the Desktop

Although it's only one system in Figure 1-1 (or two, if you count the thin client), Linux use as a desktop OS is different enough from Linux server use that it requires its own description. Several classes of differences are particularly noteworthy.

User interfaces

Generally speaking, desktop systems require better user interface devices (video cards, monitors, keyboard, and mice) than do servers. Linux usually works well with the same hardware as Windows systems, but with one caveat: the very latest video cards sometimes aren't well supported in Linux. Staying a generation or two behind the leading edge is therefore desirable in Linux.

Disk and network hardware

Many classes of servers require the very best in disk and network hardware, but this is less often the case for desktop uses. You can often get by with average ATA devices and typical Ethernet (or other network) hardware. Some desktop systems, though, do need excellent disk or network hardware. These are typically high-performance systems that run scientific simulations, specialized engineering software, and so on.

CPU and RAM

Desktop systems' needs for powerful CPUs and lots of RAM vary with the application. Generally speaking, modern GUI environments are RAM-hungry, so you should equip a modern desktop system with at least 256 MB of RAM, and probably 512 MB or even 1 GB if possible. Linux does support slimmer environments that can work well in 128 MB or less if necessary, though. Most desktop applications don't really need powerful 64-bit CPUs, but some programs are written inefficiently enough that a fast CPU is desirable. Also, certain applications are CPU-intensive.

Peripheral hardware

One of Linux's weakest hardware points as a desktop system is its degree of support for peripheral hardware that's common on desktop systems but less common on servers, such as scanners, digital cameras, video input cards, external hard drives, and so on. Drivers for all major classes of hardware exist, but many specific devices are unsupported. If you're buying or building a new system, including such peripherals, you can easily work around this problem by doing a bit of research and buying only compatible devices. If you want to convert existing systems to Linux, though, existing incompatible hardware can drive up the conversion cost.

Linux distributions

The distributions outlined earlier, in the section "Picking a distribution for server use," can all function as desktop distributions. Others, such as Mandrake and Xandros, are geared more toward desktop use.

Configuration and administration

Configuring and administering a desktop Linux system is much like handling a server system, but certain details do differ, mostly related to the specific software used to support each role. You might not even install an SMTP mail server on a desktop system, for instance; instead, you might install the OpenOffice.org office suite. The kernel, the basic startup procedures, and so on are likely to be similar for both types of system.

 The terms *desktop* and *workstation* have similar meanings in the computer world; both refer to systems that are used by end users to accomplish real-world use. Typically, *workstation* refers to slightly more powerful computers, to those used for scientific or engineering functions as opposed to office productivity, to systems running Unix or Unix-like OSs as opposed to Windows, or to those with better network connections. The exact word use differs from one author to another, though. I use the two words interchangeably, but I use *desktop* most frequently.

Traditionally, Linux hasn't been a major player in the workstation arena; however, it does have all the basic features needed to be used in this way. Over the past few years, Linux's user interface has been improving rapidly, in large part because of the K Desktop Environment (KDE; *http://www.kde.org*) and the GNU Network Object Model Environment (GNOME; *http://www.gnome.org*). These are two desktop environments for Linux that provide a GUI desktop metaphor familiar to users of Windows, Mac OS, OS/2, and other GUI-oriented OSs. These environments rest atop the X Window System (or *X* for short) that provides low-level GUI tools such as support for opening windows and displaying text. Finally, tools such as office suites (OpenOffice.org, KOffice, GNOME Office, and so on), GUI mail readers, and web browsers make Linux a productive desktop OS. All these tools, but particularly desktop environments and office suites, have advanced substantially over the past few years, and today Linux is roughly as easy to use as Windows, although Linux is less familiar to the average office worker.

Many people think of Linux as a way to save money over using a commercial OS. Although Linux can indeed help you save money in the long term, you shouldn't blindly believe that Linux will do so, particularly in the short term. Costs in the switch, such as staff time installing Linux on dozens or hundreds of computers, retraining, replacing hardware for which no Linux drivers exist, and converting existing documents to new file formats, can create a net short-term cost to switching to Linux. In the long term, Linux may save money in license fees and easier long-term administration, but sometimes Linux's limitations can put a drag on these advantages. You'll need to evaluate Linux with an eye to how you intend to use it on *your* network.

Appendix B describes in more detail some of the issues involved in using Linux on the desktop.

Comparing Linux and Windows Features

When deploying Linux, you must consider the overall feature sets of both Linux and its potential competitors. In an environment that's dominated by Windows, the most relevant comparison is often to Windows, so that comparison will be described in the rest of this chapter.

 Linux shares many of its strengths with other Unix-like OSs, and particularly with other open source Unix-like OSs, such as FreeBSD. Linux is probably the most popular and fastest-growing of these OSs because of its dynamic community and large number of distributions. If you prefer to run, say, FreeBSD, you certainly may, and much of this book is applicable to such environments; however, this book does focus on Linux, and it doesn't always point out where FreeBSD or other Unix-like OSs fit into the picture.

Linux is a powerful operating system, but Microsoft's latest offerings (Windows 2003 and Windows XP) are also powerful. Important differences between the two OS families include the following:

Cost
Linux itself is low-cost, and this fact can be a big plus; however, the cost of the software is likely to be a small factor in the overall cost of running a computer. The TCO of Linux versus Windows is a matter of some debate, but it's likely to be lower for Linux if experienced Linux or Unix administrators are already available to deal with the system.

GUI orientation
All versions of Windows are largely tied to their GUIs; administering a Windows box without its GUI is virtually impossible. This linkage can make picking up Windows administration a bit easier for those unfamiliar with text-mode configuration, but it imposes some overhead on the computer itself, and it restricts the ways in which the system can be administered. These limitations are particularly severe for servers, which may not need a flashy GUI to handle mail or deliver IP addresses, except insofar as the OS itself requires these features. Linux, by contrast, is not nearly so GUI-oriented. Many distributions do provide GUI tools, but bypassing those tools to deal with the underlying text-mode configuration files and tools is usually a simple matter, provided you know where those files and tools are located and how to handle them.

Hardware requirements
In part because of Windows' reliance on its GUI, it requires slightly more powerful hardware than does an equivalent Linux server. This factor isn't extremely dramatic, though; chances are you won't be able to replace a 3-GHz Pentium 4 Windows system with a 200-MHz Pentium Linux system and achieve similar performance. Linux also runs on an extremely broad range of hardware

platforms—IA-32, AMD64, PowerPC, Sparc, and so on. On the other hand, in the IA-32 world, the vast majority of hardware comes with Windows drivers, whereas Linux driver support isn't quite as complete. Linux drivers are available for most, but not all, IA-32 hardware.

Software choices

Both Linux and Windows provide multiple choices for many server software categories, such as mail servers or FTP servers; however, those choices are different. The best choices depend on the server type and your specific needs. Much of this book focuses on servers that work very well for Linux and for which the Windows equivalents have problems of one sort or another—cost, reliability, flexibility, or something else.

Windows client integration

This issue is really one of server features. Many Windows server programs are designed around proprietary or semiproprietary Microsoft protocols, or provide extended features that can be accessed from Microsoft clients. For these functions, Linux servers must necessarily either play catch-up or use alternative protocols. For instance, the Samba server on Linux does not provide the full features of a Windows 2000 or 2003 Active Directory (AD) domain controller. Thus, if you want such features, you must run either the Windows server or find some other way to implement the features you want.

File compatibility

Because Linux doesn't run the popular Windows programs except under emulators, file format compatibility may be an issue. This can be a factor when you read your own existing files or exchange files with other sites (with clients, say). In the office field, OpenOffice.org provides very good, but not absolutely perfect, Microsoft Office document compatibility. Appendix B describe this issue in greater detail.

On the whole, Linux makes an excellent choice for many small, mid-sized, and even large servers that use open protocols. When the server uses proprietary protocols or Microsoft extensions, the situation may change. Linux can also be a good choice as a desktop OS, particularly if your organization isn't tied to proprietary Microsoft file formats.

Summary

Linux is a flexible OS that can be deployed in many places on an existing Windows network. Its most common use is as a server to supplement or replace Windows servers, but you can also run Linux as a workstation OS. When deploying Linux, you'll have to match the Linux software to the hardware by selecting an appropriate distribution for your CPU and for the role you intend Linux to play on the network. You then need to select the server programs or end user applications you wish to run.

CHAPTER 2

Linux Deployment Strategies

Creating a plan for deploying Linux can make the difference between success and failure in that endeavor. Although it's possible to simply drop one or two isolated Linux boxes onto a network and have them work correctly, integration with other systems—particularly Windows computers—requires careful planning. You need to select particular server programs to use on the Linux computer that interact with the clients in the way you intend, so as not to disrupt existing servers. In the case of a desktop migration, careful planning and testing is in order. The problem in this case isn't so much the technical challenges of configuring a single system, but the difficulties involved in ensuring that all your existing files are accessible and that all your users are comfortable with the new systems. Finally, thin client deployment poses its own challenges. Knowing when to use thin clients, and how Linux can fit into a thin client strategy, will help you plan and implement such a plan.

One of the most fundamental aspects of deploying Linux is installing the OS. This book doesn't provide a chapter on Linux installation, both because the task varies substantially from one distribution to another and because I presume you don't need that level of detail. If you're completely new to Linux, you should probably buy a more introductory book, ideally one targeted at the distribution you've chosen. At a minimum, you should consult the documentation that came with your distribution for help on how to install it.

Linux Server Options

Chapter 1 described Linux's features as a server OS in broad strokes, including information on common server distributions and pointers to a few specific server programs. This chapter continues this examination with a closer look at the types of servers covered in this book. This information isn't enough to get the server programs up and running, though; for that, you should consult the relevant chapters of this book. Rather, these descriptions are intended to help you decide precisely what servers you should run—whether to use NetBIOS domains or Kerberos for authentication, for instance.

Linux File and Print Servers

One very popular role for Linux servers on Windows-dominated networks is as file and print servers. These computers can store users' files and Windows programs, and make printers available to all users in an area. Some server programs handle both file and print services, but others perform just one role. Common file server protocols on Linux include:

NFS

The Network File Server is a popular file server for Unix-to-Unix file sharing. It provides Unix-style file metadata, such as ownership and permissions, so it's very well suited to file sharing between Linux systems or between Linux and other Unix-like OSs. NFS is not, however, ideal for file sharing with Windows clients; NFS client software for Windows isn't common, and NFS lacks support for some Windows filesystem features, such as system and hidden bits. For this reason, this book doesn't describe configuring Linux as an NFS server or running NFS clients on Windows.

AppleShare

This protocol is a common one on Macintosh networks, particularly those with systems that run the older Mac OS Classic (that is, Mac OS prior to Mac OS X). Sometimes referred to as *AppleTalk*, which is the lower-level protocol upon which AppleShare relies, this protocol provides features required by Mac OS but not used by other OSs. This protocol isn't common on Windows-only networks. You might want to run it to support Mac OS clients, but it's not described in this book. Two AppleShare servers are common on Linux: Netatalk (*http://netatalk.sourceforge.net*) and the Columbia AppleTalk Package (CAP; *http://www.cs.mu.oz.au/appletalk/cap.html*).

NCP

The NetWare Core Protocol is a file- and printer-sharing protocol traditionally used by Novell's NetWare product. It's a server OS that delivers files to DOS, Windows, and other clients. As such, it is, in principle, a good candidate for a protocol to run on a Windows-dominated network; however, Linux's NCP server software, MARS_NWE (*http://www.compu-art.de/mars_nwe/*), has never been enthusiastically embraced. For this reason, I don't describe it in this book and instead focus on SMB/CIFS.

SMB/CIFS

The Server Message Block/Common Internet File System is the most popular file- and printer-sharing protocol in the Windows world. In Linux, it's implemented by the Samba server (*http://www.samba.org*). SMB/CIFS provides the filesystem features used by Windows, so Linux servers must find a way to implement them, and Samba provides numerous options to do so. Because of its popularity on Windows networks, this book devotes all of Part II to Samba.

AppleTalk, NCP, and SMB/CIFS all provide printer sharing as well as file sharing; however, NFS is a file sharing system *only*. To provide printer sharing among themselves, Unix systems typically use another protocol. These protocols are also used for local printing: programs submit print jobs locally to the same server that accepts remote print jobs. The most common tools for the job are as follows:

LPD

> The Line Printer Daemon is both the name of a server and the protocol it implements. This has been the most common network printer sharing protocol in the Unix and Linux worlds for a long time. Until recently, Linux systems have used LPD as the default local printing queue, as well. Two LPD server implementations are common in Linux: the original Berkeley Standard Distribution (BSD) LPD and the next-generation LPRng (*http://www.lprng.com*).

IPP

> The Internet Printing Protocol is implemented most often by the Common Unix Printing System. This protocol was designed to simplify network printer sharing configuration by supporting auto-detection of local printers. It also features mechanisms to deliver information about printers to applications so that they can set margins appropriately, give users the option of activating duplexers and other advanced features, and so on. Most major Linux distributions now use CUPS as their default printing systems. Although IPP is seldom used directly by Windows, Chapter 4 describes some basics of CUPS configuration in support of sharing printers with Windows systems via Samba.

A non-Unix printing system

> You can use a non-Unix printing system, such as AppleShare, NCP, or SMB/CIFS, to share printers between Linux systems. This approach can sometimes be convenient if you've shared a printer using one of these systems and want to make the printer available to other Linux systems. If you use CUPS, sharing between the Linux systems should be simpler.

Because of the dominant role of SMB/CIFS in Windows file and printer sharing, this book strongly emphasizes the use of Samba as a file and printer sharing tool for Windows networks. Configuring a basic Samba server requires adjusting just a few configuration options, but the server provides numerous options that enable you to fine-tune the configuration and define file and printer shares for all occasions.

Linux Authentication Servers

Maintaining local account databases can quickly become a major hassle when more than a handful of computers are involved, particularly when users frequently move between computers (as in a university's computing center). Part II of this book is devoted to *authentication servers*—servers that tell other computers whether a user has entered a valid username and password (or otherwise provided valid authentication credentials). By localizing the authentication process to just one computer (or conceivably a master computer and a small number of backups), account maintenance can be greatly simplified. Several authentication systems are in common use:

NIS and NIS+

Network Information Services and its variant, NIS+, have been the traditional Unix methods of providing centralized login services. In fact, NIS and NIS+ go beyond this duty, but providing authentication services has been one of their main purposes. Like LPD, though, NIS and NIS+ are showing their age. They're also not commonly used on Windows networks, so this book doesn't cover them.

Windows NT domains

The authentication system used by SMB/CIFS can provide network authentication. This system is built around Windows NT domains, which use a computer known as the domain controller to authenticate users on behalf of all servers. Configuring Samba to function as a domain controller is described in Chapter 5, and configuring a Linux system to authenticate accounts against a domain controller is described in Chapter 7. Note that, when Linux is configured to use a domain controller for its own accounts, that domain controller can be either a Linux (or other Unix-like) system running Samba or a Windows NT/200x domain controller.

LDAP

The Lightweight Directory Access Protocol is essentially a type of database. It's often used to store account information, and when so configured, you can set up clients to access the LDAP server. Although configuring Windows systems to directly access an LDAP server for authentication is unusual, it is possible, and LDAP is becoming increasingly common. Furthermore, LDAP is used as a component in Microsoft's Active Directory authentication system. For these reasons, Chapter 8 describes LDAP authentication.

Kerberos

This tool, named after the underworld's three-headed guard dog from Greek mythology, is a high-security cross-platform authentication and encryption system. You can configure clients to use Kerberos for a few protocols or for everything, including local logins. One of the main advantages of Kerberos is that it supports *single-login* operation; that is, you enter your username and password once, and thereafter you don't need to enter them again, even when you access new servers. For instance, after Kerberos-based local login, you don't need to enter your password when retrieving your mail from a POP server or logging into a remote system via Telnet. Kerberos is also a component of Microsoft's AD. Chapter 9 describes this system in more detail.

Active Directory

If your network already uses AD, chances are it already uses both LDAP and Kerberos (Kerberos might not be enabled in AD, but it usually is); however, Microsoft's Kerberos implementation is a bit odd, and AD configuration in Linux is complex. Windows AD servers, however, can also use the same NT domain protocols Linux systems use. Thus, if you want a Linux server to authenticate users against an existing AD domain controller, your best bet is to treat it like an NT domain controller. If you want Linux to take over AD domain controller duties, you're out of luck, at least as of early 2005. You can migrate the network to another authentication system, though.

Which authentication system should you use? In most cases, you should stick with whatever you're using now, unless that system is causing you problems. If you don't currently use a centralized authentication system but want to implement one, any of these tools should work well. NT domains are particularly useful if you've got many older Windows 9x/Me systems. LDAP's strength is in handling large numbers of users and in creating synchronized sets of login servers for redundancy in case of network problems. Kerberos was designed with security, cross-platform operation, and single-login operation in mind, but to get the most out of it, you need to use special *Kerberized* clients and servers—that is, programs that have been modified to use Kerberos.

Remote Login Servers

Remote login servers, as the name implies, enable you to log into a computer remotely. Broadly speaking, these servers come in two types: text-mode and GUI. Examples of these servers include:

rlogin

This protocol and server was once a common way to access one Unix system from another in text mode; however, its security is based on a *trusted-hosts* model, which means that the server trusts the security on the client. In today's network environment, this is an unsound assumption on any but the most private of LANs, and then only when all users can be trusted. For this reason, *rlogin* is a poor choice for remote login duties and isn't further described in this book.

Telnet

This protocol and server normally requires authentication by entering a username and password during the text-mode login process. This is a step up from *rlogin*, but Telnet (like *rlogin*) sends all data, including the password, over the network in an unencrypted form. This makes Telnet a very risky protocol on any but very well-protected LANs, and it should never be used over the Internet at large. Nonetheless, Telnet is still fairly common.

SSH

The Secure Shell protocol provides encryption for all data it passes between systems, including the username, the password, and all other data. This characteristic makes it the preferred protocol for remote text-mode logins. SSH also supports *tunnelling* data—passing data through SSH to create an encrypted connection for a protocol that doesn't normally support encryption. This ability is most easily accessed for X servers; it enables SSH to function as an encrypted link for remote GUI logins, thus straddling the line between the text-mode and GUI tools. Chapter 10 describes SSH in more detail.

The X Window System

Linux's default GUI environment, the X Window System (or X for short) is network-enabled; you can have a program (an *X client*) running on one computer and use the *X server* on another computer to display a window and accept keyboard and mouse input. One unusual feature of this arrangement is that it places the server on the computer at which the user is sitting. This fact can be confusing because most people think of servers as being remote and powerful computers. This arrangement also creates a chicken-and-egg problem: how do you tell the remote client to launch a program that uses your local X server as a display? One answer is to use a text-mode login tool, such as Telnet or SSH, to create an initial connection, as described in Chapter 11. Another answer is to use a dedicated X login server protocol, described next.

XDMCP

The X Display Manager Control Protocol is a login protocol for X. An XDMCP server runs on the X client system and accepts login requests from X servers. Linux uses XDMCP locally to provide GUI login screens for users, but you can reconfigure the XDMCP server to accept remote logins, as well. Three XDMCP servers are common in Linux: the original X Display Manager (XDM), the KDE Display Manager (KDM), and the GNOME Display Manager (GDM). All these tools are described in Chapter 11.

RFB

The Remote Frame Buffer protocol can transfer an entire desktop bitmap over the network wire and accept back keyboard and mouse inputs. RFB is most commonly implemented in a server known as Virtual Network Computing (VNC). Under Linux, VNC is implemented as a special X server that uses a network connection to a VNC client rather than a local display, keyboard, and mouse for input and output. One consequence of this arrangement is that the VNC client/server terminology is more intuitive to most people: the VNC client runs on the user's computer, and the server is the remote system the user wants to access. A conventional Linux VNC configuration involves the user running a VNC server after making a text-mode connection in some different capacity, but you can configure VNC in other ways. VNC servers for Windows are also available, enabling you to log into Windows systems from Linux. Chapter 11 describes VNC.

As a general rule, SSH is the best choice for text-mode logins because of its security features. (Kerberos ships with a version of Telnet that encrypts data, though, so the Kerberos Telnet can be a good choice, too.) You can also use SSH to tunnel an X connection, thus providing encryption for your X session. When it comes to remote GUI access, both "plain" X and VNC have their advocates. The two systems send data over the network in different ways, so their performance differs in ways that depend on the characteristics of the network. As a general rule, VNC performs well when the network has lots of bandwidth and either high or low latencies. X, by contrast, sends less data and so needs less bandwidth, but X sends lots of back-and-forth transactions and so works best when network latencies are low. You should treat these rules of thumb with some skepticism, though; variant protocols, tunneling X through SSH, and so on can alter both protocols' performance characteristics radically.

Mail Servers

Mail is an important part of many small networks, as well as on the Internet at large. Broadly speaking, mail protocols can be classified as *push mail protocols*, in which the sender initiates the transfer, or *pull mail protocols*, in which the recipient initiates the transfer. Several mail protocols exist, and for each of these, several servers can handle them:

SMTP

The Simple Mail Transfer Protocol is the most common push mail protocol on the Internet. On Linux, sendmail (*http://www.sendmail.org*), Postfix (*http://www.postfix.org*), and Exim (*http://www.exim.org*) are the most common SMTP servers to ship with Linux; qmail (*http://www.qmail.org*) is also popular. Each is a major server, so to conserve space, this book describes just two in Chapter 13: sendmail and Postfix. The most popular SMTP server on the Internet is sendmail, and it's the default with many Linux distributions; however, sendmail is also tricky to configure for anything but a basic default setup, at least for those who aren't already sendmail adepts. Postfix was designed as an alternative to sendmail using a modular design and streamlined configuration process, and distributions have slowly been switching to it as the default mail server. The default Postfix configuration file is very well-commented, and Postfix is usually easier for novice mail administrators to configure. Both sendmail and Postfix can interface with other mail server tools, which can perform virus scanning, spam checking, and other mail-related services.

IMAP

The Internet Message Access Protocol is a popular way to deliver mail to end users. In a simple configuration, a mail server computer runs an SMTP server to receive off-site mail and also runs a POP or IMAP server to deliver mail to end users who run mail clients such as Microsoft's Outlook or KDE's KMail. IMAP enables users to store mail in folders on the server, which makes it handy if users want to access their mail from different programs or computers. This feature can increase the disk requirements of the mail server computer, though. Numerous IMAP servers for Linux exist, including the University of Washington IMAP (UW-IMAP; *http://www.washington.edu/imap/*), Cyrus IMAP (*http://asg.web. cmu.edu/cyrus/imapd/*), Courier IMAP (*http://www.inter7.com/courierimap/*), and Dovecot (*http://dovecot.org*). Which one you use depends in part on your SMTP server because the IMAP server must be able to read the mail stored by the SMTP server. UW-IMAP and Cyrus IMAP both read mail in the format that's the default for sendmail, Postfix, and Exim. If you use qmail and its *maildir* format, or if you reconfigure another SMTP server to use this format, Courier IMAP is a better choice. Dovecot can handle both formats. IMAP servers are covered in Chapter 13.

POP

The Post Office Protocol is another pull mail server, similar in basic concept to IMAP. POP, though, provides no means to store mail in folders on the server; typically, the client downloads all the messages and deletes them from the server. The user then stores messages locally, if desired. The four IMAP servers just mentioned also support POP. Several others, such as Qpopper (*http://www. eudora.com/qpopper/*) and *qmail-pop3d* (which ships with qmail) are also available. POP servers are covered in Chapter 13.

Miscellaneous Linux Servers

In addition to file and printer sharing, authentication, remote login protocols, and mail servers, this book covers several others that are likely to be useful on Windows-dominated networks. These protocols don't fit into neat categories, but some are extremely important, and, in fact, entire books have been written about some of them:

Backup software

Various servers can be used for backup purposes. One of these is Samba; you can mount a shared volume and back it up using local tools or more sophisticated techniques to do so in other ways. Chapter 14 covers this topic, as well as a more specialized backup utility, the Advanced Maryland Automatic Network Disk Archiver (AMANDA; *http://www.amanda.org*). AMANDA's strength is in scheduling automated backups of many systems on a network, which can be a great boon if you need to automate the backup of a whole network. Commercial products, such as Veritas Netbackup (*http://www.veritas.com*) and Legato (*http:// www.legato.com*), are also available.

DHCP

The Dynamic Host Configuration Protocol enables a single server to deliver IP addresses and other basic TCP/IP configuration information to clients when they boot or bring their network interfaces online. Even a modest Linux system can make an excellent DHCP server for your network. The Internet Software Consortium (ISC; *http://www.isc.org*) produces a reference DHCP server that's easily the most common Linux DHCP server. Chapter 15 covers this server.

DNS

The Domain Name System converts hostnames into IP addresses and vice versa. Each DNS server functions locally, but servers usually link together to function globally, providing name resolution for systems worldwide. The ISC's DNS server, the Berkeley Internet Name Domain (BIND), is the standard one for Linux. Alternatives do exist, though, such as *djbdns* (*http://cr.yp.to/djbdns.html*). The latter can be somewhat easier to configure, although managing a full Internet domain with either package isn't trivial. Linux can make a good DNS server, but how you do this depends on your intent. If you want to run a server so that the world can resolve your domain's IP addresses, you need to create a robust DNS server with good Internet connections. If you want to run a local DNS server so that local computers can resolve each others addresses as well as addresses on the Internet, without providing your systems' names on the Internet, you can probably get by with a much simpler DNS server. Chapter 15 covers both BIND and *djbdns*.

NTP

The Network Time Protocol enables a computer to set its clock to the time maintained by an atomic clock accessible on the Internet. (In fact, many Internet time sources are available, all of which link back to highly accurate sources in one way or another.) The Linux NTP server (*http://www.ntp.org*) ships with most distributions and functions as both a client and a server. It obtains its time from one or more remote sources and can operate as a server for your own local systems. Even a modest Linux system can function as an NTP server for all but very large networks. One alternative to NTP is to use a time-setting protocol that's part of SMB/CIFS. NTP is generally the cleaner approach on Linux, but you might use the SMB/CIFS time server functionality to set clocks on Windows clients from a Linux NTP server. Chapter 15 covers NTP.

 Some protocols—most notably Kerberos—rely upon clients and servers having synchronized clocks. Thus, if you use Kerberos, you should also configure NTP or some other time protocol on all your Kerberos clients and servers.

Linux Desktop Migration

In some ways, migrating desktop systems to Linux is more difficult than migrating a server. The problem isn't the migration process itself; that's very similar, although configuration of individual programs obviously differs. The problem is the scale of the migration; if you plan to migrate all of a site's users to Linux, you need to install and configure the OS on multiple systems, train the users, and deal with the inevitable glitches that will arise.

When considering a Linux desktop migration, you should begin by examining several factors that will likely influence the likelihood of a successful transition. These factors include the availability of administrative expertise, the need and your capacity for end-user training, the availability of appropriate desktop software for your site, the need for generating Windows-compatible files or reading files generated on Windows from off-site, and Linux compatibility of your existing hardware. Any of these factors might present a real challenge to Linux migration. Other changes you're planning can also interact with these factors; for instance, if you intend to upgrade some hardware, existing hardware compatibility may not be as important. In the end, you must evaluate the feasibility of a Linux migration yourself, based on your own site's needs.

If you decide to proceed with a migration, you should begin by examining your needs and developing a plan of action. Decide what software you'll need (both the distribution and the applications you'll run) and begin the migration with a small-scale test; it's better to iron out any wrinkles you encounter on a dozen machines rather than on a hundred machines. The small-scale deployment will enable you to fine-tune your deployment strategy before scaling it up. In fact, for a very large deployment, you may want to scale it up in several stages, starting with one or two test systems, then moving to a dozen or so, then a hundred, and so on.

Linux and Thin Clients

A lot of attention has been devoted to Linux on the desktop recently. The primary goal of Linux desktop operation is to give users access to typical desktop applications—word processors, spreadsheets, web browsers, etc. An alternative exists to this configuration, though: thin client computing. In many respects, thin client computing is very old; the typical mainframe model, with a large central server and many dumb terminals attached to it, closely resembles thin client computing. Thin clients, though, give users the ability to run GUI programs. Thin client computing has certain advantages and disadvantages compared to traditional workstation configurations. You can use Linux as a thin client OS or as the OS accessed by thin clients. Before going too far with a desktop Linux deployment, you may want to consider a Linux thin client solution. It's not for everybody, but some sites can benefit from it. For more details about thin client configuration, consult Chapter 12.

In a thin client configuration, most computers are thin clients—relatively limited computers that consist of a keyboard, a mouse, a monitor, and just enough computing power to display data on the screen and communicate with a central login server. This login server is a multiuser system that can handle all of the network's users' ordinary desktop computing tasks. As such, the central system must usually be quite powerful. Because a typical desktop computer's CPU is mostly idle as a user types or reads, and because a multiuser system can save memory by using shared libraries and similar tricks, the central system doesn't need to be as powerful as the combination of all the workstations it replaces. For instance, consider an office of 10 users that require 10 2-GHz Pentium 4 computers with 512 MB of RAM. In a thin client configuration, you probably don't need a 20-GHz Pentium 4 with 5 GB of RAM (if such a computer even existed!); something along the lines of a dual 3-GHz Pentium 4 with 2 GB of RAM will suffice. Actual requirements will depend on the specific applications, the network bandwidth, and other factors.

The thin clients themselves can be either dedicated hardware devices or recycled older computers. Even an 80486 system might make an acceptable thin client. Thin clients frequently boot from the network using Ethernet cards that support network boots and an appropriate set of servers. You typically need a DHCP server and a server running the Trivial File Transfer Protocol (TFTP). One type of thin client is known as an *X terminal*. This is basically a computer that runs an X server and little else. Other thin clients can use the RFB protocol or other protocols. As described in Chapter 12, several dedicated Linux thin client distributions exist, as well as tools that enable thin clients intended for Windows to connect to Linux servers.

One big advantage of thin clients is that, by centralizing the bulk of the desktop software on one system, you can simplify system administration tasks. The thin clients themselves are simple enough that they require little in the way of maintenance, and as they download their OSs from a server, you can even administer them centrally. More important, the central login server is just one system—admittedly, one with many users, but one system nonetheless. Instead of rolling out a software update to dozens of computers, you can deal with just one. Particularly if you have a number of old computers on hand that you can recycle as thin clients, this approach can save money on hardware compared to upgrading desktop systems.

Thin clients are not without their drawbacks, though. Because GUI displays must be copied over the network, they require better network infrastructure than is required in a more conventional workstation configuration. The central login server will be particularly hard-hit by this requirement. You may need to upgrade your network to a higher speed or segment it and give the central server multiple network interfaces. As a rule of thumb, an unswitched 100-Mbps network can handle about a dozen thin clients; if you use switches, the number goes up to about 100 users. Configuring the thin clients to support sound and give users access to local floppy disks or other removable media may take extra effort. Because the entire network is wholly dependent on a single computer, a failure of that computer will be devastating.

Linux can function as a thin client OS. Typically, you'll prepare a custom Linux installation and configure it to load from the network or from a hard disk in the thin client itself. When connected to a Linux remote login server, you're likely to use X's networking capabilities to handle the communications. However, Linux can be used with RFB or with other protocols to provide users with remote access to a Windows remote login server.

Linux can also function as the central login server. Typically, you'll use X terminals (either dedicated hardware X terminals or old desktop systems configured as X terminals) as the thin clients, but you can use RFB instead, if you prefer or if you've found thin clients that support this protocol but not the X protocols. As a multiuser OS, Linux is particularly well-suited to function as a central login server. Of course, for all but the smallest network, you'll need a pretty powerful computer to fill this role—probably a multi-CPU system with several gigabytes of RAM.

Summary

Linux can be deployed in many different ways on a Windows network. One common approach is to install Linux as a server OS, supplementing or replacing Windows servers. This type of installation is often fairly well-defined in terms of its role and can be done with a modest amount of planning. You need to know the system's intended role and what server programs are available to help the system fill that role. Another type of deployment, and a much more ambitious one, is to put Linux on the desktop. This approach typically involves replacing many Windows systems with Linux and requires careful attention to detail, both in terms of Linux's technical features and in terms of users' interactions with Linux. Finally, instead of performing a workstation rollout, you can use a thin client configuration, in which Linux serves as a thin client OS or as a central login server for thin clients. This approach can save money and reduce administrative headaches, but it has drawbacks, including network bandwidth requirements and increased vulnerability to a single system's failure.

## PART II

Sharing Files and Printers

Most Windows-dominated networks use SMB/CIFS for sharing files and printers. The importance of this protocol on such networks makes Linux software for handling it a potentially valuable tool. The Linux server suite for SMB/CIFS is known as *Samba*, and it's described in the first three chapters of this part of the book. Chapter 3 describes global Samba configuration options required to get Samba to work and to take on a handful of other modest duties. Chapter 4 covers defining Samba *shares*—directories and printers to be shared with clients. Chapter 5 describes configuring Samba as a *domain controller*, which can authenticate users for other servers. The fourth and final chapter of this part of the book, Chapter 6, describes Linux SMB/CIFS client operations. These can be important both when Linux is running on a desktop system and for some types of server operations, such as a Linux backup server (which may take on the file-sharing client role in order to back up Windows systems). Between these functions, Linux can take on some of the most important server functions routinely held by Windows systems in a Windows network—sharing files, sharing printers, and authenticating users. (Part III describes other authentication protocols and also covers using Linux as an NT domain client.)

Samba is a complex server suite. This book can cover the basics of Samba operation, but if you want to take advantage of Samba's more exotic features, you may want to consult a separate book on the server, such as *Definitive Guide to Samba 3* (Apress) or *Using Samba* (O'Reilly).

## CHAPTER 3

Basic Samba Configuration

All major Linux distributions ship with Samba, the Server Message Block/Common Internet File System (SMB/CIFS) server for Unix-like systems. This server package enables Linux to serve files and printers to Windows clients, providing a reliable and low-cost platform to fill this role. In fact, despite some fundamental differences between the Linux/Unix and Windows platforms, Samba handles its duties so well that Samba servers are often more trouble-free than their Windows counterparts, so network administrators have sometimes gone to great lengths to deploy Linux running Samba rather than Windows in this role.

This chapter describes basic Samba configuration, starting with installing the server. Other topics include the configuration file format, how you identify the server to other computers on the network, minimal options to help Samba get along with other systems in terms of its browsing features, and setting password options. You must set these basic features before you can move on to the next topic, configuring file and printer shares; that topic is covered in Chapter 4.

 An experienced Samba administrator who's familiar with the local network can set all the options described in this chapter in just a minute or two. Many of these options require some time to fully describe because of changes in SMB/CIFS over time and because of peculiarities of integrating SMB/CIFS with Linux's traditional networking tools, but you'll change only a handful of Samba configuration file options. If you're impatient to get started, pay particular attention to the sections "Workgroup Name Options" and "Setting Password Options."

Installing Samba

Samba isn't a single server; rather, it's a family of servers that together provide the full functionality of the package. (Nonetheless, references to "the Samba server" or similar phrases are common.) Four daemons provide the most important Samba features.

smbd

> This daemon handles the file- and printer-serving functions per se. Clients con-
> nect to it using TCP port 139 or 445 to request the transfer of files.

nmbd

> This daemon handles most of the SMB/CIFS functionality not provided by *smbd*,
> including NetBIOS name resolution (as described in the section "Identifying the
> Server") and browsing features (as described briefly in the section "Setting Mas-
> ter Browser Options" and in more detail in Chapter 5). Iff you run *smbd*,
> chances are you'll also run *nmbd*. This server binds to UDP ports 137 and 138.

SWAT

> The Samba Web Administration Tool (SWAT) provides a web-based GUI
> administration tool for Samba. Running it isn't necessary, and I don't describe it
> further in this book. It can be a handy tool for new Samba administrators,
> though, and it provides some functions that can help ordinary users, such as an
> interface to change their passwords. It usually runs on TCP port 901.

Winbind

> This daemon, which is also known as *winbindd*, provides a way for Linux to
> access NetBIOS name and Windows NT domain information. The main upshot
> is that a system that runs Winbind can authenticate its local users against the
> Windows domain's user database, as described in Chapter 7. Although Win-
> bind is a daemon, it isn't a server for other computers; it enables extra function-
> ality solely for the computer on which it runs.

In addition to these daemons, Samba provides a number of support utilities and client programs. These include the *smbclient* client program, which provides FTP-like
access to SMB/CIFS shares; the *smbmount* utilities, which helps you mount SMB/
CIFS shares in Linux; and the *smbpasswd* utility for handling Samba passwords.
Some of these tools are described in this chapter, but others are covered elsewhere in
this book.

Most Linux distributions deliver these programs in one or more packages. Typically,
a base package is called *samba* or *samba-common*. Additional functionality often
ships in other packages, such as *samba-clients* or *swat*. Consult your distribution's
package list and descriptions to learn what you need to install for the functionality
you require. Alternatively, you can download and install Samba from its own web
site, *http://www.samba.org*. This site's download area provides links to binaries for
many distributions and to a source code tarball that should compile on any Linux
distribution. (Just one source tarball contains all the major Samba components
described here.)

Samba (or at least the *smbd* and *nmbd* daemons) is typically launched through SysV
startup scripts, and these usually install from the distribution's main Samba package. If you installed Samba from a source tarball, though, you'll need to create your
own SysV startup script, run Samba from a local startup script, or launch Samba

manually on an as-needed basis. (The *packaging* subdirectory of the Samba source package includes sample SysV startup scripts for several distributions.) Although it's possible to run Samba from a super server such as *inetd* or *xinetd*, doing so is uncommon and isn't recommended. In fact, *nmbd* tends to be a bit difficult to run in this way.

A few features related to SMB/CIFS aren't part of the main Samba package. Most notably, the ability to mount SMB/CIFS shares on a Linux system is built into the Linux kernel, although it relies on the external *smbmount* command, which is part of the Samba package. Some GUI SMB/CIFS network browsers are also available separately. Many of these tools nonetheless rely on the basic Samba configuration described in this chapter for certain default values.

The Samba Configuration File Format

Before delving into Samba configuration, you should understand the Samba configuration file format. This file is called *smb.conf*, and it's typically located in */etc/samba*, although a few distributions (particularly old ones) place it in some variant location, such as */etc/samba.d* or */etc*. When you compile from source code, it goes in */usr/local/samba/lib* unless you change a configuration option.

Wherever it's located, the *smb.conf* file is broken into several distinct sections, each of which has its purposes. Within each section, lines have a simple structure consisting of a *parameter* that's to be set and one or more *values* to be assigned to the parameter, or they may be comment lines. You should also understand the use of Samba *variables*, which enable you to set a parameter to a value you may not know when creating the configuration file.

Configuration File Sections

Example 3-1 shows a short but complete *smb.conf* configuration file. In this file, the section names appear between square brackets ([ ]). In this example, the section names are [global], [homes], and [freefiles].

Example 3-1. A short smb.conf file

```
[global]
   workgroup = GREENHOUSE
   netbios name = MANDRAKE
   server string = Free files for all
   encrypt passwords = Yes
   security = User
   os level = 2
   domain master = No
   preferred master = No
   domain logons = No
```

Example 3-1. A short smb.conf file (continued)

```
[homes]
    browseable = No
    writeable = Yes

# Put all our public files in a logical place....
[freefiles]
    path = /usr/share/samba/public
    browseable = Yes
    writeable = No
```

The [global] section of *smb.conf* is the only section that's really required. It sets *global-level parameters* that affect the operation of the server as a whole, such as setting its NetBIOS name and password encryption settings. In addition, you can place most *share-level parameters* in the [global] section, in which case the parameter effectively changes the default behavior. For instance, the writeable parameter is share-level, meaning that you can set it differently for each share. If placed in the [global] section, though, this parameter sets the default for the rest of the shares. This can be handy if you have many shares that use similar options; rather than set the same parameter in all the shares, you can set it just once, in the [global] section.

Sections after the [global] section—the [homes] and [freefiles] sections in Example 3-1—all define individual Samba shares. Each share definition begins with its name and ends with the next share definition or the end of the file. All the parameters in a share definition must be share-level parameters.

Frequently, the share names are not indented, while parameters belonging to a share are indented. This practice makes it easy to locate the parameters you want to adjust, but it's not required; Samba ignores most whitespace in *smb.conf*, including indentation of configuration lines.

Parameters, Values, and Comments

If you examine Example 3-1, you'll quickly discern the basic form of an *smb.conf* parameter line:

```
parameter = Value
```

The *parameter* is a keyword that holds particular meaning to Samba. Some Samba functions can be accessed through multiple parameter names; for instance, writeable is synonymous with writable and write ok, and read only is an antonym for these. In other words, writeable = Yes has the same effect as read only = No.

The *Value* is the value that's assigned to the parameter. Several different types of values exist:

Boolean values

Many Samba parameters require Boolean options. For these, Yes, True, and 1 are all synonymous, while No, False, and 0 are their opposites. A few Booleans also accept other options to set a feature automatically or have some other parameter-specific effect.

Numeric values

Some parameters take numeric values, such as a time in seconds or a file size in bytes or kilobytes. Both integral and real numeric values are possible, although some parameters expect one type or the other. Some parameters take values that are special numbers or sets of numbers, such as IP addresses.

String values

You can provide strings to some parameters, such as the values of the workgroup, netbios name, server string, and path parameters in Example 3-1. Sometimes these strings can be almost anything you like, as in server string. Other strings must be constrained in some way, though; for instance, path is a local Linux pathname. When a string value contains spaces, you do not normally need to enclose it in quotes, although you can do so if you prefer. Quotes may also be necessary with lists of string items that contain spaces.

Delimited values

Some parameters accept a limited range of strings as values. For instance, Example 3-1 shows the security parameter, which accepts just a handful of values.

Lists

Many parameters accept multiple values as options, such as several IP addresses or hostnames. Lists are normally delimited by commas or spaces, although a few parameters use other characters as delimiters.

For the most part, Samba doesn't care about the case of its parameters or values; domain master = No has the same effect as DOMAIN MASTER = no or any other variant. Some values, though, are case-sensitive for reasons other than Samba. For instance, a Linux filename provided as a value is case-sensitive because the underlying Linux filesystem is case-sensitive.

Similarly, parameters aren't sensitive to whitespace; you can insert or remote spaces from parameters without causing problems. For instance, server string = Free files for all is identical to serverstring = Free files for all. Whitespace may be important to parameters' values, though.

If a configuration line is very long, you can break it across multiple lines by ending the first line (and any subsequent nonterminal lines) with a backslash (\):

```
hosts allow = daisy.greenhouse.example.com, 172.24.21.27, \
              192.168.7.107
```

This example sets the hosts allow parameter to three values—a hostname and two IP addresses.

Instead of or in addition to a parameter and value, an *smb.conf* line may hold a comment. These are denoted by a hash mark (#) or a semicolon (;); Samba ignores lines that begin with one of these characters. (Whitespace before comments is ignored.)

Many sample *smb.conf* files contain numerous comments describing the function of each configuration line in the file.

 Samba provides a parameter called comment. This is not to be confused with a comment! The comment parameter sets a free-form string that's associated with a share for the benefit of users.

Variables and Their Uses

In most cases, you can set a Samba parameter to a constant value. All the parameters in Example 3-1 do this. Samba also supports variables as parameter values. A *variable* is a placeholder, denoted by a leading percent symbol (%), that can take on a particular value depending upon the machine on which Samba is running, the Samba version, the username of the person accessing the share, and so on. Table 3-1 summarizes Samba's variables. Note that variable identifiers are case-sensitive; for instance, %d and %D are distinct variables.

Table 3-1. Samba variables

Variable	Meaning
%a	The client's OS. Possible values are OS2 (OS/2), Samba, UNKNOWN, WfWg (DOS or Windows for Workgroups), Win2K (Windows 2000), Win95 (Windows 9x/Me), or WinNT (Windows NT).
%c	A print job's length in pages, if known.
%d	The daemon's process ID number.
%D	The client's workgroup or NT domain name, if known.
%f	The sender of a WinPopUp message.
%g	The primary group of %u.
%G	The primary group of %U.
%h	The server's DNS hostname, if known.
%H	The home directory of %u
%I	The client's IP address.
%J	A print job's name.
%L	The server's NetBIOS name.
%m	The client's NetBIOS name, if known.
%M	The client's DNS hostname, if known.
%N	The NIS home directory server.
%p	The path to an automounted share's root directory.
%P	The path to the share's root directory.
%R	The level of the SMB protocol in use. Legal values are CORE, COREPLUS, LANMAN1, LANMAN2, and NT1.
%s	A filename. In printer shares, this identifies the file passed by the client to be printed. It can also refer to a file that holds a WinPopUp message.
%S	The share's name.

Table 3-1. Samba variables (continued)

Variable	Meaning
%t	A WinPopUp message's destination.
%T	The current date and time.
%u	The effective Linux username. This may not be the same as %U.
%U	The username sent by the client.
%v	Samba's version number.
%z	A print job's size in bytes.
%$(*envvar*)	The value of the environment variable *envvar*.

You can use a variable much as you'd use any other value in a parameter. It will be expanded to its full replacement value when Samba needs to do so. You can even combine variables with regular text or with other variables. For instance, consider the following parameter:

```
log file = /var/log/samba/log.%m
```

A line like this is a common sight in the global sections of *smb.conf* files. If the client's NetBIOS name is *DAISY*, Samba logs information on accesses by this client in */var/log/samba/log.daisy*. (Samba usually converts NetBIOS names to lowercase.) If Samba doesn't know the client's NetBIOS name, the IP address is substituted for the Net-BIOS name. Separating logfiles in this way can be handy when debugging problems or tracing usage patterns for the server.

Some environment variables aren't guaranteed to be available. For instance, %L is only available if the client uses the NetBIOS over TCP/IP (NBT) method of connecting to the server, using TCP port 139. This variable is meaningless or will return an IP address for a client that uses the newer "raw" SMB/CIFS over on TCP port 445. Similarly, %h and %M work correctly only if your network's DNS server is working correctly. Variables that convert IP addresses to DNS names also require you to set the hostname lookups = Yes parameter to work correctly. Some parameters have meaning only in particular contexts; for instance, %S is meaningless when used with global parameters because a share name can apply only to an individual share and not to the system as a whole.

The include Parameter

Normally, a Samba server uses a single *smb.conf* configuration file; however, you can use the include parameter to merge in multiple files. This parameter takes a filename as an option. Samba reads the specified file and uses its contents as if they were part of the main *smb.conf* file, at the location of the include parameter.

Typically, you pass a variable as part of the filename that you give to include. You can use this ability to provide customized configurations for different client computers, client OSs, users, and so on. For instance, you can set options that adjust the server's delivery of filenames to clients (as described in Chapter 4) based on the client OS:

```
include = /etc/samba/smb-%a.conf
```

You then create files called *smb-Win95.conf*, *smb-Samba.conf*, or other appropriate values, and place OS-specific options in each file. You can place such a call in the [global] section or in a share definition. In fact, you can even place entire share definitions in an included configuration file. This type of configuration can be useful when one OS works better with one set of options than another. For instance, you might want to set different case-sensitivity options depending on the client OS's capabilities.

Identifying the Server

The first task you must undertake when configuring a Samba server is setting various identification options. SMB/CIFS was designed for non-TCP/IP networks and includes server identification tools that are independent of common TCP/IP naming systems, such as DNS hostnames. SMB/CIFS machines are identified by NetBIOS names, and computers belong to workgroups or NT domains (an NT domain is simply a workgroup with some extra features). Although most recent SMB/CIFS clients can contact servers using DNS hostnames or raw IP addresses rather than NetBIOS names, you must give your Samba server a NetBIOS name and a workgroup (or NT domain) name for interaction with older clients, such as DOS and Windows 9x systems. You may also want to adjust a few additional identification options, which tell the system what operating system to pretend to be, among other things.

NetBIOS Name Options

A NetBIOS name is similar to a computer's DNS hostname (without the domain name component). It's a string of up to 15 characters that can contain letters, numbers, and various punctuation marks. (Using punctuation can be confusing, though, and so is usually best avoided.) NetBIOS names are case-insensitive, although I generally present them in all-uppercase in this book to distinguish them from DNS hostnames, which I present in lowercase.

Technically, the NetBIOS name as just described is only the *base* of the NetBIOS name. The full NetBIOS name includes a one-byte code that identifies the type of service available under the name; for instance, a NetBIOS name might end with a hexadecimal 0x20 to signify a file or print service. A single computer is likely to register several NetBIOS names using a single NetBIOS base name and different type codes. Samba handles this automatically; you just give it the NetBIOS base name, and it registers the names required based on other *smb.conf* options.

You set your computer's NetBIOS name with the global `netbios name` parameter:

```
netbios name = MANDRAKE
```

If you don't include this parameter in the *smb.conf* file, the default is to use your computer's DNS hostname, minus the domain component. For instance, if your computer is called *mandrake.greenhouse.example.com*, Samba registers the NetBIOS name *MANDRAKE*. This default is usually reasonable, assuming your DNS hostname is set correctly; however, you may want to set the NetBIOS name explicitly just to be sure. (When you do so, this setting overrides the DNS hostname for NetBIOS purposes but not for other TCP/IP protocols.) In most cases, you shouldn't try to use different NetBIOS and DNS names on a single computer because it will most likely confuse your users.

Occasionally, you may want to give a computer multiple NetBIOS names. Samba supports this option via the global `netbios aliases` parameter, which enables you to specify names to be registered *in addition to* the name provided with `netbios name` (or the DNS hostname, if you omit `netbios name` from your *smb.conf* file). For instance, suppose that *MANDRAKE* should also be known as *MANDRAGORA* and *MANDRAGORIN*. You can do so by using the following line in addition to the `netbios name` line shown earlier:

```
netbios aliases = MANDRAGORA MANDRAGORIN
```

You can use this parameter to give a system multiple NetBIOS names if it also has multiple DNS hostnames. You can also use it to consolidate several servers in one. For instance, if you replace two old file server computers with one new server, you can have the new server appear under both names by assigning one name with `netbios name` and the second with `netbios aliases`. You'll need to define file or printer shares to match those found on both original servers, though.

If you use the %L variable as part of a filename in an include parameter, you can load different shares depending on which NetBIOS name a client uses to address the server. This can help minimize user confusion should you want to consolidate many servers into one; to users, your single server can look like the two old ones, complete with different shares available under each name. Be aware, though, that many newer clients, including Windows 2000 and XP, no longer use NetBIOS names by default, so this trick may not be useful on all networks. Specifying smb ports = 139 limits Samba to using port 139, and hence NetBIOS and its naming conventions. This forces the desired behavior even with most newer clients.

NetBIOS name resolution can work in any of several ways. The most common methods are broadcast name resolution and a NetBIOS Name Server (NBNS) computer, a.k.a. a Windows Internet Name Service (WINS) system. In broadcast name resolution, a client sends a broadcast that contains the name of the system it wants to contact, and that system responds to the broadcasts. Broadcast name resolution is easy to configure (no special Samba parameters are required), but it doesn't work well in networks with multiple subnets.

If your network includes an NBNS system, you should point Samba at it with the global wins server parameter, which requires the IP address (or DNS hostname, if you also set hostname lookups = Yes) of the NBNS system:

```
wins server = 172.24.21.1
```

Samba 3.0 and later supports multiple NBNS systems (separated by spaces or commas on the wins server line).

Conceptually, you can consider an NBNS system to be much like a DNS server; clients contact it to turn names into IP addresses. Unlike a DNS server, though, an NBNS system requires no explicit configuration to add hostnames to it. Instead, clients contact the NBNS system when they start up and at various times thereafter in order to register their configured names. The wins server parameter has the dual effect of telling Samba (or *nmbd*, to be more precise) to register with the NBNS system and to use that system for NBNS lookups, when they're required.

While you're setting the wins server option, you should check to be sure that wins support is set to No. If this value is Yes, Samba attempts to operate as an NBNS system. This is likely to cause confusion if your network has an existing NBNS system. Of course, if you really want your computer to take on these duties, you should set wins support = Yes, but, in this case, you should omit the wins server parameter; Samba knows to refer to itself for this function when it's configured as an NBNS system.

You can tell Samba which name lookup methods to use with the name resolve order parameter, which takes an ordered list of one to four values:

lmhosts

> This option tells Samba to use an *lmhosts* file, which is conceptually and structurally similar to an */etc/hosts* file: it's a list of IP addresses and associated NetBIOS names, one per line. The file is typically stored in the same directory as *smb.conf*.

host

> This option refers to lookups using the computer's normal TCP/IP hostname lookup mechanisms—typically */etc/hosts* and DNS. This lookup method doesn't work for some service types, so you shouldn't rely on it exclusively.

wins

> This option refers to NBNS-based lookups; it requires that you set wins server (or wins support = Yes).

bcast

> You can have Samba perform broadcast name resolution with this option.

The default name resolution order is lmhosts host wins bcast, but you can remove options or change their order by specifying them with name resolve order:

```
name resolve order = wins bcast lmhosts
```

This example causes NBNS lookups to be tried first, followed by broadcasts, followed by *lmhosts* lookups. In this example, ordinary TCP/IP hostname lookups are not attempted by Samba.

Workgroup Name Options

The NetBIOS naming system is basically flat; all computers on a network have names in the same namespace, with no hierarchical structure. This contrasts with DNS names, which provide for an arbitrary number of domains and subdomains. NetBIOS avoids name conflicts primarily by restricting the scope of the network; NetBIOS name broadcasts don't normally pass over routers, and NBNS computers typically serve just one organization's computers.

NetBIOS does provide the *illusion* of a two-tiered structure, though, through the use of workgroups and NT domains. On a conceptual level, a workgroup is a collection of computers that are related in some way, such as those in a single department. On a technical level, workgroups are implemented by having members of the workgroup register NetBIOS names based on the workgroup name and using particular service type codes.

In any event, you must tell Samba the name of the workgroup to which it belongs. You do this with the global workgroup parameter, which takes a workgroup name as its value. These names follow the same naming rules as NetBIOS machine names, but because the computer's DNS domain name is less likely to be a suitable substitute, it's not used as the default value. Instead, the default if you omit the workgroup parameter is a compile-time option, but it's usually *WORKGROUP*.

If you fail to set the computer's workgroup correctly, you may not be able to browse to the server from Windows clients, or the server may appear under its own unique workgroup in the clients' browsers. Thus, it's important that you set this option appropriately for your network. If you're configuring a new network, select a workgroup name as you see fit. Perhaps your organization's domain name will work, or maybe a subdomain name will be more appropriate. In some cases, you might even use something unrelated, but to avoid confusion, it's usually best to employ a DNS domain or subdomain name as the workgroup name.

 Windows NT domains are just workgroups with a special server, the domain controller, which handles centralized logons and typically some other tasks. If you use a domain configuration, you set the NT domain name using the workgroup parameter.

Miscellaneous Identification Options

In addition to setting the NetBIOS name, workgroup name, and related options, you may need to attend to a few miscellaneous identification parameters. These can affect how other systems interact with your Samba server:

server string
> This parameter sets a free-form string that appears along with the NetBIOS name in many operating systems' network browsers. In fact, in Windows XP, this string is more prominent than the NetBIOS name.

protocol
> This parameter sets the maximum protocol level that Samba uses. (The %R entry in Table 3-1 describes the values that this parameter accepts.) Chances are you won't need to change this value, but it's conceivable that downgrading will help when dealing with very old clients.

announce as
> You can tell Samba to announce itself as any number of different Windows OSs with this parameter. Legal values are NT Server (the default), NT (a synonym for NT Server), NT Workstation, Win95, and WfW. As with protocol, chances are you won't need to adjust this parameter except perhaps with some very old clients, which might not be able to cope with newer settings.

announce version
> This parameter sets an OS version number that goes along with the announce as value. The default value for recent versions of Samba is 4.9, and this should almost never be changed.

Chances are you'll only want to set the server string parameter, which has a direct effect on clients. This is shown in Figure 3-1, which depicts a Windows XP computer's view of the servers on a network using the My Network Places browsing tool. In most cases, the NetBIOS name appears in parentheses after the value of the server string variable. (*HALRLOPRILLALAR in* Figure 3-1 is an exception because it lacks the server string value, or rather, it lacks its equivalent because this computer is the Windows computer used to take the screen shot.) Many default *smb.conf* files place the %v variable in the server string parameter, which has the effect of displaying the Samba version number to clients, as in the *TEELA* server in Figure 3-1. This information, though, can be useful to miscreants wanting to break into the computer. To be sure, they can discover the version in some other way, but there's no point in making it easy for them; I recommend not using %v in your server string parameter.

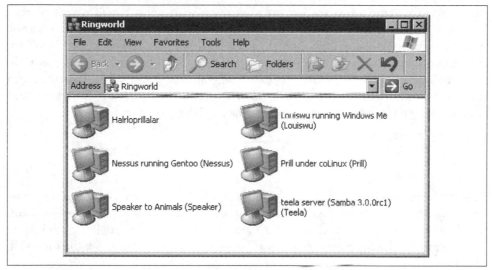

Figure 3-1. Windows displays the value of the server string variable alongside the NetBIOS name in its network browser

Setting Master Browser Options

In order to handle local network browsers like the one shown in Figure 3-1, SMB/CIFS requires one computer to be designated a *master browser*. This computer collects data on the computers on the network and provides it to any computer that asks for the information. The clients then present the data to users in one form or another (Figure 3-1 being one example).

In the context of SMB/CIFS, a network browser is a tool that provides information about, and typically a way to access, SMB/CIFS file and printer shares. Typically, it's integrated into the OS's local file manager. In Windows, it's called either *My Network Places* or *Network Neighborhood*, depending on the version of Windows. SMB/CIFS browsers use different protocols from web browsers. Although some programs, such as the K Desktop Environment's (KDE's) Konqueror, can serve as both SMB/CIFS and web browsers, the two protocols are entirely unrelated.

In fact, two types of SMB/CIFS master browsers exist. A *local master browser* handles browsing tasks on a single subnet. A *domain master browser* helps integrate multiple subnets. The local master browser is selected automatically by the computers on a network using a process known as an *election*. Samba provides options that influence how it participates in elections; you can "rig" an election so that Samba wins or loses it, as you see fit. Domain master browser status is acquired based on server configuration, and Samba provides options to control this process, as well. Chapter 5 describes these parameters in more detail. For the moment, though, if you don't want Samba to acquire either type of master browser status, you should add the following parameters to your *smb.conf* file's [global] section:

```
domain master = No
local master = No
os level = 0
preferred master = No
```

In fact, the first two options should be sufficient to keep Samba from acquiring master browser status; the last two options simply provide added insurance, should you accidentally mis-set the local master parameter. Of course, on some networks you might want Samba to acquire local master browser status; to do so, set the following options:

```
local master = Yes
os level = 33
preferred master = Yes
```

Configuring Samba to become a local master browser on a network on which browsing works fine may cause problems. If Samba acquires master browser duties over a working master browser, the result can be disruptions should that old system try to reacquire master browser status periodically. Each such attempt to reacquire master browser status will result in a temporary browsing outage. Likewise, network topology and other issues can cause problems when changing a master browser. If in doubt, configure Samba to *not* try to take on these duties.

Setting Password Options

New Samba installations are frequently plagued by two problems: incorrectly set workgroup names and password encryption difficulties. The first problem is easily corrected by changing the workgroup parameter, as described earlier. Password problems are harder to overcome because they may require changing more than just one or two Samba parameters. To address these issues, you must first understand them. You must then decide whether to use unencrypted or encrypted passwords. On some networks, you may need to decide whether to use a password server for authentication, as well.

Password Issues

Samba password issues can be complicated. SMB/CIFS provides several different ways to encode passwords, to authenticate clients using passwords, and to store them. In fact, some of these issues are negotiated between client and server, with no need for explicit configuration, but others require your attention.

The simplest case of Samba password handling, at least from the point of view of Samba administration, is to have Samba accept unencrypted (or *cleartext*) passwords from clients and authenticate users against the local Linux account database. Conceptually, this works much like Linux authentication for FTP, Telnet, SSH, or other servers that use the Linux account database. Unfortunately, this approach has some problems. Most importantly, exchanging passwords in cleartext makes them vulnerable to *sniffing*—interception by unauthorized third parties who have physical access to your network wires. (In an Internet exchange, sniffing can also occur on intervening routers or their networks.) Thus, unencrypted passwords are undesirable from a security point of view. (On the other hand, the password encryption systems used by some versions of SMB/CIFS are not much better than cleartext, so you shouldn't consider encrypted passwords to be proof against sniffing.) In terms of practicality, cleartext passwords are also a problem because recent versions of Windows use encrypted passwords by default and don't drop back to cleartext passwords. Although you can reconfigure Windows clients to use cleartext passwords, doing so on a large network can be tedious.

So, what about encrypted passwords? Unfortunately, the password encryption systems used by SMB/CIFS aren't compatible with the encrypted form of Linux passwords used in a standard Linux password database (*/etc/passwd* or, more commonly, */etc/shadow*). Therefore, in order to support SMB/CIFS encrypted passwords, Samba must maintain its own password database. Typically, this database is stored in a file called *smbpasswd* and is located in the same directory as *smb.conf* or a subdirectory of that directory. Other methods of storing this database exist but are beyond the scope of this book. If you want to use encrypted passwords, you must not only configure Samba to use them but create the encrypted password file, populate it with account information, and assign passwords to users. Because the Linux passwords are stored in a *hash* (basically, a one-way encryption system), they can't be decrypted, and you'll need to either assign random Samba passwords to users or have them enter passwords in some way. This task can be tedious on a large network.

A third approach to handling passwords is to defer to another computer. For instance, if your network is configured as a Windows NT domain or an AD domain, you can have Samba defer to the domain controller. This approach greatly simplifies Samba setup because you don't need to configure a local password database. Samba provides several options for how to defer to a remote system.

No matter what method you use, each user of your system must have a local account. (Using guest accounts can relax this restriction, but this topic is beyond the scope of this book.) Thus, you must still create local Linux accounts even if you use a Windows domain controller for authentication. If this task is tedious because you have many users, you may want to consult Chapter 7, which describes joining a Linux system to an NT domain in a way that enables the underlying Linux accounts to mirror the NT domain's accounts. Although this configuration can be a bit tricky to set up, it can greatly simplify account maintenance on a large network that has an NT domain controller (either a Windows system or a Samba server).

Using Cleartext Passwords

From a Samba configuration perspective, the simplest authentication method is to use cleartext passwords. You can do so by setting `encrypt passwords = No` in the [global] section of *smb.conf*. This configuration is the default in Samba versions prior to 3.0; however, with Version 3.0, the default setting changed to Yes. To avoid confusion, I recommend setting the value explicitly, whatever version of Samba you're using. When configured to use cleartext passwords, Samba doesn't attempt to negotiate an encrypted password exchange with clients; it does attempt to authenticate users against the passwords stored in the local Linux password database. Thus, users must have valid local Linux passwords, not just valid accounts. (With encrypted passwords, Samba users' accounts could conceivably exist but have disabled local passwords.)

Windows versions since Windows 95 OEM Service Release 2 (OSR2) and Windows NT 4.0 Service Pack 3 (SP3) require the use of encrypted passwords by default. Thus, these OSs will not work with a Samba server configured to use cleartext passwords unless you change a Windows Registry entry. One relatively painless way to do so is to use a *.reg* file that ships with Samba. In fact, several such files exist, one for each version of Windows. The filename takes the form *WinVer_PlanPassword.reg*, where *Ver* is the Windows version. For instance, *Win2000_PlainPassword.reg* is the file for Windows 2000, and *WinXP_PlainPassword.reg* does the job for Windows XP. Some distributions deliver these files in compressed form, so *.gz* may be tacked onto the end; if so, you'll need to uncompress the file with *gunzip* before you use it. Precisely where you can find these files also varies. Most place them in the *Registry* subdirectory of the Samba documentation directory, as in */usr/share/doc/samba-3.0.2a/full_docs/Registry*, but the precise path varies.

 Try using your distribution's package management tools to locate these files. For instance, on a computer that uses the RPM Package Manager (RPM), you could type `rpm -ql samba | grep PlainPassword` to locate the files in the *samba* package that contain the string *PlainPassword* in their names.

Once you've located these files, copy the ones you need to a floppy disk, put them on an FTP site, send them via email, or otherwise make them accessible to clients. On a Windows system, double-click the file from the file manager to install the changes in the Registry. You then need to reboot the computer for the changes to take effect. In a small office, you should be able to apply the patch to all the Windows clients in a few minutes by walking from one system to another with a floppy disk in your hand. Alternatively, you can make the changes manually using a Windows Registry editor; however, applying the changes automatically is almost certain to be both faster and more reliable.

Once you've configured the Samba server and your clients to use cleartext passwords, the clients should be able to access the server, assuming appropriate accounts with valid passwords exist on the server. However, a few additional parameters can affect access:

`password level`
Linux's local passwords are case-sensitive, but many SMB/CIFS clients assume passwords will be treated in a case-insensitive way. For instance, Windows 9x/Me converts all passwords to uppercase when using certain SMB/CIFS protocol levels. In order to work around this problem, the global `password level` parameter tells Samba to try case variants. The default value for this parameter is 0, which causes Samba to try the password as delivered and the password converted to all-lowercase if it was sent in all-uppercase. Higher values cause Samba to convert the password to lowercase and then to convert the specified number of letters to uppercase. For instance, if `password level` = 1 and if a client gives RHUMBA as the password, Samba tries to authenticate the user with passwords of RHUMBA, rhumba, Rhumba, rHumba, and so on. Using high numbers as the `password level` parameter can therefore improve the odds of a successful login using a valid password that's been corrupted by the client. These attempts increase the time for Samba to confirm that a password is invalid, though, and, in some cases, to verify a valid password. They also increase the odds of a successful break-in by effectively eliminating case as a security feature in your local passwords.

`username level`

> This global parameter is similar to `password level`, but it applies to usernames rather than passwords. One other minor difference is that when this parameter is set to its default value of 0, Samba tests the username converted to lowercase followed by the username converted to lowercase but with an initial capital letter. If you give higher values, Samba tries up to the number of letters converted to uppercase that you specify, just as with `password level`.

`username`

> This share-level parameter specifies a list of usernames against which to test a password. This is necessary when using some very old clients (such as some antiquated DOS clients) that don't send usernames, just passwords. Samba tries the password with each of the usernames specified. Ordinarily, this parameter isn't needed because all modern clients deliver usernames by default. This parameter can be used with encrypted passwords as well as with cleartext ones, but because the clients most likely to force its use employ unencrypted passwords, I've described it here.

On the whole, using cleartext passwords is normally undesirable on modern networks. Between the increased risks of password sniffing with cleartext passwords, and the fact that most modern SMB/CIFS clients don't use them by default, you're usually better off switching to an encrypted password system or to a password server. Encrypted passwords can be more of a hassle to configure on the Samba server, but they're easier to configure on the clients.

Using Encrypted Passwords

Because all modern versions of Windows use encrypted passwords by default, this approach is the easiest one from a client configuration point of view. You will, though, need to take some steps to get encrypted passwords working on the server.

> From a client perspective, the difference between using encrypted passwords on the file or print server and using a password server is nil. In both cases, the client engages in a challenge-response authentication exchange with the file or print server; only the configuration of that file or print server differs.

Only one *smb.conf* entry needs changing to use encrypted passwords: `encrypt passwords = Yes`. This is the default value for Samba 3.0 and later, but earlier versions used `No` as the default, so I recommend setting it explicitly to avoid confusion. A few other parameters can influence how Samba treats encrypted passwords, but they probably don't need adjustment:

smb passwd file

You can tell Samba what file to use for holding encrypted passwords with this global parameter. Ordinarily, Samba uses a file called *smbpasswd*, which is usually located in the same directory as *smb.conf* or a subdirectory thereof.

passdb backend

This parameter tells Samba how to store its password database. The usual value, smbpasswd, specifies that the *smbpasswd* file (or another file specified by smb passwd file) be used. Other options tell Samba to use more specialized types of databases, such as an LDAP directory. Fully describing these alternatives is beyond the scope of this book.

lanman auth

The LANMAN hashing scheme is one of several SMB/CIFS encrypted authentication systems. This global Boolean parameter enables or disables support for this protocol. The default value is Yes, and the parameter must be set to this value to support Windows 9x/Me systems.

ntlm auth

The NT LANMAN (NTLM) hash is an improvement on LANMAN authentication, and this parameter controls whether Samba accepts this authentication method. The default value is Yes. If this option and lanman auth are both set to No, only the newest NTLMv2 protocol will work; however, this protocol was added only to Windows NT 4.0 SP4; older clients (and many non-Microsoft clients) don't support NTLMv2.

In addition to setting encrypt passwords = Yes and, if desired, any ancillary password-related parameters, you must prepare a local Samba password database. This database is maintained using the *smbpasswd* command. In particular, you add users to the database using the *-a* parameter (which can only be used as *root*):

```
# smbpasswd -a linnaeus
New SMB password:
Retype new SMB password:
Added user linnaeus
```

This command adds a Samba password entry for the user *linnaeus*. If your system lacks a current *smbpasswd* file or its equivalent, you'll see an error message to the effect that it doesn't exist; but don't fear, the *smbpasswd* utility creates the file and adds the user to it. In any event, you should repeat this command for every user on your system. Note that Samba requires the username to match an existing Linux account, so if you're configuring a new system, you should create a Linux account first, and then create a Samba password database entry for it.

Running *smbpasswd* in this way isn't very difficult for a network with just a few users, but on a larger network, it can be quite tedious. If you want to script the operation, you can deliver a password to the utility within a script by appending the password to the username, separated by a percent symbol (%):

```
smbpasswd -a linnaeus%apassword
```

Of course, your script will need to generate passwords in some (preferably random) way. You'll then need to either communicate this information to your users or help them enter their passwords later. Another option is to use a script called *mksmbpasswd*, *mksmbpasswd.sh*, or something similar. These scripts create a new *smbpasswd* file from your regular Linux *passwd* database. Such scripts used to ship with Samba packages, but they're less common today, perhaps because they save very little time. The scripts can't convert Linux passwords to a form that SMB/CIFS can use, so they deliberately generate accounts with invalid passwords. Thus, you must still help users enter their encrypted passwords manually.

In theory, the global update encrypted parameter can help you enter encrypted passwords. When set to Yes, this parameter causes Samba to set a user's encrypted password to the value of an unencrypted password that a client computer sends when the user logs on. Unfortunately, this requires you to configure your clients to send unencrypted passwords. Thus, although update encrypted might help you convert a network from cleartext to encrypted passwords, it won't be of much help when adding a new Linux system to an existing network that already uses encrypted passwords.

The case options described earlier, in the section "Using Cleartext Passwords," are inapplicable to encrypted passwords. Depending on the hash chosen by the client, passwords may be case-sensitive or -insensitive, and Samba provides the same case sensitivity as clients. Thus, in this respect encrypted passwords are simpler than unencrypted passwords.

The *smbpasswd* command can be used to change passwords for existing accounts, as well as create new ones. Type **smbpasswd** *username*, where *username* is the username whose password you want to change, to do the job. Individual users can also use this utility to change their passwords, but they must have shell access to the server to do so.

 If users don't need shell access to the server, you can set their login shells to */usr/bin/smbpasswd*. When users log in using Telnet or SSH, they'll enter their Linux passwords and then be prompted to change their Samba passwords. Once this is done, they're immediately logged out.

Using a Password Server

Instead of using a local password database, you can defer authentication to another computer—typically a domain controller, but perhaps some other system. In fact, Samba provides three different ways to do this. You choose the method using the security parameter, but depending upon the method you choose, you may need to perform some additional configuration steps.

All these methods of authentication require you to set encrypt passwords = Yes. Instead of maintaining the account database locally, though, you point Samba at an external server.

Setting the security mode

The security parameter tells Samba what security mode to use—that is, what rules to apply for authenticating users. This parameter takes one of five possible values:

Share

> When using this security level, Samba attempts to emulate the default access control method of Windows 9x/Me, which is to assign passwords to individual shares and not use usernames. To do this, Samba tries to authenticate using the password that the client sends and a series of different accounts, such as an account used by a previous logon from the client or the name of the share itself. Share-level security is a poor match to Linux's underlying security model, though, and so it's seldom used.

User

> This security model is the default, and it corresponds to the use of a local account database—either a cleartext Linux account database or an encrypted Samba account database, depending on the value of encrypt passwords.

Server

> When using server-level security, Samba authenticates users against a remote server in much the way that Windows 9x/Me servers do. On a technical level, this authentication method is similar to a man-in-the-middle attack; the Samba server essentially passes the data on from the client as if it were making the logon request, then honors the reply from the server. This approach is easy to configure but occasionally doesn't work correctly. It can be used to authenticate against a server that's not a domain controller, but the remote server must be configured to enable remote authentication. This option is being deprecated in Samba 3.0 and later; it still works, but is likely to eventually vanish.

Domain

> In a domain-level configuration, the Samba server fully joins an NT domain, much as Windows NT/200x/XP systems do. Samba can then exchange credentials with the domain controller and use the full NT domain authentication system for its users.

ADS

> This is the latest authentication method. It links Samba to a Windows 200x Active Directory (AD) controller and uses native AD protocols for authentication. This system is also the most difficult to configure and isn't fully described in this book.

If you use server-, domain-, or ADS-level security, you must tell Samba where to find the password server. This task can be accomplished with the global password server parameter, which accepts a list of one or more names or IP addresses. If you specify a name, it's looked up in the order specified by the name resolve order parameter. If you use domain- or ADS-level security, the remote servers must be domain controllers. Alternatively, you can specify an asterisk (*) to have Samba attempt to locate its domain controller automatically.

 Don't use the `password server` parameter or domain- or ADS-level security on a system that you configure as a domain controller. Such systems should use user-level security and should omit the `password server` parameter.

Using server-level security

Server-level security can be a quick way to use a remote password server. This configuration requires you to enter options like this:

```
security = Server
password server = 172.24.21.98
```

Of course, you'd adjust the IP address for your own network. Little else is required for this configuration, at least on the Samba server that users access directly. You must ensure that appropriate user accounts exist on the password server system, though. Those accounts must also match the local Linux user accounts on the Samba server you're configuring; using a remote password server doesn't obviate the need to provide local Linux accounts for Samba's use.

 Windows networks frequently employ longer usernames than do Linux systems; for instance, *Carl Linnaeus* rather than *linnaeus*. If your password server uses such usernames, you can map them to conventional Linux usernames with the `username map` parameter. This parameter accepts a filename that contains mappings of Linux to Windows usernames, as in `linnaeus = "Carl Linnaeus"`. When Samba receives a logon request from *Carl Linnaeus*, it authenticates against the password server using that name but uses the local *linnaeus* account. Although you can use this parameter with user-level security, it's most frequently employed with server-, domain-, or ADS-level security.

Using domain-level security

A more complex configuration than server-level security looks nearly identical to it in *smb.conf*:

```
security = Domain
password server = 172.24.21.98
```

However, this configuration requires joining the Samba server to the domain using the *net* command. You can accomplish this task by passing the *join* subcommand to *net*:

```
# net join member -U adminuser
```

In this example, the system is joined as a member of the domain specified by the `workgroup` parameter in *smb.conf* and controlled by the domain controller pointed to by password server. You must specify an account to use on the domain controller for this operation with the -U parameter. This account must have administrative access to the domain controller's account database, because it must add a *machine trust account* for your Samba server. This machine trust account is used in the authentication process for individual user logons.

As a practical matter, domain-level security is a bit tougher to configure than is server-level security, but it's more reliable in some situations. If necessary, you can use the username map parameter, as described in the section "Using server-level security," to associate Linux usernames with Windows usernames.

 Chapter 5 describes configuring a Samba server as a domain controller, including the domain controller configuration options required to enable joining other Samba servers as full domain members.

Summary

If you've been making changes to your Samba server's configuration as you've read this chapter, it should now be functioning in a rather minimal way on your network. You should understand the basics of the Samba configuration file format, and you should be able to make your server appear in clients' SMB/CIFS browsers. If at least one share is defined (as is common in sample *smb.conf* files), you should also be able to log on to the Samba server from clients, thanks to appropriate settings for the password options on both client and server. Of course, these tasks aren't enough; in most cases, you run a Samba server in order to share files or printers, which means you need to be able to define appropriate shares. This task is the topic of Chapter 4.

CHAPTER 4
File and Printer Shares

Chapter 3 described basic Samba configuration—assigning NetBIOS and workgroup names to the Samba server, setting password options, and so on. In most cases, though, a Samba server's primary responsibility is to provide file and printer shares to clients. This is the topic of this chapter.

This chapter begins with a look at file shares—how to define them, set access options, and so on. Printer shares are basically just variants of file shares, but because they must interface with the Linux printing system, this chapter describes a few details of Linux's printing architecture, including the basics of configuring the Common Unix Printing System, the most popular printing software on Linux. Another printing-related feature is the delivery of printer drivers to Windows systems; SMB/CIFS and Samba support special options to handle this task. Finally, this chapter concludes with several example shares that demonstrate common file- and printer-sharing scenarios.

Common File Share Options

At many sites, file sharing is the most important duty of a Samba server. File shares can store users' data files and programs run by many users, exchange data between users, be part of a network backup system, and serve other purposes. (Examples of shares for many of these roles appear in the later section "Example Shares.") You can create a basic file share with just one line in *smb.conf*, but fine-tuning it to do what you want will take more lines. Options you may want to tune include those that control write access to the share, those that adjust how Samba reports filenames to clients, and those that influence local Linux or client filesystem security features.

Defining a File Share

A minimal file share consists of a single line that contains the share name in square brackets:

```
[sample]
```

If you include this line in *smb.conf* at the end of the file, or with another share definition immediately following it, Samba will create a file share called *SAMPLE*. This share will be a read-only share corresponding to the */tmp* directory on the server. Chances are these options aren't the ones you want. At a minimum, you'll almost certainly want to use the path parameter or its synonym, directory. These parameters tell Samba what directory to use as the root of the share you define. For instance, to share */var/samba/somedir*, you might enter a share definition like this:

```
[sample]
    path = /var/samba/somedir
```

This entry creates a file share that appears in Windows network browsers as *SAMPLE*, just like the previous definition; but this share provides read-only access to files in */var/samba/somedir*. Note that the share name (*SAMPLE* in this example) and the name of the directory to be shared (*/var/samba/somedir*) are unrelated. Of course, they *could* be related, and doing so can help you administer your system, but doing it isn't strictly necessary. Other share-level options you might want to use include the following:

available

> This parameter's value defaults to Yes, which makes the share available. If you want to temporarily disable a share, you can set available = No. (This won't work for the [homes] share, which is described in the later section "The [homes] Share.") The effect is much the same as commenting out or deleting the entire share definition.

comment

> This share-level parameter is a share's equivalent of the global server string parameter; it creates a description of the share that's visible from clients' file browsers.

browseable

> Shares that are *browseable* appear in file browsers on clients. Those that aren't browseable don't appear in browse lists but are still accessible to users who type the share name into an access tool. By default, Samba makes file shares browseable, but you can hide them by setting browseable = No. This parameter is also usually set to No for [homes] shares, as described in the section "The [homes] Share."

Setting Write Access

The default for Samba file shares is to provide read-only access. Of course, many types of shares must be read/write in order to be useful, so Samba provides a way to provide this type of access—in fact, several ways. The writeable, writable, and write ok parameters are all synonyms, and when any of them is set to Yes, read/write access to the share becomes possible. The read only parameter is an antonym for these parameters; setting read only = No has the same effect as setting writeable = Yes.

In addition to the critical writeable parameter or one of its synonyms, several other parameters affect write access to the share based on other features:

invalid users

> This share-level parameter doesn't strictly affect write access; instead, it provides a list of users who are denied all access to the share. All users who aren't explicitly listed are granted access to the share. You can specify a Linux group by preceding its name with an at sign (@) or a plus sign (+), as in @students. (The @ sign first attempts to look up a netgroup name and then uses the local group database. The plus sign uses the local group database alone.)

read list

> You can provide a list of users who are permitted only to read the files on an otherwise read/write share with this share-level parameter.

valid users

> This share-level parameter is the opposite of invalid users; it provides a list of users who are permitted to access the share. Attempts by other users to access the share are denied. You can specify a Linux group by preceding its name with an at sign (@) or a plus sign (+), as in @students.

write list

> This share-level parameter is the opposite of read list; you provide a list of users who are permitted to write to an otherwise read-only share. It's often used to specify share administrators who may add files to a share.

Setting writeable = Yes, one of its synonyms, or one of the modifier parameters, is enough to provide read/write access to a shared directory from Samba's perspective, but you must also consider the underlying Linux permissions. In most cases, Samba uses the access rights of the user who initiated a connection. For instance, if the user *linnaeus* is accessing a share, and if *linnaeus* doesn't have write access to a directory, Samba won't be able to save files in that directory for this user. Thus, you should consider user access rights from a traditional Linux permissions perspective when preparing file shares. Modifying Samba's permissions system is described in the section "Setting Access Control Features," and practical examples of some systems are described in the section "Example Shares."

 Samba provides some extremely powerful options for modifying both read and write access to its shares. As a general rule, though, it's best to keep it simple; overuse of sophisticated access control tools can create a complicated configuration that will easily break. Worse, you might inadvertently create a security hole that a user can exploit accidentally or deliberately.

Setting Filename Options

Windows and Linux make different assumptions about filenames. Because SMB/CIFS is so strongly associated with Windows and related clients, Samba is designed around the Windows assumptions. The problem comes in translating filenames stored on a Linux filesystem into the format expected by Windows. Samba provides many parameters that help you accomplish this goal. Broadly speaking, differences come in a few areas:

Filename length

> Most Linux filesystems provide long filenames—typically up to 255 characters. Windows clients can use long filenames, but they also expect to see short filenames (eight characters with a three-character extension, or so-called *8.3 filenames*) in addition to the long filenames. Older DOS clients can use only the short filenames. DOS and 16-bit Windows programs require short filenames even when they're run from more modern versions of Windows. Because Linux native filesystems store a single filename and don't automatically create shortened filenames that correspond to long filenames, Samba generates short filenames on the fly, using a process called *filename mangling*. Samba provides several parameters that enable you to fine-tune this mangling process.

Filename case

> Linux filesystems are *case-sensitive*; two filenames that differ only in case, such as *afile.txt* and *AFile.TXT*, are considered unique. Both files can exist in a single directory, and if you enter the filename's case incorrectly, Linux won't be able to access an existing file. Windows, by contrast, is *case-retentive*: filename case is preserved when you save a file, but the OS doesn't care about case when you specify a filename. This means that two files that differ only in case can't exist in the same directory. DOS is even more primitive; it uses completely *case-insensitive* filenames. DOS stores all filenames entirely in uppercase. (DOS programs can usually access lowercase filenames on a Samba server, though.) Samba provides case-sensitivity options, some of which interact with filename mangling options, to accommodate these different case-handling systems.

Character sets

> Traditionally, filenames have been stored on both Windows and Linux filesystems using the American Standard Code for Information Interchange (ASCII). ASCII is inadequate, though, for storing filenames that contain letters from non-Roman alphabets, such as Cyrillic or Arabic letters. An older solution to this problem involved *code pages*, which are basically alternatives to ASCII. A more modern solution uses *Unicode*, which uses a 16-bit encoding system for characters, thus greatly increasing the number of characters that can be used in filenames. Samba must have a way to translate between either system and the filenames actually stored on the disk.

As a general rule, Samba's default options work well. These defaults cause Samba to present the illusion of a case-retentive filesystem with both long and short filenames. Samba does this by looking for files that differ only in case when a provided filename can't be found, and by creating mangled filenames to go along with long filenames when the client requests them. Sometimes, though, you may need to tweak these settings by using some parameters:

case sensitive
> This share-level Boolean parameter controls whether Samba treats filename access in a case-sensitive way. The default value of No works well with DOS and Windows clients, and, in fact, DOS and Windows 9x/Me clients will likely misbehave in various ways if you set this option to Yes. Windows NT/200x/XP is better at handling case-sensitive filenames, but case sensitive = No is still the preferred option for it. Some Linux and Unix clients may work better with case sensitive = Yes, but this setting usually isn't required even for these clients. Samba 3.0.6 introduced the Auto value for this option and made it the default. This setting enables the server to detect some clients' preferred case sensitivity and should work with the Linux cifs filesystem, among others.

preserve case
> When set to the default value, Yes, this share-level Boolean parameter causes Samba to store new files in the same case as provided by clients. When set to No, Samba converts filenames to the case specified by default case (described shortly). Setting this option to No can be handy if you have clients that generate ugly all-uppercase filenames, and you want to access the files from other clients.

short preserve case
> This parameter works just like preserve case, but it applies only to short (8.3) filenames.

default case
> This share-level parameter accepts values of Upper and Lower. It defaults to Lower, but this default is meaningless unless you set either preserve case or short preserve case to No. If you do so, Samba converts newly created filenames to the specified case.

mangled names
> When set to Yes (the default), this share-level Boolean parameter causes Samba to generate mangled filenames for files longer than the DOS 8.3 limits. These names are delivered in addition to the regular filenames, so this option won't cause problems for clients that expect long filenames. This feature is most important for DOS clients, but it can also be important for Windows clients that run DOS or 16-bit Windows programs.

mangle case
> Ordinarily, Samba doesn't mangle short filenames that don't match the client's case expectations. If you set mangle case = Yes, though, Samba mangles filenames

that aren't entirely in the case specified by default case. Chances are this action won't be necessary, and in fact it's likely to produce very ugly results, but it's conceivable you'll run across some DOS programs that choke on lowercase names, in which case using this option may be your only solution. This option was eliminated over the development of the 3.0.x versions of Samba.

mangled map

This share-level option specifies pairs of filename wildcards that should be mangled in particular ways. For instance, mangled map = (*.html *.htm) converts all filenames that end in *.html* so that they end in *.htm* instead. Unlike other mangling options, this one applies to all filenames, not just those delivered to DOS or as short filename alternatives to Windows clients. This option is not being actively maintained and so may develop bugs in the future.

mangling method

Samba uses one of two methods to create mangled filenames. You can specify which method to use with this global parameter, which accepts values of hash and hash2. The latter option, which is the default with Samba 3.0 and later, produces filenames that bear less resemblance to the original than does the first, but hash2 is also less likely to produce *collisions*—identical hashes derived from different original filenames.

mangle prefix

This global parameter sets the number of characters to be preserved from the original filename when creating a mangled filename using the hash2 mangling method. The default value is 1, but you can improve the intelligibility of mangled filenames by increasing this value (the maximum is 6).

unicode

This global Boolean parameter defaults to Yes, which tells Samba to support Unicode filenames provided by clients. Normally there's no need to change this parameter. It's available only in early 3.0.x releases and has been dropped in later versions.

dos charset

You can tell Samba what code page to use when communicating with older clients that don't support Unicode with this global parameter. You specify code pages using three-digit codes preceded by the string CP, as in CP850 (Latin 1, which works well for most North American systems) or CP866 (Cyrillic). This option is new with Samba 3.0.

unix charset

This global parameter sets the name of the character set Linux uses for its filenames. The default value is UTF8. This value stands for Unicode Transformation Format 8, which is a method of encoding Unicode in an 8-bit character set such as ASCII. Ordinarily, you won't change this option, which is new with Samba 3.0.

client code page
> This global parameter was used through the 2.2.x versions of Samba as a way to specify what code page the client used. It's since been replaced by dos charset. This parameter takes code page numbers without a preceding CP string, as in 850 or 866.

character set
> This global parameter was used in Samba through the 2.2.x series to tell the server how to encode different code pages on the server's filesystem. Values were character set values, such as ISO8859-1 (Latin 1) or KOI8-R (Cyrillic). This parameter has been replaced by unix charset in Samba 3.0 and later.

This list of parameters may be intimidating (and I've even left out some of the more exotic options!), but in most cases, you need not change any of these values. When dealing with DOS clients, though, you might want to adjust the short preserve case option, if you want to force DOS filenames to appear in all-lowercase on the server. (This will make them look better in most non-DOS clients.) Changing mangle prefix can improve the intelligibility of mangled filenames on DOS clients. Linux and Unix clients can benefit from setting case sensitive = Yes, but this change isn't usually required. (For versions of Samba that support Auto for this parameter, using this feature is usually better, too.) If your users regularly create files with non-ASCII filenames, you may need to investigate the various character set and code page options.

You can place filename options in OS-specific configuration files and use the include parameter with the %a variable in the [global] section to load them only for appropriate client OSs. For instance, add include = smb-%a.conf to *smb.conf* and then create files called *smb-WfW.conf*, *smb-Samba.conf*, and so on, in which you store OS-specific options. Table 3-1 describes the %a variable and its possible values.

Setting Access Control Features

Linux uses Unix-style access control mechanisms, which provide read, write, and execute permissions for each of three classes of users: the file's owner, the file's group, and all other users (a.k.a. world access). Linux also provides Access Control Lists (ACLs) in most of its native filesystems, although Linux ACL support is still new and few programs are designed with it in mind.

Windows and SMB/CIFS, by contrast, originally provided little in the way of access controls; users who mounted a share were given access to all files on the share. Windows NT/200x/XP, though, provides ACLs similar to Linux ACLs. Integrating these two access control heritages can be tricky sometimes, particularly because Samba must support both older clients that don't use ACLs and newer clients that do. In order to accomplish this task, Samba provides a series of options that affect the way it treats Linux file ownership, Linux file permissions, DOS-style filesystem features, and ACLs. Recent versions of Samba also support *Unix extensions*, which are extensions to SMB/CIFS that more directly support Unix-style ownership and permissions. Samba's Unix extensions support is intended for Linux or Unix clients.

Setting Linux ownership

Linux's local file security model relies heavily on the concept of file ownership—both the file's owner and the file's group. In order to interface Samba clients with this system, Samba provides several *smb.conf* parameters that affect the ownership of files a user creates. In conjunction with existing files' permissions, Samba's ownership parameters also influence whether a user is granted the right to read or change an existing file. The most important of these parameters are as follows:

force user

> You can pass a local Linux username to this share-level parameter to have Samba treat all file accesses as if they originated with the specified user. For instance, force user = linnaeus tells Samba to give the user read access to those files that *linnaeus* can read, write access to files that *linnaeus* can write, and so on. Files created when accessing the share are owned by *linnaeus*. In addition, unless you use force group, the group used for accesses is set to the specified user's default group. The default is to use the account of the username provided by the user (or mapped by username map, if you employ that parameter).

force group

> This share-level parameter is similar to force user, but it applies to the group used for file accesses. A synonym for this parameter is group.

guest ok

> This Boolean share-level parameter tells Samba whether to accept *guest* accesses to the share—that is, accesses without the benefit of a password. If guest ok = Yes and if a guest logon occurs, Samba uses the account specified by guest account for accesses, much as if force user had been used. A synonym for this parameter is public. Note that the global map to guest parameter must also be set appropriately before this parameter will work.

guest account

> This global option sets the account used for guest accesses, as authorized on a share-by-share basis by guest ok. The default value is a compile-time option, but it's usually set to nobody.

map to guest

> This global parameter controls the conditions that trigger a guest logon. Samba accepts values of Never (Samba never accepts a guest logon; this is the default value), Bad User (Samba accepts a guest logon when a user specifies an invalid username), and Bad Password (Samba accepts a guest logon when a user specifies an invalid username or password).

Generally speaking, the best approach is to use Samba's default options. Forcing Samba to use particular users or groups can be a convenient way to avoid having to set permissions properly on files (including ensuring that Samba sets them in a sensible way), but forcing a user or group also means that you'll lose information. Should strange files begin appearing, for instance, it may become very difficult to track down who's creating the files if you use force user.

Setting Linux permissions

File ownership alone doesn't go very far in Linux. To be effective, ownership must be paired with file permissions (a.k.a. the file *mode*). Linux's traditional Unix-style permissions apply read, write, and execute permissions to each of three classes of users: the owner, the group, and the world. Each of these permissions is a single bit, for a total of nine bits of permission information. These may be expressed as a string, as in rwxr-x---, in which a dash (-) stands for no permission and an r, w, or x stands for read, write, or execute permission, respectively. Alternatively, ownership may be expressed as three octal (base-8) numbers corresponding to the 3-bit value for read, write, and execute permission, as in 750 for rwxr-x---. A leading 0 is often added to the octal form of the mode; higher values signify some special file-permission bits. A leading dash is often added to the string value. This dash is replaced by other characters to signify particular file types, such as d for a directory.

Because DOS and Windows know nothing about Unix-style permissions, and therefore don't pass information on appropriate permissions when creating new files, Samba must generate this information. It does so as specified by these parameters:

create mask

This share-level parameter specifies the default and maximum permissions to apply to new files created by the client. It's expressed in an octal form, as in create mask = 744 (the default value). Note that clients can remove write access by setting the DOS read-only flag. If you enable any execute permissions (by specifying an odd value for any of the three octal digits), they can also be removed by the client if the appropriate DOS attribute mappings are configured, as described in the section "Mapping DOS-style flags." A synonym for this parameter is create mode.

directory mask

This share-level parameter works just like create mask, except that it applies to directories rather than files. Because Linux requires the execute permission bit to be set on directories for some read operations, this parameter typically uses octal values of 7, 5, or 0, as in directory mask = 755 (the default value). A synonym for this parameter is directory mode.

inherit permissions

This share-level Boolean parameter defaults to No, but if you set it to Yes, it overrides create mask and directory mask. In this case, files and directories acquire permissions based on the values of their parent directories. (The execute bits of parent directories are stripped when creating files, however.) For instance, if a directory has a mode of 750 and a user creates a subdirectory in that directory, it will also have a mode of 750.

You should give careful thought to the values you specify for these parameters. Setting permissions too loosely can enable users who don't own the file the ability to read (or potentially even write) files and directories to which they should have no access. On the other side, setting these values too strictly can deny access to users who should be able to read or write files. Precisely what policy is right varies from one site to another, and perhaps even one share to another. Several examples appear in the section "Example Shares."

Mapping DOS-style flags

DOS and its descendent operating systems, including Windows, support several filesystem flags that don't appear in Linux or Unix filesystems. In order to support these flags, Samba can optionally map them onto the execute permission bit, which DOS and Windows don't use. Several parameters control this mapping:

map archive
> The DOS/Windows *archive bit* is set when a file is created and cleared when it's backed up with certain backup tools. If you set map archive = Yes (the default), Samba maps this bit to the owner execute bit.

map hidden
> The DOS/Windows *hidden bit* signals certain programs, such as file managers, to hide the presence of a file from users. The file is still accessible but won't appear in file listings. This bit can be used to hide files that would likely confuse users. If you set map hidden = Yes (the default is No), Samba stores this bit using the world execute bit.

map system
> The DOS/Windows *system bit* marks certain critical OS files as such. Most file managers hide these files, and some utilities treat them differently from other files. Chances are you won't be storing system files on a Samba server, so the default value of this parameter is No, but if you set it to Yes, Samba stores this bit in the group execute bit.

store dos attributes
> This share-level Boolean parameter defaults to No. When set to Yes and when the preceding three options are all set to No, store dos attributes causes Samba to store the DOS-style archive, hidden, and system attributes as extended attributes (EAs) on the Linux filesystem. EAs are supported only on the 2.6.x and later kernels and require the user_xattr filesystem mount option. They also require explicit filesystem support, which is present in ext2fs, ext3fs, ReiserFS, JFS, and XFS, but Linux doesn't support EAs in most non-Linux filesystems. One advantage of this parameter is that it supports storing attributes for directories as well as files. This parameter was added to Version 3.0.3 of Samba.

The first three of these parameters interact with the settings of the create mask parameter; if *either* create mask or the appropriate mapping parameter disables a particular execute bit, users can't set the matching DOS/Windows flag. The mapping works both ways; if you enable a mapping and then create a file under Linux that has execute permissions set (say, a script), it appears to Samba clients with the archive, hidden, or system bits set. For this reason, if you wish to let users legitimately create executable Linux files, leave these parameters at the default; this prevents the files from disappearing from view in Samba clients because of hidden or system bits appearing on these files. Disabling the archive bit (either by setting map archive = No or by setting a create mask value that disables access to the user execute bit) prevents files created on Samba clients from appearing under Linux as executable files.

Under Linux, the equivalent of hidden files are *dot files*—files whose names begin with dots (.). If a share will be accessible both from Samba clients and from Linux logins, you may want to ensure that hide dot files is set to Yes, as it is by default. This option tells Samba to set the hidden bit on all Linux dot files, no matter what the setting s of the world execute bit and the map hidden parameter are.

Using ACLs

ACLs provide a finer-grained method of access control than do Unix-style permissions. Windows NT has long supported ACLs on its New Technology File System (NTFS), and SMB/CIFS also supports ACLs. This support has only recently started to become common with Linux, though. In particular, the 2.6.x kernel series adds ACL support to most common Linux filesystems—as of the 2.6.7 kernel, ext2fs, ext3fs, JFS, and XFS all support ACLs. (With earlier kernels and most common Linux filesystems, you had to patch the kernel to add ACL support. Consult *http://acl.bestbits.at* for details.)

Samba has long supported the SMB/CIFS ACLs as a tool for accessing Unix-style permissions from Windows NT/200x/XP systems. If you use an ACL-enabled filesystem, this same support gives Windows users fuller access to the Linux filesystem's ACL features. This support is, however, a compile-time option. To determine whether your Samba binary includes ACL support, type **smbd -b | grep -i HAVE.*ACL**. The result is a list of the ACL features in the *smbd* binary. The following parameters control this support:

inherit acls
> This Boolean share-level parameter is similar to inherit permissions, but it tells Samba to copy ACLs from a parent directory when creating new subdirectories. The default value is No.

nt acl support

This Boolean share-level parameter is the key ACL feature; setting it to Yes tells Samba to enable SMB/CIFS ACL support, mapping it to the server's Unix-style permissions and, if supported, local filesystem ACLs.

security mask

This share-level parameter tells Samba which Unix-style permissions should be accessible to clients. The default value (777) gives users access to all the Unix-style permission bits.

directory security mask

This share-level parameter works just like security mask, but it applies to directories rather than files.

 Samba's ACL features require the client to know more about the underlying Linux accounts than is necessary for most other purposes. Samba can most easily provide this information in user- or domain-level security modes (set with the security parameter, as described in Chapter 3). Attempting to use ACLs when using share- or server-level security is likely to cause problems. In the case of share-level security, username mapping can vary between logins; for server-level security, the authentication against the logon server is too convoluted to be traced properly by Samba.

Whether your underlying filesystem supports ACLs or not, clients access these features using the file's Properties dialog box, which can be obtained by right-clicking the file in a Windows file browser and selecting Properties from the resulting dialog box. The Security tab provides access to the ACLs or Unix-style permissions, as shown in Figure 4-1.

Precisely how you manipulate ACLs differs between Windows versions. Figure 4-1 shows a Windows 2000 dialog box, in which users can click on the appropriate box in the Allow column to enable or disable access. If your Samba server system supports true ACLs, users can also click the Add button to add a new ACL that gives some other user access to the file. Older versions of Windows used a more awkward ACL-access mechanism that involved more dialog boxes. Even if Samba supports ACLs, these features aren't accessible from Windows 9x/Me or from the Home version of Windows XP.

Enabling Unix extensions

Most Samba features are designed with Microsoft-style clients (DOS, Windows, or OS/2) in mind. A few, though, cater to other operating systems; unix extensions is one that may be of particular interest. It's a global Boolean parameter that tells Samba whether to support a set of SMB/CIFS extensions that deliver Unix-style filesystem data—Unix-style ownership, Unix-style permissions, and a few special file types such as hard and symbolic links. This parameter defaults to Yes in Samba 3.0

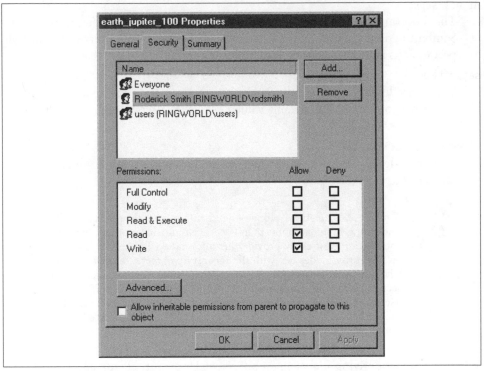

Figure 4-1. Windows ACL access tools work on Samba shares once they've been appropriately enabled

and later and shouldn't cause problems for non-Unix clients; thus, chances are you don't need to change it.

In order to do any good, the unix extensions parameter must be paired with a client that can use them. As the name suggests, these extensions are intended for use by Unix-like OSs; Windows clients can't use them. Some Linux clients can use them, though, including Samba's own *smbclient* and the cifs filesystem type code for Linux's *mount* command. Chapter 6 describes how to use the Unix extensions from a Linux client computer.

 Linux client-side Unix extensions support is still rather limited. Enabling it on the Samba server shouldn't do any harm, but for Linux-to-Linux (or Linux-to-Unix) file sharing, NFS still offers better support for Unix-style filesystem features than does Samba. This may change in the future as the Unix extensions support matures, both in Samba and in the Linux kernel.

Printing with CUPS

Although file shares are an important feature of many Samba servers, printer shares are also important. Before you can configure a Samba printer share, though, you must have a working local printer configuration. Most Linux distributions now use the Common Unix Printing System (CUPS; *http://www.cups.org*) as the local printing software. Therefore, before moving on to describing Samba printer share configuration, I present some basic information on CUPS configuration.

Installing CUPS

Because CUPS is a standard part of most Linux distributions, it may be installed on your system already. Use your package tools to look for a package called *cups*. If it's not installed, your computer either has no printing system installed or it uses an older printing system, such as LPRng or BSD LPD.

If your system uses an older printing system, you can either uninstall it and install CUPS in its place or forgo CUPS and use the older system instead. Samba configuration is similar in either case, and if local printing is working to your satisfaction, leaving your current printing system in place is likely to be the less troublesome solution, so you may want to skip ahead to the section "Creating a Printer Share." If you want to switch to CUPS, you should uninstall your existing printing software, if it's installed. In an RPM-based distribution, the -e parameter to *rpm* can uninstall the software: **rpm -e lprng** uninstalls the *lprng* package, if that's what your system uses. In Debian or its derivatives, the -r parameter to *dpkg* should do the job, as in **dpkg -r lprng**.

Once your system is shed of any printing system, the best way to install CUPS is to use a package for your distribution. These packages include SysV startup scripts designed for your distribution, as well as sample configuration files and perhaps patches. As with uninstalling programs, using your package system is usually the best approach. Some tools, such as Debian's *apt-get* and Gentoo's *emerge*, work over the network; for instance, typing **emerge cups** on a Gentoo system downloads and installs CUPS. Other tools, such as *rpm* on an RPM-based system or Debian's *dpkg*, require that you have a package file available locally. Frequently, these files are available on your installation CD-ROMs.

If you're using an older distribution, or one of the rare modern ones that doesn't yet provide CUPS as at least an option, you can obtain the CUPS source code from its web page. You must then compile and install the software locally. Consult the CUPS documentation if you need help doing this.

Linux printing, like the Unix printing systems before it, typically works on a PostScript model: printers are assumed to be PostScript printers, and programs that print generate PostScript files. (Some programs with simpler printing needs generate plain-text printing output, though.) Most printers sold today aren't PostScript models, though. For this reason, CUPS, like other printing tools, relies on Ghostscript (*http://www.cs.wisc.edu/~ghost/*) and related tools to convert PostScript into formats suitable for whatever printer you actually use. Frequently, installing CUPS automatically installs Ghostscript and perhaps a set of drivers and descriptions that CUPS uses to help pass data through Ghostscript. Particularly if you use a lower-level package management tool, you may need to install these tools manually before you can install CUPS; the package tool will complain about an unmet dependency if you haven't installed the appropriate prerequisites. In some cases, you may need to search for and manually install some driver files. One site that's likely to be helpful in this respect is the Linux Printing web site, *http://www.linuxprinting.org/printer_list. cgi*. Enter your printer brand and model in the selection boxes, and then click the Show button to obtain a report on the printer's compatibility with Linux. This page may include links to special drivers for some particularly new and exotic models. In most cases, downloading the PostScript Printer Description (PPD) file is worthwhile; it's often not necessary, but when it is, you can quickly add it to your system's printer list.

A basic CUPS installation knows how to handle generic PostScript printers and a few common non-PostScript models from a handful of manufacturers. If you begin following the options presented in the section "Adding Printers to CUPS" and can't locate your printer model, you may need to track down and install additional drivers and/or CUPS printer descriptions. These are available from several different sources:

Your distribution
> Most Linux distributions ship printer definitions in a package called *cups-drivers* or something similar. This package may just be a renamed version of one or more other printing packages.

Foomatic
> The Linux Printing site provides a series of CUPS printer definitions at *http:// www.linuxprinting.org/foomatic.html*. The information for particular printers on the Linux Printing site is likely to point you to a Foomatic driver for the printer.

GIMP Print
> The GNU Image Manipulation Program (GIMP) is a popular graphics package for Linux, and it's spawned a series of Ghostscript drivers and CUPS printer definitions that can be used even without the GIMP. Check *http://gimp-print. sourceforge.net* for more information on this package.

ESP Print Pro
> Easy Software Products (ESP) developed CUPS and released it as open source software. ESP makes commercial printer definitions available, though; check *http://www.easysw.com/printpro/* for details.

After you install one of these packages and restart the CUPS daemon, you should be able to select your printer by make and model in the CUPS configuration tools. In a few cases, though, you'll need to select a compatible model. For instance, many mid-range laser printers use the Printer Control Language (PCL) created by Hewlett-Pack-ard (HP). Thus, you may be able to get a printer working by selecting an appropriate HP LaserJet model even if yours is another make. Consult your printer's documentation to learn if it's compatible with a more popular model.

Printer Definition Files

In the case of PostScript printers, you should be able to use a generic PostScript configuration. Pointing CUPS to a definition for your specific model can improve the ability of some Linux programs to use printer-specific features, such as duplexing or wide carriages. The printer definitions just described include appropriate files for many models. If you can find a PPD file (their filenames end in ppd or PPD) on a CD-ROM that shipped with the printer or on the printer manufacturer's web site, though, you can use it. CUPS PPD files reside in subdirectories of the */usr/share/ppd* directory, so place the file in an appropriate subdirectory or create a new one. (Subdirectories are named for printer manufacturers.) The files should show up when you try to add a printer, as described shortly.

Non-PostScript printers require PPD files with a few extra features, such as a *cupsFilter line to specify the Ghostscript driver to be used. Thus, this approach is unlikely to work for non-PostScript printers, unless you can find a PPD file designed to use with CUPS and Ghostscript; that's what the printer description packages, such as Foomatic and GIMP Print, are designed to do. Some, but not all, ways of delivering drivers to Samba clients rely on the PPD files you install in CUPS, as described in the section "Delivering Printer Drivers to Windows Clients."

Adding Printers to CUPS

The simplest way to add printers to CUPS is to use the CUPS web-based administration tool. This tool runs on port 631 and is accessible by entering *http://localhost:631* in a web browser running on the computer you want to configure. (You may be able to use the hostname rather than *localhost*, or even access a CUPS server from another computer on your network, depending on the CUPS security settings.) The result is a list of CUPS server options, such as Manage Printer Classes and Manage Jobs. Click the Manage Printers item to add, delete, or modify printer definitions. If this is the first time you've done this in your current session, you'll be asked for an administrative username and password. Type **root** and the *root* password. The result should resemble Figure 4-2, although this figure shows a system with several printers already configured, and yours may show none set up.

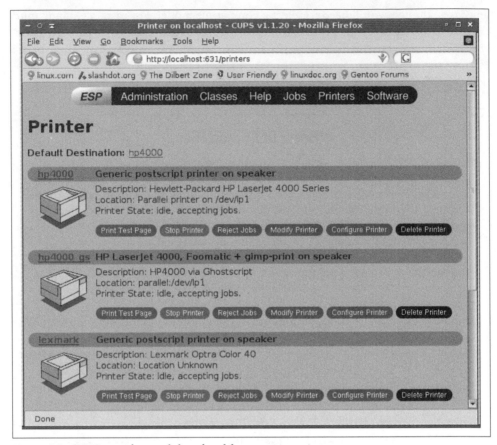

Figure 4-2. CUPS provides a web-based tool for managing printers

 CUPS can be configured to refuse all web-based administration features. Configuring CUPS access controls is covered in the section "Adjusting CUPS Browsing and Security," so check there if you can't get into the CUPS web-based interface.

To add a local printer using the web-based interface, follow these steps from the printer administration screen shown in Figure 4-2:

1. Click the Add Printer button at the bottom of the printer list. (This button is below the edge of the page shown in Figure 4-2.)

2. In the page that results, enter text for the name, location, and description of the printer. You'll use the name you enter to refer to the printer, so make it short and descriptive, such as *hp4000* if your network has just one HP 4000 printer. The location and description fields provide additional information for you and

your users, so you can enter anything you like for them. When you're done, click Continue.

3. CUPS now asks for the printer device—the hardware port to which it's connected. Chances are you'll select a parallel or USB port. You can also select various network printer options, should you want to configure a Linux system to use a remote printer queue. For this description, I assume you're configuring a parallel printer; some options (particularly for network printers) deviate somewhat from this description. In particular, you must enter a network path for a network printer device, such as *lpd://server/queue* for an LPD printer. Click Continue when you're done.

4. CUPS presents you with a list of printer makes. If you've installed Foomatic, GIMP Print, or some other printer description package, this list will be fairly long, and chances are your make will be available. If not, either install additional packages and restart the CUPS daemon or select a compatible make, such as HP or HEWLETT-PACKARD if you're using a PCL printer. Click Continue when you're done.

5. CUPS presents you with a list of printer models. Select yours. Sometimes you may need to pick between two drivers for a single model. You can pick the one that's flagged as being recommended, configure two queues so you can try both, or consult a source such as the Linux Printing web site for advice. If you don't see your model, either pick a compatible one or use your browser's back button to look for an alternate spelling for your printer make. When you've selected a model, click Continue.

6. CUPS should respond that the printer has been added. You can then click its name to bring up a control panel for the printer. Figure 4-2 shows these options for three printers.

7. Click Print Test Page to test the printer's functionality. After a brief delay, the printer should spring into action and print a test page.

Of course, the CUPS web interface, like other Linux GUI administration tools, works by modifying text files. In the case of CUPS, most configuration files reside in */etc/cups* and its subdirectories. In particular, the file *printers.conf* defines the actual printers. If you prefer to directly modify the configuration file yourself, you can do so by editing this file. Printer definitions begin with the string Printer or DefaultPrinter (the latter is for the default printer; there should be only one of these) followed by the printer name and enclosed in angle brackets (<>). Subsequent lines set the options entered in the web-based tool; each begins with a keyword and continues with a string of some sort. A few options, such as State, are adjusted by CUPS as it operates. An example entry looks like this:

```
<DefaultPrinter hp4000>
Info Hewlett-Packard HP LaserJet 4000 Series
Location Parallel printer on /dev/lp1
DeviceURI parallel:/dev/lp1
```

```
State Idle
Accepting Yes
JobSheets none none
QuotaPeriod O
PageLimit O
KLimit O
</Printer>
```

As a general rule, it's easiest to create printer definitions using the CUPS web-based tool. Directly editing the *printers.conf* file can be tricky because you must know the syntax for all of the options, as well as option names. Directly editing the file can be a handy way to quickly make a change, though, such as changing the default printer.

Adjusting CUPS Browsing and Security

In addition to *printers.conf*, another CUPS configuration file is critically important: *cupsd.conf*. This file, which also resides in */etc/cups*, controls overall server operations, including security features and *browsing*. In the context of CUPS, browsing refers to the automatic discovery of printers that are shared via the Internet Printing Protocol (IPP), the printing protocol used by CUPS for CUPS-to-CUPS printer sharing. One of the main advantages of CUPS over earlier Linux printing systems is that CUPS supports browsing. This fact can greatly simplify printer configuration on Linux clients: just ensure that the server and client support browsing, and the client will automatically detect remote printers and add them to its printer list. If you subsequently add a printer to a CUPS server, you won't need to touch the clients; they'll detect the new printers within a matter of minutes.

To enable browsing on a CUPS server, open *cupsd.conf* in a text editor, and look for the Browsing line, which will probably be about half-way through the file:

```
Browsing On
```

The default value for this option is On, meaning that browsing is enabled. Some distributions set this parameter to Off, though, presumably as a security precaution. If you want a server to announce its printers to other computers, be sure that Browsing is set to On.

 After you make a change to the CUPS configuration file and restart the CUPS daemon, it may take several seconds for clients to see the new printers.

You may also want to adjust the BrowseAddress lines, which appear shortly after the Browsing option. This parameter specifies the network addresses to which browse lists should be broadcast. On a small LAN, a value of @LOCAL should do well. This option tells CUPS to broadcast browse lists to its local network interfaces. You can also specify network blocks using broadcast IP addresses, as in 192.168.17.255 to

---

send broadcasts to the 192.168.17.0/24 network. In fact, you can include several BrowseAddress lines to specify multiple networks:

```
BrowseAddress @LOCAL
BrowseAddress 192.168.17.255
```

On the client side, the BrowseAllow and BrowseDeny options specify addresses from which browse packets should or should not be accepted. You can set these options as DNS hostnames, as domain names preceded by dots (as in *.example.com*), as IP addresses, as IP address/netmask pairs, or in various other forms. You can also use the same @LOCAL notation accepted by BrowseAddress. Typically, you'll set a CUPS client to accept browse packets from your local network, and perhaps from some others:

```
BrowseAllow @LOCAL
BrowseAllow 192.168.17.0/24
```

The default for BrowseAllow is All, which accepts all browse packets. This configuration is appropriate for CUPS clients on small LANs, but if you're configuring a system on a larger network, you may want to restrict the remote printers it adds by explicitly setting BrowseAllow.

Most of the options in *cupsd.conf* are global; they apply to the CUPS configuration as a whole. CUPS also supports more fine-grained control in sections that are delimited by Location directives. These begin with the keyword Location and a location name, surrounded by angle brackets (<>), and end with </Location>:

```
<Location /printers>
Order Deny,Allow
Deny From All
Allow from 127.0.0.1
Allow from 192.168.1.0/24
Allow from 172.24.21.0/24
Allow From @LOCAL
</Location>
```

This example uses the Allow directive to tell CUPS to grant access to the specified computers and networks. This example also controls access to the /printers location, which, as you might expect, provides the means to access printers. Other locations of interest include the root (/), which sets the default security policy; /jobs, which controls the ability to adjust job priorities, delete jobs, and so on; and /admin, which controls administrative functions such as adding new printers. This last section frequently includes AuthType and AuthClass options, which tell CUPS to require authentication; after all, you don't want to let just anybody access the printer administration tools.

If you can't access the CUPS administration web page, try examining the /admin location. Be sure that an Allow line grants access to the computer used to access the server. Frequently, this is set to 127.0.0.1, for localhost access only, but you can add more lines to grant access to other computers. I recommend doing so with caution, though; granting other computers access to a CUPS server is a potential security risk.

Creating a Printer Share

Now that you've got printers working on the Samba server using CUPS or some other printing software, it's time to begin configuring a printer share in Samba itself. Printer shares are very much like file shares, so you can configure printer shares much as you would configure file shares, but with a few key differences. You'll also need to decide whether to share a non-PostScript printer as a PostScript model (using Ghostscript to convert PostScript into the printer's native format) or using native drivers on the clients (bypassing Ghostscript on the server).

File Shares Versus Printer Shares

SMB/CIFS printer shares are virtually identical to file shares from a Samba configuration perspective. The difference is what the server does with files sent to the share by clients. In the case of file shares, the files are stored in a local directory and then ignored—at least, until they're accessed by the same or another client. In the case of printer shares, though, the server stores the file and then passes that file to the local printing system. The printing system typically prints the file and then deletes it. (Samba supports specifying an arbitrary command as the printing system, though, so you can use "printer" shares to perform unusual tasks, such as creating a CD-R.)

Because SMB/CIFS printer shares are so similar to file shares, they're defined just as you would define a file share, by placing the share name in square brackets, as in [okidata] to create a printer share called *OKIDATA*. In order to create a printer share, though, you must set one or more additional parameters:

printable
> This share-level Boolean parameter, when set to Yes (the default is No), defines a printer share; it alone will create a printer share, although it might not work, depending on other parameters and the overall computer configuration. This parameter overrides the writeable parameter and its synonyms; all printable shares are necessarily read/write. A synonym for this parameter is print ok.

printing
> This parameter sets the printing system that Linux uses. Samba supports 11 values (BSD, AIX, LPRng, PLP, SysV, HPUX, QNX, SoftQ, CUPS, OS2, and NT), but only BSD, LPRng, and CUPS are common in Linux. (The SoftQ option was removed early in

---

the 3.0.x series, while OS2 and NT are recent additions.) This parameter sets the defaults for several other parameters, enabling Samba to most efficiently submit print jobs to your local print queues. Until Samba 3.0.3, this parameter was global, but it's a now a share-level parameter.

print command

This share-level parameter sets the command that's used to print a file. The default depends on the printing parameter. You can tweak this option to achieve special effects, such as setting duplex printing. If you try changing this parameter, be sure that the command you specify deletes the input file (identified by the Samba %s variable).

printer name

You can specify the name of the local print queue with this parameter. If you omit it, the default is based on the share name; for instance, if the share is called *OKIDATA*, Samba will try to submit the job to a queue called *okidata*. One important exception is described shortly. This option actually sets the %p variable, which specifies the print queue in the print command.

printcap name

This parameter points Samba at a file that defines local printers. It's important only if you define a [printers] share, as described shortly. Ordinarily, this parameter points to */etc/printcap*, but if you set printing = CUPS, you can also set printcap name = CUPS to have Samba use the CUPS API to obtain a printer list. This requires CUPS support in the Samba binary, which may be added or omitted as a compile-time option. If this support is missing, you may still use printing = CUPS, but Samba won't use the CUPS API, and you may need to set printcap name = /etc/printcap.

load printers

This global Boolean parameter tells Samba whether to load the printers specified in printcap name for browsing. This parameter defaults to Yes, and if you intend to use a [printers] share, you shouldn't change it.

min print space

To minimize the risk of problems due to insufficient disk space, you can specify a minimum that must be present before Samba will accept a print job. This parameter takes disk space in kilobytes; if less space is free in the target directory, Samba will refuse the print job. The default value is 0, which disables this check.

Several other options are available to tweak features, such as the commands used to delete print jobs, pause the print queue, and so on. Consult the *smb.conf* manpage for details. In addition, some common file share parameters are important. Most notable of these is directory or its synonym, path. These parameters tell Samba where to store the print job before it's submitted to the print queue. The default value of /tmp usually works, but you may want to change this to a Samba-specific directory, such as /var/spool/samba. You should *not* try pointing Samba to your CUPS, LPRng, or other local printing system's queue! If you create a new Samba printer queue directory, be sure it's readable to all users who are authorized to use the printer. You may also want to set the *sticky bit* on the directory, which will prevent users other than the files' owners from deleting a file:

```
# mkdir /var/spool/samba
# chmod 777 /var/spool/samba
# chmod o+t /var/spool/samba
```

One unusual printer share is defined as [printers]. If this share is present, Samba creates individual shares for all of the shares in */etc/printcap* (or another file specified by printcap name). Using a [printers] share can greatly simplify printer configuration, particularly on a server with many printers you want to share. This share is described in more detail in the section "The [printers] Share."

Sharing PostScript Printers

In Linux's native printing system, most programs treat printers as PostScript models. Part of the job of CUPS (or any other Linux printing queue) is to pass PostScript files through Ghostscript to convert them into formats that the printer can actually understand. (Of course, if the printer is a PostScript model, this conversion process isn't necessary when programs generate PostScript output.) From a purely Linux point of view, Samba is just another program; the fact that the files Samba prints originate from another computer is unimportant.

The result of this arrangement is that sharing a printer as a PostScript printer is usually fairly straightforward. If you can print from the Samba server computer itself using commands like *lpr* or the CUPS test page printout, you can share a printer with a fairly basic *smb.conf* entry:

```
[epson]
    directory = /var/spool/samba
    printable = Yes
```

This entry makes a printer share called *EPSON* available to clients. On the clients, you must use a PostScript driver to print to the printer, whether or not the printer is really a PostScript model; to the client, it *looks like* a PostScript printer. (Windows printer drivers are described in more detail in the section "Delivering Printer Drivers to Windows Clients.")

Some Windows PostScript drivers generate output that can confuse a normal Linux queue into thinking the file is not, in fact, PostScript. If your Windows printouts to genuine PostScript printers consist of PostScript code rather than the documents you intended, one workaround is to use a raw queue like the one described in the section "Sharing Non-PostScript Printers," on the Samba server.

Sharing printers as PostScript models means that print jobs are sent over the network as PostScript. In the case of text documents, this is generally fairly efficient because the content is mostly text, rather than text converted to bitmaps. Using PostScript can also simplify driver installation and maintenance on a network with many printers; you may be able to use just one driver for several different printers. On the other hand, if the printer isn't really a PostScript model, the Samba server computer will need to convert the text into some other form (usually a printer-specific bitmap), which can consume a fair amount of CPU time on the server.

Sharing Non-PostScript Printers

When sharing a non-PostScript printer, another option is available: you can share the printer using a "raw" Linux printer queue. This queue uses the local Linux printing system, such as CUPS, but it bypasses Ghostscript. The result is that programs, such as Samba and its clients, must produce files the printer can parse. Typically, you do this by installing and using a printer's native drivers, as supplied by the manufacturer, on the Windows clients.

The Samba printer share configuration for a non-PostScript printer is likely to look much like the configuration for a PostScript printer. The main difference on the Samba server side is in the Linux printer queue configuration. In the case of CUPS, when you provide CUPS with the printer's make (in Step #4 of the procedure in the section "Adding Printers to CUPS"), you select Raw, followed by Raw Queue as the model. Alternatively, in Samba 3.0.3 and later, you can use the Samba cups options = raw parameter if you set printing = CUPS. This option tells CUPS to handle the input as if it were to a raw queue. If you're using LPRng or BSD LPD, omit the if line in /etc/printcap to create a raw queue.

When sharing printers in this way, the client generates printer-specific codes. For many low-end printers, this means that the clients generate bitmaps, even when printing text. These bitmaps are likely to be larger than PostScript files describing the same page, so raw printer queues may increase the network bandwidth requirements of printing. On the other hand, because Ghostscript isn't involved on the print server, the CPU requirements on the server are likely to be reduced. Non-PostScript Windows printer drivers are also likely to provide access to printer features that aren't easily adjusted through PostScript drivers, such as a printer's resolution.

When deciding between PostScript and raw queues, your best bet is to set up both types of queue and evaluate performance yourself. Try printing some documents in both ways and judge the output quality, print speed, and network load. You can then decide which method to use when you make the printers available to all your users. In some cases, you may want to make a printer accessible in both ways. This will enable your users to pick the optimum driver—say, to use a PostScript driver when printing text but to use a printer-specific driver when printing graphics.

Delivering Printer Drivers to Windows Clients

One critically important part of Samba printer configuration is distributing drivers to Windows clients. This task can be accomplished in several different ways. One approach that requires little explanation is to use the driver CD-ROM that came with the printer (or a generic PostScript driver for Ghostscript-driven printers) to install the driver on all the clients. This approach is simple enough on a small network, but it becomes awkward when many clients are involved. For these cases, SMB/CIFS provides mechanisms to help deliver drivers to many clients, and Samba supports these mechanisms.

 If you fail to configure Linux to deliver a Windows printer driver, Windows NT/200x/XP clients may display spurious "unable to connect" error messages. To avoid this problem, set use client driver = Yes. However, you should *not* use this option if you configure Linux to deliver printer drivers to Windows NT/200x/XP clients.

You can take a middle ground. Instead of using the semiautomated driver installation mechanisms described here, you can create an ordinary file share that holds the printer drivers. You can then install the drivers from that share on all the clients. This procedure obviates the need to carry a CD-ROM around from one computer to another, or to keep track of the CD-ROM for the benefit of computers you add after setting up the printer.

Picking a Driver

The first task you must undertake in driver installation is to select the drivers you want to install. To a large extent, this decision depends on whether you share the printer using a PostScript queue or a raw queue. (This difference is moot, of course, in the case of PostScript printers.) In many cases, though, you can choose between drivers from more than one source:

OS drivers
> Windows (and most other operating systems) ship with an array of printer drivers. You may be able to select a driver from among those that ship with the OS. This is true for both PostScript and non-PostScript drivers.

Printer manufacturer drivers
> Printer manufacturers invariably ship Windows drivers with their printers. For older printers, you may need to check the manufacturer's web site to obtain drivers that can work with more recent versions of Windows.

Adobe's PostScript drivers

Adobe makes drivers for PostScript printers available from its downloads page (*http://www.adobe.com/support/downloads/*). These drivers are generic PostScript drivers that require PPD files to operate. (Adobe makes these available for printers with Adobe interpreters, as well.) They're also licensed only for printers that use PostScript interpreters written by Adobe.

The CUPS PostScript driver

A Windows PostScript driver is associated with the CUPS project. Because you can install this driver from the Samba server computer without the help of a Windows system, it's particularly simple to install, as described in the section "Installing drivers from Linux." The CUPS driver works only on Windows NT/200x/XP systems, however; if you need to deliver drivers to Windows 9x/Me systems, you'll need another driver source, at least for those clients.

Because of the array of printers available today, I can't make a blanket recommendation for what driver to use; any of the preceding classes of drivers might work well. In fact, chances are any of them will work well with most printers, with the exception of PostScript drivers if you already know you want to share a non-PostScript printer raw.

Defining Necessary Shares

Samba 2.2 and later use a special file share to deliver printer drivers. This share is defined as [print$]. Ultimately, printer driver files will reside in this share, but for the moment you must simply create it. A typical [print$] share looks like this:

```
[print$]
    comment = Printer Driver Storage
    directory = /usr/share/samba/drivers
    browseable = No
    read only = Yes
    write list = gutenberg
```

The location of the shared directory is somewhat arbitrary, but the key point is that it must exist. This directory must also be readable to all those who might want to add printers to their machines. You'll typically give one or more users write access to the share (gutenberg in this example). These users are the printer administrators; they're authorized to add printer drivers to the share. Be sure that the printer administrators have Linux write privileges to the location you've chosen as the PRINT$ share directory. You should also list these users on the printer admin line in the [global] section of *smb.conf*:

```
printer admin = gutenberg
```

Before adding drivers, you must also define some printer shares. If you want to share all the printers on the server, a [printers] share, as described in the section "The [printers] Share," should do nicely.

```
[printers]
   comment = All Printers
   path = /var/spool/samba
   printable = Yes
```

After you make these changes to *smb.conf*, you must either wait a minute or two for Samba to discover and implement the changes or force Samba to restart or reload its configuration file.

 Samba stores printer driver files in the *PRINT$* share, but it stores information about these files in Trivial Data Base (TDB) files located elsewhere—typically in */var/cache/samba* and */var/cache/samba/printing*. In theory, you can edit these files with the help of Samba's *rpcclient* command, but unless you're an expert with this tool, doing so is extremely tedious. In case of errors when installing printer drivers, you may need to delete these files and start from scratch.

Installing the Driver on the Server

Once you've reconfigured Samba with the PRINT$ share and one or more printer shares, you can install Windows printer drivers in Samba. You can perform this task from the Samba server, from another Linux or Unix system, or from a Windows client. The CUPS driver can only be installed from a Linux or Unix system, the Adobe PostScript driver can be installed in either way, and most other drivers can be most easily installed from a Windows client.

Installing drivers from Linux

CUPS ships with a program, called *cupsaddsmb*, which can install Windows printer drivers on a Samba server computer. This command's syntax is as follows:

```
cupsaddsmb [-H samba-server] [-U samba-user] [-h cups-server] [-v]
   {-a | printer-list}
```

In the simplest case, you can type **cupsaddsmb -a** on the server system as the printer administrator. The system defaults to installing the CUPS drivers from *localhost* to *localhost*. The -a parameter tells the program to add drivers for all available CUPS printers. If you don't share all these printers, you must specify them individually. The -v parameter increases the verbosity of the program's output, which can be handy for debugging problems.

Of course, *cupsaddsmb* can't conjure printer drivers out of thin air; you must place them somewhere the program can find them *before* executing the program. By default, *cupsaddsmb* looks for drivers in */usr/share/cups/drivers*. These drivers can come from one of two sources:

The CUPS PostScript drivers for Windows

These drivers can be found at *http://www.cups.org/windows.php*. The CUPS documentation recommends using them. As of CUPS 1.1.20, though, these drivers support only Windows NT/200x/XP.

The Adobe PostScript drivers for Windows

You can find Adobe's drivers at *http://www.adobe.com/support/downloads/*. These drivers support Windows 9x/Me as well as NT/200x/XP.

In either case, you must install driver files in */usr/share/cups/drivers*, but how you place them there depends on the driver. In the case of the CUPS drivers, you download a tarball from the CUPS web site, extract the tarball, and run the *cups-samba. install* script from the tarball. This script asks for confirmation and installs the files in */usr/share/cups/drivers*. You can then run *cupsaddsmb* to install the drivers on the Samba server.

The Adobe drivers, on the other hand, were designed to be installed from a Windows system to a Windows system. They come in the form of a Windows executable (.*EXE*) file. This file is a self-extracting Microsoft Cabinet archive, which can be extracted in Linux using the *cabextract* program. (Check your distribution for this program, or visit *http://freshmeat.net/projects/cabextract/* to download the source code or a binary package.) When you extract the drivers file, you must copy several files into */usr/share/ cups/drivers*, as detailed in Table 4-1. Note that *cupsaddsmb* expects these files to appear in all-uppercase, but some of them are in lowercase or mixed case in the archive; you need to rename some of the files to change their case. Also, these files are scattered about in the *Windows* and *WinNT* subdirectories. In my experience, this option works well for Windows NT/200x/XP, but Windows 9x/Me tends to complain about a missing .*INF* file when installing the drivers installed in this way. If you run into this problem, you may need to install Windows 9x/Me drivers another way.

Table 4-1. Adobe PostScript driver files

Windows 9x/Me	Windows NT/200x/XP
ADFONTS.MFM	ADOBEPS5.DLL
ADOBEPS4.DRV	ADOBEPSU.DLL
ADOBEPS4.HLP	ADOBEPSU.HLP
DEFPRTR2.PPD	–
ICONLIB.DLL	–
PSMON.DLL	–

Once you've installed the CUPS or Adobe driver files, you can type **cupsaddsmb -a** or whatever variant you need to type, given your printer administration username and other variables. The program should ask for your password on the Samba server, copy the driver files, and configure the server to deliver the files to clients when they connect, as described in the section "Installing Drivers on Clients."

Unfortunately, *cupsaddsmb* is rather delicate and sometimes doesn't work correctly. Likely problems include missing driver files, an attempt to install drivers without appropriate privileges on the server, and a mismatch of CUPS and Samba printer names (*cupsaddsmb* assumes that these names match). If you have problems, check these items. You may also want to add the -v parameter and check your Samba log files for clues to the cause of the problem.

 Whenever possible, *cupsaddsmb* copies the PPD files used by CUPS as part of the driver installation. Both the CUPS and Adobe PostScript drivers for Windows use PPD files. It's possible, though, that the PPD file used by CUPS for Linux clients will not work well from Windows. If you suspect this is the problem, try replacing the PPD file on the Samba server and then re-install the driver on the clients. Look for a PPD file with your Windows PostScript driver package and copy it to the name and location in which Samba looks for the PPD file for that driver.

Installing drivers from Windows NT/200x/XP

In theory, any Windows driver can be installed from Linux. The *cupsaddsmb* command merely copies files to the server and issues a few commands using the *smbclient* utility. You should be able to do the same for any printer driver files. In practice, though, the task is tedious without the help of *cupsaddsmb*, and it only supports the CUPS and Adobe PostScript drivers. For this reason, you may want to install some drivers from Windows clients. (This task can be accomplished only from Windows NT/200x/XP clients; Windows 9x/Me doesn't support this operation.) Doing so employs the same facilities on the Samba server *cupsaddsmb* uses, but the Windows driver-installation tools use these features.

 Some drivers, particularly for older printers, come with installation programs that assume the printer will be connected locally or that don't support network installations. These drivers can be very difficult to install on a network print server. If you have such drivers and can't find more network-friendly updates, you may want to consider creating an ordinary Samba file share in which you can place the installer. You can then run the installer from each client that needs to use the printer.

When installing drivers from Windows, you must take one extra step on the Samba server computer. Windows printer drivers are installed in fixed directories on the Samba server's *PRINT$* share. You must create these directories and set their permissions so that the user adding the drivers can write to them. Table 4-2 summarizes the directories you must add.

Table 4-2. Windows driver directories in PRINT$ share

Client OS	Directory name
Windows 9x/Me	win40
Windows NT/200x/XP for x86 CPUs	w32x86
Windows NT for Alpha CPUs	x32alpha
Windows NT for MIPS CPUs	w32mips
Windows NT for PowerPC CPUs	w32ppc

Before proceeding, you should obtain the driver installation files. If you choose to use a driver that ships with Windows, you need only the Windows installation CD-ROM. Alternatively, you can download drivers from the printer manufacturer, from Adobe, or conceivably from some other source. Once you've obtained the drivers, follow these steps on the Windows computer to install drivers for the OS you're running:

1. In My Network Places, browse to the Samba server on which the share you want to install is located, and open the Printers and Faxes or Printers folder.

2. Right-click the printer you want to install and select Properties from the resulting pop-up menu. If no driver is installed, Windows asks if you want to install one.

3. Click No in response to the question about installing a driver. Clicking Yes will install a driver locally, not to the print server. Windows now displays a Properties dialog box.

4. Select the Advanced tab in the Properties dialog box.

5. Click the New Driver button in the Advanced tab of the Properties dialog box. Windows launches an Add Printer wizard to help guide you through the driver installation process.

6. Click Next in the Add Printer wizard's introductory screen. The result is a dialog box in which you can select the make and model of your printer from a list of standard Windows drivers, as shown in Figure 4-3.

7. Select the driver for your printer from the list and click Next. Alternatively, click Have Disk to point the wizard at driver files you've obtained from another source.

If you can't find your printer in the list and don't have a disk, try using the Apple LaserWriter IINT driver for monochrome PostScript printers or the QMS magicolor driver for color PostScript printers. These drivers are fairly generic and usually produce acceptable results.

8. The Wizard informs you that you're about to add drivers. Click Finish to do so.

This procedure adds drivers for the OS that the client you used to install them is running. If you want to add drivers for additional operating systems, follow these steps.

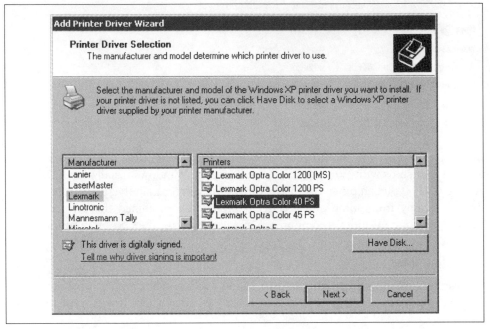

Figure 4-3. Windows ships with a large number of printer drivers

1. Open the Properties dialog box for the printer in question, if necessary.

2. Click the Sharing tab in the Properties dialogue box.

3. Click the Additional Drivers button in the Sharing tab. This action brings up an Additional Drivers dialog box, as shown in Figure 4-4.

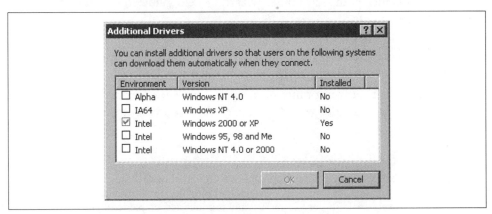

Figure 4-4. You can install drivers for additional Windows OSs

4. Check the box next to the Windows version for which you want to install drivers.

5. Click OK. Windows will ask for the location of the drivers.

6. Enter the path to the driver files or browse to them. The system will present a list of printers similar to that shown in Figure 4-3.

7. Select the printer and click OK. Windows should install the drivers.

Installing Drivers on Clients

Windows printer drivers, by their very nature, are Windows programs and so must be installed on Windows print clients. Installing them on a Samba server merely makes the drivers available for semiautomatic installation on Windows clients, thus obviating the need to keep track of driver installation CD-ROMs or files. Despite the fact that installing the drivers on the Samba server simplifies client driver installation, this task isn't wholly automatic, at least not when using SMB/CIFS printing. To install a driver on a Windows client, follow these steps:

1. Browse to the print server that hosts the printer you want to add to the computer. You should see an icon for the printer you want to add. If you don't, chances are the server is misconfigured.

2. Double-click the icon corresponding to the printer you want to add. The result is a notice that you're about to connect to a printer and add a driver for it.

3. Click Yes to continue the setup process. In some versions of Windows (most notably Windows 9x/Me), you'll be asked some additional questions, such as whether you intend to print to this printer from DOS programs.

If all goes well, you'll see a dialog box summarizing the progress as the client transfers files from the server. An icon for the printer should then appear in your Printers or Printers and Faxes window, which you can open from the Control Panel. Windows 9x/Me asks if you want to print a test page during the install process. You should probably do so to test the printer's operation, particularly on the first client you install. If you skip this step during installation but want to do so afterwards, right-click the printer icon in the Printers or Printers and Faxes window and select Properties from the resulting menu. This action opens a Properties dialog box. Click Print Test Page from the General tab in this dialog box to print a test page.

 Under Windows NT/200x/XP, one reason you may not be able to print is because the printer data in the Registry didn't get set correctly. You can set this data by setting the default page orientation in the printer control dialog box.

Some Windows PostScript printer drivers generate PostScript that can confuse Linux printer queues into thinking the file is plain text. The result is a printout of PostScript commands, rather than the file you'd intended to print. If this happens, you can try several solutions.

- Look for client-side options to disable a Ctrl-D before the print job. This character, if present, can be the cause of problems.

- Look for client-side options to disable printer mode-setting features. Some printer drivers generate special code to kick dual-language printers into PostScript mode, but this code can have the effect of confusing the Linux printer queue.

- Define a new raw printer queue on the Samba server and share the printer using that queue rather than the normal queue used from Linux.

- Change the driver used on the Windows client. If you've installed it in Samba, this action requires reinstalling the driver in Samba, which itself may require deleting TDB files.

Example Shares

Knowing what the parameters are that control Samba share definitions and knowing how to use those parameters are two different things. Failing to see the forest for the trees, as it were, is easy to do when confronted with a list of Samba parameters. For this reason, this chapter concludes with a look at several common uses of Samba file and printer shares: the [homes] share, which provides users with data storage space for their own files; a share that can store program files, templates, and other shared read-only files; shares for exchanging files between users; a closer look at the [printers] share introduced earlier; and a "printer" share that generates PDF files rather than paper printouts.

The [homes] Share

Many Samba server computers function, in whole or in part, as centralized storage locations for users' files. Users store their important files on the Samba server, enabling them to store more or larger files than would fit on their clients' disks and to move from one client to another and access their own home files. This strategy can also greatly simplify backup; if users' data files are on a single server, that server can be backed up more easily than can an entire network's worth of files, thus providing more reliable insurance in case of hardware failure.

The user data storage function is so important that Samba provides a special share name just for this purpose: [homes]. This share functions much like an ordinary file share but with several important differences:

- The share can be accessed via the user's username, as in *LINNAEUS* for the user *linnaeus*. The share can also be accessed by the name *HOMES*, but this name is usually considered secondary.

- In a Windows-dominated network, the username-based share name is typically what appears in network browsers. The *HOMES* name might not appear in browsers; this detail depends on configuration options, as described shortly.

- The default path for the share is the user's home directory, as specified in */etc/ passwd* or other account-definition files.

A typical [homes] share definition can be quite short:

```
[homes]
    comment = Home Directories
    writeable = Yes
    create mask = 644
    browseable = No
```

The Samba default is to make shares read-only, but because the intended [homes] shares enable users to store files that they create, changing this default is particularly important for these shares. The create mask = 644 parameter isn't necessary, and, in fact, it's undesirable if you want to preserve the archive bit on files. Using this parameter keeps the owner execute bit from being set, though, which may be desirable if users make heavy use of shell access or access via NFS or some other means that preserves this bit as such.

Ordinarily, shares on which you set browseable = No aren't visible in file browsers, but [homes] shares are exceptions to this rule. Specifically, the browseable parameter applies to the share called *HOMES*; if you omit the browseable = No parameter or set it to Yes, a share called *HOMES* appears in clients' network browsers. Part of the definition of the [homes] share is that a share named after the user who accesses the server appears in the user's browse lists. (*Only* the home share for the user who accesses the server is displayed; users won't see other users' home shares, although they can be accessed by entering their names directly.)

This example share doesn't specify a directory or path; it relies on the [homes] default. Although you can set a directory for the share, setting a static directory is usually undesirable. If you want to provide users with different home directories for remote text-mode or GUI logins than for Samba access, you can specify a Samba directory that is unique for each user by including variables such as %S, %u, or %U; these variables all expand to values related to the username. (In many cases, they expand to the same value.) For instance, you might set the path like this:

```
path = /home/samba/%u
```

 Some clients, such as the BeOS network browser, don't deliver a username until after they've retrieved lists of shares. For these network browsers, a [homes] share will be invisible unless you set browseable = Yes. Such clients might also not work well if you use a %S (share name) variable in a [homes] share's path or directory parameter.

Many sample *smb.conf* files include [homes] shares, so this share may already exist on your server. Of course, if you don't need it, you can delete it or change the definition to suit your particular needs.

A Windows Program Share

Samba servers can also be used as central repositories for files that many clients must access in a read-only manner—program executables, templates, clip art, fonts, and so on. Most users have no need to write to such shares, so most users receive read-only access. Somebody must maintain these shares, though, so a write list parameter provides an exception to the rule:

```
[programs]
    comment = Program Files for All Users
    path = /usr/share/samba/windows-programs
    write list = linnaeus, mendel
    force user = linnaeus
    force group = users
    read only = Yes
    create mask = 660
    directory mask = 770
```

In addition to the write list, this example share includes force user and force group parameters. These parameters force all files to be owned by a single user and group; even those files written by *mendel* will be owned by *linnaeus*, which makes for a cleaner on-server set of ownerships; however, this also means you can't track whoever installed a particular file. These parameters also guarantee that all users will be able to read the files in the share, at least assuming that no files are written to the share through non-Samba means. Note that the force user parameter in conjunction with write list does *not* give all users write access to the share; write list applies to users' true logon usernames, not their identities as determined by force user.

If you create a share like this, be sure to set appropriate permissions on the share's directory (*/usr/share/samba/windows-programs* in this example). If you don't give *linnaeus* write access to the directory, neither *linnaeus* nor *mendel* can store files in the share. You may also want to consider local Samba server security issues. For instance, if the share contains files that shouldn't be accessible to some non-Samba users of the server, you should set create mask and directory mask parameters that deny world access (as in the example) and ensure that these users aren't in the group specified by force group.

File-Exchange Shares

A read-only share such as the [programs] share is relatively straightforward to configure. A share that's used for data exchange between users is much more complex because you must decide how to set ownership and permissions that enable those who should be able to write to files to do so, while preventing those who shouldn't. Several approaches to solving this problem exist:

Shared access to [homes] directories

You can set permissions on users' home directories such that they can read each others' files. If necessary, you can create local Linux groups and enable read access to group members while denying world access, thus providing support for groups of users. One drawback to this approach is that users will have to type in their collaborators' usernames when accessing shares; they won't be able to browse directly to those directories. (Creating symbolic links between users' home directories from Linux may provide a partial fix to this problem.)

Multiple file exchange shares

You can create several shares for file exchange, giving different groups access to different shares. You can use `valid users` or `invalid users` to control access. Using Linux groups and permissions on files in shares also works to this end. Depending on your needs, using multiple sharing directories can be awkward because it clutters your list of shares if you need to create shares for many different groups

One big happy file exchange share

You can create a single share with lenient permissions—say, setting create `mask=666` and `directory mask=777` or using `force user` to set ownership of all files to a single user. The effect is that all users can read and write all files in the share. This can be a good approach on servers on which you don't need to worry too much about keeping files from particular groups of local users. Even if that's the case, judicious use of such a share may be acceptable, but users will have to be warned against placing sensitive files on the data-exchange share.

One big exchange share with internal security

If you use the `inherit permissions = Yes` parameter, you can use a single file-exchange share but maintain internal security by setting up subdirectories with different ownership and modes. For instance, one subdirectory might have 777 (`rwxrwxrwx`) permissions, enabling anybody to read and write it, whereas another subdirectory might have 770 (`rwxrwx---`) permissions, enabling members of its group to use it to exchange files while keeping it off-limits to other users. This approach is very flexible, but you need to give some thought to the local Linux permissions on the subdirectories. You also need to create these subdirectories from Linux. Users are likely to find this scheme confusing, but giving the subdirectories descriptive names, such as *dna-analysis-group* or *instructors-only*, should help on that score.

Precisely how you would configure such a share depends on which approach you take and on your Linux server's local security configuration. For one example, consider this file share:

```
[sanescientists]
    comment = Share for Use by Sane Scientists Only
    path = /usr/share/samba/sane
    valid users = @sane, linnaeus, mendel, curie
    writeable = Yes
    force group = sane
    create mask = 660
    directory mask = 770

[madscientists]
    comment = Share for Use by Mad Scientists Only
    path = /usr/share/samba/mad
    valid users = @mad, morbius, moreau, frankenstein
    writeable = Yes
    force group = mad
    create mask = 660
    directory mask = 770
```

These two shares, in combination, provide separate file-exchange areas for two groups of users. The first grants access to all members of the Linux *sane* group, plus three others who might or might not be members of that group. The second share does the same for the *mad* group and three other users. You can include a user in both groups if you like, in which case that user has access to both shares. For instance, you can place the user *jekyl* in both the *sane* and *mad* groups, or add the user explicitly to one or both shares' valid users lines. If you want to give one group read-only access to another group's shares, add the members of both groups to the share's valid users line but use read list to restrict some users' access to the share.

Another way to implement a similar system is to create a single share:

```
[scientists]
    comment = Share for Use by All Scientists
    path = /usr/share/samba/scientists
    valid users = @sane, @mad
    writeable = Yes
    inherit permissions = Yes
```

You then create subdirectories within the share's directory with appropriate permissions set to enable only members of particular groups to access the directories. The result might look like this, as viewed using Linux's *ls*:

```
# ls -l /usr/share/samba/scientists
total 8
drwxrwx---  2 root mad  4096 May  2 14:47 mad
drwxrwx---  2 root sane 4096 May  2 14:47 sane
```

The result is that members of the *mad* group can exchange files in the *mad* subdirectory, and members of the *sane* group can exchange files in the *sane* subdirectory. As configured, members of each group can't view the contents of or read files from the other group's subdirectory unless the individual is a member of both Linux groups. By changing permissions on the directories to 775 (rwxrwxr-x) rather than 770 (rwxrwx---), you can enable members of the groups to read but not write files in each others' directories. Because of the reliance on the local Linux groups, this scheme doesn't work well if some users aren't members of the underlying groups; this is the reason the individual users (*linnaeus*, *morbius*, and so on) were omitted from the valid users line in the share definition. You should also attend to ownership and permissions on the share directory itself; depending on its settings, users could create new subdirectories, which can complicate your security settings.

 Both examples omit the nt acl support parameter, which defaults to Yes. As a result, Windows NT/200x/XP users can set ACLs on their files, which will complicate access permissions. Of course, these ACLs won't help users read files if the users can't read the shares or directories in which they're stored, but if users can read the directories, ACLs can broaden or restrict access to specific files, particularly if the underlying filesystem supports ACLs.

These are just two examples of common-access file shares. Many variants and alternatives are possible, that use Samba's security features, Linux's security features, or an interaction of the two. As a general rule, it's best to start with a simple security system; trying to use too many sophisticated features can lead you into trouble if you forget an important consequence or interaction.

The [printers] Share

Most print servers use a single [printers] share to make all printers available. This share can consist of just a few lines, but it relies on a few global settings, and some of its implications deserve elaboration. First, before defining a [printers] share, be sure to set the following parameters in the [global] section of *smb.conf*:

```
printing = CUPS
printcap name = CUPS
load printers = Yes
printer admin = gutenberg
guest ok = Yes
```

In this example, the printing and printcap name parameters are both set to CUPS, which tells Samba to use CUPS for printing, including using CUPS' own API for determining what printers are available. Of course, if you use another printing system, you'll change these parameters appropriately—say, to printing = LPRng and printcap name = /etc/printcap.

Samba provides CUPS support as a compile-time option. If Samba wasn't compiled on a system with appropriate CUPS development libraries installed, or if CUPS support was explicitly disabled, Samba won't include the necessary tools to use the CUPS API. In this case, you can still use printing = CUPS (Samba will use old-style printing commands rather than the CUPS API to submit print jobs). You may need to set printcap name = /etc/printcap, though. If Samba doesn't find your printers, try making this change. In fact, CUPS provides compatibility commands, so it should work even if you set printing = LPRng, printing = BSD, or certain other values.

The load printers = Yes parameter tells Samba to read information on available local printers from the file pointed to by printcap name (or, if printcap name = CUPS, to read the data using the CUPS API). By itself, this doesn't do anything; only if you provide an explicit [printers] share does this parameter have any effect.

The printer admin line is optional; it sets the Linux username of a printer administrator—a user whose accesses to printer shares are done as if by *root*. This user should be able to delete others' print jobs and otherwise perform maintenance on the queues.

The guest ok = Yes parameter tells Samba to accept guest access to the printer shares. This can be handy if you don't want to maintain a user database on a dedicated print server, but you'll need to adjust the global map to guest and guest account parameters. Enabling guest access also opens the system to potential abuses, particularly if the server is accessible to the Internet at large. (Imagine coming in one morning to discover that a high-speed, high-capacity printer has printed its entire load of paper with completely black pages, wasting both paper and toner or ink.)

Once you've set the global options, you can create a [printers] share. This share is likely to be fairly uninteresting on the surface:

```
[printers]
    comment = All Printers
    path = /var/spool/samba
    printable = Yes
```

Once this share is defined, and Samba either detects the changes (which it should do after a few minutes) or is restarted, you should see printer shares corresponding to all of your local printers that appear in clients' network browsers. The shares won't be usable, though; you must first install printer drivers on the clients, as described in the section "Delivering Printer Drivers to Windows Clients."

Using a [printers] share doesn't mean that you're restricted from creating other printer shares. You can do so in either of two ways:

- You can create a separate printer share using a name that doesn't correspond to a print queue on the underlying Linux computer. This share will be presented to users in addition to the shares created by the [printers] share.

- You can create a printer share that uses the same name as one of the printer queues on the underlying Linux computer. This share will override the share of the same name created by the [printers] share.

The shares generated by [printers] may be PostScript printers, non-PostScript printers that appear to clients as PostScript printers because of the use of Ghostscript in the Linux printer queue, or non-PostScript printers with raw Linux printer queues for which native printer drivers are necessary on the clients. In fact, you can provide a mixture of share types; the [printers] share simply doesn't care.

A PDF-Generation Printer Share

Samba printer shares can be unusually flexible. This flexibility is derived, in part, from the print command parameter, which enables you to bypass the usual print processing. In fact, you can do some extremely complex and unusual things with this parameter, but in this section I describe a use that's at least related to printing: creating Portable Document Format (PDF) files.

Several tools exist to generate PDF files from various formats. One of these is almost certainly already installed on your Linux computer: Ghostscript. In addition to generating output in formats that can be printed by your printer, Ghostscript can generate several common file formats, such as Tagged Image File Format (TIFF), Portable Network Graphics (PNG), and PDF. To create a Samba share that generates a PDF file, you call Ghostscript (with appropriate parameters) as the print command:

```
[makepdf]
    comment = Share to Make PDFs
    path = /var/spool/samba
    printable = Yes
    print command = gs -dNOPAUSE -dBATCH -q -sDEVICE=pdfwrite \
                    -sOutputFile=%H/%s.pdf; rm %s
```

When the *MAKEPDF* share receives a PostScript file, it passes it through Ghostscript (*gs*), specifying various parameters to generate PDF output without prompts and saving the output as *%H/%s.pdf*. Because %H is the user's home directory and %s is the print job's filename, the result is a file whose name begins with the Samba print job name and ends in *.pdf*. This filename is likely to be ugly, but it will at least be unique. The print command line ends with rm %s, which deletes the original print job, keeping it from cluttering the disk.

Of course, the [makepdf] share, as just presented, requires users to have access to their home directories, presumably through a [homes] share. If this isn't true of your system, you can deliver the results in some other ways. For instance, you might have Samba email the PDF files to users. If necessary, you can write a script that passes the file through Ghostscript, looks up users' email addresses in a list, and sends the file. Then call the script on the `print` command line, passing it whatever Samba variables you need, such as the print job filename (%s) and the username (%u or %U).

To clients, this particular share is indistinguishable from a real printer's share. Because it expects PostScript input, you should install PostScript drivers on clients—ideally a fairly generic PostScript driver. Instead of printed output, though, users will find PDF files in their home directories soon after printing documents. This share can be a good way to provide basic PDF-generation capabilities to all users in all their programs that can print. It might not be enough for all functions; some dedicated PDF-generation tools support features that aren't available through Ghostscript or Windows PostScript printer drivers.

 You may want to install drivers in Samba for the share for automated delivery to clients, as described in the section "Delivering Printer Drivers to Windows Clients." You can do so from a Windows client, as described in the section "Installing drivers from Windows NT/200x/XP." If you create a CUPS queue with the name of the PDF-generation share and set it up using a generic PPD file, you can then install the CUPS PostScript drivers for Windows as described in the section "Installing drivers from Linux." You can then delete the bogus CUPS queue. Alternatively, you can generate the queue to print to a networked SMB/CIFS queue to begin with and point it as the Samba queue you're creating. If you do the latter, CUPS clients can create PDFs by printing to CUPS, which then submits the print job to Samba.

Summary

Samba was created as a file and print server for Linux and other Unix-like operating systems, enabling these systems to fill an important role on many LANs. Although Samba has grown over the years to take on many other SMB/CIFS duties, such as domain controller and NetBIOS name server, sharing files and printers remains at the core of Samba's functionality. Creating these shares requires that you understand the basic Samba share-creation parameters. File shares are likely to use many of these options, but printer shares are likely to use a smaller subset of these options, along with a few printer-specific options. Printer shares also require configuring a local Linux printer queue, which in the case of modern Linux distributions usually means CUPS. Actually using printer shares usually requires driver installation on clients, and Samba provides tools to help automate this process.

Managing a NetBIOS Network with Samba

Samba makes a fine file and print server for Windows clients, as described in the previous chapter. Samba's capabilities go further than that, though; the software can also take on many of the ancillary roles on a NetBIOS LAN. Many of these duties are associated with NT domain controllers. *Domain controllers* are basically centralized logon databases for systems on a NetBIOS network; servers consult the domain controller when asked to authenticate users. This topic is first up in this chapter. A couple of additional roles that are often associated with domain controllers, but can exist even in a nondomain configuration, are described next: providing NetBIOS name resolution services and collecting browse lists for delivery to clients. Finally, this chapter concludes with a look at configuring Windows clients to use these features of a Samba server.

 A domain controller can serve as an authentication tool for both Windows and Linux clients. In fact, you can use a Linux computer running Samba as an authentication server for other Linux computers. To do so, you must configure the Samba domain controller features, as described in the section "Enabling Domain Controller Functions"; the Linux client configuration is described in Chapter 7.

Linux can make an excellent NT domain controller on a Windows network for many of the same reasons that Linux is an excellent platform for other network roles: Linux is reliable, less vulnerable to security problems than Windows, and low in cost. Samba is also more flexible than Windows in certain domain control details; you can set many options individually that aren't available or that are linked to other options in Windows. On the other hand, Linux and Samba don't yet implement full Active Directory (AD) domain controller support, only the older NT domain support. (Linux can function on an AD network, but it can't function as an AD controller.)

Enabling Domain Controller Functions

Samba's domain control features enable it to provide authentication services for Windows 9x/Me, Windows NT/200x/XP, Linux, and various other operating systems. Used in this way, the domain controller client (which may itself be a server to other computers) uses the account database on the domain controller to authenticate users. In order to support this functionality, Samba requires that you set a few *smb.conf* parameters. This part of the domain controller configuration isn't the tough part, though; you must also maintain an encrypted password database for your users and also keep *machine trust accounts*, which enable Samba to authenticate the machines that are asking for authentication services. Many domain controllers also deliver a few special share types, which you might want to configure on your domain controller.

The Role of a Domain Controller

An NT domain controller serves as a backend for authentication requests directed at an SMB/CIFS server, as illustrated by Figure 5-1. Samba servers can actually take on the role of the NT domain controller, the SMB/CIFS server (a.k.a. the *domain member server*), or both systems. Linux or other Samba-using systems can also function as SMB/CIFS clients, as described in Chapter 6.

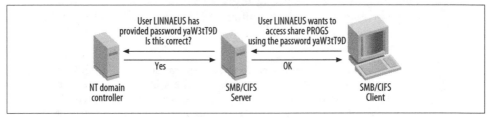

Figure 5-1. NT domain controllers regulate access to other servers' shares

Figure 5-1 most accurately depicts one of two major authentication methods supported by NT domain controllers and Samba. Specifically, this figure depicts *pass-through authentication*, which is used by Windows 9x/Me domain members and Samba file servers when you set security = Server in their *smb.conf* files. Even in this case, Figure 5-1 presents a simplified view of the exchanges involved. Windows NT/200x/XP computers and Samba servers configured with security = Domain use a more complex arrangement, known as *NetLogon authentication*, in which the domain member server contacts the domain controller and obtains enough information from the domain controller to authenticate users itself, using data from the domain controller, rather than a local password file. Both systems look the same to SMB/CIFS clients. In fact, from the client's point of view, these systems are also indistinguishable from one in which servers use local authentication databases.

Not all Windows networks use domain configurations. Simpler networks use workgroup configuration, which are essentially NT domains without domain controllers. Workgroups are easier to configure, but they're missing some of the features provided by domain controllers, such as the ability to use a central authentication database and to store local user configurations on a central server.

The advantage of a domain configuration, at least in terms of authentication, is that you need to maintain a user password database only on one system. Consider a network with half a dozen SMB/CIFS servers. If your users had to maintain separate passwords on all these servers, they'd either never change them or they'd forget all the different passwords. Your system administration task would also be more difficult in this case, because you'd need to explicitly create and delete accounts on all six servers. In a domain configuration, though, only one password database needs to be maintained, which greatly simplifies administration and users' own account maintenance tasks.

 Samba domain member server computers must maintain local Linux user accounts as well as Samba passwords (or defer to a domain controller for the latter). Thus, the administration benefits of a domain configuration are somewhat lower for Samba than for Windows SMB/CIFS servers—at least, unless you take additional steps. As described in Chapter 7, you can configure Linux to use an NT domain controller for the Linux account database. This can be more effort to set up but will reduce long-term administrative effort if your network hosts several Samba servers or if you want to integrate Linux and Windows accounts into one system. Alternatively, you can point the global add user script parameter to a script that creates an account for users who are authenticated by the domain controller but who don't already have local accounts. For instance, setting add user script = useradd -m %u in the [global] section of *smb.conf* may do the trick, although you may want to write a script that does more than this.

Frequently, the domain controller serves as a file and print server, in addition to functioning as a domain controller. This part of the Samba domain controller configuration is described in Chapter 4. It also delivers other NetBIOS functions on the LAN; specifically, it typically functions as a NetBIOS name server and as a domain master browser. These duties are described in the sections "Enabling NBNS Functions" and "Assuming Master Browser Duties."

Domain Controller Parameters

In order to function as a domain controller, Samba must be configured with certain options set in its *smb.conf* file's [global] section.

`security = User`

> This parameter, described in Chapter 3, sets the local authentication system. Because the domain controller serves as an authentication tool for other servers, user-level security is appropriate for the domain controller. Setting this parameter incorrectly causes the domain controller to function incorrectly.

`encrypt passwords = Yes`

> You must tell Samba to use encrypted passwords; if you don't, it won't be able to parse the encrypted password exchange initiated by domain member servers. On a domain controller, this setting also requires you to maintain a local encrypted password database, as described in the next section.

`passdb backend`

> This parameter specifies how Samba is to store its password database. The default value, `smbpasswd`, is simple and easy to administer compared to the alternatives, but it tends to be slow. This speed problem is extremely minor for networks with a few dozen, or even over a hundred, users. If your network has many hundreds or thousands of users, though, you may want to look into alternatives, such as `tdbsam` and `ldapsam`. These alternatives also support additional features, such as the ability to deliver time-based restrictions on user access. These alternatives require additional configuration, though, and such configuration is beyond the scope of this book.

`domain logons = Yes`

> This parameter is the defining one for a domain controller; it tells Samba to accept remote logon requests. The default value is `No`, so be sure to change it on your domain controller. Conversely, be sure *not* to change it on domain member servers and clients.

In addition to setting these parameters, you should be sure *not* to set the `password server` parameter. This parameter tells a Samba domain member server where the domain controller is, so it isn't needed for a domain controller. In fact, setting it can cause confusion because you're telling Samba to do two contradictory things—function as a domain controller and function as a domain member server.

> Because most domain controllers also take on name server and master browser duties, you must also set *smb.conf* parameters related to these functions, as described later in this chapter.

Maintaining the Password Database

Fortunately, maintaining the password database on a domain controller isn't much different from maintaining a password database on an isolated Samba server that uses local (user-level) authentication. This task is described in more detail in Chapter 3.

One point that deserves reiteration is that Samba's password database, whether for an isolated server or a domain controller, relies upon corresponding entries in an underlying Linux account database. Thus, you must maintain *both* Linux and Samba accounts on the system, and they must match. Normally this means that the usernames must be identical for both systems, although you can use the username map parameter and the mapping file to which it points to link together dissimilar usernames. This requirement also exists on Samba domain member servers, although you can use Winbind on them so that the domain controller provides the basis for the Linux accounts, if you like. (This topic is covered in Chapter 7.) Alternatively, domain member servers can set the add user script to add accounts automatically when the user authenticates and no matching Linux account exists. Windows servers can use the domain controller exclusively, as described in the section "Configuring Windows Clients and Servers as Domain Members."

Perhaps the toughest challenge in maintaining the password database relates to actual maintenance—adding and deleting users, enabling users to change their passwords, and so on. This task, although easy on a user-by-user basis, can become a time-consuming chore on larger networks. Fortunately, several procedures can help minimize the effort required to handle this task:

Adding users
> If you add users on a regular basis, you can write a simple shell script that adds both Linux and Samba accounts at once. Something as simple as Example 5-1 might serve well. This example requires you to type users' passwords twice, though, at least if they should have access to the server system both through Samba and through some other means. A more complex script can disable the Linux account for non-Samba logins, prompt for a password and deliver it to both *useradd* and *smbpasswd*, or otherwise work in a way that's suitable for your network.

> *Example 5-1. Sample script for adding Linux and Samba users*

> ```
> #!/bin/bash
> useradd -m $1
> passwd $1
> smbpasswd -a $1
> ```

Deleting users
> As with adding users, you should be sure to delete both the Samba and the Linux accounts when you do this. If you forget to delete the Linux account, users who should no longer have access to the server might be able to get in. A simple script that calls *userdel* and *smbpasswd* with appropriate options can help on this score.

Changing user passwords
> You can enable users to change their passwords several ways. One grants users shell access to the Linux domain controller, in which case they can call

smbpasswd themselves. If users shouldn't have shell access to the server, access to another Linux system can do as well; passing the -r parameter and a machine name causes *smbpasswd* to change the password on the specified remote system. Setting users' login shells to *smbpasswd* is another way to let them change their passwords; they can log in using Secure Shell (SSH), Telnet, or even console access, and they'll immediately be prompted to change their passwords. The Samba Web Administration Tool (SWAT) is another way to enable users to change their passwords. When users access this server with a web browser, they can change their Samba passwords. SWAT doesn't support encryption, though, which is a potentially important limitation.

Synchronizing Linux and Samba passwords

Keeping Linux and Samba passwords synchronized can be a tricky proposition. Setting the global Samba unix password sync parameter to Yes can help. This setting requires one of two additional options, though. One is the pam password change parameter, which should be set to Yes. Instead of setting pam password change = Yes, you can set passwd program to specify the local password-changing program, and set passwd chat to a chat script that controls the password-changing exchange.

When creating or modifying Linux accounts, remember to consider Linux groups. Depending on your shares' security settings and your overall server security policy, you may need to specify particular groups for your users. This detail is highly site-specific, though. If you don't specify a group, chances are the group will be either *users* or a group created specifically for the user you've added, depending on your Linux distribution.

Configuring Machine Trust Accounts

As noted earlier, Samba supports two methods of interacting with domain member servers: pass-through authentication and NetLogon authentication. (Technically, systems that use pass-through authentication aren't domain member servers, but they fill the same role in the network as a whole, so I don't try to draw a distinction in this chapter.) Windows 9x/Me servers and Linux servers configured with security = Server use pass-through authentication. If your network contains nothing but such servers, you can safely skip this section. Windows NT/200x/XP servers and Samba servers configured with security = Domain, though, use the NetLogon authentication method. This method requires that servers have accounts on the domain controller. Thus, to support such servers, you must create appropriate accounts, which are known as *machine trust accounts*.

 Technically, machine trust accounts are required only by servers; however, many Windows NT/200x/XP systems configured as clients try to use these accounts when you log onto them. Thus, you may need to create these accounts for all your Windows systems.

Like ordinary user accounts, machine trust accounts must exist both in the underlying Linux account database and in Samba. The Samba-side accounts are created in a semiautomated way once certain Samba options are set, though.

Typically, you create a special Linux group to hold the Linux-side machine trust accounts. For instance, you might call the group *trust*:

```
# groupadd trust
```

You should then create Linux-side accounts for all the domain member servers and any clients that you expect to require such accounts. These accounts are named after the computers' NetBIOS names, but they are in lowercase and with dollar signs ($) appended to the names. For instance, you'd create an account called *tulip$* for the computer whose NetBIOS name is *TULIP*. These accounts would be members of the machine trust group you created. They can also be non-login accounts, so they can be configured to refuse logins. A command to add such an account might look like this:

```
# useradd -g trust -d /tmp -s /bin/false tulip$
```

This command creates a new account (*tulip$*) in the *test* group (*-g test*) using the */tmp* directory as the account's home directory (*-d /tmp*) and */bin/false* as the default shell (*-s /bin/false*). Some of these parameters, such as setting the default shell to */bin/false*, provide an extra measure of security. Of course, you may want to tweak these options for your local system's requirements.

If you must add many machine trust accounts, you can streamline the process by placing the command in the [global] section of *smb.conf*, using the add machine script parameter:

```
add machine script = useradd -g trust -d /tmp -s /bin/false %u
```

This parameter enables Samba to create a machine trust account itself when a machine attempts to join the domain. The joining machine must present appropriate authentication first, though—presumably indicating that you or another authorized administrator is sitting at its console.

Once you add the Linux-side machine trust accounts, you should configure an administrative user. You can either add *root* to the list of Samba user accounts (a potentially risky proposition), or you can specify an administrative user with the admin users parameter in the [global] section of *smb.conf*: admin users = linnaeus. This user then has *root* privileges when accessing the server.

 For added security, comment out the admin users line when you don't need it, and specify an account you don't normally use for this purpose. That way, the risks of system compromise due to a compromise of this account are minimized. You can reduce the risk of using the *root* account if you employ that approach, using different Samba and Linux passwords for *root*.

Once these tasks are accomplished, Samba begins accepting domain member server requests to be added to the domain. This process is described in the section "Configuring Windows Clients and Servers as Domain Members," for Windows systems, and in Chapter 7, for Linux systems.

Common Domain Controller File Shares

NT domain controllers can and often do function as ordinary file and print servers, in addition to handling domain logons. If you want to configure home shares, file-exchange shares, and the like, consult Chapter 4. However, a couple of shares are common to domain controllers: domain logon shares and roaming profile shares. The former deliver domain logon scripts to clients, enabling you to provide consistent environments to all domain members. The latter enable you to store user desktop settings (icon placement, theme selections, and so on) on the domain controller, which can help provide users with consistent settings in environments in which users frequently move from one physical computer to another.

 The roaming profile share is optional. Although some documentation refers to the netlogon share as required, in practice, the domain controller can function without one. These shares both provide functionality that's important for some domains, though.

Configuring domain logon shares

A domain logon script is a Windows script (a.k.a. a *batch file*) that the Windows client retrieves and runs automatically when a user logs onto the computer. Clients retrieve these scripts from a share called *NETLOGON*, so if you want to use this feature, you must create this share:

```
[netlogon]
    comment = Network Logon Share
    path = /usr/share/samba/netlogon
    writeable = No
    write list = linnaeus
```

This share definition is fairly ordinary; it's a typical read-only file share, but with a user appointed with write privileges. The unusual feature of the share is actually defined in the [global] section of *smb.conf*, with a pointer to the logon script's filename:

```
logon script = LOGON.BAT
```

This line tells Samba to deliver the *LOGON.BAT* file from the *NETLOGON* share to clients when they log on. Note that you can use Samba's variables to deliver different logon scripts to different clients. For instance, specifying LOGON-%a.BAT tells Samba to deliver files with the clients' OS codes in the filenames, such as *LOGON-Win95.BAT* for Windows 9x/Me systems or *LOGON-Win2K.BAT* for Windows 2000 systems.

What should go in domain logon scripts, though? Anything you want. These scripts are Windows batch files, so you can run any command accessible on all the Windows client computers (or on any network share accessible to them). A simple example might set the systems' clocks and open users' home directories:

```
NET TIME \\TULIP /SET /YES
NET USE M: \\TULIP\HOMES /YES
EXPLORER M:
```

This example uses the *NET* command on Windows to set the time and mount the *HOMES* share from the *TULIP* server, then launch the Windows *EXPLORER* file manager on the share. You can do more or less, though; it's up to you.

Configuring roaming profiles

Normally, Windows stores users' preferences for user interface settings like icon placement and window themes on the local hard disk. This configuration works perfectly well on networks whose users generally have their own systems, such as office workers who have their own offices or cubicles. In other environments, though, users may regularly move from one computer to another—for instance, in a college computer center. In such cases, roaming profiles are handy. These enable users to store their personalized settings on the domain controller, so that they appear on whatever client they use, even if a user has never used a particular computer before.

Unfortunately, roaming profiles work slightly differently for Windows 9x/Me as opposed to Windows NT/200x/XP systems. (They're also completely unavailable for Windows XP Home systems, which technically can't participate in domains, although they can treat a domain as a workgroup.) To support Windows 9x/Me systems, Samba uses the global logon home parameter, which typically points to a subdirectory of the user's home directory:

```
logon home = \\%L\%U\.roamingprofile
```

This parameter specifies a Windows-style share locator (note the backslashes in the path). In this example, %L expands to the server's own name, and %U expands to the user's username; thus, this example should point to the *.roamingprofile* subdirectory in the user's home directory.

Windows NT/200x/XP requires a somewhat different definition. This is provided by a global parameter called logon path:

```
logon path = \\%L\PROFILES\%U\%a
```

This definition requires that a share called *PROFILES* exist on your server. The logon path includes the %a variable, which expands to the OS name, because Windows NT, 2000, and XP profiles aren't interchangeable. The profile share can be a fairly ordinary file-storage share, but for security purposes, it's best to set create mode and directory mode to fairly restrictive values:

```
[profiles]
   comment = NT Roaming Profiles
```

```
directory = /usr/share/samba/profiles
read only = No
create mode = 0600
directory mode = 0700
browseable = No
```

The share directory itself (*/usr/share/samba/profiles* in this example) must be write-able to all users; if it's not, users can't create their roaming profiles. In theory, you can point Windows NT/200x/XP systems to a subdirectory of users' home shares; however, Windows NT/200x/XP doesn't always completely disconnect from shares when users log out, which can complicate such an arrangement.

Configuring Windows Clients and Servers as Domain Members

Configuring Samba as a domain controller won't do any good unless you also config-ure computers as members of the domain. In theory, only domain member servers need to be so configured; however, in practice, clients may need to be configured in this way, too. Precisely how you accomplish this goal varies with the OS you're using. In particular, Windows 9x/Me and Windows NT/200x/XP have different domain membership requirements and options.

 Samba servers can also join domains, as described in Chapter 3. To use a domain controller as a way to control non-Samba access to a Linux system, consult Chapter 7.

Activating Windows 9x/Me domain membership

Ordinarily, when a Windows 9x/Me system is configured to use a workgroup, it pre-sents a logon screen with a two-field logon prompt, as shown in Figure 5-2. This logon screen provides no real security, though; clicking Cancel bypasses the logon screen and gives you full local access to the computer. This screen merely provides a way for Windows to cache your username and password for network accesses. Switching to a domain configuration won't change this lack of security.

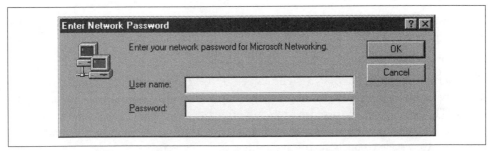

Figure 5-2. The Windows 9x/Me logon screen for a workgroup configuration

To reconfigure a Windows system with a workgroup-style logon to use a domain, follow these steps:

1. Open the Network item in the Control Panel. Windows displays a Network dialog box.

2. Select the Client for Microsoft Networks item in the Network dialog box and click Properties. Windows displays a Client for Microsoft Networks Properties dialog box, as shown in Figure 5-3.

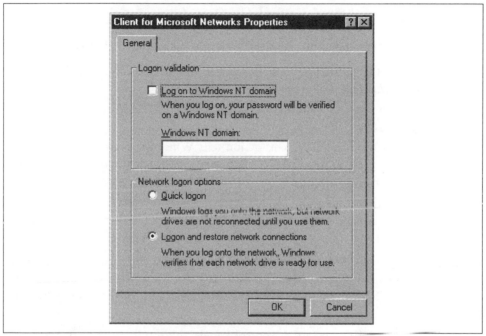

Figure 5-3. The Windows 9x/Me Client for Microsoft Networks Properties dialog box

3. Check the "Log on to Windows NT domain" check box.

4. Enter the name of your NT domain in the Windows NT domain field.

5. Click OK in the two open dialog boxes. Windows will inform you that it must reboot in order to implement the changes.

6. Allow Windows to reboot, or do so yourself. When the system starts up again, you should see a new logon dialog box, similar to the one shown in Figure 5-4.

Configuring Windows 9x/Me systems as just described doesn't improve security or change the system's logon procedures. It does, however, tell the Windows client to use a domain logon script, if you've configured your domain controller to provide one. It also enables the client to use roaming profiles, although extra configuration steps are required to actually use them.

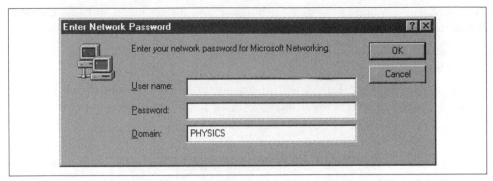

Figure 5-4. In a domain configuration, Windows 9x/Me provides a three-field logon dialog box

1. Double-click the Passwords item in the Control Panel. Windows displays the Passwords Properties dialog box.

2. Click the User Profiles tab in the Passwords Properties dialog box.

3. Click the Users Can Customize Their Preferences... radio button in the Passwords Properties dialog box. This action tells Windows to store different desktops for each user. In a domain configuration in which the domain controller supports roaming profiles, these are stored on the domain controller.

4. Click OK. Windows informs you that it must reboot. Do so.

5. When Windows starts up again and you log on, the system tells you that you haven't logged on before. Click Yes to tell Windows to create the roaming profile.

Ordinarily, Windows 9x/Me assigns passwords to any drives you share, using share-level security. Once you've configured a Windows 9x/Me system as a member of a domain, though, you can tell it to defer to the domain controller for authenticating its share access:

1. Open the Network icon in the Control Panel. The result is the Network dialog box.

2. Click the Access Control tab in the Network dialog box.

3. Click the User-Level Access Control radio button.

4. Enter the name of your domain in the "Obtain List of Users and Groups From" field.

5. Click OK in the Network dialog box. Windows displays a dialog box warning that you'll need to reconfigure your shared directories.

6. Click Yes in the warning dialog box. You'll then be asked to restart the computer. Do so.

After making this change, you'll need to redo your sharing configuration. The changes add the ability to specify user-based access control, so you can grant or deny access to the share to particular users.

Activating Windows NT/200x/XP domain membership

Windows 9x/Me systems use the pass-through authentication protocol, whereas Windows NT/200x/XP uses NetLogon authentication. For this reason, Windows NT/200x/XP systems require that you prepare a machine trust account on the domain controller, as described in the earlier section "Configuring Machine Trust Accounts," before you add the computer to the domain. (Windows XP Home doesn't support domain configurations, though, so you can't configure it this way. You can only treat a domain as if it were a workgroup from Windows XP Home.) Once you've created domain trust accounts on the domain controller, you can add a computer to the domain as follows:

1. Log onto the Windows system as Administrator. Don't open any shares on the domain controller.

2. Open the System object in the Control Panel. Windows should display the System Properties dialog box.

3. Click the tab called Network Identification or Computer Name, depending on the version of Windows you're running.

4. Click the Properties or Change button. Windows should display the Identification Changes or Computer Name Changes dialog box shown in Figure 5-5.

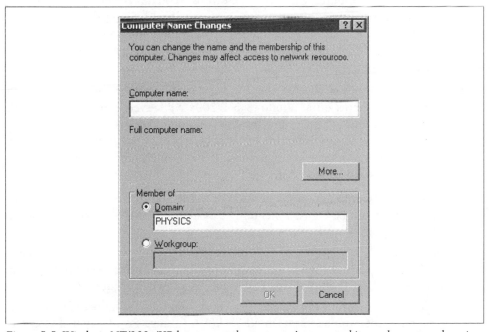

Figure 5-5. Windows NT/200x/XP lets you set the computer's name and its workgroup or domain affiliation in a single dialog box

5. If it's not already set, enter the computer's NetBIOS name in the "Computer name" field.

6. Click Domain in the "Member of area," and enter the name of the NT domain. If the computer is configured as a member of a workgroup of the same name as the domain you enter, Windows may complain. If this happens, try changing the workgroup name to a fictitious one, reboot, and start again.

7. Click OK in the Identification Changes dialog box. Windows opens a dialog box asking for a username and password.

8. Enter the username of the administrative user you specified with `admin users` on the Samba domain controller, along with the associated password. After you do this, you should see a message welcoming you to the domain and a notice that you must reboot the computer.

9. Dismiss the dialog boxes, and reboot the computer.

After you've made these changes and rebooted, Windows displays a new three-field logon window similar to the one shown in Figure 5-4. (Some versions of Windows NT/200x/XP differ in certain details; in fact, some hide the third logon field in an advanced options area.) Unlike the Windows 9x/Me logon screen, the Windows NT/200x/XP logon screen provides real security; you can't simply click Cancel to gain access to the computer without a password. You may want to bypass the domain authentication, though, and use the system's local account database. This is particularly handy when performing administrative tasks as the Administrator. To do so, select the computer's name rather than the domain name in the new Log On To field at the bottom of the logon prompt.

Windows should automatically use the domain controller for authentication when users try to access shares on a Windows NT/200x/XP server; thus, you shouldn't need to reconfigure the system to use the domain controller, as you do with Windows 9x/Me systems. Recent versions of Windows NT/200x/XP also use roaming profiles by default in a domain configuration. If you want to reconfigure a client to use local profiles instead, follow these steps:

1. Right-click My Computer on the desktop or in the Start menu and select Properties from the resulting context menu. The System Properties dialog box should appear in response.

2. In Windows 2000, select the User Profiles tab. In Windows 2003 or XP, select the Advanced tab and then click the Settings button in the User Profiles area. The result is a User Profiles dialog box or tab, as shown in Figure 5-6.

3. Double-click the line for the account you want to modify. (Figure 5-6 shows just one account, for Administrator on *NESSUS*.) A Change Profile Type dialog box appears, enabling you to select a roaming or a local profile.

4. Click the profile type you want to set in the Change Profile Type dialog box, and then click OK in all the open dialog boxes.

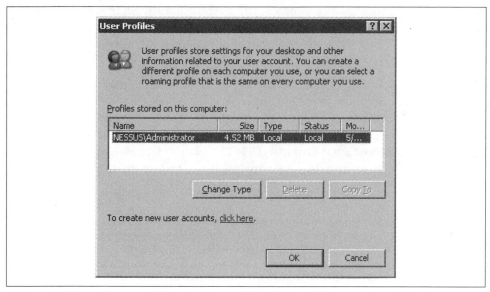

Figure 5-6. The Windows NT/200x/XP User Profiles selection dialog

Enabling NBNS Functions

Name resolution—converting computer names into IP addresses—is a problem that must be solved with any networking system. NetBIOS supports several methods of name resolution. One of these, the use of a NetBIOS Name Server (NBNS) system, is often associated with running a domain controller, although you don't need a domain configuration to use NBNS. Naturally, Samba can function as an NBNS system. Doing so requires setting just a couple of Samba options; the rest is fairly automatic, from Samba's perspective. Client configuration may be another matter, though; you must know how to tell clients to use the NBNS system.

The Role of the NBNS System

NetBIOS and Samba support several methods of name resolution, as described in Chapter 3. The simplest of these to configure is *broadcast name resolution*, in which computers needing to contact other computers broadcast the names, and the so-named computers respond to these broadcasts. Windows systems use broadcast name resolution by default. Broadcasts work well on small networks with just one subnet, but in a multisubnet configuration, broadcasts are typically blocked at the routers between subnets. Thus, other methods are used in such situations.

One type of solution to this problem is to use an NBNS computer. The NBNS system fills a role similar to that of a DNS server, but the NBNS system is specific to NetBIOS name resolution. It listens for name registrations from clients, caches them, and then delivers those names to other clients who ask for them. Because clients are told where to find NBNS systems, broadcasts aren't needed in NBNS-based name resolution. This means that NBNS is a superior name resolution system when a network spans multiple subnets.

NBNS-based name resolution is designed to work in a conceptually similar way to broadcast name resolution, in that clients register the names they want to use. Unlike a DNS server (described in Chapter 15), there's no need to explicitly tell an NBNS system about the names or IP addresses it's to share. If your network uses the Dynamic Host Configuration Protocol (DHCP) to deliver IP addresses to computers, they may change from time to time. An NBNS system automatically tracks these changes.

 You can configure Linux to use an NBNS system or broadcast Net-BIOS name resolution (instead of or, more commonly, in addition to DNS) even for non-Samba name resolution. This can be a convenient way to get name resolution working on a network on which IP addresses are likely to change from time to time. This topic is covered in Chapter 6.

Defining Samba NBNS Functions

Because the name resolution features of SMB/CIFS, including NBNS functions, were designed to work fairly automatically, Samba provides relatively few options related to these features. Only one option is required to activate NBNS features, although a few more will help fine-tune the operation:

wins support
> This global Boolean parameter controls NBNS functions. (Microsoft refers to the NBNS features as the Windows Internet Name Service, or WINS, hence the parameter name.) This option defaults to No; setting it to Yes causes Samba to function as an NBNS system.

wins proxy
> This global Boolean parameter tells Samba whether it should respond to broadcast name resolution requests on behalf of its NBNS clients. The default value is No, which is usually fine, but sometimes setting it to Yes improves the reliability of name resolution; try that if you're having problems.

dns proxy
> Ordinarily, the NetBIOS and DNS name spaces are logically distinct, although most administrators prefer to use the same names for specific computers in both spaces to avoid confusion. If you specify dns proxy = Yes (the default is No), though, Samba configured as an NBNS system will perform DNS lookups on any names it can't resolve using its NBNS name cache. This practice can improve reliability in some cases, but it can also slow down lookups, particularly

if the DNS server is slow. This feature only works for lookups of file and print servers, though, not for lookups of other types of systems, such as domain controllers.

 If you set wins support = Yes, be sure not to set the wins server parameter (described in Chapter 3). This parameter tells Samba what computer to refer to as an NBNS system. Ordinarily, an NBNS system automatically uses itself in this role, so specifying both parameters will likely result in malfunctions.

Overall, the NBNS system only needs to have wins support = Yes set; additional options just tweak the operation of the server. You should set this option on one server only; configuring multiple servers as NBNS systems is likely to cause confusion unless they can communicate with one another, which Samba doesn't support—at least as of the early 3.0.x versions. If two different clients are configured to use two different NBNS servers, they won't be able to locate each other via these servers, and possibly not at all if they aren't configured to use broadcasts as fallback or if they aren't on the same subnet.

Delivering NBNS Information via DHCP

Just as with DNS, the clients of NBNS systems must know how to contact their servers. Also just as with DNS, this task is accomplished by giving the clients the IP addresses of their servers. You can do this by entering the information on each client manually, but if your network uses DHCP, a simpler solution is to deliver the information via DHCP. (Even in this case, some client configuration may be necessary.)

 In Linux, you specify the NBNS system using Samba's wins server parameter, as described in Chapter 3. This is true even if you use DHCP to configure the Linux system.

DHCP server configuration

If your network uses DHCP for assigning IP addresses to Windows systems, the simplest way to configure those systems to use your NBNS system is to deliver the information via DHCP. Doing so requires modifying your DHCP server's configuration, though. Chapter 15 describes DHCP configuration generally, so you should consult that chapter first if you need to get your DHCP system operational. This section assumes you're using the Internet Software Consortium's (ISC) DHCP server, which is the most common one on Linux systems. Its configuration file is usually called /etc/dhcpd.conf, although it's likely to be stored in /usr/local/etc if you compile it from source rather than install it via a package for your Linux distribution.

Don't confuse the ISC DHCP server, *dhcpd*, with the ISC DHCP client, *dhcpcd*. The one-letter difference in the daemons' names, and similar differences in their configuration filenames, can be easy to overlook.

The */etc/dhcpd.conf* file is composed of several parts. At the top of the file are a series of global options. Chances are you'll include the NBNS options with these. The configuration file is likely to contain one or more declarations for particular subnets, which begin with the subnet keyword and include options for the subnet within lines delimited by curly braces ({ }). If you want to configure different NBNS servers for separate domains on different subnets, you can place the configuration options within these subnet declarations. In any event, to point DHCP clients at your NBNS system, add these lines:

```
option netbios-name-servers 192.168.1.1;
option netbios-node-type 8;
```

The first of these options specifies the IP addresses of your NetBIOS name servers. You would change the IP address as appropriate for your network, of course. Although the ISC DHCP server supports delivering multiple NBNS addresses (separated by commas), you're likely to deliver one only if you use Samba as an NBNS system, because Samba doesn't yet support exchanging NetBIOS name information with other Samba servers, so you're effectively limited to one NBNS system.

The netbios-node-type option specifies a code for the order in which the client attempts various lookup methods. Specifically, passing 1 as this value tells clients to use broadcasts alone; 2 means to use the NBNS system alone; 4 means to try broadcasts first and then to try the NBNS system if the broadcast fails; and 8 means to try the NBNS system and then to use broadcasts if the NBNS attempt fails. In most cases, 8 is the appropriate option.

Once you've made these changes, you need to restart the DHCP server. In most cases, passing restart to a SysV startup script, as in */etc/init.d/dhcpd restart*, does the trick.

Windows client configuration

Unless they're told otherwise, Windows clients use broadcast name resolution by default. Even if you configure DHCP to deliver NBNS information to clients, Windows 9x/Me systems ignore this information by default, so you must make a change to such systems' configurations to have them use DHCP-provided information. Windows NT/200x/XP, though, uses DHCP-provided information by default. Thus, you may not need to change these clients' configurations if you configure a DHCP server to deliver NBNS information.

If your network is dominated by older Windows 9x/Me systems, you might think that using DHCP to deliver NBNS information is pointless because you must reconfigure clients to use this information. Using DHCP does have certain advantages, though. For one thing, you can't mistype the IP address on a client, so misconfiguration of individual systems is less likely. Another advantage of using DHCP is that you can easily change the configuration of all clients merely by changing the server, should the NBNS system's IP address ever change.

To set NBNS information in a Windows 9x/Me client, follow these steps:

1. Open the Control Panel, and double-click the Network icon. Windows should display a Network dialog box in which you can select various drivers, network stacks, and so on.

2. Select the TCP/IP network stack for your local network's network card.

3. Click Properties. Windows should display a TCP/IP Properties dialog box.

4. Click the WINS Configuration tab in the TCP/IP Properties dialog box. The result should resemble Figure 5-7.

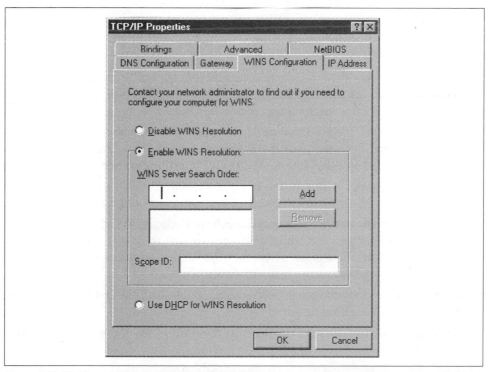

Figure 5-7. Windows 9x/Me lets you disable an NBNS system, specify an NBNS system explicitly, or obtain the information from a DHCP server

5. If you don't want the client to obtain information from a DHCP server, click the Enable WINS Resolution radio button, enter the IP address for your NBNS system in the WINS Server Search Order box, and click Add.

6. If you want to have Windows obtain information from the DHCP server, click the "Use DHCP for WINS Resolution" radio button.

7. Click OK in the TCP/IP Properties dialog box and then in the Network dialog box.

Windows must be restarted for the changes to take effect, and it should prompt you to do so. After the restart, Windows should use your NBNS system for name resolution.

If you use Windows NT 4.0, the method of setting the NBNS system is similar to that in Windows 9x/Me, although there are a few differences. For instance, you must select the tab called WINS Address rather than WINS Configuration, and the field in which you enter an NBNS system's IP address is configured slightly differently.

Windows 200x and XP use a substantially different way to specify NBNS information. These OSs use the information delivered by the DHCP server by default, so you shouldn't need to adjust them if you use this method. If you must specify IP addresses explicitly, though, you can do so:

1. Open the Control Panel, and then open the Network and Dial-Up Connections (Windows 2000) or Network Connections (Windows XP) object in the Control Panel.

2. Right-click the Local Area Connections object. This action produces a context menu, in which you should select the Properties item. Windows should now display a Local Area Connection Properties dialog box.

3. In the Local Area Connection Properties dialog box, select the Internet Protocol (TCP/IP) component and click the Properties button. This action should bring up a new dialog box called Internet Protocol (TCP/IP) Properties.

4. Click the Advanced button in the Internet Protocol (TCP/IP) Properties dialog box. Windows displays the Advanced TCP/IP Settings dialog box.

5. In the Advanced TCP/IP Settings dialog box, click the WINS tab. The result should resemble Figure 5-8, although chances are no addresses will appear in the address list. (Some details are different in the Windows 2000 version of this dialog box; Figure 5-8 was taken on a Windows XP system.)

6. Click the Add button to add an NBNS system to the list. The result is the TCP/IP WINS Server dialog box.

7. Type your NBNS system's IP address in the TCP/IP WINS Server dialog box, and click Add.

8. Click OK or Close in each of the open dialog boxes.

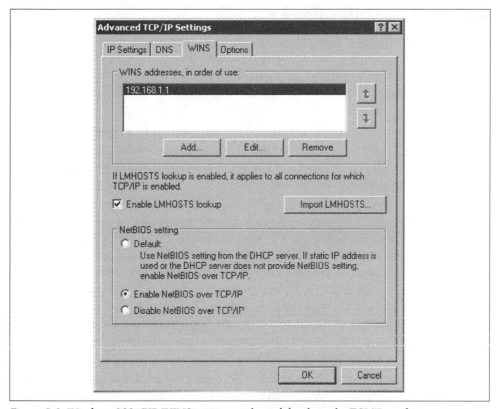

Figure 5-8. Windows 200x/XP WINS options are buried deeply in the TCP/IP configuration system

Assuming Master Browser Duties

Windows networks use a system known as the *master browser* to help maintain *browse lists*—lists of computers, the workgroups or domains to which they belong, and the types of services they offer. This may sound a lot like the duty of the NBNS system, but it's not quite the same. The master browser's list doesn't include mappings to IP addresses; it's used by clients to present lists of computers on the local network in network browsers.

In fact, there are *two* types of master browser: the *domain master browser* and the *local master browser*. The domain master browser is most often associated with networks that use an NT domain configuration, and in such configurations, the domain controller takes on this role. If you use a workgroup configuration, chances are you won't have a domain master browser. All NetBIOS networks have local master browsers, though. Samba provides configuration options that affect its ability to function in both roles.

The Role of the Master Browser

Master browsers maintain lists of computers and the services they offer. In this context, *services* refers to the types of SMB/CIFS duties they perform, such as file server, NBNS system, and so on. Master browsers don't maintain lists of the specific shares offered on particular servers; for that detail, clients must contact the servers themselves.

As mentioned earlier, two types of master browsers exist: local master browsers and domain master browsers. Domain master browsers normally also function as local master browsers. Both types deliver basically the same information, but domain master browsers add more methods of operation.

Local master browsers serve just one subnet on a LAN. The computers on a single subnet automatically determine which system is to function as the local master browser via an *election*, in which each computer broadcasts a set of credentials to the entire subnet, and the system with the best credentials claims victory. Because of this automatic selection system, you can't simply set a Samba parameter or two and be sure the system will become a local master browser. You can, however, set Samba parameters that will make it more or less likely to win—ideally, so likely to win that it's all but a sure thing, if that's what you desire. You can also tell Samba not to participate in elections, if you like. The next section describes configuring a system to win or lose local master browser elections.

Domain master browsers integrate information from local master browsers on multiple subnets, providing a way to enable browsing across subnets. They're usually part of an NT domain configuration, although you can configure a domain master browser in a workgroup. You must explicitly configure one computer as a domain master browser; they aren't selected through an election process. The section "Configuring Samba Domain Master Browser Features" describes how to do this.

No client-side configuration is required to point clients at either type of master browser. Clients should be able to find local master browsers by using broadcasts. Domain master browsers can be found via any NetBIOS name lookup method.

Winning (or Not Winning) Local Master Browser Elections

The local master browser election process is designed to give local master browser status to the computer that's best able to handle this duty. Election criteria include the OS version, whether the computer is functioning as a domain controller, whether the computer is functioning as an NBNS system, and so on. The most important factor is the OS version, so adjusting this detail is a critical step in "rigging" an election that you want a Samba server to win. Several other factors are important as well, though. Overall, you should consider these global parameters:

local master

This Boolean parameter tells Samba whether it should participate in local master browser elections. The default value is Yes, so you should change this parameter only if you want to ensure that a server doesn't become the local master browser.

os level

This parameter sets the OS version. It takes an integer as a value, with higher values making the server more likely to win. OS levels for Microsoft OSs vary; for instance, Windows 9x/Me is 1, Windows 2000 Professional is 16, and Windows 2000 Server is 32—the highest value of any Microsoft OS, at least as of late 2004. Samba's default os level is 20, so Samba will win over Windows 9x/Me or Windows 2000 Professional by default, but it will lose against Windows 2000 Server. If you want Samba to acquire local master browser status, you should set this value to 33 or above. If your network contains only one Samba server, any value above 32 should work fine. Inexpertly managed Samba servers may have higher values set by mistake, though, so you may need to use a higher value. This may also be necessary to win against future versions of Windows or other OSs. The highest value this parameter accepts is 255.

domain logons

This Boolean parameter is described earlier in this chapter, in the section "Domain Controller Parameters." The local master browser election procedure gives an edge to domain controllers, but this factor is less important than the OS level.

wins support

This Boolean parameter is also described earlier in this chapter, in the section "Defining Samba NBNS Functions." A domain master browser doesn't have to be an NBNS system, but the election criteria give these systems a slight edge.

preferred master

If this Boolean parameter is set to Yes, *nmbd* calls for an election whenever it's started, and periodically thereafter. This setting also gives the server a slight boost in the election. The default value is No.

> Setting preferred master = Yes inappropriately can cause problems because master browser elections take time, during which browsing ceases to function. Therefore, you should be sure that you don't use this setting on a system unless you're reasonably sure it will win the election (by setting a high os level value).

browse list

The default for this Boolean parameter is Yes, which causes Samba to maintain a browse list for the network. Maintaining the browse list does no harm if the computer doesn't function as a master browser, so there's normally no need to change this option. If you do set it to No, the system won't participate in browser elections.

The os level parameter trumps all the others, aside from local master and browse list. That is, in a contest between computers with os level parameters set to say, 32 and 33, the system with os level = 33 will win every master browser election, even if the other system is configured with domain logons = Yes, wins support = Yes, and preferred master = Yes. Overall, you can be fairly certain that a system will function as a local master browser if you set options like these in the [global] section of *smb.conf*:

```
local master = Yes
preferred master = Yes
os level = 64
```

If your network has some Samba systems with inappropriately high os level parameters, you may need to increase that value. (On the other hand, tracking down the offending systems and fixing their configurations may be a preferable solution.) If the computer also functions as a domain controller or NBNS system, you may need to set appropriate options for those functions, too. These settings shouldn't be necessary to have the system take on local master browser duties, though.

Configuring Samba Domain Master Browser Features

The domain master browser isn't elected by all the computers on the network; it's assigned by a network administrator. For this reason, Samba provides a parameter that tells Samba to take on this duty: domain master. This parameter is a global Boolean, and you should be careful about setting it. Don't set this parameter to Yes if you're not certain the system should be functioning as a domain master browser; do set it to Yes if the computer takes on this role.

Normally, the domain controller takes on domain master browser duties. Some workgroup configurations also use domain master browsers, even though they don't have domain controllers. This configuration can be helpful if your network spans multiple subnets, but you don't want to use a full domain configuration.

You should be sure to configure a domain master browser to win the local master browser election for its subnet, as described in the previous section. That section describes some options related to domain controller status as factors in browser elections; however, these factors are small ones, and they're completely irrelevant if two systems' OS levels don't match. Thus, you should be sure your domain controller has the highest os level parameter of any computer on the network.

Summary

Samba can take on many duties that are helpful or even necessary on Windows networks but that don't relate to sharing files or printers directly. Most of these duties are related to handling NT domain controller functions, and, in fact, functioning as a domain controller is one of these key functions. Related functions include handling NetBIOS name resolution as an NBNS system and becoming the local master browser or domain master browser. Using Linux as the operating system for any of these functions can help improve your network's overall reliability because of its excellent overall stability.

CHAPTER 6

Linux as an SMB/CIFS Client

Linux often functions as a tool for running Samba as a server on a network that's otherwise dominated by Windows systems. Sometimes, though, you might need to reverse this role and have Linux function as the client in an SMB/CIFS environment. Perhaps a few Linux desktop systems must access Windows servers; maybe a Linux system that works as a server for other protocols must do so. Whatever the details, the Samba package includes client tools, and the Linux kernel also supports accessing SMB/CIFS file shares. Thus, Linux can function in the client role, using Windows, Samba, or other SMB/CIFS servers on other computers.

This chapter covers several specific client roles for Linux on an SMB/CIFS network: using NetBIOS name resolution, accessing file and printer shares, and using GUI network browsers for Linux.

Using NetBIOS Name Resolution

As described in Chapters 3 and 5, NetBIOS provides a computer-naming system that's independent of DNS, which is used by most TCP/IP protocols. In fact, Windows enables its clients to use these NetBIOS names in place of DNS names for most protocols, at least for local computers. For this reason, some LANs rely heavily on these names, and if you want to refer to computers by name rather than by IP address from Linux, you may need to know how to configure Linux utilities to use these addresses. For the most part, this task can be handled with a setting or two in *smb.conf*. If your LAN doesn't use DNS hostnames for its local computers, though, you may want to expand this configuration to enable Linux to use NetBIOS names in non-SMB/CIFS tools, such as web browsers and email clients.

Setting Name Resolution Options in smb.conf

Most SMB/CIFS client tools in Linux support the use of NetBIOS names. These tools rely on libraries that ship with Samba and that are configured in the [global] section of your *smb.conf* file. In particular, you should review the name resolve order, wins server, and hostname lookups parameters, all of which are described in Chapter 3. For the most part, the default settings work well on small LANs that are configured to use broadcast name resolution. You might want to set hostname lookups = Yes if you want to specify computers by their DNS hostnames in *smb.conf*, though. If your network hosts an NBNS system, you may also want to point Linux systems to it with wins server.

 If a computer functions as an NBNS system, do *not* set wins server. Even pointing the server to itself with this parameter can result in odd behavior.

The parameter that requires the most attention is name resolve order. This parameter takes one to four of several values: lmhosts, hosts, wins, and bcast. The default lookup order is lmhosts host wins bcast, which minimizes the use of network resources. You can change this order if you like, though, or even omit options entirely. For instance, suppose you know your *lmhosts* file is empty, and suppose you don't want to use DNS except as a last resort because of possible name conflicts. You might then include these lines in *smb.conf*:

```
name resolve order = wins bcast hosts
wins server = 192.168.24.1
```

Using NetBIOS Name Resolution in Non-Samba Programs

In most cases, the NetBIOS name-resolution methods you set with name resolve order and other options in *smb.conf* apply only to Samba and related tools. These name-resolution methods have been split off into a library, though, and it's possible to splice this library into Linux's normal name-resolution system. When you configure Linux this way, you can use NetBIOS names in any Linux program that employs the normal name-resolution system, such as web browsers, mail clients, FTP clients, and so on. This can be a handy way to get name resolution working on a small network that doesn't have its own DNS server. (You'd presumably use your ISP's DNS server for handling names on the Internet, but it might not have entries for your local computers.)

Using NetBIOS names for non-SMB/CIFS tools can be convenient, but it can also cause problems. NetBIOS names lack Internet domain names, and so a few programs that rely on Internet domain names can choke if they're fed NetBIOS names. If DNS and NetBIOS names don't match, you can also cause problems when reverse lookups don't match forward lookups or when one name masks another one. These problems aren't always serious, but if you see strange error messages about failed lookups, you might want to consider using local */etc/hosts* files or running your own DNS server for local use, as described in Chapter 15.

The first step to using NetBIOS name resolution in non-Samba programs is to check for the presence of the necessary support libraries. These appear under the name *libnss_wins.so* (typically with a symbolic link called *libnss_wins.so.2*), usually in */lib*. If you can't find these files, you may need to install additional or newer Samba packages for your distribution. If you compiled Samba from source code, try typing **make nsswitch** from the Samba source directory, copying the resulting *nsswitch/libnss_wins.so* file to */lib*, and creating a symbolic link called *libnss_wins.so.2*. Usually, you will need to type **ldconfig** to have the system recognize the new library.

Once the library is installed, you must configure Linux to use it. This task can be accomplished by editing */etc/nsswitch.conf*. Look for the hosts line in this file. It probably contains entries for files, dns, and perhaps other name-resolution methods. Add wins to this list:

```
hosts: files dns wins
```

Linux tries name lookups in the order specified, so this example uses NetBIOS name lookups as the last resort. You might want to move wins earlier in the list, but doing so increases the odds for problems should a name be resolved in multiple ways and a program needs an Internet domain name.

 Although the option in */etc/nsswitch.conf* is called wins, the name-resolution system it enables works with both NBNS systems and broadcast name lookups. The *libnss_wins.so* library uses the NBNS computer specified by the wins server parameter in *smb.conf*, but it ignores the name resolve order parameter.

Accessing File Shares

One of the most complex topics in Linux SMB/CIFS client operations is file share access. Several tools exist to handle such accesses: the Samba *smbclient* utility, the *smbmount* tool for mounting shares, the standard Linux *mount* command, and the standard Linux */etc/fstab* file. (These final three methods are all closely related to one another.) No matter what method you use, you should be aware of some of the limitations of file accesses using SMB/CIFS, as described later.

Using smbclient

The *smbclient* program ships with Samba and is usually installed in the main *samba* package or in a package called *samba-clients*. This program is modelled after text-mode FTP client programs such as *ftp*. Basic use is fairly straightforward: type **smbclient**, followed by a NetBIOS name and share name in the form *//SERVER/SHARE*. The result is a prompt for a password followed by *smbclient*'s own prompt. You can then type FTP-style commands, such as *dir*, *get*, *put*, and *exit*. A typical session looks like this:

```
$ smbclient //MANDRAGORA/DDRIVE
Password:
smb: \> put chapter06.xml
putting file chapter06.xml as \chapter06.xml (613.4 kb/s) (average 613.4 kb/s)
smb: \> dir
  _Restore                       DHS        0   Sat Oct 18 13:15:50 2003
  Recycled                       DHS        0   Sat Oct 18 13:17:28 2003
  utils                          D          0   Sat Oct 18 13:37:28 2003
  APPS                           D          0   Sun Oct 19 00:07:20 2003
  drivers                        D          0   Sat Oct 18 15:47:42 2003
  chapter06.xml                  A      11935   Fri May 14 22:20:28 2004
  chapter05.xml                  A      64236   Fri May 14 22:19:50 2004
  flashplayer7installer.exe      A     658586   Sat Oct 25 11:20:54 2003
  RECYCLED                       D          0   Sun Nov  2 12:07:38 2003
  Font Navigator                 D          0   Mon Mar  1 12:55:40 2004

          47889 blocks of size 65536. 44706 blocks available
smb: \> del chapter05.xml
smb: \> exit
```

By default, *smbclient* uses your login username as the SMB/CIFS username. You can change this detail, and several others, with *smbclient* parameters, including:

-I *IP-address*

If you use this parameter, *smbclient* connects to the IP address you specify, rather than resolving the machine name.

-N   This parameter suppresses the normal prompt for a password, which can be handy if you know the share doesn't require one.

-U *username[%password]*

If your username on the server is different from your Linux username, you can specify the correct username with this parameter. If you like, you can also include your password after the username, using a percent symbol (%) as a separator.

-A *auth-file*

The *auth-file* specified with this parameter contains a username, password, and optionally a domain, one to a line and labeled, as in username = linnaeus. You can use this option to deliver authentication information to *smbclient* in scripts.

-c *command string*

This option passes a series of commands to *smbclient*, separated by semicolons (;). This feature is most commonly used by scripts. It implies -N, so you must usually deliver a password to *smbclient* in some other way, such as via -A.

-L *server*

This parameter causes *smbclient* to display a list of services available on the specified *server*. You omit the usual server and share specification if you use this parameter.

-M *server*

You can send text to another system to appear as a WinPopUp message with this parameter. When you use this option, *smbclient* accepts text you type until you press Ctrl-D. Alternatively, you can use redirection operators to send a file to another computer. When you use this parameter, you omit the usual server and share specification.

 This list of options only hits on the highlights; *smbclient* supports many more options, some of which are highly specialized. Consult the *smbclient* manpage for more details.

Once *smbclient* is running, you can type any of about 50 FTP-style commands. The most useful of these commands are:

? *or* help

You can obtain a list of commands by typing one of these commands. If you follow it by the name of a command (as in **help cd**), *smbclient* displays basic usage information on the requested command.

cd [*directory*]

Type this command to change into a directory on the server.

lcd [*directory*]

This command changes the working directory on the Linux client.

put *local-name* [*remote-name*]

Upload a file from the client to the server with this command.

get *remote-name* [*local-name*]

This command transfers a file from the server to the client.

ls [*mask*] *or* dir [*mask*]

These commands are equivalent; they produce a directory listing from the server, optionally of a subset of files or from a subdirectory if you include an appropriate *mask*.

rm *mask*

This command deletes a file or set of files matching the specified *mask* on the server.

rmdir *directory*

This command deletes the specified *directory* on the server.

rename *old-name* *new-name*

Unsurprisingly, this command renames a file on the server.

print *filename*

This command submits a local file as a print job to a printer share. It's covered in more detail in the section "Printing Using smbclient."

These commands should be sufficient for most casual uses of *smbclient*. For information on more exotic commands, consult the *smbclient* manpage or use its internal ? or help commands.

Mounting Shares Using smbmount

Accessing SMB/CIFS shares with *smbclient* is sufficient in some cases, but sometimes you need more. For instance, you might want to directly access a clip art collection using a word processor or graphics program, without having to copy files to the local computer using a separate program. For this purpose, Linux supports mounting SMB/CIFS shares as filesystems in the Linux directory tree. You can do this using the *smbmount* or *mount* commands or by adding an entry to */etc/fstab*.

All these SMB/CIFS mounting options rely on your kernel having SMB/CIFS client support. In 2.6.x kernels, this option appears in the File Systems → Network File Systems menu in the kernel configuration system, under the name SMB File System Support. (One option relies on the CIFS Support option instead, as described in the section "Using the cifs driver.") Most distributions' stock kernels include this support, but if yours doesn't, you need to recompile your kernel or at least add this support as a module and compile it that way. Once you've added the necessary support to the kernel, you can use *smbmount*, which takes the following syntax:

```
smbmount //SERVER/SHARE mount-point [-o options]
```

As an example, typing **smbmount //MANDRAGORA/DDRIVE /home/linnaeus/mandragora** mounts the *DDRIVE* share from *MANDRAGORA* on */home/linnaeus/mandragora*. Normally, though, this command prompts you for a password, so you must enter it. What's more, like *smbclient*, *smbmount* passes your current Linux username as the username for the server. Because only *root* may run *smbmount* by default, this means you may need to pass another username to the command or change the default in order to run it as an ordinary user. The former task can be accomplished by passing a parameter to *smbmount* with the -o parameter. Some of the more useful options you can pass in this way include:

username=*user*
> You can specify a remote username other than your current username with this option.

password=*pass*
> You can specify a password to be used with this option. (If you omit it, *smbmount* normally prompts for a password.)

 Delivering a password on the command line is potentially risky; it briefly appears in *ps* outputs and also appears in your shell's command history. For this reason, you should avoid using the password option whenever possible.

`credentials=auth-file`

You can deliver a username and password in a file with this option, which points to a file with the same format as the credentials file for *smbclient*—the string `username=` followed by the username, and the string `password=` followed by the password on the next line.

`uid=UID`

This option sets the user ID (UID) that will own all the files on the share you mount. If you omit this option, files are owned by the user who runs *smbmount*.

`gid=GID`

This option works like `uid`, but it sets the group ID (GID) rather than the UID.

`fmask=mode`

You can set the mode (specified in octal format) of files on the remote share with this parameter. The default—if you omit this option—is based on the current umask.

`dmask=mode`

This option works like `fmask`, but it sets the mode for directories on the share.

`guest`

Pass this option if you know the share doesn't require a password; *smbmount* won't prompt for one.

`ro` This option causes *smbmount* to mount a share read-only, even if the share supports write access.

`rw` This option attempts a read/write mount and is the default.

The *smbmount* command accepts several additional parameters, most of which set fairly obscure options. Consult its manpage if you need more details.

As an example, consider this scenario: you want to mount the *DDRIVE* share from *MANDRAGORA* at */usr/share/clipart* in such a way that all users can read the share and the user with a UID of 1027 can write to it. You want to use the username *linnaeus* and the password *bu9N!nEp* on the server. The following command accomplishes this goal:

```
# smbmount //MANDRAGORA/DDRIVE /usr/share/clipart \
   -o uid=1027,fmask=644,dmask=755,credentials=/etc/samba/mandragora.creds
```

This command requires a credentials file (*/etc/samba/mandragora.creds*) with the following contents:

```
username=linnaeus
password=bu9N!nEp
```

 Credentials files are extremely sensitive. They should be set to be readable only by the user who'll use the SMB/CIFS client programs that read them.

When you're done using a share, you can unmount it with the *smbumount* command, which works much like the standard Linux *umount* command:

```
# smbumount /usr/share/clipart
```

One problem with the *smbmount* command as just described is that only *root* may use it. This problem can be overcome by setting the set-user-ID (SUID) bit on the *smbmnt* helper program and on *smbumount*:

```
# chmod a+s /usr/bin/smbmnt /usr/bin/smbumount
```

After you make this change, ordinary users may run *smbmount* and *smbumount*. They must, however, own their mount points. This configuration can be handy on multiuser systems or when shares should be mounted and unmounted on a regular basis. On the other hand, any SUID *root* program is a potential security risk, so you shouldn't set this option unless it's necessary. If a share should be mounted at all times, you might consider adding it to */etc/fstab*, as described in the section "Editing /etc/fstab."

> Some versions of *smbumount* often have problems identifying shares that are mounted by *smbmount*. If you see the error message:
>
> ```
> /mount/point probably not smb-filesystem
> ```
>
> you need to use *umount* as *root* to unmount the filesystem.

Mounting Shares Using mount

An alternative to *smbmount* that's very similar is to use the standard Linux *mount* command. To use this command, specify the smbfs or cifs filesystem type codes. These codes correspond to two different SMB/CIFS clients in the Linux kernel. The first, smbfs, is the older of the two. It works with any common SMB/CIFS server, using TCP port 139 and NetBIOS over TCP/IP, and is quite reliable. The cifs code is much newer (it was only added as a standard part of the kernel with the 2.6.x series) and isn't quite as reliable. This driver works using newer "raw" SMB/CIFS over port 445, which isn't supported by older servers such as those that ship with Windows 9x/Me. The cifs driver supports some more recent low-level SMB/CIFS features, though, and so it might eventually provide faster operation.

> Ordinary users can't use *mount* as described here; however, if you add an entry to */etc/fstab*, as described in the section "Editing /etc/fstab," and if that entry includes the user, users, or owners option, ordinary users can use *mount* to mount a share. To do so, users specify the mount point only, rather than the full set of options *mount* normally accepts.

Using the smbfs driver

To use the smbfs driver, you must include support for it in the kernel, as described in the section "Mounting Shares Using smbmount." Once that's done, you can use *mount* to do the job by passing it a filesystem type code of smbfs and a share specification like the one you'd pass to *smbmount*. You can also use the same options that *smbmount* supports. For instance, you might issue a command like this:

```
# mount -t smbfs //MANDRAGORA/DDRIVE /usr/share/clipart \
   -o uid=1027,fmask=644,dmask=755,credentials=/etc/samba/mandragora.creds
```

This command is equivalent to the similar one shown in the previous section. Like that command, it relies on a credentials file (*/etc/samba/mandragora.creds*). In fact, as a practical matter, the two commands are virtually identical. One practical difference, when typed at a shell prompt by *root*, is that you use *umount* rather than *smbumount* to unmount a share mounted via *mount*. Using *mount* also enables you to use *mount*-specific options not provided by *smbmount*, such as the remount option to -o, which tells Linux to remount a filesystem with different options.

Using the cifs driver

The cifs driver was added to the 2.6.x kernel series as a way to support certain features not supported by the smbfs driver. Most of these are low-level features relating to protocol operational details, though, so they have no obvious consequences to users or system administrators. (Some features, such as Kerberos and DFS support, are under development or are important in some environments, though.) This driver works exclusively with recent servers, such as Samba and Windows 200x/XP. The driver uses "raw" SMB/CIFS over TCP port 445, rather than the port 139 that's used by earlier SMB/CIFS implementations. As a practical matter, the main reason to use the cifs driver is if you want to close off port 139 on the server (say, for security reasons). One other practical difference between the drivers is that cifs accepts DNS hostnames but not NetBIOS names for the server specification; smbfs accepts both name forms. (However, if you configure NetBIOS name resolution for Linux TCP/IP applications, as described in the section "Using NetBIOS Name Resolution in Non-Samba Programs," cifs will accept NetBIOS names.)

The cifs driver works with a helper application, *mount.cifs*. Recent distributions and versions of Linux ship with this tool. If yours didn't, you can find it at *http://linux-cifs.samba.org*, along with assorted other cifs documentation and tools, including the latest version of the driver. (This may be more recent than the version included in the latest Linux kernel.)

In theory, cifs accepts basically the same set of mount options as smbfs, so you should be able to use it in precisely the same way. In practice, though, cifs is still new enough (at least, as of the 2.6.7 kernel) that some options don't work or have only recently begun working. The credentials option didn't work properly until somewhere between the 2.6.4 and 2.6.6 kernel, for instance. If you run into problems with the cifs driver, therefore, you may want to drop back to the smbfs driver, at least for troubleshooting purposes.

My experience with cifs is that it's not as stable as smbfs. Sometimes it refuses to mount a share for no apparent reason, and when a share does mount, file accesses are sometimes unreliable. All in all, then, I recommend you avoid cifs if possible. On the other hand, raw SMB/CIFS over TCP port 445 supports features that aren't supported using the older NetBIOS over TCP port 139, such as Unicode filenames, better locking, and so on. Thus, it's possible that cifs will one day provide superior features and performance, compared to smbfs.

Editing /etc/fstab

Both *smbmount* and *mount* can be used by *root* to mount shares on an as-needed basis, and *smbmount* can be used by ordinary users if its support programs are given SUID *root* status. What if you want to make a share available at all times, though? You can place a *mount* or *smbmount* command in a startup script, of course, but as a general rule, the way filesystems are mounted automatically in Linux is to use entries in */etc/fstab*. You can do the same with SMB/CIFS shares, using the filesystem type codes smbfs or cifs, just as you would with the *mount* command.

An */etc/fstab* entry for an SMB/CIFS share looks much like any other */etc/fstab* entry, except that it uses an SMB/CIFS server/share specification rather than a device filename and smbfs or cifs options—which are the same as those for *smbmount*, as described earlier. All told, entries might resemble these:

```
//MANDRAGORA/SHARED    /mnt/shared    smbfs \
credentials=/etc/samba/creds/shared,uid=1027,gid=100,fmask=666,dmask=777  0 0
//tulip/CLIPART        /mnt/clipart  cifs  guest  0 0
```

This example mounts two shares: *//MANDRAGORA/SHARED* is mounted using smbfs at */mnt/shared*, while *//tulip/CLIPART* is mounted using cifs at */mnt/clipart*.

The first mount's options are so lengthy that the */etc/fstab* entry is split across two lines in this book, using a backslash (\) as a line-continuation indicator. You'd replace this character with the second line's contents in a real */etc/fstab* file. This entry uses credentials stored in the specified file, assigns ownership of all files to the user with UID 1027, and gives everybody full read and write access to the share. The idea is that this is a share to which everybody should be able to write, probably on an old Windows 9x/Me system, although it could be a Windows NT/200x/XP server or a Samba share.

The second mount's options are shorter because the assumption is that file ownership and permissions will be acquired from the server using Unix extensions (as described in the next section). Thus, there's no need for the uid, gid, fmask, or dmask options. This share supports guest access, and so this entry uses the guest option to access the share. (This option began working between the 2.6.4 and 2.6.6 kernels; on earlier versions, the guest option didn't work with the cifs driver.)

 If a share requires a password, you should store it in a credentials file and restrict access to that file. Storing anything but bogus passwords in */etc/fstab* is potentially quite risky because it's readable to all users of the system.

After making changes to /etc/fstab, you should unmount the shares if they're already mounted. You can then type **mount -a** to have Linux mount all your filesystems using the new values. If the operation doesn't succeed, check the */var/log/ messages* file on the client and the relevant Samba log files on the server for clues to what went wrong. The cifs filesystem can be particularly troublesome, in my experience; you might want to try smbfs instead, at least for testing purposes.

Normally, shares specified in */etc/fstab* are mounted at boot time. (Some distributions seem to have problems mounting SMB/CIFS shares at boot time, though. To do so, you may need to add a call to *mount -a* to a startup script.) If you include the noauto option along with user, users, or owner, though, the share doesn't mount automatically. However, users can mount the share by typing **mount */mount/point***, where */mount/point* is the mount point specified in */etc/fstab*. The user and users parameters both permit any user to mount a share. They differ in that users enables any user to unmount the share, whereas user gives this authority only to *root* and the user who mounted the share. The owner option requires that the user who mounts the share own the mount point.

File Share Access Limitations

SMB/CIFS was originally designed with non-Unix systems in mind, and so most SMB/CIFS servers don't support Unix-style filesystem features, such as ownership, permissions, and symbolic links. (SMB/CIFS does support NT-style equivalents to some of these features, but they don't yet integrate cleanly with Linux clients.) Some features, such as ownership and permissions, are fundamental to Linux filesystem handling, so Linux SMB/CIFS mounting tools provide parameters to set these options on a filesystem-wide basis—effectively, giving ownership of all files to a particular user and setting all files' permissions identically. (Setting the DOS-style read-only bit, though, removes all write permissions.)

Depending on how you want to use an SMB/CIFS share, these limitations might or might not be a problem. For instance, if you want to give individual users access to their home shares on a remote server, you can enable them to mount their own shares with *smbmount*. These shares are then owned by the users in question, which is probably just fine for access to ordinary files. Setting up such access in */etc/fstab* can be tedious, though. You probably can't simply mount all a server's home shares with one entry, and even if a server were set up to enable such access, the ownership of all files would be assigned to a single user, which is probably unacceptable. Thus, you need to create separate */etc/fstab* entries for each user, and give users some way to set their passwords (presumably in a credentials file in their own home directories). Maintaining such a configuration is tedious at best. If the server is a Unix or Linux system, chances are you should use NFS rather than SMB/CIFS.

On the surface, *Unix extensions* can help with these problems. These are extensions to the SMB/CIFS parameters that support Unix-style ownership, permissions, symbolic links, and so on. On a Samba server, you can enable Unix extensions by setting unix extensions = Yes, which is the default as of Samba 3.0. These extensions aren't available on Windows servers, though.

When the cifs driver, or recent versions of smbfs or the *smbmount* command mount a share that's delivered by a remote server that supports Unix extensions, the server delivers ownership and file permissions information to the client. Unfortunately, this system only goes so far; the server still authenticates a single user for file accesses. Therefore, files are accessed in that user's name, which may not be the same as the user who's really accessing the file. For instance, suppose you use the *linnaeus* account to mount a remote share. If *mendel* tries to access a file that's owned by *mendel* with 600 (rw-------) permissions, access is denied, because from the server's point of view, it's *linnaeus*, not *mendel*, who's trying to access the file, and *linnaeus* lacks appropriate permissions. Samba's developers are working to overcome this limitation, but it still exists, at least as of the 2.6.8 kernel and Samba 3.0.7.

Nonetheless, using Unix extensions can still be a useful security tool for preventing unauthorized access to files. You can change ownership and permissions on the server to restrict access to files from the client in ways that can't be done using SMB/CIFS alone. File owners can set their Unix-style permissions, including the execute bit, within limits imposed by the create mask and directory mask parameters on the server, which can be handy if users need to store program executable files on the server. The Unix extensions also support hard and symbolic links. On the other hand, if you prefer to rely on Samba's server-side security features, you can set unix extensions = No to disable this support, in which case client-side options, such as the uid and fmask mount options, begin working again.

Printing to Printer Shares

A popular SMB/CIFS client feature on Linux is the ability to print to printers that are connected to Windows systems or to other systems that support SMB/CIFS printing. (Many dedicated print server appliances support SMB/CIFS printing, for instance.) Precisely how this task is accomplished depends on the software installed on your Linux system. One way that should always work, given an appropriately formatted file, is to use *smbclient* to submit a print job. You can also configure your

Linux print queue to submit jobs to a remote server via SMB/CIFS, but the details vary with your local print queue. This section describes how to configure CUPS to configure an SMB/CIFS printer, as well as how to do the job with BSD LPD or LPRng.

Printing Using smbclient

If you have a one-time need to print to a Windows printer from Linux, you may want to consider using *smbclient* to do the job directly. As described earlier, *smbclient* is a basic text-mode tool for transferring files using SMB/CIFS. Many *smbclient* features and commands are modelled after those in text-mode FTP clients. One command in particular, though, is of interest here: *print*. Once you've started *smbclient* and connected to a print server, you can use this command to transfer a print job to the server. The transaction looks something like this:

```
$ smbclient //MANDRAGORA/HP4000
Password:
Domain=[GREENHOUSE] OS=[Unix] Server=[Samba 3.0.3]
smb: \> print myoutput.ps
putting file myoutput.ps as myoutput.ps (29.8 kb/s) (average 29.8 kb/s)
smb: \> quit
```

This operation is fairly straightforward for printing a single file (or even a few files), but it does have a few caveats. Most obviously, it requires that you have a file on hand. Most Linux programs that can print can also "print" to a file, so this requirement is seldom a problem. A more important caveat is that the file you submit (*myoutput.ps* in this example) must be in a format that the remote printer can parse. Most Linux programs generate PostScript output, so if you're printing to a Post-Script printer, this will probably work fine. If the printer isn't a PostScript model, though, you may be in a bind. Many printers can handle ASCII (a.k.a. plain text) files, so if you want to print simple text (such as the output of an *ls* command), you may be fine; just put the information in a text file and submit it. For more complex data, you may need to use Ghostscript (*gs*) to convert PostScript to the remote printer's native format. For instance, to convert PostScript to PCL, which is used by many mid-range laser printers, you might type a command like this:

```
$ gs -dNOPAUSE -dBATCH -sDEVICE=ljet4 -sOutputFile=myoutput.pcl myoutput.ps
```

The -sDEVICE option sets the output driver; ljet4 stands for *LaserJet 4*—one of Hewlett-Packard's (HP's) PCL printers (and for which one PCL version's Ghostscript driver is named). If you don't know what driver to use, you may need to check *http://www.linuxprinting.org* for advice, or at least type **gs --help** to obtain a list of drivers available in your Ghostscript executable. With luck, one of the abbreviations will be familiar to you.

Using *smbclient* directly can become tedious. If you need to print to an SMB/CIFS printer on a regular basis, you can configure your local Linux printing queue to do so

---

automatically. To do so, manually configure a queue or use a configuration tool, as described in the next two sections.

Defining SMB/CIFS Printers Using CUPS

Most Linux distributions today ship with the Common Unix Printing System, which provides both local and remote printing services for Linux systems. Chapter 4 describes basic CUPS configuration, so if you're not already familiar with CUPS, you should consult the relevant section of that chapter before proceeding.

Configuring an SMB/CIFS printer from CUPS works much like configuring a local printer. Instead of selecting the local printer port (such as a parallel or USB port), though, you pick the "Windows Printer via SAMBA" option as the device. Once you do this, the CUPS GUI asks you for the printer device's uniform resource identifier (URI). In theory, this is the same as the share name, as delivered to *smbclient* and other tools, except that it's preceded by smb:. This basic form, though, works only with printers that are shared for anonymous users. If your printer share requires a username and password, you must add this information to the URI, so that it takes the form smb://*username:password@NetBIOS-name/share-name*. For instance, you might enter **smb://linnaeus:bu9N!nEp@BIRCH/EPSON** to print to the *EPSON* share on *BIRCH* using the *linnaeus* account and the password *bu9N!nEp*. Several variants on this form are possible; consult the *smbspool* manpage for details (*smbspool* is a part of the Samba package that helps CUPS by submitting the print job to the remote server). If you include a username and password in the device URI, they won't appear in subsequent pages of the CUPS web-based configuration tool; they're hidden from view, but used internally.

 When you enter the password as part of the device URI, it appears in the web browser's text-entry field. Worse, the username and password are both stored in */etc/cups/printers.conf*. For these reasons, it's best to use a dedicated printing-only account that has no other access to the print server. (Windows 9x/Me print servers normally ignore the username and provide share-level access to the printer, using a password only.)

When printing to a printer on a Windows server, you should normally select a CUPS printer definition for the printer in question, as described in Chapter 4. This causes the Linux system to pass programs' output through Ghostscript, if necessary, and turn it into a form that's acceptable to the remote printer. If the server is a Linux or Unix system running Samba, though, a raw queue may work better than a printer-specific queue. This is true even for genuine PostScript printers and their printer-specific definitions; sometimes these definitions add lines to the PostScript file that can confuse the server's print queue and cause it to print PostScript code rather than the file you want to see. Of course, when printing from Linux to another Linux or Unix system, chances are you'll use Unix-centric printing protocols rather than SMB/CIFS, but you can use SMB/CIFS if you have some reason to do so.

Defining SMB/CIFS Printers Using LPRng or BSD LPD

Although CUPS has become the most popular printing package in Linux, some distributions still provide an option to use LPRng or even BSD LPD. These printing systems weren't designed with much thought for printing to non-LPD remote printers, but they can do so by bypassing the normal local printer queue and calling a remote-printing tool as part of a print filter. For instance, a normal local printer queue using LPRng or BSD LPD is defined by a set of lines in */etc/printcap*:

```
lp|lp0|hp4000:\
    :sd=/var/spool/lpd/hp4000:\
    :mx#0:\
    :sh:\
    :lp=/dev/lp0:\
    :if=/var/spool/lpd/hp4000/filter:
```

The if line defines an *input filter* for the queue—a program that processes the print jobs for printing. Normally, this filter attempts to identify the file's type and passes it through programs such as Ghostscript to convert it to a format that's appropriate for the printer, whereupon the print job continues on to the output device specified by lp. To print to an SMB/CIFS printer, you instead point if at a program that delivers the print job to the remote queue, bypassing the lp line entirely.

Normally the task of submitting the print job to an SMB/CIFS queue is fairly complex: the submitted file's type must be identified, the file must be converted into a format suitable for the printer, and the file is delivered via an SMB/CIFS client program. Printer configuration tools can handle all these tasks. In the past, distributions such as Red Hat and SuSE shipped with distribution-specific tools for printer configuration. (These tools frequently called *smbprint* as part of their operation, but this detail was hidden from the user.) Most such tools have now been altered to configure CUPS rather than BSD LPD or LPRng, though, or omitted entirely in favor of CUPS web-based tools. If you're still using a non-CUPS print queue, you should check your distribution's documentation and look for options akin to those provided by CUPS.

If you've deliberately installed BSD LPD or LPRng on a distribution that normally uses CUPS, you may want to look into Apsfilter (*http://www.apsfilter.org*). This package is a set of configuration tools and smart filters that can identify various file types and apply appropriate transformations to them. Once you've installed Apsfilter, you should be able to launch its configuration utility by typing **/usr/share/apsfilter/SETUP** (the *SETUP* utility might exist in another directory on some systems, though). When you set up a queue, select the Windows/NT (Samba) option and then enter the appropriate information about the server's name, the queue name, etc.

Configuring GUI Workgroup Browsers

If you're migrating desktop users from Windows to Linux, chances are your users will be familiar with the Windows Network Neighborhood or My Network Places network browsers. These browsers enable users to easily locate network resources in a friendly visual manner. The core Linux SMB/CIFS client tools, though, are purely textual, and hence decidedly unfriendly to users who aren't comfortable with text-mode commands. Fortunately, some tools exist that provide GUI frontends to the text-based tools or that integrate SMB/CIFS functionality into primarily GUI tools. Installing and configuring such tools can help make former Windows users feel at home on a Linux desktop system.

A Rundown of GUI Network Browsers

Fitting with the Unix tradition of creating small programs that work together, many SMB/CIFS network browsers serve as frontends to the text-mode tools. Others use functions that are now provided in Samba libraries to handle much of the grunt work of SMB/CIFS interactions. These tools differ in their levels of sophistication and precise feature sets. Examples include:

Konqueror
> This program is the file manager and web browser in the K Desktop Environment (KDE; *http://www.kde.org*) package. It supports accessing SMB/CIFS shares when the user enters an SMB/CIFS URI, such as *smb://MANDRAGORA/ SHARED*, in a window's path specification. Konqueror doesn't actually mount shares on the Linux filesystem.

Nautilus
> The GNOME file manager, Nautilus, supports SMB/CIFS access. You may need to select the File → Open Location option in the program and enter a URI for your share. Like Konqueror, Nautilus doesn't actually mount the SMB/CIFS share, but it does provide drag-and-drop access to files.

LinNeighborhood
> This program provides a GUI frontend to several Samba and related utilities, the end result being a system that's similar to Network Neighborhood or My Network Places in overall capabilities. It uses *smbclient* to mount remote shares, so they're accessible to all programs. If LinNeighborhood doesn't ship with your distribution, you can obtain it from *http://www.bnro.de/~schmidjo/*.

Gnomba
> Like LinNeighborhood, Gnomba is an SMB/CIFS network browser that supports mounting shares you discover in the Linux filesystem tree. You can obtain it from its home page, *http://gnomba.sourceforge.net*.

xSMBrowser

This program doesn't actually mount remote shares, but it enables easy browsing of the network. Check the project's home page, *http://www.public.iastate. edu/~chadspen/*, for more information.

SMB2WWW

This tool is unusual in that it's an interface between HTTP, which is used by web browsers, and SMB/CIFS. The program runs as a Common Gateway Interface (CGI) program from a web server, giving web browsers that access the server the ability to browse the local SMB/CIFS network. You can obtain more information and download the program from *http://www.scintilla.utwente.nl/ users/frank/smb2www/*.

There are several more GUI tools for Linux SMB/CIFS interfacing, including some very specialized ones. Check *http://www.samba.org/samba/GUI/* for brief descriptions and links to those tools that have been registered with the main Samba project.

Using LinNeighborhood

LinNeighborhood provides fairly typical network-browsing features, although its user interface isn't quite as polished as some users might expect. Still, it works with a variety of desktop environments, which can be a big plus. Before you can use it in any significant way, you must install and configure it:

1. Check your distribution or the LinNeighborhood web site itself for the program. The web page includes binaries in several different formats, or you can download and install the source code.

2. As an ordinary user, type **LinNeighborhood** in an *xterm* or similar window. The result is the main LinNeighborhood window.

3. Click the Prefs button in the LinNeighborhood window. LinNeighborhood displays its main Preferences dialog box, as shown in Figure 6-1.

4. Enter the information in the Scan tab. The workgroup is particularly important, but you may want to enter the IP address of your NBNS system. LinNeighborhood should be able to find the primary master browser automatically, and because this can change unexpectedly, it's probably best to leave this field alone. Adjusting the various checkboxes can also help in some cases; for instance, you might want to perform scans as your logon user rather than anonymously.

5. Click the Programs tab, and check the entries there; they relate to the programs LinNeighborhood uses to do the real work. Chances are you won't need to adjust these entries.

6. Click the Miscellaneous tab, and check the items there. Particularly if you checked "Always scan as user" on the Scan tab, you may want to enter a default user. If you enter a default password, be aware that LinNeighborhood will store

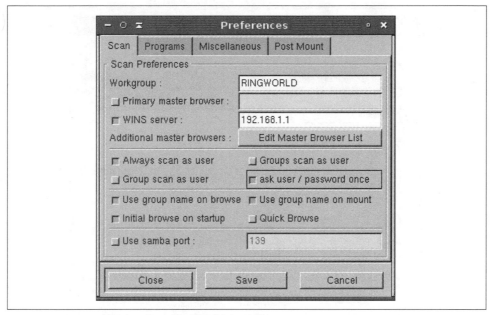

Figure 6-1. LinNeighborhood configuration

it in a plain-text file, ~/.LinNeighborhood/password, in your home directory. Be sure that file is readable only to you!

7. Click the Post Mount tab, and adjust the items there. This tab enables you to launch a file manager on shares you mount, or conceivably perform other arbitrary actions.

8. When you're done with the Preferences dialog box, click Save, followed by Close.

The LinNeighborhood configuration files are in the ~/.LinNeighborhood directory, and in particular, in the *preferences* file. You can configure LinNeighborhood as you like and then copy this file to all users' home directories. You may need to omit or customize the default_user line from this file, though.

LinNeighborhood should now be configured and ready to function. If you don't yet see a list of systems in the main window, as shown in Figure 6-2, try right-clicking the machine name, and select Rescan Groups from the resulting pop-up menu.

You can browse the network in a way that should be familiar to those with GUI file manager or network browser experience: double-click machine names (such as *HALRLOPRILLALAR* and *LOUISWU* in Figure 6-2) to open them, or click the plus or minus symbol next to the name to open or close a machine that's already been visited. Depending on your settings, you may be asked to enter a username and

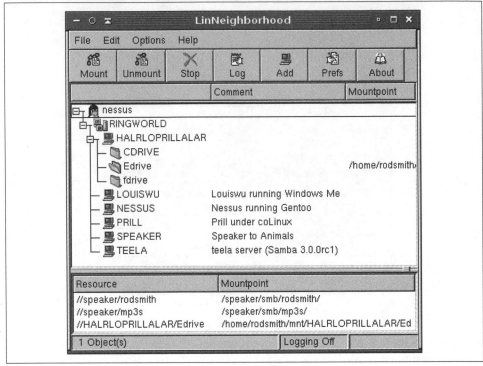

Figure 6-2. The main LinNeighborhood window provides point-and-click network browsing

password when you do this. Double-clicking a share's folder under a machine (such as *CDRIVE* or *EDRIVE* in Figure 6-2) brings up a mount dialog box in which you specify the mount point, username, password, and so on. LinNeighborhood then mounts the share and displays it in the bottom pane of its main window, along with other SMB/CIFS mounts. If you configured LinNeighborhood to launch a file manager after mounting a share, your file manager window should appear.

 To mount shares, LinNeighborhood requires that you either enter the *root* password in the mount dialog box or set the SUID bit on the *smbmount* binary, as described in the section "Mounting Shares Using smbmount."

To unmount a share, right-click the share or its mount point in the bottom pane of the window, and select Unmount from the resulting pop-up menu. LinNeighborhood should unmount the share—if it can. If any programs have open files on the share, LinNeighborhood won't be able to comply.

On some systems, *smbumount* won't be able to unmount the filesystem, despite the fact that it was mounted with *smbmount*. This appears to be a bug in *smbumount*.

Using Konqueror

Konqueror, the primary web browser and file manager for KDE, also supports SMB/CIFS; however, this support is fairly recent and is still improving. Konqueror's support also doesn't actually mount the share in the Linux filesystem. This means that if you attempt to directly access a file (say, by double-clicking it), either Konqueror must copy the file to a temporary local location and then copy it back when you're through or the application used to access the file must implement its own SMB/CIFS support. Konqueror, like other GUI SMB/CIFS tools, also relies on other support libraries. For the most part, these are installed with your main Samba or Samba clients package.

To use Konqueror's SMB/CIFS features, you should first launch it. Most Linux distributions place a link for Konqueror in a menu or on the desktop, particularly when you run KDE rather than GNOME or some other desktop environment. If you can't find a link, type **konqueror** in an *xterm* or similar window.

Once Konqueror is running, type a URI (beginning with smb://) for the machine or share you want to access in the Location field. If you enter a complete share specification, Konqueror asks for a username and password, which you must enter correctly. (If you enter a machine name without a share name, Konqueror defers asking for a username and password until you try to access a share.) Konqueror should then present a list of file shares on a server or files and folders in a share. For instance, Figure 6-3 shows Konqueror's display of the shares on the *SPEAKER* server. You can browse your entire network by entering smb:/ as the device URI (the number of slashes is critically important: you must place one slash after smb:).

In theory, you should be able to use an SMB/CIFS share much as you'd use a local directory, by clicking folders to open them and clicking files to launch applications that will read the files. In practice, though, this sometimes doesn't work correctly. Konqueror may hang during file transfers to temporary locations, or programs may fail to load the files. These problems will likely diminish as Konqueror's SMB/CIFS support matures.

Summary

Although Linux often functions as an SMB/CIFS server with the help of Samba, the Samba suite and Linux kernel both provide support for SMB/CIFS client operations. You can use these features to enable NetBIOS name resolution for ordinary TCP/IP applications, to access files on Windows or other SMB/CIFS file servers, and to print

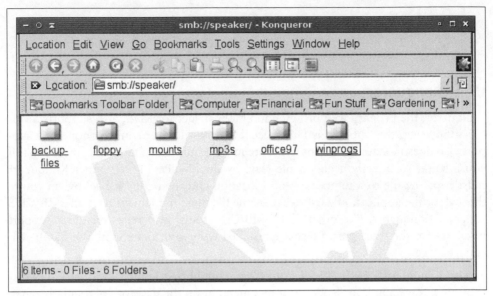

Figure 6-3. Konqueror displays shares and their files much as it displays local files

to shared printers. An array of GUI tools can also make accessing SMB/CIFS resources easy for less computer-savvy users, although these tools may require configuration by more experienced users.

## PART III

Centralized Authentication Tools

Networks with many computers frequently set aside one system as an *authentication server*—a computer that authenticates users for the benefit of other computers. This practice can greatly simplify account maintenance, because you need to maintain only one set of user accounts rather than separate accounts on each computer. This goal is more complex on a multi-OS network than in a single-OS environment, though, because different OSs support different protocols for performing these tasks. This part of the book looks at three protocols that can be used in a mixed Windows/ Linux environment: Chapter 7 describes using an NT domain controller, Chapter 8 describes using the Lightweight Directory Access Protocol (LDAP), and Chapter 9 describes using Kerberos. Chapter 7 emphasizes Linux configuration as an authentication client; the Linux server and Windows client sides are covered in Chapter 5. Chapters 8 and 9 describe both client and server configuration for Linux and client configuration for Windows.

Which tool should you use? All can do the job, but each has its strengths and weaknesses. Broadly speaking, using an NT domain controller works well when you have an existing NT domain controller for file share access and want to apply this existing account database to other purposes. LDAP provides the best support for Linux account data and can also work well with Windows 200x/XP systems, but it doesn't support Windows 9x/Me very well. Kerberos was designed to provide a single sign-on—that is, to enable users to enter their passwords once per session, even if they log in and out of multiple servers during this session. It doesn't maintain all the necessary account data, though, and it can be tricky to use for some cross-platform tasks.

## CHAPTER 7

Using NT Domains for Linux Authentication

If your existing network uses an NT domain or an Active Directory domain, you may want to tap into your existing domain controller for Linux authentication. For instance, you might want a Linux POP server to use your existing Windows domain accounts. Doing so presents certain challenges, though; the Windows and Linux authentication systems require different types of information, so some information Linux needs isn't available from the domain controller. Fortunately, Samba's Winbind software helps bridge this gap. Winbind links together the domain controller's database and Linux's native authentication system, the Pluggable Authentication Modules (PAM). Using Winbind requires configuring Samba options for Winbind, as well as for PAM and another helper tool, the Name Service Switch (NSS).

> Active Directory, introduced with Windows 2000, is the successor to NT domains. AD domain controllers support the older NT domain controller protocols for the sake of backward compatibility, so you can authenticate Linux systems against an AD controller using the methods described in this chapter. You can also authenticate Linux systems against an NT domain controller that runs Samba.

Because Winbind is part of Samba, you should understand the basics of Samba configuration before proceeding, even if you don't want to run the full Samba server suite on the system you're configuring. If you're not already familiar with the basics of Samba, you should read Chapter 3. If you want to have Linux fill the role of the NT domain controller, you should read Chapter 5.

The Principles Behind Winbind

When configuring a Linux system to authenticate users against an NT domain controller, you should understand the basic principles behind this operation—that is, how Linux can work with an account database that wasn't designed with Linux or other Unix-like OSs in mind. Essentially, the problem is one of integrating two dissimilar systems—the NT domain system and Linux's PAM. Winbind is a tool that performs most of this integration, although some details are left to other tools.

The Problem: Linux Users on an NT Domain

As a practical matter, the desirability of running Linux as an NT domain controller's client (that is, as a *domain member server*) varies from one network to another. The most common use for this approach is limited to file shares on a Samba server, and that procedure is described in Chapter 3. This configuration, though, works only for Samba shares, not for other services the computer might offer, such as a POP server, an SSH login server, or console logins. If a computer should be used in any of these ways in addition to or instead of being used as a Samba server, you must normally maintain local Linux-only accounts. On a network that already uses NT domain authentication for Windows systems, this separation can be a serious problem. You need to recreate your NT domain accounts on your Samba server—a tedious undertaking for you and for your users, who will have to reenter their passwords. If you want to run multiple Linux server computers or add Linux desktop systems, you need to either maintain separate Linux account databases on each Linux system or use some other network authentication database. In other words, you'll be throwing away the benefits of the NT domain controller for the new Linux systems.

Using an NT domain controller can be a good way to minimize the account maintenance difficulties when you start adding Linux systems. Instead of using a Unix-centric centralized account system or using local Linux account databases, you can tap into the NT domain controller. Once you've done this, a Linux POP server, SSH server, or most other servers automatically accepts logins using the usernames and passwords supported by the NT domain controller. You can even use this method to enable console logins using the NT domain's accounts.

 Typically, some accounts are still maintained locally. Most notably, you should leave the *root* account defined only in the local Linux account database. This practice enables you to log in even if network problems exist. It also enables you to set different *root* passwords for each Linux system, which can help improve your overall network security; a breach of one system won't necessarily translate into a breach of all your systems.

NT domain authentication was designed with the needs of Windows computers in mind. These authentication tools provide some information that Linux requires, such as a username and password. This information isn't always available in a form the Linux system will find immediately useful, though; for instance, the password is encrypted using a method that's foreign to Linux. Worse, NT domain accounts lack some information that's critical to Linux, such as the Linux account's home directory and default shell. Thus, Winbind must make up some of this information using values set in Samba's *smb.conf* file. Other differences, such as NT domain password encryption, are handled by Winbind's PAM integration modules.

Linux's PAM and NSS Systems

Linux relies on two systems to help manage accounts: PAM and NSS. PAM is described in detail in Appendix A. In brief, PAM tells login services whether a user may log in or not, helps programs change passwords, and handles a few related tasks. PAM is a modular system, so you can reconfigure PAM to use authentication modules based on authentication tools other than the common */etc/passwd* and */etc/shadow* files. In particular, this chapter describes how to configure PAM modules that link to an NT domain controller with the Winbind tool.

In addition to PAM, Linux relies on another software component, NSS, for account information. Rather than authentication information, though, NSS provides more mundane information, such as a mapping of UIDs to usernames and the account's default shell. Like PAM, NSS is designed in a modular way and sits between applications that ask for this information and the actual account databases. Although you may think in terms of domain authentication, which is what PAM provides, this ancillary information is just as important, so you must configure NSS to query Winbind. Most of the information NSS delivers is made up rather than pulled out of the NT domain controller, though, because this is the information the domain controller doesn't support.

Winbind: Linking PAM and NSS to an NT Domain

Winbind is implemented as a daemon, *winbindd*. This daemon ships with the official Samba source code tarball, although some Linux distributions split it off into its own package, such as *winbind*. As described in the later section "Running the Winbind Daemon," this daemon runs at all times on any server that authenticates users against a domain controller. Although *winbindd* is a daemon, it's not an externally accessible server; it doesn't bind to a port and listen for external connections. It does, though, use Unix domain sockets to communicate with local processes—namely, the PAM and NSS libraries that are also part of the Winbind package.

Winbind connects to the domain controller to authenticate users and thus functions as a domain member server to a domain controller. Winbind works in this way only when the computer on which it's running is fully joined to a domain using the Samba *net* command, which is described in a later section, "Winbind Options in smb.conf."

Samba Winbind Configuration

Much of the configuration of Winbind is done using Samba. The main Winbind options appear in *smb.conf* (although, as described earlier, some options are set in the PAM and NSS configuration files, as well). Thus, you must know how to set these Samba options. Running the Winbind daemon is also critically important to getting the system running.

> This configuration occurs on the domain member server—the Linux system you want to configure to use a domain controller's account database. If you use a Samba server as the domain controller, it requires its own configuration, which need not include most of the options described here.

Winbind Options in smb.conf

You should configure the *smb.conf* file on the domain member server much as you would for any Samba server on a domain, as described in Chapter 3. Most notably, you should set the workgroup, security, encrypt passwords, and password server global options:

```
workgroup = GREENHOUSE
security = Domain
encrypt passwords = Yes
password server = 192.168.1.1
```

You should adjust the values of the workgroup and password server parameters for your network, of course. The security parameter must be set to Domain, and encrypt passwords must be set to Yes.

> If your domain controller supports AD, you can set security = ADS instead of security = Domain, but this configuration requires setting additional options and can be finicky. It provides somewhat better security on your LAN because it uses the extremely robust Kerberos authentication system.

In addition to these options, which are the same as those you must set for any Samba domain member server, you may want to set several other global parameters. These parameters set values for information required by Linux accounts but not provided by the domain controller:

winbind use default domain
> Ordinarily, Winbind returns Linux usernames that are based on a combination of the NT domain name and the NT username. This feature enables you to maintain multiple domains and support users with duplicate usernames in these domains without causing conflicts. If you set this Boolean parameter's value to

Yes, though, Winbind omits the domain name from usernames, which results in shorter and more sensible usernames. Doing this is safest when you have just one domain or when you're sure that no usernames are duplicated on multiple domains. This parameter's default value is No.

winbind separator

This parameter specifies a character that separates domain names from usernames when winbind use default domain = No. The default character is a backslash (\).

winbind enum users

Linux provides certain system calls that enable programs to enumerate users on a system. Winbind supports these features if this parameter is set to Yes (the default), but this support can be slow. Thus, if the programs you run on a system don't require this support, setting this parameter to No can improve performance.

winbind enum groups

This parameter works much like winbind enum users, but it affects system calls for enumerating groups rather than users.

idmap uid

Linux uses UIDs internally for tracking users. NT domains use a number called a Security Identifier (SID) for a similar purpose; however, the two numbers aren't identical. Thus, you can give Winbind a range of local UID numbers to use for the accounts it handles. This range is given as two numbers separated by a dash, as in 2000-5000. You should never create local Linux accounts in the range you reserve for Winbind in this way. This parameter's default range is undefined. Prior to Samba 3.0.6, this value had to be set, but in Samba 3.0.6 and later, an undefined idmap uid causes Winbind to try to map NT domain usernames to locally defined accounts, which can be useful if you have existing Linux accounts but want to rely on a domain controller for password authentication. A synonym for this parameter is winbind uid.

idmap gid

This parameter works much like idmap uid, but it reserves a range of GID numbers rather than UID numbers. This parameter's default value is undefined. A synonym for this parameter is winbind gid.

Winbind makes no guarantees about the UIDs and GIDs assigned to particular users and groups. In particular, two Linux systems might assign completely different UIDs and GIDs to a user, even if you specify the same range of UIDs with idmap uid. This can complicate certain Linux-to-Linux protocols, such as NFS, which identifies accounts by UID rather than username. You can overcome this problem using the idmap backend parameter to point to an LDAP directory that holds the UID mapping information.

Samba maintains information about UID and GID mapping in Trivial Database (TDB) files, typically in */var/cache/samba* or a similar location. If these files are damaged or deleted, Winbind has to rebuild these mappings, and they may not match the originals. If this happens, you have to reassign ownership of all your users' files and home directories.

template shell

> An */etc/passwd* file normally specifies a default shell for a user; this program is run when a user logs in at a text-mode console, via SSH, and so on. NT domain controllers don't maintain this information, though, so you must tell Winbind what value to provide. The default is /bin/false, which is a conservative choice from a security point of view and may be good for some functions. However, for systems that should support shell access, another value, such as /bin/bash, will function better. You can't customize this value on a per-user basis; all accounts mediated by Winbind must use the same shell.

template homedir

> Just as with the default shell, NT domain controllers don't maintain information on the users' home directories. You specify this information with this parameter, which defaults to /home/%D/%U. Because %D is a Samba variable for the domain name and %U stands for the username, this value sets a unique home directory for each user. As of Samba 3.0.6, only the %D, %N, %U, and %u variables are supported in this option.

winbind cache time

> This parameter sets the amount of time, in seconds, that Winbind will cache authentication information before querying the server again, should a new authentication request occur. The default value is 300 (five minutes). You may want to reduce this value during testing.

The most important of these parameters to set or change are usually idmap uid, idmap gid, and template shell. Setting other parameters can sometimes be desirable, though. For instance, you might use parameters like these for testing in a one-domain configuration:

```
winbind use default domain = Yes
idmap uid = 2000-5000
idmap gid = 2000-5000
template shell = /bin/bash
template homedir = /home/%U
winbind cache time = 5
```

Once you're convinced everything is working, you should increase the cache time so as to reduce the number of queries the system makes of the domain controller. Changes to some other parameters might require additional system changes; for instance, if you alter template homedir, you have to move users' home directories yourself.

Before proceeding, remember to add a machine trust account to the domain controller for the Linux computer. This can be done from the Linux system using the *net* utility. For instance, to join a computer to the domain specified by the workgroup parameter in *smb.conf*, type this command:

```
# net join member -U adminuser
```

This command needs to be run just once. In this example, *adminuser* is the username of an account on the domain controller that may add machine trust accounts. (This topic is covered in more detail in Chapter 3.) If the domain controller is a Samba server, consult Chapter 5 for information on configuring the necessary machine trust accounts.

Running the Winbind Daemon

Because Winbind relies on a running daemon, you must configure it to run at all times. For testing purposes, though, you may want to run it manually:

```
# /usr/sbin/winbindd -i
```

 The *winbindd* program file may be in another directory on your system. */usr/local/samba/sbin* is common if you compiled Samba from source code yourself. If you can't find the binary on your system, check your distribution's Samba packages; you might not have installed the package in which the daemon ships.

To run the daemon permanently, you should do one of two things:

* Add a line to launch the program to a local startup script, such as the */etc/rc.d/rc.local* script in Fedora Core, Mandrake, or Red Hat; */etc/init.d/boot.local* in SuSE; or */etc/conf.d/local.start* in Gentoo.

* Configure a SysV startup script to launch the daemon. Many distributions' Samba packages include such scripts, usually called *winbind* or something similar. Create appropriate symbolic links or use whatever SysV startup script management tools your distribution provides to do the job.

In either case, you should remove the -i option from the line that launches *winbindd*. This option causes the daemon to log information on its operation to standard output and to not detach from the current terminal, which is handy when testing the daemon but not when using it in normal operation.

Once Winbind is running, you can test its basic operation using the *wbinfo* command. This command supports numerous options that return information on accounts maintained by the domain controller. Some options enable you to modify those accounts, as well. To test the most basic operation, use the -t option to test the trust account you've created and the basic Winbind functionality:

```
$ wbinfo -t
checking the trust secret via RPC calls succeeded
```

If this call returns an error message, review your *smb.conf* options and check the logs on the Linux system and the domain controller for clues to the cause. A subsequent testing step involves -u; this option returns a list of accounts maintained by the domain controller:

```
$ wbinfo -u
linnaeus
mendel
britton
```

 This example shows output consistent with a setting of winbind use default domain = Yes. If this option is set to No, the usernames include domain names, as in GREENHOUSE\linnaeus rather than linnaeus.

If **wbinfo -u** returns a list of users, you can be confident that Winbind is operating, at least minimally. If you receive an error message, though, you should look into the matter. Review your *smb.conf* entries, and check the logs on both the Linux system and the domain controller for clues.

PAM and NSS Winbind Options

Getting the Winbind daemon up and running is only part of the configuration required on the domain member server. Once Winbind is functioning, you must configure PAM and NSS to use Winbind to authenticate users and return additional account information to programs that need it. These tasks are handled by special modules and configuration of these two subsystems. You may also want to configure Linux to create home directories automatically when they don't exist.

NSS and PAM Winbind Modules

PAM and NSS both rely on modules to interface with Winbind. These module files, *pam_winbind.so* and *libnss_winbind.so*, are usually installed as part of a Samba package, such as *samba-common*. The *pam_winbind.so* file usually appears in */lib/security* or */usr/lib/security*. The *libnss_winbind.so* file usually resides in */lib* and is linked to another file, *libnss_winbind.so.2* (either file may be a symbolic link to the other).

If you've installed Samba from source code, you may need to install these libraries independently. The source code appears in the *source/nsswitch* subdirectory of the Samba source code package, and the compiled libraries should appear there after you build the main Samba package. (These files appear only if you select the --with-pam configure option.) Copy the files to appropriate directories, and create an appropriate link for the *libnss_winbind.so* file. You can then type **ldconfig** to force Linux to reexamine the library directories and register the new libraries.

Configuring NSS

NSS provides nonauthentication information on accounts to tools that require it. Before PAM allows you to log in using Winbind, you must configure NSS to use Winbind. This can be done by editing the */etc/nsswitch.conf* file. Locate the passwd and group lines in this file. (The shadow line usually separates them, but you won't edit this line.) Add winbind to the passwd and group lines:

```
passwd:  files winbind
shadow:  files
group:   files winbind
```

 Some distributions place other options on these lines in addition to files. Some use compat instead of files. If yours is so configured, simply add winbind to the end of the list, or to an earlier position if you prefer. (NSS consults each source in turn for account information.)

Configuring PAM

PAM enables you to customize authentication options on a service-by-service basis. For instance, you can tell Linux to use only the local account database for console logins, to use only the NT domain controller for FTP logins, and to use either method for remote SSH logins. PAM accomplishes this goal by using one or more configuration files: either a file called */etc/pam.conf* or files in the */etc/pam.d* directory named after the particular systems they control. Modifying these files to use additional PAM modules, such as those that support NT domain authentication, is described in Appendix A.

 When reconfiguring PAM, you can easily render your system unable to support logins. Thus, I recommend experimenting with one login server at a time, leaving yourself some way to log in should you create an inoperable system. For instance, experiment with the login service and leave the gdm or xdm service alone.

As an example of adding NT domain authentication, consider Example 7-1. This listing shows the contents of the */etc/pam.d/login* file on a Debian system, which defines how PAM handles authentication for text-mode console logins and logins via such servers as Telnet.

Example 7-1. Sample PAM configuration file

```
auth      requisite  pam_securetty.so
auth      requisite  pam_nologin.so
auth      required   pam_env.so
auth      required   pam_unix.so nullok

account   requisite  pam_time.so
account   required   pam_unix.so
```

Example 7-1. Sample PAM configuration file (continued)

```
session    required    pam_unix.so
session    optional    pam_lastlog.so
session    optional    pam_motd.so
session    optional    pam_mail.so standard noenv

password   required    pam_unix.so nullok min=6 max=255 md5
```

 PAM configurations vary both from one service to another and from one distribution to another. If your PAM configuration file doesn't look exactly like Example 7-1, don't panic. The most important part of PAM Winbind configuration is adding lines, as described shortly.

To add NT domain authentication to this system, you should add a couple of lines to this file. These lines tell PAM to use the *pam_winbind.so* library for authentication and account validity checks. The result of adding these lines appears in Example 7-2, with the added or changed material shown in bold.

Example 7-2. Sample PAM configuration file with Winbind support

```
auth       requisite   pam_securetty.so
auth       requisite   pam_nologin.so
auth       required    pam_env.so
auth       sufficient  pam_winbind.so
auth       required    pam_unix.so nullok try_first_pass

account    requisite   pam_time.so
account    sufficient  pam_winbind.so
account    required    pam_unix.so

session    required    pam_unix.so
session    optional    pam_lastlog.so
session    optional    pam_motd.so
session    optional    pam_mail.so standard noenv
session    required    pam_mkhomedir.so skel=/etc/skel umask=0027

password   required    pam_unix.so nullok min=6 max=255 md5
```

This configuration adds an auth line just before the existing auth line that references pam_unix.so and adds the try_first_pass parameter to that existing line. These changes add Winbind to the authentication system and cause pam_unix.so to use the password entered for Winbind if Winbind authentication fails. A second set of changes is in the account stack, which adds a Winbind call to it. Finally, this configuration adds a call to pam_mkhomedir.so, which creates a new home directory for the user if one doesn't already exist. You need to make these changes for every service that should use the NT domain controller.

Some distributions, including Red Hat, Fedora, and Gentoo, now use the pam_stack.so module rather than pam_unix.so or pam_unix2.so. If you see calls to this module, you can either add your calls to pam_winbind.so to the file as described here or modify the */etc/pam/system-auth* file instead of the file for the individual servers. The pam_stack.so module pushes part of the PAM configuration into the *system-auth* file, as described in Appendix A.

You should also change the */etc/pam.d/passwd* file, which controls the *passwd* command's actions. As described in Appendix A, this change requires adding references to *pam_winbind.so* to the auth, account, and password stacks.

You normally don't need to change the */etc/pam.d/samba* configuration. The Samba server provides its own tools for authenticating against the domain controller, and in fact, if you configure Winbind properly, Samba is automatically configured to use the domain controller directly. Thus, although it has one, there's no need to edit Samba's PAM configuration file.

Winbind in Action

In theory, Winbind should now be working. In practice, though, various problems can occur. You can perform tests to check on Winbind's operation that will point you to likely solutions for any problems that might exist. Once the system is up and running, you can begin using it, but you should understand its capabilities and limitations in day-to-day operation.

Testing Winbind Operation

We looked at the *wbinfo* tool that tests Winbind operation in the section "Running the Winbind Daemon." This tool queries the domain controller via Winbind without using the NSS or PAM libraries, and as such, it's a good test of "pure" Winbind operation. It provides several options you can use to test basic Winbind operations:

-a *username%password*
    This option performs a test authentication using the provided *username* and *password*. If it succeeds, Winbind can authenticate users. This option only works when run as *root*.

-g This option displays all groups available on the current domain.

-n *name*
    Winbind returns the SID of the specified *name*, which is normally a username but could be a group name.

-p   This option checks for the presence of Winbind; if it's running and working at least minimally, the program responds `Ping to winbindd succeeded`.

-t   Use this option to check the validity of your domain trust account. If it's valid, *wbinfo* responds:

    `checking the trust secret via RPC calls succeeded`

-u   As described earlier, this option displays a list of usernames managed by Winbind.

Some additional options provide more features for converting between SIDs, Unix usernames, and Unix UIDs. Still more options can be used for account management. Consult the *wbinfo* manpage for more information.

When debugging problems, I recommend using the -p, -t, -u, and -g options to check for basic functionality. (The last of these may return an empty list under some circumstances, though.) Using options that work on specific accounts or groups, such as -a and -n, can help you verify that more advanced features are working. If any tests fail, the pattern of failures can be informative. For instance, if -t fails, but -p works, you should check your machine trust account, and if necessary recreate it.

A second layer of tests uses the *getent* command. This tool returns the contents of administrative databases, such as */etc/passwd* or */etc/group*. The tool works through NSS, though, so when you configure NSS to use a domain controller, *getent* should return information from the local */etc/passwd* or */etc/group* files, followed by constructed entries for the NT domain accounts and groups. You obtain these lists by typing the command followed by the database—that is, **getent passwd** or **getent group**. Check the outputs of these commands for the accounts and groups that are defined on your domain controller. If either output lacks entries that should be present, you might have mistyped an entry in */etc/nsswitch.conf*, or your system might be missing the appropriate library. Remember to type **ldconfig** after adding libraries.

You should also check the output of *getent* for appropriate UID and GID numbers. The NT domain accounts and groups should use numbers specified in the `idmap uid` and `idmap gid` parameters, respectively, in *smb.conf*. If these numbers overlap those of locally defined accounts, reconfigure *smb.conf* so they don't overlap.

 Sorting the *getent* output by UID can sometimes be helpful. Typing **getent passwd | sort -t: -k3 -n** will do this.

Winbind Logins

Once you've performed these tests, you can try logging in using Winbind. Doing so may require you to restart the login process you're using, though. If you can't seem to log in, try terminating the server you're using and restarting it. (The local *login* process, which handles text-mode logins, normally starts anew whenever you log out. The same is true of processes run from a super server.)

If all goes well, you should be able to log into your system using the NT domain controller just as you would using the local login database; you should see absolutely no difference. To be sure you're using the NT domain controller, use an account that exists on the domain controller but not in the Linux system's local account database.

 Some PAM configuration errors enable you to log into an account with no password or with an incorrect password, so be sure to test not only your ability to log in, but Linux's response to incorrect passwords.

If you set winbind use default domain = No, you'll have to provide the domain name as part of each username, as in *GREENHOUSE\linnaeus* rather than *linnaeus*. This can be awkward, so you should set this parameter to Yes, if possible.

If your server should support multiple login services, such as text-mode console, GDM, and FTP accesses, be sure to test all of them. Of course, you'll also have to adjust each service's */etc/pam.d* file.

 Some servers require unusual configurations, either in their PAM configuration files or in their own configuration files. For instance, OpenSSH requires you to set UsePrivilegeSeparation no in its */etc/ssh/ sshd_config* file. Some servers also provide optional PAM support, which must be enabled either in a configuration file or when building the server. If you find that most servers work with NT domain authentication but some don't, try a web search on *Winbind* or *PAM* and the server name for clues about any server-specific quirks.

If your domain controller is a Samba server, you might find that your NT domain accounts don't belong to an explicitly defined group. The usual symptom is a GID number rather than a group name in *ls* listings:

```
$ ls -l
total 0
-rw-r--r--  1 linnaeus 2009 0 May 23 15:55 myfile.txt
```

Note the GID number (2009) in this output where a group name normally appears. This problem is a result of the fact that Samba doesn't automatically map its local Linux groups to NT domain groups. You may be able to safely ignore this problem, but if groups are important to you, you can overcome it using the *net* utility to set up a mapping of Linux to NT domain groups. First, create NT groups using the GROUP ADD subcommand:

```
$ net GROUP ADD Botanists
```

Now, set up a mapping of existing Linux groups to the NT domain groups:

```
$ net GROUPMAP ADD ntgroup=Botanists unixgroup=botany
```

Of course, the Linux group must exist before you type this command; if it doesn't, you should create it first, using *groupadd* or some other tool. You may be asked for a password after typing these commands. You may also need to add the -U *adminuser* option to perform this action as the specified administrative user. If you want to configure multiple groups, you must set up each individually. In any event, after performing these steps, group mapping should operate in a fairly straightforward way.

Another approach to the problem of missing group mappings is to use NIS, LDAP, or some other tool to share group information between the Samba server and the Winbind client. This approach requires either setting `winbind trusted domains only` = Yes or not setting the `idmap gid` parameter. In either case, the Winbind client then uses the GID information distributed via the alternative protocol, such as NIS or LDAP.

In normal operation, Winbind attempts to authenticate users against the NT domain controller. This attempt can fail, though. This can happen because of a failure of the domain controller, network problems, or local configuration problems or because the account doesn't exist on the domain controller. In such situations, if you've configured Winbind as described in this chapter, Linux falls back on its local account database. You may want to keep this database populated with a few critical accounts—most importantly, the *root* account, so that you can perform system maintenance even if the domain authentication system fails. However, if you maintain redundant accounts (for instance, if *linnaeus* is defined both locally and on the domain controller), which account is used depends on the order of entries in the PAM configuration file and the */etc/nsswitch.conf* file. As a general rule, defining an account in both ways is likely to lead to confusion, so this practice should be avoided.

Summary

Many Windows networks use NT domain controllers or AD domain controllers to provide authentication services to Windows systems. You can tap into this existing resource to provide automatic account creation and password authentication on a Linux system—even one that doesn't function as a Samba server. To do this, you must adjust some *smb.conf* entries, run the Winbind daemon, and configure the PAM and NSS systems to use Winbind for account authentication and information queries. Once this system is configured and running, users shouldn't be able to tell that Winbind is in use; everything should work just as it does with a local account database.

## CHAPTER 8

Using LDAP

The Lightweight Directory Access Protocol is the second of three cross-platform authentication tools described in this book. In reality, though, LDAP is much more than an authentication tool; it's a protocol for accessing *directories*, which in this context are essentially databases designed to be read more often than they're written. As such, LDAP can store many different types of information—Unix or Windows account databases, mappings of hostnames to IP addresses, employee contact information, and so on. This chapter focuses on one narrow use for LDAP, as a network-accessible account authentication system. LDAP makes a viable alternative to NT or Active Directory domains for network authentication of both Windows and Linux servers and desktop systems. It can provide better Linux account database integration, so it's the smarter choice if you use many Linux systems. It can also provide much more than account authentication information, although such configurations are beyond the scope of this book. Using Linux as an LDAP platform gives you all of Linux's usual advantages, such as its reliability and low cost.

When setting up an LDAP authentication system, you should first understand some LDAP basics. Despite the word *lightweight* in the protocol's name, LDAP is a complex system, with its own terminology and peculiarities. In fact, several LDAP implementations exist, so you must pick one and install it on your Linux LDAP server. You must then set up your directories to handle authentication. Only then can you begin configuring your LDAP clients to use your network's account directory. (Note that LDAP clients can be servers for other protocols.) Of course, the details of this configuration vary between Linux and Windows clients, so you must know how to handle both.

You can use a non-Linux LDAP server for authentication. In fact, if you currently use a Windows 200x Active Directory domain controller, it already runs LDAP. You can use this server to authenticate users on Linux systems, but you need to add Unix-style account information to the LDAP directories. Alternatively, you can configure the Linux systems to access the Windows server as an NT domain controller, as described in Chapter 7. This solution requires no changes on the Windows LDAP server and so is likely to be slightly simpler to configure.

The Principles Behind LDAP

At its core, LDAP is a protocol for exchanging data between computers. The LDAP protocol has been independently implemented in several packages, but understanding what problems LDAP is intended to solve will help you understand its features and implementations. As a practical matter, you must also pick an LDAP implementation to run on your LDAP server, as well as LDAP clients for systems that should authenticate against the server.

The Problem: Providing a Network-Accessible Directory

Directories, and LDAP in particular, are tools for storing data. At this level of analysis, directories are similar to databases. In order to understand directories, though, you should understand a couple of key differences between directories and databases:

- Directories are designed to be read more often than they're written; databases are designed for more equal distribution of read and write accesses. This characteristic simplifies many aspects of a directory's design and can lead to faster lookups in directories.

- The internal structure of databases is designed to support easy sorting and cross-referencing, but the entries are otherwise unstructured. Directories, by contrast, use a hierarchical structure but are less easily sorted than database entries.

LDAP provides tools that enable accessing directories across a network, with the goal of centralizing this information. The central directory can host a variety of information. For instance, it might hold individuals' computer account information, telephone numbers, office numbers, birth dates, departmental affiliations, and so on. This information is unlikely to change frequently, and individuals throughout an organization may have need to access it. Thus, a network-accessible directory protocol is the ideal way to store such information.

 LDAP, and directories more generally, can handle more than just account or even personal information. For instance, you might store computer help documentation in a directory. This chapter focuses on LDAP as a tool for storing computer account information. For more information on LDAP, including additional potential uses, consult a book on the subject, such as *LDAP System Administration* (O'Reilly).

One important characteristic of LDAP is that it's a protocol description. The actual data storage can be in any of several different forms, depending on the features of the LDAP server you choose. For instance, an LDAP server might use plain-text files, a proprietary binary format, or a well-documented database file format. The choice of backend data file format doesn't affect the operations that can be performed by clients, but it may influence the server's overall performance level.

LDAP Terminology and Features

LDAP documentation is filled with its own jargon. Some LDAP terms should be familiar to most Linux administrators, but some of it is unique or used oddly:

Directory

This term, as already described, refers to a data-storage system. Note that the term is unrelated to a filesystem directory, although the two types of directories do have certain common features, such as being methods of data storage. A *directory tree* refers to the entire collection of structured entries in the directory.

Attributes

An LDAP *attribute* is similar to a variable in a programming language; it's a named identifier for data stored in the directory. Attributes, though, can sometimes hold multiple values.

Object class

Every entry in a directory is a member of an *object class*, which defines a collection of attributes for data. You set the object class by setting the objectClass attribute to a particular value. For instance, when using LDAP to handle accounts, you'll use the posixAccount class, among others. This class defines attributes called uid, userPassword, and so on, to store account information.

Schema

This is a way to define several object classes at once. LDAP implementations ship with standardized schema files that provide many predefined object classes, including some that are useful for handling user accounts. (The schema is a structure for holding data, not the data itself.)

DC

A *domain component* identifies the scope of an entry or of an entire tree. Typically, you'll set dc= attributes that correspond to your DNS domain or subdomain name.

DN

A *distinguished name* is the name of an attribute along with a description of where the entry belongs in the directory tree. It's described in more detail later in this chapter.

OU

An *organizational unit* is a common subdivision in a directory. It's often used to separate departments from one another within a single organization, enabling (for instance) duplication of usernames in two different departments.

LDIF

The LDAP Data Interchange Format describes information in a way that LDAP can understand. It's covered in more detail later in this chapter.

LDAP directories are often represented in graphical form, such as that shown in Figure 8-1. In practice, these trees are constructed through the data you place in individual entries, which appear at the nodes in the tree. The topmost entry in the tree (dc=pangaea,dc=edu in Figure 8-1), or its root, defines the naming context of the directory. In this example, the naming context includes two DCs, which together are equivalent to the *pangaea.edu* DNS domain.

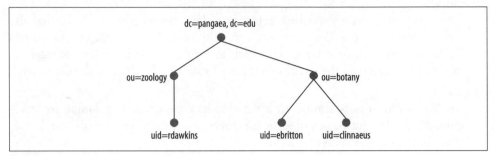

Figure 8-1. LDAP enables you to define a hierarchical tree of entries

LDAP Software

Of course, you need actual software to implement an LDAP server. In Linux, the most popular LDAP package is OpenLDAP, which is headquartered at *http://www.openldap.org*. Other LDAP packages are available, though, and some are popular on non-Linux systems. The most notable of these is probably Microsoft's Active Directory, which incorporates LDAP and Kerberos functionality. Other products include Sun's SunOne and Novell's eDirectory.

Because OpenLDAP is the most common LDAP package for Linux, the rest of this chapter uses it as an example, at least for server operations. In particular, this chapter describes OpenLDAP 2.2. LDAP client configuration should be the same even if you use another LDAP server, though. Many details differ for other LDAP servers, so if you choose to use one, you'll have to consult its documentation to learn how it differs from OpenLDAP.

Configuring an OpenLDAP Server

The first step in using LDAP as a distributed login database is to get the server software running. This process entails obtaining and installing the software, setting it up to handle your domain, setting encryption options, and running the server. The section "Creating a User Directory" will show you how to create a directory that contains all your site's user accounts.

Obtaining and Installing OpenLDAP

OpenLDAP's official home page is *http://www.openldap.org*. You can obtain the OpenLDAP source code from this site, but the OpenLDAP site doesn't host any precompiled binaries. Fortunately, most major Linux distributions provide such binaries, usually under the name *openldap* or *openldap2* (the current OpenLDAP major version number is 2, hence that digit at the end of some OpenLDAP package names). Because most Linux distributions ship with OpenLDAP packages, the assumption in this chapter is that you're installing the server in this way. If you compile the server from source code, you may need to adjust some filesystem directory paths in the coming descriptions because OpenLDAP installs in */usr/local* by default, compared to */usr* for most precompiled Linux OpenLDAP binaries.

Whether you install a binary package or compile OpenLDAP from source code, you may need to install several dependencies. These programs are either required for proper OpenLDAP functioning or are optional tools that OpenLDAP can use to provide improved security or other features:

SSL and TLS

The Secure Sockets Layer and Transport Layer Security are cryptography tools. They're used to encrypt connections between two computers on a network—a useful feature for a network authentication system. In Linux, OpenSSL (*http://www.openssl.org*) is the most common implementation of both protocols.

SASL

The Simple Authentication and Security Layer is a tool for mediating between applications and authentication systems. It's optional if you compile OpenLDAP from source code, but your distribution's binary packages may require it. The main reasons to include it are if you want to enable Kerberos authentication with OpenLDAP or if you want to use other SASL-enabled applications, such as SASL-enabled SMTP or IMAP mail servers. Check *http://asg.web.cmu.edu/sasl/* for more information on SASL.

Kerberos

This tool, described in more detail in Chapter 9, is an encryption and remote login tool. It's possible to integrate Kerberos with LDAP authentication (in fact, that's what Microsoft's AD does), but such integration isn't necessary. However, binary OpenLDAP distributions may require that you install a Kerberos package as a dependency.

Database backends

LDAP is primarily a tool for computer-to-computer communication. To do any good, though, LDAP requires data to be stored on the server, and OpenLDAP relies on a *database backend* to do this job. Several database backends are supported, but the most common is the Berkeley DB package (*http://www.sleepycat.com*). Most Linux distributions provide this software in a package called *db*.

In addition to these packages, binary distributions are likely to have more mundane dependencies, such as a requirement that *glibc* be installed. If you're using a tool such as the Advanced Package Tool's (APT's) *apt-get* (used mainly with Debian but also available for many RPM-based distributions) or Gentoo's *emerge*, dependencies should be installed automatically when you install OpenLDAP. If you use a lower-level tool such as *rpm* or *dpkg*, however, you may see errors about missing dependencies. To correct them, you need to locate and install the dependencies.

The OpenLDAP package contains several programs. Only one is the actual server program; others are support tools of various types, including:

slapd
    This program is the main LDAP server.

slurpd
    This server, which helps synchronize LDAP directories on multiple computers, is an advanced LDAP feature that's beyond the scope of this book.

ldapadd
    This program adds entries to an LDAP directory. Normally, you pass it an LDIF file containing one or more account entries, as described in the later section "Creating the Directory."

ldapmodify
    This program modifies entries in an LDAP directory.

ldapdelete
    This program deletes entries from an LDAP directory.

ldapsearch
    This program searches an LDAP directory for entries that match criteria you specify.

ldapcompare
    This program compares entries in an LDAP directory using criteria you specify.

ldappasswd
    This program changes the password attribute in an LDAP entry. It's similar to the standard Linux *passwd* command.

ldapwhoami
    This program reports your identity as passed to the LDAP server. It can be a useful diagnostic tool when you can't seem to obtain the results you expect.

slapadd
    This local program adds entries to an LDAP directory, using an LDIF original file as input.

slapcat
    This local program displays entries in an LDAP directory, displaying them as LDIF files.

slapindex
    This local program creates an LDIF index file from the current LDAP directory.

slappasswd
> This utility generates a password suitable for inclusion in an LDIF file and subsequent addition to an LDAP directory via *slapadd*.

You needn't be too concerned about the details of how these programs work just yet. The upcoming pages describe how to use some of them to help create and maintain your OpenLDAP server and an account directory for it. For more information, consult these programs' manpages. One point to note, though, is that the utilities whose names begin with *slap* operate on the directory that's housed on the local computer; that is, they must be run from the OpenLDAP server computer. The programs whose names begin with *ldap*, by contrast, are network tools; you can run them on the OpenLDAP server or any of its clients, provided they've been properly configured to refer to the LDAP server.

Basic OpenLDAP Configuration

OpenLDAP's main server configuration file is *slapd.conf*. It usually resides in */etc/openldap*, but it might appear in another location, particularly if you compile from source.

 LDAP client tools, including programs like *ldapmodify* and *ldapsearch*, use the *ldap.conf* file rather than *slapd.conf*. This file is described in more detail in the section "Account Maintenance."

The *slapd.conf* file is a typical Linux text-mode configuration file. Hash marks (#) denote comments; lines beginning with this character are ignored. Parameters are identified by name with one or more values following them; equal signs are not used. One unusual feature of the *slapd.conf* format is that a line that begins with a space is interpreted as a continuation of the preceding line. This convention is used instead of the more common backslash (\) at the end of the first line to denote a line continuation.

The *slapd.conf* file begins with a series of lines that specify the server's overall performance—what schemas it uses, where it stores its PID number, and so on. Following this global configuration are one or more sections, each beginning with the keyword database, that define directories. Each database section continues until the next database section or until the end of the file. These sections include options that specify the backend database type (the database directive itself does this, in fact), where the database is to be stored, the root of the directory tree, and so on.

Consider Example 8-1. This listing is a complete (if simple) *slapd.conf* file that's suitable for handling an LDAP server that functions solely as a remote authentication system.

Example 8-1. A Sample slapd.conf file

```
####
# Global section

# Load schemas for storing user accounts
include /etc/openldap/schema/core.schema
include /etc/openldap/schema/cosine.schema
include /etc/openldap/schema/nis.schema

# Logging options
loglevel 296
pidfile  /var/run/slapd/slapd.pid
argsfile /var/run/slapd/slapd.args

# TLS options
TLSCipherSuite        HIGH
TLSCertificateFile    /etc/openldap/ssl/slapd-cert.crt
TLSCertificateKeyFile /etc/openldap/ssl/slapd-key.pem

# Set high security
security ssf=128

# Miscellaneous security options
password-hash {SSHA}

# Default access level
defaultaccess search

####
# Database section

database bdb

# The root suffix for the directory
suffix "dc=pangaea,dc=edu"

# The root DN for administration
rootdn "cn=Manager,dc=pangaea,dc=edu"

# The password used for administrative access
rootpw {SSHA}vHVUhjRetxArbQCTPOhyXC1aOs9z3Ej1

# Linux directory housing database files
directory /var/lib/ldap/

# Ensure that files may be read ONLY by their owner
mode 0600

## ACLs to control access to the directory

# Allow users to authenticate against and modify their own
# passwords
access to attrs=userPassword
```

Example 8-1. A Sample slapd.conf file (continued)

```
by self write
by * auth

# Allow users to read all non-password data
access to *
  by * read
```

Of course, Example 8-1 is only a starting point; you'll need to customize several of its entries for your system. The meanings of these options are:

Loading schemas

The first few lines of Example 8-1 load three schema files: *core.schema*, *cosine. schema*, and *nis.schema*. The last of these is the critical one, but it depends on the first two. The *nis.schema* schema provides a framework for handling all the data an NIS server normally manages. Because this includes Unix-style account information, it's a common choice for implementing an authentication server. These schema files ship with OpenLDAP, but their location may not be as shown in Example 8-1 on your system; adjust the directory paths as required.

Logging options

The loglevel line sets logging options. These are set using bit flags converted to decimal notation. A value of 296 is reasonable for most production systems. This value logs information on connection statistics, filter processing, and connection management. (Consult the *slapd.conf* manpage for details.) The pidfile and argsfile options specify files in which *slapd* stores its PID and the arguments with which it was run. If your OpenLDAP binary includes a sample configuration file that sets these values in a particular way, you should probably leave them as such; it's possible that your SysV startup scripts or other tools rely on this location.

TLS options

The next three options set TLS features; the assumption in Example 8-1 is that the server will use TLS or SSL encryption, which is a reasonable configuration in most cases. (If you want to use another encryption system, you'll have to consult OpenLDAP's documentation.) As with other Linux directory paths, you may need to adjust the path shown in Example 8-1 for your system. Preparing the TLS certificates is described in the next section.

Security level

The security keyword sets security options. Example 8-1 sets security ssf=128, which sets the server's overall security strength factor (SSF) to 128—a code that stands for a class of encryption algorithms that includes Blowfish, RC4, and others that are fairly strong. If you must use less robust encryption algorithms, you can change 128 to 112 or 56. A value of 0 disables the encryption requirement.

Password hashing

The password-hash option specifies how OpenLDAP hashes passwords it stores. {SSHA} means that OpenLDAP uses the Salted Secure Hash Algorithm (SSHA), which is the preferred means of storing passwords on an LDAP server. Other possible values include {CRYPT} (the method used by the system crypt( ) call), {MD5} (the Message Digest 5 system, which is often used in */etc/passwd* or */etc/ shadow* files), {SHA} (a less-secure variant of SSHA), and {CLEARTEXT} (no encryption). Of these, {CLEARTEXT} is the least secure and should be avoided. Note that individual users' passwords may be stored using any method; the password-hash option only sets the default.

The database definition

The database bdb line begins the one and only database definition in Example 8-1. This line tells OpenLDAP to use the Berkeley DB (hence, bdb) system for its backend. Other possible backend codes are ldbm (an older variant of bdb that can be handled by the BerkeleyDB software or the GNU Database Manager), passwd (a quick-and-dirty interface to your existing */etc/passwd* file), and shell (an interface to other database tools).

The root suffix

The suffix line specifies the DN for the directory. In most cases, this root suffix is built from your network's domain name. In the case of Example 8-1, OpenLDAP is configured to manage passwords for the *pangaea.edu* domain.

The administrative DN

You can specify a root DN for administration with the rootdn parameter. This DN is built from the root suffix's DN by adding a cn value, typically Manager (as in Example 8-1) or admin. This line and the following rootpw entry are useful mainly for initial OpenLDAP configuration; once the system is working, you may want to remove them to improve the server's security.

The administrative password

The rootpw line sets an administrative password that's associated with the rootdn item. You can generate a password with the *slappasswd* command; type it and enter a password twice, then paste it into the file in place of the password shown in Example 8-1. The password you generate should begin with {SSHA} (or possibly some other value in curly braces); replace everything from {SSHA} on with the output of *slappasswd* from your system.

The Linux database directory

The directory line refers to a Linux filesystem directory, not an LDAP directory; it's the location of the database files maintained by the database system specified by the preceding database line. This directory must be specified as an absolute path. You may need to adjust this option for your system.

The database mode

The mode line specifies a Linux file mode for the database files. Normally, 0600 is appropriate: it prevents unauthorized snooping or modifications.

ACLs

Access Control Lists specify who may access particular types of data in the directory and in what way. They're conceptually similar to filesystem ACLs, but the details differ. The last few lines of Example 8-1 define two ACLs, each of which begins with the keyword access. The first of these sets accesses conditions to the userPassword attribute: users may modify their own passwords (by self write), and all users may access this attribute for authentication (by * auth). The second ACL gives all users read access to all other attributes. ACLs are applied in order, with the earlier ACLs taking precedence over the later ones. In the case of Example 8-1, the more restrictive ACL for the userPassword attribute must precede the read-only ACL for other attributes, lest users be granted the ability to read each other's passwords.

Once you've tweaked Example 8-1 for your system, OpenLDAP is basically configured. You must still prepare the TLS certificates, though. Once that's done, you can start the slapd server.

Preparing Keys and Certificates

Although it's possible to run an LDAP server without using encryption, doing so is inadvisable, at least when the LDAP server is functioning as a network authentication tool. Encryption keeps your passwords secure; without it, passwords will be sent over the network in cleartext, which makes them susceptible to sniffing.

> Use of SASL generally includes its own encryption mechanism, so if you use SASL, preparing encryption as described here isn't necessary. This chapter doesn't cover LDAP's SASL capabilities, though.

In Example 8-1, the three lines under the TLS options comment set options related to SSL and TLS encryption, enabling OpenLDAP to engage in encrypted communications. In order for this configuration to work, though, you must first configure the TLS and SSL encryption tool, which is provided by the OpenSSL package (*http://www.openssl.org*). This package should be a dependency of any binary OpenLDAP package that can use SSL or TLS encryption, and it's also required to compile OpenLDAP with support for these methods of encryption. (If you compile OpenLDAP yourself, you may need to install a separate OpenSSL development package.)

As described in the earlier section, "Obtaining and Installing OpenLDAP," LDAP supports encryption methods other than SSL and TLS. In order to keep this chapter manageable, though, and because SSL and TLS are popular and well-respected encryption tools for LDAP, they're the only ones described here.

SSL and TLS support a set of encryption tools, some of which require one-time manual preparation before they can be used. Most notable among these are *keys* and *certificates*. A key is a numeric code that can encrypt or decrypt data. Once data is encrypted with a key, it can only be decrypted with a matching key. Keys can be generated fairly automatically, but certificates require at least minimal input from users. They're designed to authenticate a site's identity and are essentially files with information on the owner of a server, signed and encrypted with a key that the other system trusts. One type of certificate is created by Certificate Authorities (CAs), which are organizations founded to create certificates for the sake of e-commerce and the like. web sites that use encrypted transmissions usually employ certificates created for them by CAs; web browsers can then decrypt the certificates sent by web sites and verify that they were signed by a trusted CA. If a certificate's signature doesn't check out, the web browser notifies the user that the site might not be trustworthy.

For in-house use, though, you don't need to go to a CA; you can create a certificate yourself. The OpenSSL package includes the tools necessary to do so. The simplest and most direct way is to call *openssl* with a series of options that cause it to generate a certificate and a key:

```
# openssl req -x509 -days 365 -newkey rsa: -nodes \
  -keyout slapd-key.pem -out slapd-cert.crt
Generating a 1024 bit RSA private key
.........................++++++
.....++++++
writing new private key to 'server.key'
-----
You are about to be asked to enter information that will be incorporated
into your certificate request.
What you are about to enter is what is called a Distinguished Name or a DN.
There are quite a few fields but you can leave some blank
For some fields there will be a default value,
If you enter '.', the field will be left blank.
-----
Country Name (2 letter code) [AU]:US
State or Province Name (full name) [Some-State]:RI
Locality Name (eg, city) [ ]:Woonsocket
Organization Name (eg, company) [Internet Widgits Pty Ltd]:Very Old University
Organizational Unit Name (eg, section) [ ]:CS Dept
Common Name (eg, YOUR name) [ ]:ldap.pangaea.edu
Email Address [ ]:johndoe@pangaea.edu
```

Of course, you should customize the information in the certificate to describe your organization. Pay particular attention to the data you enter at the Common Name (eg,

YOUR name) prompt; some clients, including the Windows LDAP authentication client, require this to match the hostname or IP address of the LDAP server. The result of running this command is two files: *slapd-key.pem* and *slapd-cert.crt*. These files contain a private key and a public certificate, respectively. Be sure that the private key can be read only by its owner; 600 (rw-------) permissions are appropriate, so type **chmod 600 slapd-key.pem** to set this file mode. (Some other OpenLDAP files, such as *slapd.conf*, should be readable to all users, though.) Ordinarily, *slapd* runs as a specific user (such as *ldap*, although this username varies from one distribution to another), so you should give ownership of the file to that user. If you run into problems launching the server you should check to see what user is running the server and adjust ownership of this file accordingly. You should now move the *sldapd-key.pem* and *slapd-cert.crt* files to the location specified by the TLSCertificateKeyFile and TLSCertificateFile parameters in *slapd.conf*—*/etc/openldap/ssl* in Example 8-1.

Running the Server

At this point, it's time to run the server. You can run *slapd* on a one-time basis by typing the server's filename (you may need to include the full path) or by using a SysV startup script. For instance, on a SuSE system, the SysV startup script is */etc/init.d/ldap*, so the following command does the trick:

```
# /etc/init.d/ldap start
```

As you test the server, you're likely to start and stop it frequently. Once it's running the way you want it to run, you'll probably want to configure your system to launch *slapd* at startup. You can do this as you would any other server that runs constantly. (Typically, *slapd* is run from a SysV or local startup script, not from a super server.) Typing **chkconfig ldap on** will do this on many systems, but some distributions use other commands instead of or in addition to *chkconfig*. Consult distribution-specific documentation if you need help with this task.

One problem you may encounter is getting the server to bind to appropriate ports, particularly if you intend to use SSL encryption. By default, *slapd* binds to port 389, which is used for cleartext connections and those that negotiate TLS encryption after making an initial connection. Some clients, though, including the pGina tool that's described in the section "Configuring Windows to Use LDAP for Login Authentication," must use a dedicated SSL LDAP (that is, LDAPS) encryption port, 636. To force *slapd* to bind to this port, you must pass an appropriate parameter to the server with the -h option. Passing -h ldap:/// causes *slapd* to bind to port 389 only, whereas passing -h ldap:/// ldaps:/// causes it to bind to both ports 389 and 636. You may need to modify your *slapd* SysV startup script to add this option. Some SysV startup scripts, such as the one for SuSE Linux, include a variable in which you can pass these options; in the SuSE script, you edit the SLAPD_URLS variable to include ldaps:///.

Creating a User Directory

Once the server is running, you must populate the directory with information about your network's users. To do this, you must understand distinguished name notation. Understanding at least the basics of LDIF files, which can be used to enter information into the directory, is also a necessity. With these pieces of information, you can actually begin populating the directory with user accounts.

Distinguished Names

Distinguished Names (DNs) are the pointers to data in a directory. They're similar in many ways to filenames in hard-disk filesystems. For example, the Linux filename */etc/X11/xdm/Xaccess* refers to the *Xaccess* file in the */etc/X11/xdm* directory, which in turn can be broken down into a series of subdirectories leading to the root directory of the Linux directory tree. Similarly, DNs are typically composed of multiple elements that enable an LDAP implementation to quickly locate the data. In the case of DNs, though, these elements are labeled according to type. Common types in an LDAP directory used for authentication include Domain Class (DC), Common Name (CN), User ID (UID, which is equivalent to a username rather than a numeric UID), and sometimes Organizational Unit (OU). Each abbreviation is converted to lowercase and separated from its value by an equal sign; these are then strung together with commas and identified as a DN by using the dn code and a colon:

    dn: cn=Carl Linnaeus,dc=pangaea,dc=edu

This example refers to an entry for the common name Carl Linnaeus in the *pangaea.edu* domain. You may have noticed that this notation is similar to the one for the rootdn item in the *slapd.conf* file, as illustrated in Example 8-1. This is no accident; the rootdn entry identifies a DN for a user with special privileges on the server.

Although the DC components of DN frequently combine to form an Internet domain name that's associated with the LDAP server, this isn't a requirement.

Occasionally, variants on this notation are necessary. One of these occurs when the CN for a user is not unique. For instance, suppose your organization has two users named Carl Linnaeus, one in the Botany department and one in the Genetics department. You might then create two DNs that add the appropriate OUs:

    dn: cn=Carl Linnaeus+ou=Botany,dc=pangaea,dc=edu
    dn: cn=Carl Linnaeus+ou=Genetics,dc=pangaea,dc=edu

In practice, you'll create these DNs in files with intervening lines that specify other account characteristics, as described in the section "Understanding LDIF."

In this example, the DN begins with a Relative Distinguished Name (RDN)—cn=Carl Linnaeus+ou=Botany or cn=Carl Linnaeus+ou=Genetics. An RDN uses a plus sign (+) to separate two attributes, neither of which is unique by itself. In this example, two users named Carl Linnaeus exist, and presumably both the Botany and Genetics OUs host other users.

 The use of the plus sign to separate RDN components means that this symbol can't be used within an element without taking special steps. Specifically, if an element must contain a plus sign, the plus sign should be preceded by a backslash (\). Other special characters that should be preceded by a backslash include a hash mark (#) at the start of a string, a space at the end of a string, a comma (,), a double quote ("), a backslash, a semicolon (;), and angle brackets (< or >). Chances are you won't need to use any of these symbols in the DN elements for a Unix-based account database, although spaces are common in databases that originate on Windows systems.

DNs are usually case-insensitive, but case is preserved in storing them. Thus, cn=carl linnaeus,dc=pangaea,dc=edu is equivalent to cn=Carl Linnaeus,dc=pangaea,dc=EDU. This characteristic is based on matching rules defined in the schema, though, so it's not always true.

Understanding LDIF

Behind the scenes, OpenLDAP may use any of several databases for data storage; but to examine and modify data, a common plain-text format is desirable. This is where LDIF comes into the picture; it represents LDAP directory entries that are invariant across OpenLDAP backends, and even across LDAP implementations. For the most part, it consists of a series of attribute names and values, separated by colons. Entries begin with the DN entry, as described earlier. Subsequent entries' content depend on the schemas a directory uses. The NIS schema defines several object classes, each of which defines several attributes. For the purposes of this chapter, the posixAccount object class is one of the most important of these object classes. This object class's attributes roughly correspond to entries in the traditional Linux /etc/passwd file, as shown in Figure 8-2.

Every field in the /etc/passwd file maps to an attribute in the posixAccount object class, although the names aren't always intuitive. In particular, the uid attribute maps to the Linux username; the uidNumber attribute holds the Linux UID number. The posixAccount object class also defines two attributes, cn and description, that aren't present in /etc/passwd. Of these, cn is required and typically holds the user's real name.

Figure 8-3 shows a mapping of the shadowAccount object class to entries traditionally found in /etc/shadow. All these entries except uid are optional. This attribute,

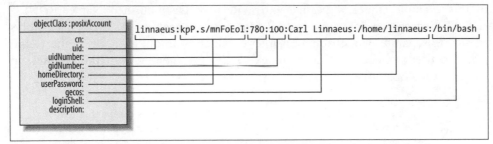

Figure 8-2. The posixAccount object class defines data traditionally found in /etc/passwd

though, as well as the `userPassword` and `description` attributes, are in fact shared with the `posixAccount` object class. Specifying values for all the required attributes in these two object classes creates a user account.

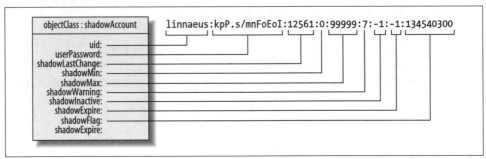

Figure 8-3. The shadowAccount object class defines data traditionally found in /etc/shadow

In traditional Linux accounts, using shadow passwords and the */etc/ shadow* file increases security. The equivalent use of the `shadowAccount` object class in LDAP does *not* have this effect, though. When properly configured, an LDAP account directory should be at least as secure as a Linux shadow passwords system, whether or not you place data in the `shadowAccount` structures. What `shadowAccount` does provide is a place to store password aging and expiration information.

Between these two object classes, you can define an account. To do so in an LDIF file, you create one line per attribute, plus a few `objectClass` attributes pointing to the objects upon which the `posixAccount` and `shadowAccount` objects rely. The result looks something like this:

```
dn: uid=linnaeus,ou=People,dc=pangaea,dc=edu
uid: linnaeus
cn: Carl Linnaeus
objectClass: account
objectClass: posixAccount
objectClass: top
objectClass: shadowAccount
```

```
userPassword: {crypt}KpP.s/mnFoEoI
shadowLastChange: 12561
shadowMax: 99999
shadowWarning: 7
loginShell: /bin/bash
uidNumber: 780
gidNumber: 100
homeDirectory: /home/linnaeus
gecos: Carl Linnaeus
```

 Don't start generating accounts by copying this entry. As described in the section "Creating the Directory," there are easier ways to populate your directory than creating LDIF files by hand.

Figure 8-4 shows a mapping of the posixGroup object class to entries traditionally found in */etc/group*. These entries are necessary if the server is to deliver group information as well as account information to clients. Note that these objects are not directly related to accounts, although they do refer to accounts; the memberUid attribute points to user accounts. (Likewise, the gidNumber field in the posixAccount object class points to a posixGroup via its gidNumber field.)

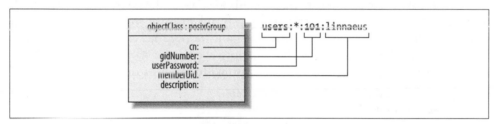

Figure 8-4. The posixGroup object class defines data traditionally found in /etc/group

The NIS schema file defines several object classes in addition to those described here. These object classes enable an LDAP server to deliver information that's traditionally contained in */etc/fstab*, */etc/hosts*, */etc/protocols*, and more—in short, the data that's normally delivered by an NIS server. Configuring OpenLDAP to deliver this information is similar to configuring it to deliver account and group information, but such configurations are beyond the scope of this chapter.

Creating the Directory

The simplest way to populate an OpenLDAP directory with account and group information is to convert this information from existing account and group files. You can perform this task with scripts available on the Internet. If you're not migrating accounts directly, you may want to use these tools on a dummy password file to create a template you can use to create new accounts in piecemeal fashion.

The scripts you use to migrate an existing set of Linux accounts can be obtained from *http://www.padl.com/OSS/MigrationTools.html*. The download links at the bottom of this page retrieve a file called *MigrationTools.tgz*. This tarball contains a series of Perl scripts, each of which reads the contents of one or more system configuration files and creates an equivalent LDIF file.

> The migration tools package described here has a project version number of 45, as revealed in the *CVSVersionInfo.txt* file. If you obtain a more recent version, you may find that some of the details have changed.

Before running the conversion scripts, you must edit one of them (*migrate_common. ph*) so that it holds appropriate site-specific information. Specifically, change the $DEFAULT_MAIL_DOMAIN and $DEFAULT_BASE variables, defined on lines 71 and 74, to point to your DNS domain and your directory's base. For instance, to conform to the options shown in Example 8-1, set these options as follows:

```
$DEFAULT_MAIL_DOMAIN = "pangaea.edu";
$DEFAULT_BASE = "dc=pangaea,dc=edu";
```

Once this task is done, you can create LDIF files using the appropriate scripts. Of particular interest are the *migrate_passwd.pl* and *migrate_group.pl* scripts, which migrate your account database (including both */etc/passwd* and */etc/shadow*) and your */etc/group* file, respectively. Both scripts accept the name of the source file (just */etc/passwd* in the case of *migrate_passwd.pl*) followed by an output file:

```
# ./migrate_passwd.pl /etc/passwd passwd.ldif
# ./migrate_group.pl /etc/group group.ldif
```

You can examine the contents of these LDIF files, if you like. At a minimum, you might want to perform a quick check to verify that all your users have entries in the password file. You might also want to eliminate system accounts that don't require authentication and those that you don't want to be authenticated via the LDAP server. If you eliminate such accounts, though, be sure that they either exist in your clients' local account databases or aren't required by your clients.

> The migration scripts can't decrypt the already encrypted passwords in the password database. Therefore, they're entered into the LDIF file using the {crypt} encoding notation.

These scripts don't create entries for the top-level DNs. If you haven't created them already, you should add them to the start of each file. For the password file, the entries for the example domain are these:

```
dn: dc=pangaea,dc=edu
objectClass: domain
dc: pangaea
```

```
dn: ou=People,dc=pangaea,dc=edu
objectClass: organizationalUnit
ou: People
```

The entry to add to the start of the groups file is similar:

```
dn: ou=Group,dc=pangaea,dc=edu
objectClass: organizationalUnit
ou: Group
```

Of course, in both cases, you must make changes to the dn and dc lines suitable for your organization. Once you've done this, you're ready to add the LDIF files to your LDAP directory. You can do this with either the *ldapadd* command or the *slapadd* command, using the -f or -l parameters (respectively) to pass the name of the LDIF file you want to add. You might also want to use -v, which provides feedback on the success of the operations. (If you use *ldapadd*, though, you'll first need to perform additional client configurations, as described in the next section.) For instance, these commands add both the files created earlier:

```
# slapadd -v -l passwd.ldif
# slapadd -v -l group.ldif
```

Account Maintenance

Account maintenance on an OpenLDAP server uses various utilities whose names begin with *ldap*, as described earlier. Of particular interest are *ldapadd*, which adds accounts; *ldapmodify*, which modifies existing accounts; and *ldapdelete*, which deletes accounts. You can run these commands on any LDAP client computer (including the LDAP server itself, if it's properly configured as a client); they use the network protocol to communicate with the server.

These tools rely on the */etc/openldap/ldap.conf* configuration file. Before you can use these tools, therefore, you should edit this file. Normally, you must set the BASE and URI options, and possibly point the system to a certificate file:

```
BASE        dc=pangaea,dc=edu
URI         ldaps://ldap.pangaea.edu
TLS_CACERT  /etc/openldap/ssl/certs/slapd-cert.crt
```

The first of these entries should be familiar by now; it's the root of the LDAP directory you'll be using. The URI entry points to the LDAP server, using a URI format similar to that used to express web addresses, except that it begins with the ldaps:// keyword. You can use ldap:// rather than ldaps:// if you don't want to require the use of SSL encryption. (The system may still negotiate TLS encryption during the session, however.) If you specify an LDAPS port in the URI, you must point the server to a file that contains certificates (via TLS_CACERT) or to a directory that contains certificate files (via TLS_CACERTDIR). You must copy the certificate you generated on the server to this location. If you don't, the client tools will refuse to communicate with the server.

In order to perform most account maintenance tasks, you must access the server with sufficient privileges; by default, the LDAP utilities perform anonymous accesses. You can specify a suitable high-privilege DN with the -D option. When you do, you must also include the -W option to have the utility prompt you for a password. You can use the administrative DN and password you specified in your *slapd.conf*.

To add an account, you should prepare an LDIF file. You can use an entry from an LDIF file created from */etc/passwd* using *migrate_passwd.pl* as a model, if you like. You can then pass this file to *ldapadd*:

```
$ ldapadd -D cn=manager,dc=pangaea,dc=edu -W -f acct.ldif
```

 Because you're passing the authentication information to the server, you don't need type this command as *root*.

The *ldapmodify* command works in much the same way, except that the file you pass to the utility contains modifications to an existing entry rather than new account information. To delete an account, you use the *ldapdelete* command, omit the -f parameter, and instead pass the DN of the account you want to delete:

```
$ ldapdelete -D cn=manager,dc=pangaea,dc=edu -W
uid=linnaeus,ou=People,dc=pangaea,dc=edu
```

This example deletes the *linnaeus* account in the *People* unit on the LDAP server. Changing a password is similar, but you must also pass the -S option to be prompted for the new password, as well as changing the name of the tool:

```
$ ldappasswd -D cn=manager,dc=pangaea,dc=edu -S -W
uid=linnaeus,ou=People,dc=pangaea,dc=edu
New password:
Re-enter new password:
Enter LDAP Password:
Result: Success (0)
```

Unlike the standard Linux *passwd* command, *ldappasswd* prompts for the new password *before* prompting for the administrative LDAP password. As with most password-handling tools, this one doesn't echo the passwords to the screen.

 The *ldappasswd* command isn't intended as a full replacement for *passwd*. If you configure the */etc/pam.d/passwd* file to use LDAP, as described in the section "Configuring the LDAP PAM Modules" and Appendix A, the standard Linux *passwd* command will change users' passwords on the LDAP server instead of or in addition to changing the local password when an ordinary user calls this tool. The *ldappasswd* command is useful mainly when a user has forgotten a password; you can use your LDAP administrative access to replace the forgotten password.

If you're used to normal Linux account maintenance tools such as *useradd* and *userdel*, these LDAP account maintenance tools may seem awkward at first. If you keep a template LDIF file handy and prepare scripts with the necessary options, DNs can save you a lot of typing and make using these tools far more intuitive.

Various additional tools exist that help manage LDAP accounts. For instance, phpLDAPadmin (*http://phpldapadmin.sourceforge.net/*) is a web-based tool that provides a point-and-click interface to your account database. You could also write some scripts yourself to help simplify these tasks.

Configuring Linux to Use LDAP for Login Authentication

At this point, your LDAP server should be running and should contain account information for your site. In order to do any good, though, you must be able to use that LDAP server for user authentication. In the case of Linux systems, this entails configuring the Pluggable Authentication Modules system and the Name Service Switch system to interface with LDAP. This requires understanding the basic relationships between these systems, installing necessary modules, and configuring the modules.

 To use Windows as an LDAP login client, consult the section "Configuring Windows to Use LDAP for Login Authentication."

LDAP, PAM, and NSS

The PAM and NSS systems are at the core of Linux's account management. These systems are described in Chapter 7 and in Appendix A. In brief, PAM is a set of libraries that sits between applications and the account database for authentication purposes. Instead of accessing account databases directly, PAM-enabled applications consult PAM. This arrangement enables you to modify your authentication system (such as adding LDAP) with relative ease, by reconfiguring PAM rather than rewriting all the programs that require authentication. Similarly, NSS manages access to nonauthentication account information, such as home directory locations.

In order to configure a Linux system to use LDAP, you must tie LDAP into these two systems. This is done by installing PAM and NSS support modules and by modifying PAM and NSS configuration files to call the LDAP modules.

Basic LDAP Client Configuration

Most Linux distributions make PAM and NSS modules for LDAP available in one or two packages that are separate from the main LDAP package. Packages that are called *pam_ldap* and *nss_ldap* are common, but some variants exist, such as Debian's *libpam-ldap* and *libnss-ldap*.

The PAM and NSS modules both rely on a configuration file called *ldap.conf*, which is normally stored in */etc*. (Instead of a single *ldap.conf* file, though, Debian uses two: *libnss-ldap.conf* and *pam_ldap.conf*, both in */etc*. You must make similar changes to both files.) Before configuring PAM- and NSS-specific options, you should load this configuration file into an editor to customize it for your network.

 The OpenLDAP package also includes a configuration file called *ldap.conf*, but this file is likely to reside in the same directory as *slapd.conf*—usually */etc/openldap*.

The */etc/ldap.conf* file might be installed as part of any number of different packages. Most frequently, it's installed with the NSS LDAP package, but Debian places its two configuration files in the *libnss-ldap* and *libpam-ldap* packages, and SuSE distributes the file in the *pwdutils* package.

For the basic configuration described earlier in the chapter, you must modify two items, host and base, in the */etc/ldap.conf* (or equivalent) file:

```
host 192.168.1.1
base dc=pangaea,dc=edu
```

The host item points the LDAP clients to the LDAP server by IP address or hostname. (The system must be able to locate the server without the use of LDAP, so if you're using LDAP for local hostname resolution, it's particularly important that you use an IP address.) The base item specifies the base of the directory tree that's served by your LDAP server.

If you've configured your system for high security, you must also set security options. Most importantly, you must uncomment one of two ssl lines:

```
ssl start_tls
ssl on
```

The first of these lines tells the client to negotiate TLS encryption after making a connection to the traditional LDAP port (389); the second tells the client to use SSL and connect to the LDAPS port (636). Several other security options also reside in this file; for instance, you can point the tools to a certificate file or directory with the tls_cacertfile or tls_cacertdir options. One of these options is required if you set tls_checkpeer yes, which makes the server refuse connections to a server if it has an unknown certificate.

Configuring the LDAP NSS Modules

NSS provides basic account information to the Linux system. It's controlled via its configuration file, */etc/nsswitch.conf*. To tell NSS to use LDAP as part of its operation, you must change just three lines in this file. Specifically, you should look for the lines beginning with the keywords passwd, shadow, and group. Each line contains a list of tools NSS uses to look up account information, and you should add ldap to each of these lines:

```
passwd:  files ldap
shadow:  files ldap
group:   files ldap
```

 As with PAM configuration files, the */etc/nsswitch.conf* file varies from one distribution to another. If yours contains entries instead of or in addition to the files entry, the safest course is to add ldap to the end of whatever entries already exist. (The compat source is common with distributions based on *glibc* 2.3, for instance.) If you want LDAP to replace an existing authentication tool, though, you can remove the reference to that old tool.

If you want to use LDAP to take over additional duties, you can add ldap to additional appropriate lines in */etc/nsswitch.conf*. If you add ldap to the hosts line, for instance, the system attempts to use LDAP for hostname resolution. Of course, such configurations require adding appropriate directory entries to the LDAP server, much as you added user accounts to the server.

Configuring the LDAP PAM Modules

Once you've configured */etc/ldap.conf* or its equivalent and modified */etc/nsswitch.conf*, you can begin telling PAM to use LDAP for authentication of various services. This process is described in Appendix A, so look there for details of PAM configuration. This section describes some LDAP-specific features. In most cases, you'll modify files in */etc/pam.d*; each file is named after the login or account maintenance service you want to adjust.

To add LDAP to the login authentication, you must add a couple of lines to the PAM configuration file for the service you want to use LDAP:

```
auth     sufficient  /lib/security/pam_ldap.so try_first_pass
account  sufficient  /lib/security/pam_ldap.so
```

 Modifying your PAM configuration modifies how Linux authenticates you. A mistake can result in an inability to log into the computer. For this reason, I recommend modifying these files one at a time, leaving at least one known-working login tool unmodified. This way, if you create a nonfunctional service, you'll still be able to log in using another tool to correct the problem. Backing up the original files can also help you recover from such an error.

Typically, you'll modify all your active login services' PAM modules in analogous ways. These are likely to include *login*, *gdm*, *xdm*, *sshd*, *ftp*, and perhaps some others.

If your system uses the pam_stack system, though, you may be able to get away with modifying just one file: *system-auth*. However, you might want to keep some authentication tools local. For instance, you might want to use the local database only for *sudo*, which is often used to obtain *root* privileges; if your LDAP directory doesn't include information on the *root* account, it obviously won't be useful for *sudo*'s typical uses.

Verifying Proper Functioning

At this point, the Linux system should be using the LDAP server for user authentication. One way to check this is to type **getent passwd**. This command returns user account information. (A similar command, **getent group**, returns group information.) On a system that uses only its local account files, the result is similar to typing **cat /etc/passwd**; however, on a system that uses an LDAP server, you should see additional entries for LDAP-accessible accounts. A partial output might look like this:

```
# getent passwd
root:x:0:0:root:/root:/bin/bash
bin:x:1:1:bin:/bin:/bin/false
linnaeus:x:500:100:C. Linnaeus:/home/linnaeus:/bin/bash
linnaeus:x:500:100:Carl Linnaeus:/home/linnaeus:/bin/bash
```

This output reveals an oddity: the user *linnaeus* has two entries. One entry is in the computer's local */etc/passwd* file; the other originates on the LDAP server. (If the two lines are different, you can tell which is which by comparing the lines to the contents of the local */etc/passwd* file.) In this case, no harm comes of this because information from the two sources is identical, aside from the minor detail of the user's full name. If the entries had different data, though, such as different UIDs or home directories, confusion can result. Thus, it's best not to duplicate accounts between the LDAP server and the local system. If duplicates do occur, the first one takes precedence. NSS orders accounts according to the order specified on the passwd, shadow, and group lines in */etc/nsswitch.conf*, so placing ldap after files in this file gives local files precedence over LDAP entries.

If you've been able to verify your LDAP-generated accounts with *getent*, you can proceed to testing the login tools. Use whatever login tool you've modified to use LDAP and try to log in. Try entering accounts that are defined only via LDAP and only via the local account files, to be sure both work. Try entering both correct and incorrect passwords to be sure that the system is correctly handling the case of login failures. If a password is correct for one system (such as LDAP or your local files) but incorrect for the other, the behavior will vary depending on your precise configuration, as described in Appendix A.

Configuring Windows to Use LDAP for Login Authentication

All this talk of using LDAP for Linux authentication is well and good, but this book is about integrating Linux and Windows on a network. How, then, does LDAP help you with Windows clients? The answer is that Windows—or at least, Windows NT/200x/XP—uses an authentication system known as Graphical Identification and Authentication (GINA). Supplements to the Microsoft-supplied GINA are available, and you can use one of these to have Windows authenticate against your LDAP server.

One of the most flexible GINA supplements is known as pGina (*http://pgina. xpasystems.com*), which is a modular open source GINA tool. You can find pGina modules that support LDAP, MySQL, NIS, SecurID, and many more authentication systems. The following pages are devoted to pGina's LDAP functionality. Unfortunately, pGina is limited to working with Windows 200x/XP; it doesn't work with Windows 9x/Me. (In theory, pGina should work with Windows NT, but its LDAP module requires features that were added with Windows 2000.) Using pGina requires installing it and configuring it to use your LDAP server.

Obtaining and Installing pGina

You can obtain pGina from its web site. You'll need to download both the main pGina package (available from *http://pgina.xpasystems.com/files/*) and the LDAP plugin module (available from *http://pgina.xpasystems.com/plugins/*). Both packages come in the form of installer applications. This chapter uses pGina 1.7.6 and the LDAPAuth 1.4-beta plugin as references; some details may differ if you use another version of the package.

 To work with Windows XP SP2, pGina Version 1.7.7.4 or later is required for best functionality.

Once you've downloaded the two installer programs, you should run them both as the Windows *Administrator*. These are typical Windows program installers; they ask you to accept a license agreement (the GPL), where to install the program, and so on, then drop the files in the appropriate locations. The main pGina installer then runs the pGina configuration utility, but if you install it first, you'll have to run the LDAP plugin installer before you can configure pGina to use LDAP.

As with configuring PAM in Linux, installing and configuring pGina incorrectly can produce a system you can't access. You should prepare an emergency recovery disk and be prepared to use it with the Windows Safe Mode should problems occur. Completely backing up the Windows boot partition may be wise, as well. If you're preparing to install pGina on an entire network, try installing it first on a test system that holds no important data.

Registering Your Certificate

If you're using strong encryption, as is wise on most networks, you must register your SSL certificate with Windows. This step is necessary because Windows is fussier about certificates than are the Linux PAM and NSS LDAP modules; if Windows can't verify your certificate, you won't be able to establish an encrypted SSL connection with the LDAP server.

To do the deed, you should begin by making the LDAP certificate file (*slapd-cert.crt*), which you created earlier. You can place it on a file share, move it around on a floppy, or whatever's convenient. (This file is not sensitive from a security point of view, so you needn't take any precautions to prevent it from being seen by others.) Once the file is available in Windows, follow these steps:

1. Double-click the certificate file. This action should bring up the Certificate dialog box shown in Figure 8-5. If it doesn't, check the filename; it should end in a *.crt* extension. If it doesn't, correct the matter, and try again.

2. Click Install Certificate. This action yields a certificate installation wizard.

3. Click Next in the wizard. The result resembles Figure 8-6, except that this figure shows some data entered as described in the next few steps.

4. Click Place all certificates in the following store.

5. Click Browse. The wizard displays a dialog box called Select Certificate Store.

6. In the Select Certificate Store dialog box, check the Show Physical Stores checkbox.

7. In the Select Certificate Store dialog box, expand the Trusted Root Certification Authorities item.

8. An object called Local Computer should now be visible. Highlight it and click OK in the Select Certificate Store dialog box. Your wizard should now show the same path in the Certificate Store field as is shown in Figure 8-6.

9. Click Next. The wizard presents a summary screen.

10. Click Finish. A message stating that the import was successful should appear.

At this point, your certificate should be installed, which should enable you to use SSL encryption with your LDAP server, provided the server is properly configured to accept this encryption.

Figure 8-5. Windows provides a tool for registering certificates you generate

Figure 8-6. The certificate installation wizard lets you select how to categorize your certificate

Configuring pGina for LDAP Client Use

Before proceeding to actual pGina configuration, I recommend you test the LDAP module. To do so, select Start › Programs → pGina → PluginTester from the

Windows desktop. The result is a large pGina Plugin Simulation dialog box. Click the Browse button to locate the LDAP plugin, which by default is installed in a subdirectory of your main pGina installation directory. You can then click the Configure button, which brings up the pGina LDAPAuth configuration dialog box, shown in Figure 8-7.

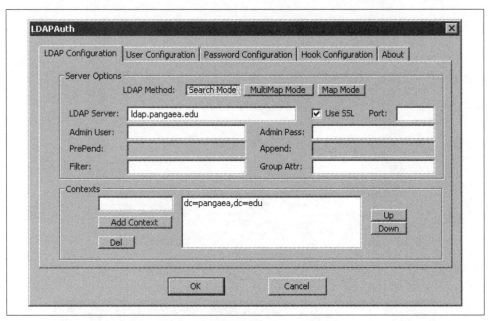

Figure 8-7. To configure pGina's LDAP module, use a dialog box to enter many of the options you enter in Linux LDAP client configuration files

You must give pGina's LDAPAuth dialog box some basic information on your LDAP server. The most important information items are the LDAP Server, Use SSL, and Contexts items. The other items can be important in some situations, but are beyond the scope of this chapter to describe; consult the pGina documentation for details. Enter your server's IP address or hostname in the LDAP Server field. If you're using SSL encryption, you *must* use the name you specified in the Common Name (eg, YOUR name) item when you created your certificate, as described in the section "Preparing Keys and Certificates." You must also check the Use SSL checkbox to enable SSL encryption. For the Contexts, you must enter a context in the field just above the Add Context button, then click that button. Your entry will then be moved to the larger field to the right of the button. Typically, the context you enter will be your root DN, as shown in Figure 8-7.

After entering this information, click OK. The system says it's saved the settings. You can then type a username and password into the large pGina Plugin Simulation dialog box, and click Login. (Note that your password will echo when you type it, and it will also appear in the dialog box once it's been authenticated.) If all goes well, the program reports "plugin reported success", along with information on the account in the main dialog box. If the tool instead reports a failure, you should click Configure to go back to the configuration dialog box and make changes. Because of pGina's insistence on verifying the server's certificate, this can be a problem area. You may want to temporarily disable SSL encryption (on both the client and the server) to simplify matters while you troubleshoot. Once you can authenticate users, click Exit.

To fully configure pGina, select Start → Programs → pGina → Configuration Tool. (The installer launches this program automatically by default, so it may already be running.) The result is the main pGina configuration dialog box, shown in Figure 8-8. Basic configuration at this point is fairly simple: click Browse to locate the LDAP plugin. If you haven't tested the plugin, though, you'll also need to click Configure to configure it. Testing your configuration can be tricky unless you use the plugin tester program, as just described.

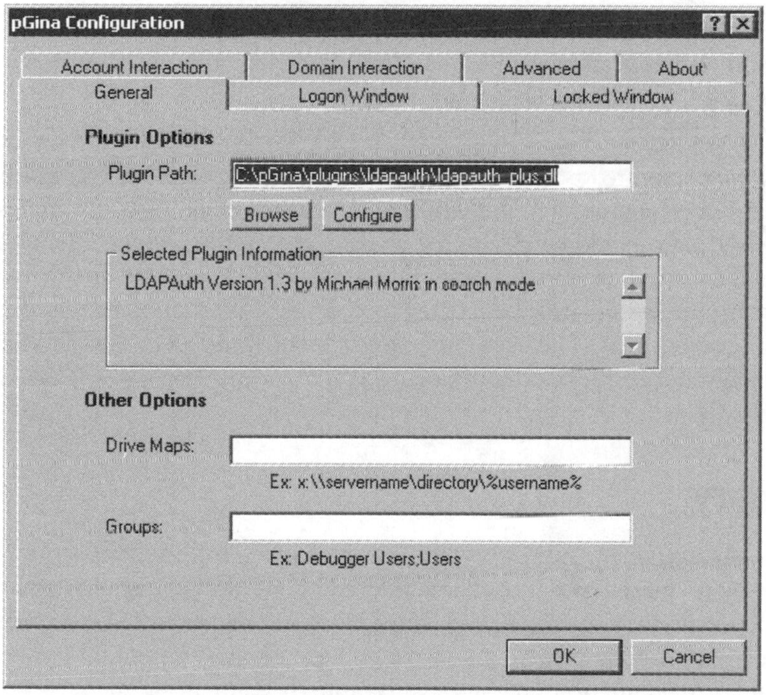

Figure 8-8. The main pGina configuration dialog box

In addition to the basic configuration, you may want to adjust some of the more advanced features of pGina:

- You can tell pGina to map network drives by entering a mapping in the Drive Maps field. For instance, entering **M:\\MANDRAGORA\SHARED** maps the *SHARED* share on the *MANDRAGORA* server to the local *M:* drive letter. (This requires that the SMB/CIFS server use the same password that's stored by the LDAP server.)

- You can force all users to belong to a specified set of groups by entering those groups in the Groups field. Separate groups with semicolons (;), as in Users;Staff to make all users members of both the *Users* and *Staff* groups.

- You can set features of the logon display, such as the graphic shown and any login messages, by using the Logon Window tab.

- By default, pGina keeps users' profiles between logons, meaning that users can customize their desktops and keep these settings. If you want users to see a standard desktop at each logon, you can uncheck the Keep Profiles item on the Account Information tab. The Force Login checkbox on this tab tells pGina to store the authenticated password locally, which should enable local logins even if the LDAP server goes down, provided the user has authenticated before. (This option might be handy on laptop computers.)

- The Domain Interaction tab presents options that enable pGina to perform domain authentication, as well as LDAP authentication. If your network hosts both an LDAP server and an NT Domain controller, each with its own set of accounts, this option enables a client to authenticate against either server.

Once you've configured pGina, you need to reboot the computer for the changes to take effect. Once you do, you'll be greeted by a new pGina login prompt, as shown in Figure 8-9. You should be able to log on using any of the accounts defined on your LDAP server, as well as any accounts that are defined locally on the Windows system. When you log on using an LDAP account, pGina automatically generates a matching local account. The user thereafter appears in the local user database unless you manually delete the accounts or uncheck the Keep Profiles checkbox, as just described.

Summary

LDAP is an extremely powerful tool for managing information on a network. Although by no means its only possible role, one good way to begin using LDAP is as a cross-platform authentication tool. In order to configure an LDAP server for this role, you must begin by installing a server package, such as OpenLDAP. Much of the tedium of LDAP configuration comes with properly configuring the server; you must set basic server configuration options, enable security options, and create an initial account database backend for the server. Only then can you configure your clients, which is a relatively straightforward task involving setting options in a few configuration files. Windows clients require a helper application, such as pGina, to integrate with an LDAP server, but once this software is installed, these servers can work quite nicely. The result of all this work is integrated Linux/Windows account information and simplified account maintenance, particularly on a mid-sized or large network.

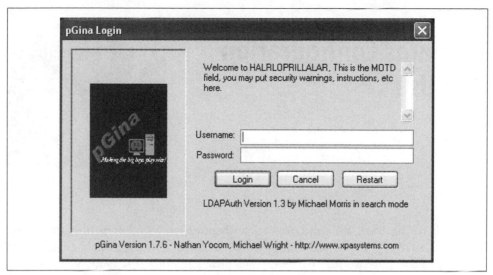

Figure 8-9. Once pGina is working, it presents its own logon screen rather than the default Windows logon screen

On a complex or large network, the savings in day-to-day administrative hassles more than compensates for the time you invest in configuring LDAP.

## CHAPTER 9

Kerberos Configuration and Use

The Kerberos protocol, the third network authentication tool described in this book, is named after the three-headed dog from Greek mythology, which guarded the entrance to the underworld. Like its mythological namesake, the modern Kerberos is a gatekeeper. Its principles and the problems it solves are different from those of NT domains and LDAP, though, which means that Kerberos's best areas of application are also different. Broadly speaking, Kerberos works best as a way to manage logins to multiple systems using multiple protocols; Kerberos provides single-sign-on capabilities that aren't well matched by competing protocols. As with NT domain configurations, Kerberos requires software on three classes of systems: the main Kerberos server; Kerberos *application servers* which are servers for other protocols that defer to the Kerberos server for authentication; and clients of the application servers. You can use either Linux or Windows in any of these roles, although not all combinations work equally well. Some Microsoft application servers and clients, in particular, don't work as well with Linux Kerberos servers as with their Microsoft counterparts. This chapter presents Kerberos first from a Linux perspective and concludes with Windows-specific information.

This chapter emphasizes setting up the basic Kerberos environment, using a few Kerberized tools that come with Kerberos, and configuring basic login authentication via Kerberos. It can be used for more protocols, though, such as providing single-sign-on for POP email retrieval. Going beyond the protocols provided with the Kerberos package requires installing additional software.

Kerberos Fundamentals

Kerberos is a centralized login tool. This statement, although true, is deceptively simple. Kerberos was designed to solve certain authentication problems that aren't easily handled by other protocols. Understanding these problems, and how Kerberos solves them, will help you configure a Kerberos server, as well as determine whether you want to do so. You'll also have to decide what Kerberos software you want to run, both in terms of the server itself and the Kerberos application servers and clients you'll run with it. Many of these decisions are likely to be Linux-centric, but depending on your needs, chances are you'll need to make Windows-related Kerberos decisions, as well.

The Problem: Centralized Single-Authentication Logins

Large local networks are likely to host many servers. This arrangement makes centralized authentication tools, such as NT domains and LDAP, desirable. However, centralizing login control in one server is just part of the answer. Kerberos was actually designed to meet three major needs:

Centralize authentication

> The most fundamental Kerberos design goal is to centralize authentication. This goal is basically the same as the primary goal of NT domains and is one of the many possible functions of LDAP. Kerberos also gives considerable weight to a sort of reverse authentication: providing an assurance to clients that the servers they connect to are the ones they claim to be. This identity verification helps ensure that, for instance, you're actually saving your departmental budget on your real departmental file server, rather than on the laptop of an industrial spy who's pretending to be a photocopier technician.

Protect passwords

> One problem with many network protocols that require authentication is that they're susceptible to password sniffing. To be sure, the last few years have seen great strides in this area, with secure protocols such as SSH largely displacing less secure protocols, such as Telnet. Still, Kerberos was designed with a high degree of attention to password security. It's also designed as a tool that can be used by many protocols, so any *Kerberized* client and server (that is, programs that have been designed to use Kerberos authentication) can gain the Kerberos password security benefits. Many Kerberized applications also provide encryption of non-password data, although this isn't a necessary feature of such tools.

Provide single-login operation

> This is arguably Kerberos's most unusual design feature. The idea is that users frequently log into a computer and proceed to use it to access many other computers. You might retrieve your email from a POP server, use a remote login protocol to run programs on another system, upload files to a third computer using FTP, submit print jobs using a printing protocol, and so on. Typing a password for each access becomes tedious at best. To be sure, some tools save your password on disk to mitigate the problem, but this practice is a potential security risk. Kerberos was designed to solve the problem by enabling single logins: once you've authenticated yourself to the Kerberos server, you don't need to do so

again with any Kerberos application server that defers to the main Kerberos server.

Of these features, the first two are handled reasonably well by both NT domains and LDAP, although neither really addresses the issue of server authentication for clients. (The NT domain controller and LDAP servers' identities may be authenticated, but other servers are not.) The single-login feature of Kerberos isn't well addressed by either of these alternatives. (Windows caches passwords for file server access, which presents the illusion of a single logon to the NT domain. This caching only helps with certain protocols, though.)

On the flip side, Kerberos wasn't designed with account management at the forefront. In particular, tools for delivering full account information to Linux clients—the tasks performed by NSS in Linux—are lacking in Kerberos. Although you can use Kerberos as part of a workstation login procedure, you need to maintain local accounts using local databases, LDAP, or some other tool.

 Microsoft's Active Directory uses LDAP in conjunction with Kerberos. These two tools provide some overlap in function, but they also complement each other very well. Unfortunately, Microsoft's Kerberos implementation is a bit odd and doesn't interact well with some non-Microsoft versions. These matters are described in the later sections "Windows and Kerberos" and "Windows Kerberos Tools."

An Overview of Kerberos Operation

Discussions of Kerberos, like those of LDAP and NT domains, tend to be filled with lots of jargon. Understanding these terms is necessary for understanding how Kerberos works and how to configure it.

KDC
> The *key distribution center* is the heart of Kerberos; it's the system that manages Kerberos logins. In other words, it's the Kerberos server. Some networks host multiple KDCs, in which case one is a *master* KDC, and the others are *slave* KDCs. For brevity's sake, this chapter describes only master KDC configuration. Slave KDCs are configured in much the same way as their masters, but both master and slave require additional components to propagate the password database to all KDCs.

Kerberized
> This adjective describes server or client programs that support the Kerberos protocols. They rely on the KDC for authentication, albeit in an indirect way, as described shortly. They can often also authenticate users in more conventional ways as a backup to their Kerberos functionality.

Kerberos application server
> An application server runs Kerberized servers.

Kerberos client

This term refers to any computer that obtains a ticket (described shortly) from a KDC. Normally, the Kerberos client is a client program run by a user.

Realm

A Kerberos realm is the range of the KDC's responsibility. Kerberos realms are often named after DNS domains or subdomains, but realm names are case-sensitive and are conventionally uppercase. For instance, if you're configuring a Kerberos system for the *example.com* domain, you'd probably call the realm *EXAMPLE.COM*. The realm need not correspond exactly to the domain, though; it can include or exclude specific computers, as you see fit.

Tickets

Tickets are at the heart of Kerberos authentication. A ticket is an encrypted hunk of data that's passed between systems as a mode of authentication. Most tickets are encrypted using a password, meaning that proper encryption of the ticket is proof of the ticket's validity.

TGT

A *ticket-granting ticket* is a special type of ticket that can obtain additional tickets. The KDC delivers a TGT to a user; the Kerberos client tools use the TGT to request tickets for accessing specific servers.

TGS

The ticket-granting service is the KDC subsystem that's responsible for granting TGTs.

Principals

A Kerberos principal is a user or server identification. Principals take the form *primary/instance@REALM*, where *primary* is a name (frequently a username), *instance* is an optional expansion that enables one user to have multiple principals, and *REALM* is the realm name. For instance, *fluffy@EXAMPLE.COM* is a possible principal for the user *fluffy* on the *EXAMPLE.COM* realm. Administrators frequently have a secondary principal with the instance name of *admin*, so if *fluffy* were an administrator, the account's administrative instance would be *fluffy/admin@EXAMPLE.COM*. Principals for application servers are named after the server, as in *telnet/mandragora.example.com@EXAMPLE.COM* for the Telnet server on *mandragora.example.com*. Computers that run application servers also require principals, on which the primary name is *host*, as in *host/ mandragora.example.com@EXAMPLE.COM*. Much of the administrative work of running Kerberos involves managing principals.

The fact that Kerberos is reliant on tickets makes its operation a bit different from that of most other network authentication tools, although many details can be hidden from users. In broad strokes, the system works like this: the user requests a TGT from the KDC, which delivers the TGT to the Kerberos tools on the user's system. When the user then initiates a connection to an application server, the Kerberos utilities on the client pass the TGT back to the KDC along with information on the server the user wants to connect to. The KDC replies with a new ticket, which is encrypted with the application server's password. This ticket includes the username and other relevant information. The user's system then forwards this ticket to the application server, which knows the ticket is valid because it's been encrypted with its own password (which is known only to the application server and the KDC). At this point, the user is authenticated to use the application server, and the session can proceed much as it would with a more direct username/password exchange. (The application server can, of course, apply its own local security rules to limit access on a user-by-user basis, up to and including denying specific users access even if they've been authenticated by the KDC.)

 Kerberos tickets include time stamps, and they expire after a limited period of time, which varies depending on your Kerberos options and the type of ticket. Thus, if a computer's clock is set incorrectly, it may not be able to authenticate on a Kerberos network. For this reason, if you use Kerberos, you should also use a network clock-setting tool to ensure that your systems' clocks are all set correctly. Chapter 15 describes one tool you can use for this purpose, the Network Time Protocol.

In practice, and from a user's point of view, using Kerberos involves two operations: authentication with the KDC and accessing servers. Tools for the former, and for managing Kerberos sessions, are described in the section "Using Kerberized Clients." Some tools can integrate KDC authentication with a desktop system's basic login, so the process can be quite seamless from a user's perspective. Still, the focus for Kerberos is on providing centralized *network* accesses, whereas the focus for LDAP, and to a lesser extent NT domains, is in providing centralized authentication for desktop logins. This distinction can be subtle, but is important in understanding when and how to deploy Kerberos, as opposed to other tools. Kerberos is best suited to environments in which users must frequently access a variety of password-protected servers for which Kerberized variants are available. Kerberos is less useful in environments in which users log into their desktop systems and then seldom need to access other password-protected computers. For desktop authentication alone, LDAP or NT domains do a better job. (NT domain logins, particularly for Windows desktop systems, also provide the illusion of password-less access to file and printer shares, but not to most other types of servers.)

Kerberos Tools for Linux

One of the difficulties with Kerberos is in deciding *which* Kerberos to use. Broadly speaking, Kerberos packages can be classified as V4 or V5, V5 being the latest. Linux implementations of both versions include:

MIT Kerberos

Kerberos originated at MIT, and so many people consider the original MIT Kerberos to be the standard. You can peruse its official web site, *http://web.mit.edu/kerberos/www/*, and download it from there. Kerberos is available in source code form and as binary packages for several OSs, including Linux, Windows, and Mac OS (both pre-X and X versions). MIT's Linux binaries, though, are available only in the form of a tarball. The latest version, 1.3.5, is a Kerberos V5 implementation.

Heimdal

This version of the Kerberos V5 protocol is hosted in Sweden, at *http://www.pdc.kth.se/heimdal/*. This site hosts source code and some binary packages, including versions for Linux, Solaris, DEC Unix, and Mac OS X. Version 0.6.3 is the latest as I write.

eBones

This package, headquartered at *http://www.pdc.kth.se/kth-krb/*, is a Kerberos V4 implementation. It's sometimes released with Linux distributions under a package name such as *krb4*. As a Kerberos V4 implementation, it's a bit dated, but if your site uses Kerberos V4, you might consider using it. The latest version as I write is Version 1.2.2.

Many distributions ship with one or more of these implementations in binary form. Typically, MIT Kerberos is available under the package name *mit-krb5* or *krb5*, whereas Heimdal is available as *heimdal* or something similar. Some distributions split the Kerberos package into parts, separating base tools, application servers, and clients. In theory, you should be able to mix and match Kerberos V5 implementations (MIT Kerberos and Heimdal, for instance); however, in practice you may find it easier to stick to a single product whenever possible. Problems are most likely to crop up in administrative tools and trying to mix master and slave KDCs of different types; problems between clients and KDCs or application servers are less common. Likewise, cross-OS mixes (using Linux MIT Kerberos clients and a MacOS MIT Kerberos KDC, for instance) should work, although problems sometimes crop up. Because Kerberos V4 is becoming rather elderly and has some protocol security bugs, this chapter describes V5 exclusively.

 This chapter uses Heimdal and MIT Kerberos V5 implementations as references. The reference realm's primary KDC runs Heimdal 0.6 on SuSE 9.1, but this chapter describes both Heimdal and MIT Kerberos tools and commands for most tasks.

Linux Kerberos packages ship with several Kerberized servers and clients, including Telnet, *rlogin*, FTP, *rsh*, and *rcp* programs. Subsequent sections of this chapter describe some of these tools in greater detail.

Kerberos was designed to enable just about any protocol that requires authentication to use it. Thus, the list of Kerberized protocols isn't limited to those that ship with the main Kerberos package. If you want to use Kerberos in conjunction with a protocol that's not supported by a client or server that ships with Kerberos, you should search for support elsewhere. Although Kerberos support is far from universal, many clients and servers do support the protocol. Sometimes this support comes in the form of a compile-time option, so you may need to recompile your software to include the Kerberos features. In other cases, you may need to switch from one client or server package to another one. Unfortunately, Kerberos support, although far from restricted to the clients and servers provided with Kerberos packages, is also far from universal; you may need to search long and hard to find Kerberized tools for a particular task.

Windows and Kerberos

In theory, Windows can fit into a Kerberos realm as easily as Linux. In practice, of course, you'll need to learn to configure both Linux and Windows; configuration file locations and the like will differ between the two platforms. You might also run into compatibility problems related to specific Kerberos implementations.

Of particular note along these lines is the fact that Windows 2000 and later ship with AD support, and AD includes Kerberos as one of its components. Microsoft, however, implemented Kerberos in a slightly different way than did other providers. Some notable areas of divergence include:

Encryption algorithms
> For political and technical reasons, Microsoft chose to support a different set of encryption algorithms than did the versions of Kerberos available in 2000. The practical upshot of this decision is that, if you use an AD controller as your KDC, you must either enable Data Encryption Standard (DES) encryption on the KDC and change users' passwords or use a recent version of Kerberos (such as MIT Kerberos 1.3 or later) on the non-Microsoft systems.

The PAC
> Perhaps the biggest Windows/non-Windows Kerberos compatibility issue is the Privilege Access Certificate (PAC). This is an extra field added to tickets returned by a Windows KDC. Microsoft's own Windows clients typically refuse to work with a KDC that doesn't return a PAC, which makes interoperating with a Linux KDC difficult, for example. Microsoft developed the PAC in a proprietary way, but in late 2003 some documentation on the PAC became available, so this problem is also fading in importance. Fortunately, non-Microsoft Kerberos implementations typically ignore the PAC, so Linux Kerberos application servers and clients should be able to operate with a Windows KDC.

Cached credentials
> Windows systems cache their login credentials as a way of supporting logins on laptops or in case of a KDC or network failure. Ordinarily, this practice poses no problems, but if a user logs on using a cached credential and a non-Microsoft KDC then becomes available, the system isn't likely to notice the KDC, resulting in an inability to access network resources.

Overall, using Microsoft's own KDC as your network's KDC in conjunction with Linux application servers and clients works well. If you're using older Kerberos implementations, though, you may need to enable DES support and then change users' passwords so that the new password is encoded in DES form. This step shouldn't be necessary with recent Kerberos V5 implementations for Linux, though. (If in doubt, check whether the Kerberos implementation supports the RC4-HMAC encryption algorithm.) For the most part, the details of administering a Windows KDC are beyond the scope of this book.

Using Windows clients with a non-Microsoft KDC is a bit trickier, but it is possible. You must create local Windows accounts on the Windows system for your users and use special tools to configure Windows to use the KDC for authentication. This process is described later in this chapter, in the section "Windows Kerberized Clients." Alternatively, you can install a non-Microsoft Kerberos package and run it without using Kerberos for logon authentication. Instead, you'd use regular Kerberized clients and servers under Windows, much as you would their equivalents under Linux.

Linux Kerberos Server Configuration

The single most complex task when you implement Kerberos on your network is to set up the Kerberos server—the KDC. To do this, you start by editing a server configuration file. This isn't the end of the job, though. You must also create a *master key*, which is used to encrypt the KDC's communications. Practical use of a Kerberos realm also requires such administrative tasks as creating principals and configuring access control rules. Finally, you must run the Kerberos servers (the main server and, typically, a separate administrative server).

Kerberos Realm Configuration

MIT Kerberos uses two configuration files: *krb5.conf* and *kdc.conf*. Heimdal, though, dispenses with the latter file, so you needn't be concerned with *kdc.conf* if you're configuring Heimdal. The *krb5.conf* file contains assorted information about your realm and the server's operation, while the *kdc.conf* file contains KDC-specific information.

Application servers and clients need to know much of the realm information in *krb5.conf*, and so these systems use this file, as well, although some sections are missing or ignored on these systems.

Editing krb5.conf

The KDC's main configuration file is called *krb5.conf*. If you install Kerberos from a package, chances are this file will reside in */etc*. A sample *krb5.conf* file appears in Example 9-1.

Example 9-1. Sample krb5.conf listing

```
[logging]
 default = FILE:/var/log/krb5libs.log
 kdc = FILE:/var/log/krb5kdc.log
 admin_server = FILE:/var/log/kadmind.log

[libdefaults]
 ticket_lifetime = 28800
 default_realm = EXAMPLE.COM
 dns_lookup_realm = false
 dns_lookup_kdc = false

[realms]
 EXAMPLE.COM = {
  kdc = kdc.example.com:88
  admin_server = kdc.example.com:749
  default_domain = example.com
 }

[domain_realm]
 .example.com = EXAMPLE.COM
 tropical.pangaea.edu = EXAMPLE.COM
```

This file is broken into sections, with each section denoted by a section name within square brackets ([ ]). Most options span a single line and consist of an option name followed by an equal sign and its value. Some, though, use compound values, which themselves span multiple lines. These are denoted by curly braces ({ }), as in the EXAMPLE.COM item within the [realms] section. Many of the *krb5.conf* parameters are self-explanatory, but some deserve additional elaboration:

Logging options

> The options in the [logging] section tell the server where to log data related to Kerberos operation. This section is not required for application server and client installations, just for KDCs.

Ticket lifetime

> The ticket_lifetime option sets the default lifetime for most tickets issued by the KDC, in seconds. The value of 28800 shown in Example 9-1 corresponds to eight hours. A too-long lifetime increases the risk of security breaches caused by

stolen tickets, while a too-short lifetime will be inconvenient for users because they have to reinitialize their Kerberos sessions.

Default realm

The default_realm option sets the realm that the KDC is to manage. This is likely to be named after your DNS domain name, but it doesn't have to be.

DNS lookup options

The dns_lookup_realm and dns_lookup_kdc options tell Kerberos to use DNS to help locate systems.

Realm definitions

The [realms] section defines realms. In Example 9-1, one realm is defined: *EXAMPLE.COM*. This definition includes pointers to a single KDC and one administrative server. (If your realm has slave KDCs, they're defined just like the master, using a kdc line.) The administrative server handles administrative functions, such as adding principals; it's normally the same as the master KDC. These definitions include port numbers—88 for the KDC and 749 for the administrative server. The default_domain option specifies the DNS domain name that's associated with Kerberos principals, when appropriate. A single *krb5.conf* file may define multiple realms. In such cases, you'd define each in its own set of lines, in a single [realms] section.

Domain/realm mapping

The [domain_realm] section specifies a mapping of computers to realms. In Example 9-1, all computers in the *example.com* domain and the computer *tropical.pangaea.edu* are included in the *EXAMPLE.COM* realm. Subdomains are indicated by a leading dot (.); entries lacking this dot are interpreted as referring to individual computers.

In addition to the entries shown in Example 9-1, MIT Kerberos is likely to have an additional section that points to the *kdc.conf* file:

```
[kdc]
    profile = /var/kerberos/krb5kdc/kdc.conf
```

You may also see a section called [appdefaults] in sample configuration files. This section modifies settings for individual application servers and clients. For instance, you might increase or decrease a ticket lifetime based on the likely session length for a particular service.

Editing kdc.conf

MIT Kerberos implementations typically place some KDC options in a separate file, called *kdc.conf*, which are referred to by a profile option in the [kdc] section of *krb5.conf*. Example 9-2 shows a typical example of this file. You should leave most of these options alone, but you can change the name of the Kerberos realm on the first line of the [realms] section to match your needs. The master_key_type and supported_enctypes options relate to the encryption methods that Kerberos supports.

Example 9-2. Sample kdc.conf listing

```
[kdcdefaults]
 acl_file = /var/kerberos/krb5kdc/kadm5.acl
 dict_file - /usr/share/dict/words
 admin_keytab = /var/kerberos/krb5kdc/kadm5.keytab
 v4_mode = nopreauth

[realms]
 EXAMPLE.COM = {
  master_key_type = des-cbc-crc
  supported_enctypes = arcfour-hmac:normal arcfour-hmac:norealm arcfour-hmac:onlyrealm
des3-hmac-sha1:normal des-hmac-sha1:normal des-cbc-md5:normal des-cbc-crc:normal des-cbc-
crc:v4 des-cbc-crc:afs3
}
```

Creating a Master Key

Because of the high priority Kerberos places on security, it uses a cryptographic *master key* to control access to itself. Without this key, Kerberos won't start. The key is generated from a password, and it's possible to store this password in a *stash file*. Using a stash file, Kerberos can start automatically when the computer boots; without a stash file, you must enter a password whenever you start the server.

In Heimdal, the utility to create a master key and a stash file is called *kstash*. (Heimdal actually creates a single file for both purposes.) To perform this task, type this command:

```
# kstash
Master key:
Verifying - Master key:
kstash: writing key to `/var/heimdal/m-key'
```

As with most utilities that ask for passwords, *kstash* doesn't echo the password you type. MIT Kerberos uses another utility, *kdb5_util*, to create its master key and stash file:

```
# kdb5_util create -r EXAMPLE.COM -s
Loading random data
Initializing database '/var/kerberos/krb5kdc/principal' for realm 'EXAMPLE.COM',
master key name 'K/M@EXAMPLE.COM'
You will be prompted for the database Master Password.
It is important that you NOT FORGET this password.
Enter KDC database master key:
Re-enter KDC database master key to verify:
```

The master key, stash file, and password are all extremely sensitive. The utilities should create files with appropriate permissions to protect them (typically 0600), at least assuming the Kerberos server isn't compromised. You should be extremely careful to both remember the password and not let it fall into unauthorized hands. Pick a password that's as close to a random collection of letters, digits, and punctuation as possible without running the risk of forgetting it, and don't reuse this password for any other account or server.

Realm Administration

At this point, your KDC is nearly ready to be used; however, you must still set up principals and define access control rules. Both tasks are critical for normal Kerberos operations. In fact, you're likely to return to these tasks, and particularly principal creation, many times in the future.

Creating principals

Principals are, essentially, Kerberos accounts. Kerberos requires certain principals in order to function, and you'll presumably want to create principals for your ordinary users. This section describes both tasks. Application servers also require principals, but this task is described in the section, "Preparing Application Server Principals."

Kerberos provides a tool called *kadmin* to manage principals. Ordinarily, this tool connects to the Kerberos administrative server (specified by the admin_server option in *krb5.conf*) to manage principals. At this point, though, this server isn't running because it's not yet fully configured, so you must create principals without using this server. In Heimdal, this task is accomplished by passing the -l option to *kadmin*. In MIT Kerberos, you use a variant command, *kadmin.local*. In Heimdal, the interaction for initializing the realm looks like this:

```
# kadmin -l
kadmin> init EXAMPLE.COM
Realm max ticket life [unlimited]:
Realm max renewable ticket life [unlimited]:
kadmin> add admin/admin@EXAMPLE.COM
Max ticket life [1 day]:
Max renewable life [1 week]:
Principal expiration time [never]:
Password expiration time [never]:
Attributes [ ]:
admin/admin@EXAMPLE.COM's Password:
Verifying - admin/admin@EXAMPLE.COM's Password:
```

The *init* command initializes the Kerberos database; it should be the first command you type when you use this program for the first time. The *add* command adds a principal for the administrative user. (You can use other primary and instance names if you like, though the principal should be in your realm.) If you're using MIT Kerberos, there's no need to begin with the *init* command, and the *add* command is called *addprinc*. You do, however, need to use the *ktadd* command to prepare a *keytab*, which is a special key Kerberos uses to handle administrative principals:

```
kadmin.local: ktadd -k /var/kerberos/krb5kdc/kadm5.keytab kadmin/admin kadmin/
changepw
```

The system should respond with a rather verbose report concerning the creation of the keytab files.

Whether you're using Heimdal or MIT Kerberos, you might want to take the time now to create at least one or two test accounts. These accounts might not have instance names for simplicity's sake. You can also omit the realm name, if you're adding a principal to your default realm:

```
kadmin> add fluffy
```

Heimdal is more verbose in the questions it asks at this point, and you can select the default for most of these. Whichever server you're using, though, you'll have to enter a password.

 Once you've started the KDC and the *kadmind* server, you can use *kadmin* to administer the server remotely, with one caveat: you can't use the *kadmin* from MIT Kerberos to administer a Heimdal server or vice versa; the administrative protocols aren't compatible.

ACL definitions

Kerberos uses ACLs to determine who may access the server (that is, *kadmind*, not the KDC as a whole) and in what ways. Kerberos ACLs are conceptually similar to filesystem ACLs, but they're not identical, nor do they rely on filesystem ACLs. Kerberos ACLs are defined in a special ACL file. In Heimdal, this file is normally */var/heimdal/kadmind.acl*; in MIT Kerberos, it's the file pointed to by the acl_file entry in *kdc.conf*. (You can specify the same parameter in a [kdc] section in Heimdal's *krb5.conf* file, if you want to use another file in Heimdal.) The ACL file consists of a series of lines, each with two or three entries:

```
Kerberos-Principal Permissions [Target-Principal]
```

The first entry, `Kerberos-Principal`, is the principal to which the ACL applies—that is, the user whose permissions are being defined. The `Permissions` string is a collection of one or more letters (in MIT Kerberos) or a comma-separated list of codes (in Heimdal), as summarized in Table 9-1, that define the operations the user can perform. If no third option is present, these permissions apply to all other principals. If a third entry is present, however, it refers to the principals that the first principal may modify in the specified ways. For instance, you might want to give some users the ability to modify certain classes of principals but not others.

Table 9-1. Kerberos ACL permission codes

MIT Kerberos code	Heimdal code	Meaning
a	add	Principals or policies can be added.
A	–	Principals or policies can't be added.
d	delete	Principals or policies can be deleted.
D	–	Principals or policies can't be deleted.
m	modify	Principals or policies can be modified.
M	–	Principals or policies can't be modified.
c	cpw or change-password	Passwords can be changed.
C	–	Passwords can't be changed.
i	get	Database inquiries can be made.
I	–	Database inquiries can't be made.
l	list	Principals or policies can be listed.
L	–	Principals or policies can't be listed.
x or *	all	Wildcard for all "can" ACLs (admcil).

In the case of both principal specifications, an asterisk (*) can be used as a wildcard for part of the specification. For instance, you can give all users in the *admin* instance the ability to do anything in MIT Kerberos:

```
*/admin@EXAMPLE.COM  *
```

In MIT Kerberos, an entry similar to this is the default, but you should modify it to point to your realm. You might also want to fine-tune the ACLs to suit your own needs—for instance, providing different groups of administrators different levels of access to the server's administrative functions. In Heimdal, the ACL file is absent by default, so you'll probably want to create it. A failure to create this file means that you can't perform administrative tasks from other systems, including adding principals and extracting keytabs—tasks that are required for adding application servers to a Kerberos realm. (You can still perform these tasks from the KDC itself, but then you'll have to move highly sensitive keytab files to the application server in some other way, such as on a floppy disk or via a network file transfer.)

Running the KDC

The KDC must be run in order to be useful. On most Linux distributions, you can do this by running a SysV startup script:

```
# /etc/init.d/kdc start
```

Details vary from one distribution to another, though; the script may be called *kdc*, *krb5kdc*, *mit-krb5kdc*, or something else. You may need to use your distribution's package system or simply peruse your SysV startup scripts to locate the correct script.

Some KDC startup scripts start the Kerberos administrative server along with the KDC server. Others, though, provide a separate script to start the administrative server. This second script may be called *mit-krb5kadmind*, *kadmin*, or something else. Again, checking the SysV scripts installed with your package or perusing the startup scripts may be necessary. Normally, you'll want to run the administrative server on the master KDC; without it, your ability to administer your realm from anything but the KDC itself will be limited.

Starting the KDC and administrative server manually is fine for testing, but, in operation, you'll probably want to configure your system to start the servers on a regular basis. On many distributions, the *chkconfig* command can be used to do this:

```
# chkconfig --add kdc
```

Other distributions use other tools to do this job. Consult distribution-specific documentation if you need help with this task.

Kerberos Application Server Configuration

Setting up a master KDC is the most involved part of configuring a Kerberos realm; however, by itself, a KDC doesn't do much good. The next step in this process is to configure one or more application servers. Each application server computer must have a basic Kerberos configuration, which is similar in some details to the KDC's configuration. You must also create principals for each application server and set up appropriate keytabs. Once this is done, you can run the server programs to make them available.

Setting Up Kerberos

Any Linux system that runs a Kerberos application server requires certain basic preparation, some of which is the same as that for the KDC. In particular, you must set up the */etc/krb5.conf* file in much the same way, as described in the earlier section, "Editing krb5.conf." You can, however, omit some sections from this file, namely the [logging] and [kdc] sections.

Preparing Application Server Principals

Before you can run an application server, you must prepare principals for the server (both the server computer and the individual server programs). Furthermore, you must install keytabs for these principals on the application server computer.

The first step in this process is to create the principals. You do this much as you do for ordinary users, with the help of the *kadmin* or *kadmin.local* command. To simplify the procedure, pass the -r (in Heimdal) or -randkey (in MIT Kerberos) option. This assigns a random password to the principal. Because the password need only be "known" to software on the server computer, this practice should work well. Generally speaking, you must create principals with the instance name of the computer's DNS hostname and primary names of host (for the computer as a whole) and named after each server. Some specific servers don't need their own principals, though. For instance, to enable *gingko.example.com* to function as a Kerberized Telnet server, you can type (using Heimdal's *kadmin*) the following:

```
kadmin> add -r host/gingko.example.com
Max ticket life [1 day]:
Max renewable life [1 week]:
Principal expiration time [never]:
Password expiration time [never]:
Attributes [ ]:
kadmin> add -r telnet/gingko.example.com
Max ticket life [1 day]:
Max renewable life [1 week]:
Principal expiration time [never]:
Password expiration time [never]:
Attributes [ ]:
```

 The Kerberized Telnet server doesn't need its own principal. Thus, you can still run it if you omit the second *add* command in the preceding example.

With the principals created, you must then extract them to a keytab file. You do this with the *ext_keytab* (Heimdal) or *ktadd* (MIT Kerberos) command within *kadmin*:

```
kadmin> ext_keytab -k gingko.keytab host/gingko.example.com telnet/gingko.example.com
```

The -k option tells the utility what file to use to store the keytab. If you perform this step from the application server itself, you can give the filename */etc/krb5.keytab* directly. If you do this job from another computer, such as the KDC, you can store the keytab under any convenient name, but you must then transfer the file to the application server and store it as */etc/krb5.keytab*. Be sure this file is readable only by *root* (or by the account that will be used to run the server). If you add new Kerberized server programs to an application server, you need to add new principals and repeat this step, specifying principals for all of your server programs. Alternatively, you can combine multiple files using *cat* or similar tools, adding only the new principals, as needed.

Keytab files function as proof of a server's identity. For this reason, they're extremely sensitive. Never transfer them using unencrypted network protocols, such as an unencrypted FTP or NFS server. For network transfers, *scp* (part of the SSH package) is an acceptable choice. You can also use a floppy disk or other removable media, but when you're done, be sure to do a low-level reformat of a floppy disk or otherwise securely wipe the keytab file from the disk (say, using *wipe*); don't just delete the file with *rm*. Also, if you use a KDC to generate the keytabs, delete the keytab file from the KDC's disk, ideally using *wipe* or another tool that completely destroys the data in a file. The KDC stores a copy in its principals database, and a copy in a disk file might fall into the wrong hands if not given sufficient protection.

Running the Servers

Once the application server's keytab is in place, you can run the server programs. Doing so is much like running non-Kerberos servers. The servers that come standard with Kerberos are typically run from a super server (*inetd* or *xineted*). For instance, Example 9-3 shows a file, stored in */etc/xinetd.d*, that will launch the Kerberized Telnet server (*ktelnetd*) that ships with MIT Kerberos.

Example 9-3. Sample xinetd configuration for the Kerberized Telnet server

```
service telnet
{
    disable      = no
    socket_type  = stream
    protocol     = tcp
    wait         = no
    user         = root
    group        = root
    server       = /usr/sbin/ktelnetd
    server_args  = -a valid
}
```

The standard Kerberos servers support additional options you must use to enable Kerberos authentication:

klogind

> This program works in conjunction with the *rlogin* command. You'll ordinarily use the options -k (enable Kerberos authentication), -e (enable encryption), and -c (require a cryptographic checksum from the client, which improves security).

kshd

> This remote shell server is used with *rsh* to enable remote program execution. You'll probably use the same -k, -e, and -c parameters described for *klogind*.

kftp

> This program is a Kerberized FTP server. With some versions of this program, you'll probably use it with the -a valid option, which enables Kerberos authentication. Other versions of the server don't require this option. Consult your package's documentation to learn which option is required.

ktelnetd

> This server provides Kerberized Telnet access to a computer. Like *kftpd*, it may require a -a valid option to enable Kerberos authentication.

These servers support encryption, but only when used with matching Kerberized clients, such as those that ship with Kerberos packages. When used with ordinary non-Kerberized clients, these servers provide no advantages over their non-Kerberized counterparts.

These servers support additional options, too, some of which aren't related to Kerberos operation. Depending on their configuration options, they might or might not accept non-Kerberos logins. If you need more details, consult their manpages or other documentation. (Some packages lack manpages for their servers.)

 Some Kerberos packages (notably Heimdal) omit the leading *k* from the server filenames. In addition, the server files' locations vary depending on the Kerberos package. Check your package's contents to learn the details.

In addition to these basic servers, Kerberized versions of other servers are available. In some, Kerberos support is part of the main server, although it may be a compile-time option. For instance, Samba supports Kerberos authentication, but only if you provide appropriate compile-time options. (The details of Samba's Kerberos features are actually rather complex and are beyond the scope of this book.) For some protocols, Kerberos support is available in some servers but not others. Thus, if you want to support Kerberos for particular protocols, you should check the documentation for your preferred servers. If they don't support Kerberos, try performing a web search. Precisely how you might activate Kerberos support for these tools varies greatly from one server to another, so you'll have to consult your server's documentation.

Linux Kerberos Client Configuration

Kerberized clients are simpler to configure than KDCs or Kerberized application servers. Nonetheless, these tools do require some basic configuration to work. You may even need to track down Kerberized versions of clients for specific protocols, particularly if you want to use tools that aren't provided with Kerberos. Once everything's set up, you should know something about the basic Kerberos user management tools, because they control user access to the realm.

Preparing Kerberos Clients

The main requirement for Kerberos client configuration is to set up the Kerberos configuration file, *krb5.conf*, as described earlier. Note that there's no need for a [logging] or [kdc] section, and, consequently, no need for a *kdc.conf* file—even if you're using MIT Kerberos.

You can mix and match an MIT Kerberos KDC with Heimdal clients, or a Heimdal KDC with MIT Kerberos clients. As described in the section "Windows Kerberos Tools," still other Kerberos implementations can interact with these common Linux Kerberos tools.

Because the Kerberos clients don't maintain Kerberos databases, you don't need to use *kadmin* or *kadmin.local* to set up local Kerberos databases on the clients. You do, though, need to create principals for your users, as described earlier in this chapter.

Installing Kerberized Clients

Kerberized clients can be classified in two categories: those that ship with the main Kerberos package and third-party tools. The "official" Kerberized clients are those that match the "official" Kerberized servers, as described earlier in the section "Running the Servers." If you install Kerberos from source code, these clients install with the main Kerberos package, so the easiest way to install them is to compile the whole Kerberos package. Some Linux distributions, though, split the Kerberos clients into a separate package, such as Fedora's *krb5-workstation*. (Such tools may depend on others, such as Fedora's *krb5-libs*.) Other distributions place everything in one huge package.

If you want to use additional protocols, such as POP or IMAP, you need to track down Kerberized clients—in the case of POP or IMAP, this is a Kerberized mail reader, such as Pine (*http://www.washington.edu/pine/*). As with matching Kerberized servers, tracking these down can be tricky. A web search on appropriate terms, such as *Kerberos IMAP*, may help.

Many clients and servers provide Kerberos support as a compile-time option. If you can't seem to get Kerberos support working, particularly if you're using precompiled binaries and the documentation says that the client supports Kerberos, you can try recompiling the program locally. This may require that you install a Kerberos development package, though.

Using Kerberized Clients

Kerberos is a network login protocol, but Linux Kerberos packages don't automatically enable Kerberized authentication for desktop logins. (This option is described in the next section.) Instead, you can manage a Kerberos session *after* you've logged into your normal Linux (or other OS) session. Once you've done this, you can use the following four Kerberos client tools to manage your Kerberos session:

kinit
    This program initializes a Kerberos session. More precisely, it obtains a TGT from the KDC. Once you've acquired a TGT, the Kerberos utilities can easily—

and transparently—obtain tickets to specific servers. Thus, *kinit* manages the "single sign-on" feature of Kerberos. To use the tool, type its name; it will ask you for a password, using your Linux username as the primary of the principal and the default realm defined in *krb5.conf*. You can obtain a TGT for another principal by passing its name to *kinit*, as in **kinit linnaeus/admin@EXAMPLE.COM**. This is handy if you have multiple principals, such as one for regular use and another for administrative functions.

klist

This program displays information on your current tickets, including the TGT. If you can't seem to log in using a Kerberos client, using *klist* can be a good starting point. You might discover that you're missing a necessary ticket.

kpasswd

This command is the Kerberos equivalent of the Linux *passwd* command; it changes your Kerberos realm password. You must have a TGT to use it.

kdestroy

This command destroys all your tickets. In theory, you should run this command just before logging out of the computer from which you're managing your Kerberos session. If you fail to do so, the tickets might remain in memory and could, in theory, be misappropriated by somebody with sufficient privilege. Some session management tools destroy tickets automatically, though, so this may not be necessary. You can also use this tool to destroy tickets you no longer need, which enables you to authenticate using a "clean slate" for testing purposes.

Of these commands, only *kinit* is necessary for using Kerberos as a client, and it can be replaced by other tools, as described later. To illustrate the use of these tools, though, consider the following sequence of commands:

```
$ kinit
Password for fluffy@EXAMPLE.COM:
$ klist
Ticket cache: FILE:/tmp/krb5cc_500
Default principal: fluffy@EXAMPLE.COM

Valid starting      Expires           Service principal
06/23/04 19:24:42  06/24/04 19:24:39  krbtgt/EXAMPLE.COM@EXAMPLE.COM

Kerberos 4 ticket cache: /tmp/tkt500
klist: You have no tickets cached
$ kpasswd
Password for fluffy@EXAMPLE.COM:
Enter new password: :
Enter it again: :
Password changed.
$ /usr/lib/heimdal/bin/telnet -af mandragora
Trying 192.168.1.3...
Connected to mandragora (192.168.1.3).
Escape character is '^]'.
[ Kerberos V5 accepts you as ``fluffy@EXAMPLE.COM'' ]
```

```
Last login: Wed Jun 23 19:24:25 from halrloprillalar
fluffly@mandragora> logout
Connection closed by foreign host.
$ klist
Ticket cache: FILE:/tmp/krb5cc_500
Default principal: fluffy@EXAMPLE.COM

Valid starting       Expires            Service principal
06/23/04 19:24:42  06/24/04 19:24:39  krbtgt/EXAMPLE.COM@EXAMPLE.COM
06/23/04 19:26:16  06/24/04 19:24:39  host/mandragora.example.com@EXAMPLE.COM

Kerberos 4 ticket cache: /tmp/tkt500
klist: You have no tickets cached
$ kdestroy
$ klist
klist: No credentials cache found (ticket cache FILE:/tmp/krb5cc_500)

Kerberos 4 ticket cache: /tmp/tkt500
klist: You have no tickets cached
```

This example begins with a call to *kinit*, which obtains the initial TGT (*krbtgt/EXAMPLE.COM@EXAMPLE.COM*, as revealed by the first call to *klist*). The call to *klist* also displays the TGT's starting and ending times—one day apart in this example. The call to *kpasswd* results in a password-change exchange much like the one that results from the standard Linux *passwd* command.

The Kerberized *telnet* command works much like the stock *telnet*, but passing the -a and -f parameters are necessary to have the client attempt an automatic login and forward its credentials to the server, respectively. Without these options, you'll be prompted for your username and password. Note also that this example includes the complete path to the Kerberized binary. Depending on your PATH environment variable and where your Kerberized and normal *telnet* binaries are located, this may or may not be necessary to ensure use of the Kerberized tool. After logging out of the remote system, a second call to *klist* reveals that the system is still holding onto the TGT but has acquired a new ticket, *host/mandragora.example.com@EXAMPLE.COM*, which corresponds to the server system to which you've connected. After using the *kdestroy* command, *klist* reveals that no tickets are present. At this point, an attempt to use Kerberized clients will either fail or result in a conventional login prompt, or at least a request for a password. If this happens, Kerberos is *not* being used for authentication.

 Of the clients that ship with Kerberos, *ftp* provides the most verbose information while connecting to the server. This fact can be useful when you're debugging problems.

Many of the stock Kerberos client programs (*telnet*, *rlogin*, and so on) require the -a and/or -f options to enable automatic logins using Kerberos credentials. Some packages use a leading *k* to differentiate the Kerberized programs from their non-Kerberized counterparts, as in *ktelnet*. You'll need to consult your local documentation and package information to learn the details for your system.

Using Kerberos for Network Logins

One of the limitations of Kerberos, at least as it's delivered in the main Kerberos package, is that it isn't a very good tool for logging into individual desktop systems. To use Kerberos as just described, you must log into your desktop system, including entering a password, and then use *kinit* to initialize a Kerberos session. Ideally, you should be able to enter your username and password just once, when you log into the computer. This ideal is achievable using any of several tools; however, some of them require additional configuration to use. Even at their best, though, these tools aren't complete replacements for your local Linux accounts; you must still maintain some information locally or via some other tool, such as LDAP.

Kerberized login tools

Linux requires authentication for many different tools. In terms of local login, two broad classes of tools are most notable: text-mode login, which is handled by the *login* program, and GUI login, which is handled by an X Display Manager (XDM) program. In addition to these login tools, though, other local authentication tools exist, such as screen-locking programs, which lock the console after a period of activity, much like screen savers, but require a password to unlock the screen.

The stock Heimdal and MIT Kerberos packages ship with a replacement for the standard *login* tool. This replacement is called *login* in Heimdal and *login.krb5* in MIT Kerberos. It's installed in an out-of-the-way directory or under an unusual name to prevent interference with the standard *login* program. To use the new tool, you must copy it over the original, which is typically located in */bin*, but I recommend you first back up the original in case you run into problems:

```
# mv /bin/login /bin/login-original
# cp /usr/sbin/login.krb5 /bin/login
```

> Adjusting your system's login tools is potentially risky. You should ensure that you have some alternate way to log in that doesn't use *login* (such as via an XDM program or an SSH session) when adjusting *login*. You may also want to leave a *root* login running in one virtual terminal while you make changes.

Once you make this change, your system should begin using Kerberos for all text-mode console logins, with the caveat that any currently running *login* processes may need to be restarted first. (Typically, logging in and then logging out should do the job.) The *login* program is used by some other tools, too, such as non-Kerberized Telnet servers. Using a Kerberized *login* program, though, doesn't provide you with any extra security; the client still sends the username and password to the server unencrypted, and the resulting session will also be unencrypted.

 One good way to test whether you're using the Kerberized *login* tool is to use *klist*. If you destroy your tickets, log out, log in, and then find you have a new TGT after logging in, you can be sure you're using the Kerberized *login*.

After making these changes, you should test all your user accounts, or at least all of those you can test. Be sure to test your *root* account, too, and if it doesn't work, create an appropriate Kerberos principal for *root*.

 Using PAM for Kerberized logins, as described next, enables you to use a local *root* account along with Kerberos for other users. This can make the PAM solution a bit safer because you won't be denied *root* access if a Kerberos problem develops. This solution also lets you set different *root* passwords for each computer.

Unfortunately, the standard Kerberos packages don't ship with an equivalent to the Kerberized *login* for GUI logins. To implement Kerberized GUI logins, you must either track down a Kerberized XDM (they're rare) or implement Kerberos via PAM. The latter is a more flexible approach, and it can also be used in place of the explicitly Kerberized *login* program, but PAM takes more effort to set up.

Kerberos and PAM

Several third-party Kerberos PAM modules exist, but the most popular is the *pam_krb5* package, which is available under that name with most distributions. (Debian calls its version *libpam-krb5*, though.) Its main web site is *http://sourceforge.net/projects/pam-krb5/*, should you need to install it from source code.

The Kerberos PAM package installs very few files; aside from documentation files, the only important file is */lib/security/pam_krb5.so*. Some versions also install a variant known as *pam_krb5afs.so*, which also supports logins via Andrew File System (AFS) authentication.

You can configure the Kerberos PAM modules by adding references to *pam_krb5.so* for the auth and account items in the files in */etc/pam.d* corresponding to the services you want to use Kerberos authentication. This topic is described in more detail in Appendix A, so consult it for details.

The primary advantage of using PAM for local Kerberos authentication is that you can use Kerberos for just about any service that requires authentication. The list of likely services includes *login*, XDM (or its GNOME or KDE variants, GDM or KDM), *su*, *sudo*, *passwd*, *vlock* (a text-mode, console-locking program), *xlock* (an X-based console-locking program), and *xscreensaver* (another X-based, console locking program). Using the Kerberized PAM modules for these services (and particularly for the *login* and XDM, GDM, or XDM services) means that users will have TGTs the moment they log in; they won't need to use *kinit* to obtain them.

In theory, you can use the Kerberized PAM module to support network-accessible login servers, such as POP, IMAP, FTP, and SSH. In practice, though, the advantages to doing so are slim, because the communication between the client and server is still done in whatever way it would be done if you used the normal PAM configuration. In particular, a protocol that delivers the password in unencrypted form will continue to do so. If possible, you should instead replace the client and server programs with explicitly Kerberized versions. This configuration bypasses PAM and uses Kerberos directly, giving you more Kerberos benefits. Alternatively, you can set up an encrypted tunnel to encrypt all data, including passwords. This protects your passwords and enables you to use the Kerberos database, but won't extend the single-sign-on advantages of Kerberos to non-Kerberized clients.

Kerberized account maintenance

If you've read Chapters 7 or 8, you may have noticed an omission in the preceding description of Kerberos and PAM: no mention has been made of the Name Service Switch. This Linux component provides account information, such as UID-to-username mapping, to programs that need it. Unfortunately, no Kerberos NSS modules are available, which means that you can't rely on Kerberos to maintain the sort of information NSS normally handles. The practical upshot of this limitation is that you must either maintain local accounts (in */etc/passwd*) for your Kerberos-authenticated users, or you must rely on another tool (such as LDAP) to handle this job.

This limitation can be a serious one for many potential uses of Kerberos; if you want to maintain full user account information in a central database, so that you needn't modify desktop systems' configurations when adding or deleting users on your network, Kerberos by itself isn't a complete solution, at least not when you're using Linux desktop systems. Some possible solutions to this problem include:

- You can maintain a central Kerberos database and deal with conventional Linux */etc/passwd* files manually. This approach may be acceptable if users seldom or never use anything but their own desktop systems; you need to update only a user's own desktop system and the Kerberized servers when adding or deleting network users. For instance, when adding the user *bbode*, you don't need to modify *fluffy*'s desktop system.

- You can abandon Kerberos entirely, at least as a login tool, and switch to another protocol, or relegate Kerberos to secondary duty (say, for use by just a few users). You can still use Kerberos as a tool for managing server accesses subsequent to desktop logins, but the servers will still need local accounts to match the Kerberos principals.

- You can use another protocol, such as LDAP, as a supplement to Kerberos. You'd use Kerberos for authentication via PAM but configure NSS to use the other protocol. This approach can be an effective one and can be a useful way to take advantage of Kerberos's single-sign-on capabilities while minimizing account maintenance. Unfortunately, configuring both systems is likely to be tedious in the short term, and this approach also seems to require that you maintain two account databases, at least at first glance—one for Kerberos and one for the secondary system. In practice, you can link LDAP and Kerberos more tightly (much as AD under Windows does), but this topic is well beyond the scope of this chapter.

 If your network hosts a Windows 200x AD controller, you can use it as the KDC and configure Linux systems as Kerberos application servers. If you also configure Winbind's NSS features and use the AD controller as a domain controller, as described in Chapter 7, the Linux system will maintain Linux user accounts automatically.

Ultimately, you'll have to decide for yourself just how to balance your priorities: Kerberos's unique features, such as single-sign-on, versus simplified local account information. If the former isn't very important but the latter is, LDAP or NT domains will probably be a better solution than Kerberos; if the former is very important, Kerberos is the better tool in addition to or instead of another one.

Windows Kerberos Tools

Up to now, this chapter has presented Kerberos largely from a Linux perspective. Kerberos, though, is a cross-platform tool, and you can use it to help integrate Linux and Windows systems. You can use Windows in any of the main Kerberos roles (KDC, application server, or client).

Windows Kerberos Implementations

Broadly speaking, three approaches to Kerberos are possible under Windows:

Microsoft's Kerberos implementation
    Microsoft provides a Kerberos implementation as part of Windows 200x/XP (but not Windows XP Home). As described in the earlier section, "Windows and Kerberos," Microsoft's Kerberos implementation deviates from others, which can make using it with a non-Microsoft KDC tricky. In the section "Windows Kerberized Clients," some pointers for using Microsoft's Kerberos clients with non-Microsoft KDCs are presented.

Conventional non-Microsoft Kerberos implementations

You can obtain non-Microsoft Kerberos implementations for Windows. For instance, a Windows binary version of MIT Kerberos (*http://web.mit.edu/kerberos/*) is available for all versions of Windows since Windows 98. (Windows 95 and earlier are not supported.) This tool can be configured and used much like Linux versions of Kerberos. The main difference is that configuration file locations differ. Most importantly, instead of editing */etc/krb5.conf*, you edit *C:\WINDOWS\krb5.ini*. (This file may reside in another directory if you installed Windows to a directory other than *C:\WINDOWS*.) This package also includes a GUI tool called *Leash*, which manages Kerberos tickets.

Limited non-Microsoft Kerberos implementations

Some tools provide limited Kerberos support—typically, Kerberos-enabled versions of a handful of protocols, with their own Kerberos libraries. One of the more popular of these is Kerberos Telnet (*http://www.stacken.kth.se/~thn/ktelnet/*), which provides Kerberized Telnet, FTP, and POP implementations for Windows. Tools like this don't work in conjunction with either Microsoft's Kerberos or broader non-Microsoft Kerberos tools on the same system, although, of course, they can interact with such systems as KDCs and application servers.

Each tool type has its advantages and disadvantages. Broadly speaking, you're most likely to find Kerberized Windows clients and application servers that work with the Windows implementation of Kerberos; however, this implementation is limited to just a few recent versions of Windows, and it doesn't always interoperate well with non-Microsoft KDCs. Kerberized Windows clients and servers can also be very difficult to locate, aside from those provided with Windows. Microsoft's Kerberos implementation can function well as a KDC for non-Microsoft application servers and clients. Full non-Microsoft Kerberos implementations work best with Unix tools ported to Windows (say, running in conjunction with Cygwin) or with Kerberized Windows clients and application servers. These tools interoperate well with Kerberized Linux programs, but the implementation is awkward when it comes to providing single-login authentication for Windows desktop systems. Limited non-Microsoft Kerberos implementations can be handy on desktop systems when you want to use Kerberos authentication for security reasons or to provide single-login authentication but when you're not concerned about Kerberizing the initial logon to Windows.

Windows Kerberized Servers

Windows 200x/XP systems that are members of an AD domain automatically use the AD controller's Kerberos features to authenticate file and printer sharing access. Thus, configuring this aspect of Kerberized server use is relatively straightforward.

By treating the AD controller as an NT domain controller, Linux systems running Samba and older Windows NT servers can authenticate against the AD controller even if these domain member servers don't use Kerberos. Thus, many of the benefits of Kerberos extend even to some non-Kerberos systems.

As with Linux servers, Kerberos support in most third-party servers is a hit-or-miss proposition. Windows doesn't ship with Kerberized Telnet, FTP, or other servers, and these servers are lacking even in some third-party Kerberos packages.

Windows Kerberized Clients

In principle, Windows Kerberos clients can be as varied as Linux Kerberos clients. If you have specific needs, you may need to consult the documentation for the Kerberized clients you've selected. It's even possible that your choice of client programs will dictate your choice of overall Windows Kerberos implementation (Microsoft's, a third party's, or Kerberos integrated into a server). As a couple of examples, I present information on using Microsoft's Kerberos to authenticate against a non-Windows KDC and using the Kerberos Telnet package.

Using Windows' Kerberos

Microsoft supports Kerberos as part of its Active Directory domain authentication. If you're using an AD domain controller, Windows clients automatically use the AD controller's KDC features when they're configured as members of the domain. This support also extends to use of Windows file and printer shares offered by domain members.

You can use a non-Windows Kerberos KDC as a way to authenticate Windows 200x/XP users' initial sign-ons, but the process is awkward. One way to do it is to establish a cross-realm trust relationship between a Windows AD controller and the non-Windows KDC. This procedure is quite advanced, though, and is beyond the scope of this book. A somewhat simpler, but more limited, approach is to configure local user accounts on the Windows desktop system and tell it to use the KDC, thus centralizing the password database. The following list shows you how:

1. Create a host key for the Windows client using *kadmin* on the KDC. This key must use DES encryption. In MIT Kerberos, you can do this with the -e option to *addprinc*, as in **addprinc -e des:normal host/mimbulus.example.com@EXAMPLE.COM** to add a principal for the Windows system *mimbulus.example.com*. Don't randomize the password when you create this principal, as you do when creating a principal for a Linux application server.

2. Run the *ksetup* program on the Windows client, and tell it how to locate the KDC. In the last step, you'll need to enter the password you used when you created the host key for the Windows system:

```
C:\>ksetup /setdomain EXAMPLE.COM
C:\>ksetup /addkdc EXAMPLE.COM kdc.example.com
C:\>ksetup /addpasswd EXAMPLE.COM kdc.example.com
C:\>ksetup /setmachpasswd password
```

3. Use the Windows *ksetup* tool to map a Kerberos principal name to a local username. For instance, typing **ksetup /mapuser fluffy@EXAMPLE.COM Cerberus** maps the Kerberos principal name *fluffy@EXAMPLE.COM* to the local account *Cerberus*. As a shortcut, you can type **ksetup /mapuser * *.** This command maps local users to like-named Kerberos principals; for instance, the local user *fluffy* maps to the *fluffy@EXAMPLE.COM* principal.

Once this is done, you should be able to log on and have the Windows desktop system use the KDC for authentication. You will, however, have to maintain local accounts corresponding to those on the KDC, or at least mapped to it using *ksetup /mapuser*.

Using Kerberos Telnet

If you want to use Kerberos only for Telnet, FTP, or POP access, Kerberos Telnet (*http://www.stacken.kth.se/~thn/ktelnet/*) may be just what you need. This program, shown in Figure 9-1, is a Kerberized POP proxy, FTP, and Telnet implementation for Windows that doesn't rely on any other local Kerberos tools.

When you install Kerberos Telnet, you'll be asked for basic information, such as your realm name. The tool then uses that information when you request a connection to a server. The first time you do this, you'll be asked for principal information (in the "User data" dialog box shown in Figure 9-1. Thereafter, you won't have to type your password again. Kerberos Telnet provides integrated ticket management tools (also shown in Figure 9-1), so you can check on tickets' expiration dates, destroy them, and so on.

Summary

Compared to other remote authentication tools, Kerberos is unusual; it's designed to manage entire network logins, rather than desktop computer logins. As such, it's best suited for environments in which users frequently use multiple servers, with protocols such as Telnet or FTP. Kerberos configuration requires configuring three computer classes: the KDC, the application servers, and the clients. All have certain commonalities, such as the *krb5.conf* file, but each has its unique features, as well. Considered as a cross-platform tool, Kerberos can be an integrative tool, but Microsoft's non-standard Kerberos implementation throws a monkey wrench into the equation. Cross-platform Kerberos use works best with a Microsoft KDC (in the form of an AD controller) and non-Microsoft application servers or clients; using

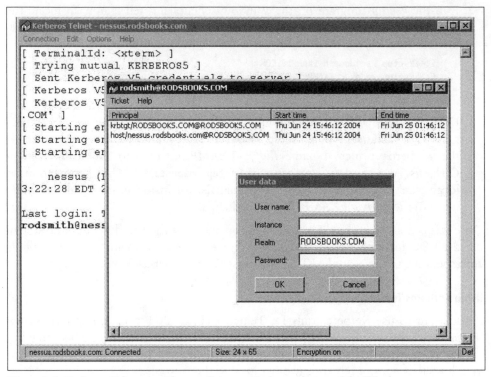

Figure 9-1. Kerberos Telnet provides an all-in-one Kerberos client tool for Windows

Microsoft application servers or clients with a non-Microsoft KDC is trickier, although it's still possible, and sometimes worthwhile, for some purposes.

## PART IV

Remote Login Tools

One of Linux's features that differentiates it from Windows is that Linux has long supported remote logins. By using a remote login protocol, you can log into a Linux computer and run almost any program you could run if you were sitting at the Linux machine's console. The computer you use to access Linux could itself be running Linux, or it could be running Windows, Mac OS, or just about any other OS. This feature can be a tremendous boon in many environments, because it enables you to devote a small number of Linux systems to running important but seldom-used or resource non-intensive software that's not available for Windows. Users can then log into Linux from their Windows systems. As a system administrator, you can use this same feature to remotely administer a Linux system from a nearby office or from the other side of the world. Although Linux leads Windows in the area of remote logins, remote access servers are also available for Windows, so you can use these tools to access a Windows system from another computer, too.

Chapters 10 and 11 describe two broad classes of remote login protocols: those that work only in text mode and those that handle GUI accesses. The emphasis in these chapters is on accessing Linux systems, but both also describe some Windows remote-access tools. The third chapter of this part, Chapter 12, describes a way to stretch your hardware dollars or extend the life of old computers, by turning them into dedicated remote login clients, or *thin clients* as they've come to be known. Linux can function as a thin client OS or as a remote server accessed by thin clients.

## CHAPTER 10

Remote Text-Mode Administration and Use

The simplest form of remote login access is text-mode access, in which only textual data and a few simple control codes are exchanged between computers. Text-mode access is ideal for running text-mode programs, and it has the added advantage of consuming little in the way of network bandwidth, which makes it suitable to use across slow network links, such as dial-up Internet connections. This type of access can be very handy for administering a Linux system; Linux can be configured entirely using text-mode tools, so text-mode login methods can be a good way to do the job remotely. Perhaps your servers are scattered about the building (say, print servers located near the printers they manage) and you need to make changes without running around. Perhaps you need to log in over a dial-up line or even from a PDA while on the road. In such cases, remote administration is critical, and the ability to do the job without a lot of flashy (and bandwidth-intensive) GUI overhead can help you get the job done quickly. Remote text-mode access can also be useful for running many nonadministrative programs, although most ordinary users are more comfortable with GUI tools.

This chapter begins with a look at the principles behind text-mode logins—tools for implementing it and why you might want to use it. This chapter then looks at two common protocols for implementing remote text-mode access, Telnet and the SSH, with a focus on Linux configuration. This chapter concludes with information on Windows tools for handling remote text-mode access, including both clients and servers.

What Can Text-Mode Logins Do?

In today's world of POP email, the World Wide Web, file shares that are virtually indistinguishable from hard drives (from a user's perspective), and so on, text-mode login protocols may seem quaint at first. Nonetheless, these tools still have life left in them, at least in some environments. Text-mode user access can still be a useful way to enable users to get work done, and such access is particularly helpful for remote administration of Linux systems, which can typically be administered entirely using text-mode tools. Assuming you've decided that text-mode logins are worth implementing, you should know a bit about the most common protocols so that you can pick the one that's right for your needs.

Remote Text-Mode User Access

Most Linux users today run GUI programs using the X Window System (or X for short). This wasn't always the case, though. In Linux's early years, most programs were text mode. Some of these programs were quite powerful, having been inherited from earlier Unix systems. Many of these programs have been maintained over the years and can still be useful tools for remote text-mode users. Indeed, even users who run X often make heavy use of text-mode tools, running them in *xterm* or similar command-line windows under X.

 Many text-mode user programs are also useful, or even required, for administrative functions.

What, then, are these programs? Examples of some of the more notable programs and classes of programs include:

Text editors
> Text-only text editors for Linux are plentiful and include such stripped-down tools as *vi*, *jed*, and *nano*, as well as much more powerful programs such as Emacs.

Document processing
> Word processing as we know it today is usually implemented in GUI programs, but you can create, edit, and print documents using a text editor and a text-mode document processing system such as LaTeX. Indeed, some people prefer using such tools to using the more popular word processors. Even for word-processor fans, a few are available in text mode, although they tend to be old. The commercial WordPerfect for Linux, although best-known as a GUI program, had a text-mode variant, for instance.

Office tools
> In addition to word processing, other traditional office tools are available in text-only versions. For instance, the SC and SS spreadsheets run entirely in text mode. Even some graphics programs run in text mode, but typically just to convert between file formats and the like.

Development tools
> Most Linux compilers are, first and foremost, text-mode tools. Although GUI frontends are available, the GNU Compiler Collection (GCC) and many other development tools run just fine from text-mode logins.

Network tools

Most network protocols have text-mode clients available. A Linux system can function as a limited door onto the Internet for a network that's otherwise restricted in access; users can log into a Linux system and run mail clients such as Pine and Mutt, FTP clients such as *ftp*, and even web browsers such as *lynx*.

Overall, most tasks that Linux can accomplish using GUI tools can also be accomplished in text mode. The main exception is graphics-intensive tasks like bitmap graphics editing.

Why, though, would users want to restrict themselves to text mode? Sometimes the text-based tools simply are the best available, at least for particular users. For instance, a user who's accustomed to creating documents in LaTeX and who doesn't need or want the GUI add-ons might be quite happy to do so from a remote system using a text-mode login protocol. In many cases, though, the question boils down to one of available bandwidth, and hence speed. Text-mode access tools are quite zippy on modern networks, and they're even tolerable on 56-Kbps dial-up connections. GUI access tools, by contrast, are bandwidth hogs. They may work reasonably well on fast and unsaturated local network connections, but over slow links or when the local network is under heavy load, GUI tools can become intolerably slow. Thus, one common reason to use text-mode tools is to make remote use of a Linux system tolerable over slow or heavily loaded network links. For instance, you might give users who travel frequently remote login access to a Linux box, from which they can access your network's files, read email, and so on. To be sure, using other protocols directly from the remote systems might be an equally good or even superior solution in many cases, but using the remote login protocol can help simplify matters and may help security, particularly if you use a protocol that incorporates encryption.

Another reason to implement text-mode login tools is to provide a necessary "foot in the door" for running GUI login tools. In particular, some methods of running X remotely or starting a VNC session require that users have text-mode access to the Linux system. This issue is covered in more detail in Chapter 11.

Remote Text-Mode Administration

A second broad class of reasons to use text-mode login tools is to enable remote administration of a Linux computer. All major Linux distributions are built around configuration files that you can edit with a text editor, so administering them via a text-mode login is almost always an option. Even when distributions provide GUI administrative tools, they also often supply text-based equivalents. For instance, SuSE's YaST2 GUI tool has a text-based counterpart in YaST, and most of Red Hat's and Fedora's small administrative applications come in both GUI and text-based versions. Remote administration has many more specific types of application:

Headless servers

You can run a server computer without a monitor, and sometimes even without a keyboard, as a way to save space and money. Such systems *must* be administered remotely, although you may have a choice of text-based, GUI, web-based, or perhaps other methods of remote administration.

Side-by-side comparisons

Sometimes it's helpful to have access to two systems' configurations on one screen. You can open a pair of *xterm* windows in a GUI window, use a text-mode access protocol to log into one system from another, and compare the systems' configurations in the two windows. This can be a handy approach even if the two computers are just a few feet apart.

Administering desktop systems or widely separated servers

If your site uses Linux desktop systems, remote administration of those systems can be a real time-saver. Rather than run around your site to investigate problems, you can log into computers remotely and run text-based diagnostic commands. The same approach is helpful if you've got multiple server computers in different locations.

Inaccessible servers

Sometimes a computer must be located in a physically inaccessible location. A common example is a colocated web server, which is housed at an Internet Service Provider's (ISP) office to gain access to that ISP's high-speed Internet connection. Systems housed at branch offices, used for automated remote data collection, and so on also qualify in this category.

Emergency situations

If you're at home or on vacation when a dire problem occurs on a Linux system at work, you may be able to use a remote text-mode protocol to quickly fix the problem. Of course, chances are you won't like getting the call during your off hours, but being able to fix the problem remotely beats having to go in to work on your day off!

Telecommuting

Just as ordinary users can telecommute with the help of remote access tools, you may be able to do the same with your system administration duties.

Text-mode access protocols are arguably more appealing for remote system administration than for ordinary work. Because of Linux's text-based heritage, administrative tools are exceptionally well represented in text-based versions. Also, many Linux system administrators are as or more comfortable with text-based tools than with GUI tools. The same bandwidth and speed issues apply to remote system administration as apply to remote end user access.

Tools for Remote Text-Mode Access

If you've decided you want to implement remote text-mode access, your next decision is how to do it. Two protocols, Telnet and SSH, dominate remote access today. Other tools are available to do the job, though, and in some cases they're appropriate. Overall, the most common tools are:

Telnet

This is one of the oldest protocols in common use, and also one of the simplest. It basically sets up a two-way text link, in which the characters you type are passed over the network to the remote system, and remote program responses are relayed to your screen. Basic Telnet supports very little in the way of encryption or other complications to this simple model. This simplicity is Telnet's major flaw; without encryption, data passed over a Telnet session can easily be sniffed by computer miscreants on your network or on intervening networks if the client and server aren't on a single network.

Kerberized Telnet

The Telnet clients and servers that ship with Kerberos implementations support data encryption, although the encryption features aren't always implemented automatically. If your network already uses Kerberos, switching to Kerberized Telnet makes sense and can provide much-needed encryption to these sessions. Chapter 9 covers Kerberos and its version of Telnet.

rlogin

The *rlogin* protocol, named after its client command, is an extremely simple remote access tool. It provides no-password access from an account on one system to a like-named account on another system. This security model is, by modern standards, appallingly lax, so *rlogin* is almost never used today. (A Kerberized variant is much better in this respect, though.)

rsh

A variant of *rlogin*, this command enables you to run a single program from a remote computer on your local computer. Like *rlogin*, its security is poor, so it should almost never be used.

SSH

SSH may be the most popular remote text-mode access tool in use, having displaced Telnet as the tool of choice. SSH's most important advantage over Telnet is that it supports encryption, making the protocol a much safer choice than Telnet. SSH also supports tunneling non-SSH protocols (including X sessions), file copying (via the *scp* command), and the ability to replace *rsh*'s functionality.

RS-232 serial connections

This tool isn't a network protocol; instead, it's a method of physically connecting two computers. In days of old, mainframe computers served a collection of potentially dozens of *dumb terminals*, which were connected to the mainframe via RS-232 serial connections, or something similar. Linux can work in the same way, which can give two users access to one computer if you've got an old dumb terminal or if you run a *terminal emulator* on another computer (even an extremely old one). RS-232 connections are usually fairly secure because they're direct physical connections without intervening networks. They're inflexible, though; you can't easily use them to connect to a server from other arbitrary systems.

This chapter emphasizes the Telnet and SSH servers because they're very popular. Kerberized Telnet is described briefly in Chapter 9.

 You should *never* use Telnet or any other unencrypted remote access tool to transfer sensitive data. (Remember that data travels both ways; for instance, your password is retrievable from a Telnet login session even though it's not echoed back to your screen.) Although this chapter describes Telnet for the sake of completeness, I don't recommend using it unless you absolutely can't use SSH for some reason. This caution applies even more strongly to use of Telnet for remote system administration, which necessarily involves transferring the highly sensitive *root* password.

SSH Server Configuration

In most cases, SSH is the preferred remote text-mode access method; this protocol implements security at its core, and it's become almost as widely available as Telnet. SSH is, though, a much more complex protocol, and its server program implementations reflect this fact. Configuring and running an SSH server is therefore a more complex task than configuring and running a Telnet server, although the default SSH server configurations for most Linux distributions require little work to get running.

SSH Server Options for Linux

If you want to use SSH, you must first decide which of several SSH server packages to use:

SSH Tectia
    SSH was developed by a company called SSH Communications Security (*http:// www.ssh.com*), which sells its commercial SSH server under the name *SSH Tectia*. (Versions prior to 4.0 used the name *SSH* alone.)

OpenSSH
    This may be the most popular SSH server in Linux. It was originally developed in association with OpenBSD, but most Linux distributions include it under the package name *openssh* or something similar. Its official web site is *http://www. openssh.org*, and it's distributed under the BSD license.

FreSSH
    This server, headquartered at *http://www.fressh.org*, is an independent SSH implementation that's distributed under the BSD license.

lsh

> For GPL fans, *lsh* is an SSH implementation under that license. You can learn more at *http://www.lysator.liu.se/~nisse/lsh/*.

Any of these servers should work well and interoperate with common SSH client programs, but their configuration details differ. This chapter describes OpenSSH configuration, which is similar to SSH Tectia in its configuration file locations and formats. If you elect to use FreSSH or *lsh*, you need to consult your server's documentation. If you need more information on SSH than is in this chapter, consult the package's manpages or a book on the subject, such as *SSH, The Secure Shell: The Definitive Guide* (O'Reilly).

 SSH has seen protocol version changes over time. As I write, SSH Version 2 is the latest major protocol release in widespread use. Older systems may require use of SSH Version 1, but its use isn't recommended. Major SSH servers should support both protocols, but configuration options are available to disable one or the other version.

Configuring an SSH Server

Once you've installed your SSH server package, you should look for its configuration file: */etc/ssh/sshd_config*. Do not confuse this file with the configuration file for your SSH *client* program, */etc/ssh/ssh_config*. This one-character difference in filenames can lead to a great deal of confusion if you don't notice it.

The OpenSSH configuration file format is fairly straightforward: non-comment lines begin with a keyword and end with an argument. Comment lines are denoted by a leading hash mark (#). For the most part, the default SSH configuration should work reasonably well for most installations; however, you might want to look through the file to be sure everything's set reasonably. Pay particular attention to these options:

AllowTcpForwarding

> This option defaults to yes, which tells the server it may forward connections to ports specified by the client. This is a useful feature if you want to use SSH to tunnel other protocols. Disabling it might seem to be one way to improve security, but if users have shell access, they can install their own port forwarders, so disabling this feature isn't likely to provide any significant security benefit.

AllowUsers

> You can provide a list of users who are given access by using this option. This may be a handy security tool if only some users should have remote access. (A similar option for groups is called AllowGroups.)

Banner

> If you pass a filename to this option, OpenSSH displays its contents to the client before authenticating the user.

Compression

This option takes a yes or no argument, which tells the server whether to accept a client request to compress data transfers. The default value is yes, which is usually desirable; however, if your server has a weak CPU, you might want to set this value to no.

DenyUsers

This option is the opposite of `AllowUsers`; you can blacklist specific users by listing them as arguments. A similar option for groups is `DenyGroups`.

GatewayPorts

This option defaults to no, which causes remote port forwardings to bind only to the loopback address (127.0.0.1). For some tunneling applications, though, these forwards should bind to all local network addresses, which requires this option to be set to yes.

KerberosAuthentication

If set to yes, this option tells SSH to try to validate a user's password with the help of a Kerberos server. The default value is no.

ListenAddress

This option takes a hostname or IP address, optionally followed by a colon and a port number (as in 192.168.1.7 or 192.168.1.7:22) to specify the network hardware to which the server should bind. If this option is not specified, SSH binds to all network interfaces. To bind to multiple interfaces but not to all of them, you can provide multiple `ListenAddress` lines.

LogLevel

This option determines how much information the server logs. Possible values, in increasing log level, are QUIET, FATAL, ERROR, INFO, VERBOSE, DEBUG, DEBUG1, DEBUG2, and DEBUG3, with the default being INFO.

PasswordAuthentication

This option, which defaults to yes, determines whether the system should accept passwords for authentication.

PermitRootLogin

This option tells SSH whether and under what circumstances to accept direct *root* logins. The default value is yes, but you may want to set this option to no to reduce the risk of abuse. (You can still log in as a normal user and run *su*, *sudo*, or other tools to administer a Linux system.) Intermediate values are without-password, which disables password-based authentication in favor of public key authentication, and forced-commands-only, which disables *root* logins but permits public key authentication only for running specific commands. That can be handy for enabling remote backups or other tasks that require running specific programs as *root*.

Protocol

> You can tell SSH which protocol levels to support by passing their numbers. If you want to support both Versions 1 and 2, you must separate the numbers with a comma, as in 2,1. Order is unimportant; protocol preference is set by the client.

PubkeyAuthentication

> This option takes a yes or no value and defaults to yes. It determines whether the server accepts public key authentication. This option affects SSH Version 2 only.

RSAAuthentication

> This option is similar to PubkeyAuthentication, but if affects protocol Version 1 only. (SSH protocol Versions 1 and 2 require different public key file formats.)

UseDNS

> If set to yes (the default), this option causes the server to look up a client's hostname using its IP address and then look up the IP address from that hostname and check that it matches the IP address the client uses. This improves security because it makes it harder for an attacker to pretend to be an authorized client, however, this option can also cause problems if your DNS configuration is broken or slow.

UsePAM

> This option defaults to no, but you may need to change it to yes if you want to use an NT domain controller, LDAP server, or other advanced authentication tools, as described in Appendix A. If you do this, the documentation recommends also setting PasswordAuthentication to no.

X11Forwarding

> This option, which defaults to no, tells SSH not to forward X traffic. This configuration helps protect the client's X server from attack; however, to use SSH as part of a remote X access method, as described in Chapter 11, you must change this option to yes.

SSH in general, and the OpenSSH server implementation in particular, is complex enough that this list is incomplete. If you need to perform more advanced tasks, you may need to consult the relevant documentation.

Launching an SSH Server

You can launch an SSH server using a super server, much as you launch a Telnet server; however, SSH is slower to start up than is Telnet, so the more common approach is to start SSH using a SysV or local startup script. Most Linux SSH packages include such a script, typically called *ssh* or *sshd* and stored in */etc/init.d* or */etc/rc.d/init.d*. To start or stop the SSH server on a one-time basis, pass the start or stop option to the SysV startup script, and most distributions respond with some sort of status report:

```
# /etc/init.d/sshd start
 * Starting sshd...                      [ ok ]
```

Most distributions provide a tool called *chkconfig* to manage which servers start in common runlevels; to tell your system to start the SSH server, type a command such as **chkconfig --add sshd**. Consult distribution-specific documentation if this command doesn't work or if you need to perform other special tasks. Instead of *chkconfig*, Gentoo Linux uses *rc-update*; you'd type **rc-update add sshd default** to add the SSH server to the default runlevel.

Once the server is running, you should be able to access it from another computer:

```
$ ssh linnaeus@mandragora.pangaea.edu
Password:
Last login: Mon Dec 27 11:24:40 2004 from pointer.example.com
Have a lot of fun...
linnaeus@mandragora:~>
```

This example uses the *username@hostname* form of address to specify both the username and the server's hostname. In many cases, you can omit the *username@* part, though; Linux's *ssh* clients use your current username if you don't specify one. To execute a single command rather than log into the remote system, specify the command after the other options, as in **ssh root@mandragora.pangaea.edu shutdown now -r** to shut down and reboot the remote computer. (Note that this particular example requires that direct *root* access be enabled.)

Telnet Server Configuration

As one of the oldest and most popular remote text-mode login tools available, Telnet is an excellent choice for compatibility—just about every OS with a TCP/IP stack comes with a Telnet client, so using a Telnet server under Linux makes your system accessible from just about everywhere. Telnet's unencrypted nature, though, is a major drawback. Thus, you should use Telnet only when you have no other choice (say, because of limited client OS software options) or on highly protected local networks.

Telnet servers are simple and easy to configure in Linux; the worst complication is knowing whether you're using the *inetd* or *xinetd* super server. Although Telnet's security features are severely lacking, you may be able to improve matters using a Kerberized Telnet or by implementing limited access controls in your super server.

Launching a Telnet Server

All major Linux distributions ship with a Telnet server, although many don't install it by default. Likely package names include *telnetd*, *telnet-server*, *netkit-telnetd*, *telnet-bsd*, and *utelnetd*, among others. (Kerberized or other encrypting variants are also available.) The server program itself is usually called *telnetd* or *in.telnetd*, and is usually stored in */sbin* or */usr/sbin*. Although Telnet servers come from several different sources, basic configuration and use is fairly consistent.

Typically, Telnet servers are launched from super servers—usually *inetd* or *xinetd*. If you're not sure which super server your system runs, type **ps ax | grep inetd** and examine the output for a process called *inetd* or *xinetd*. If neither is present, you may need to install, or at least launch, your distribution's super server package.

The *inetd* super server is controlled through the */etc/inetd.conf* file, which devotes one line to each server it manages. A typical Telnet server configuration looks something like this:

```
telnet stream tcp nowait root /usr/sbin/tcpd in.telnetd
```

This example calls the server via the TCP Wrappers (*tcpd*) program, which provides added security options. An equivalent configuration for a system that uses *xinetd* doesn't use TCP Wrappers because *xinetd* incorporates features similar to those provided by TCP Wrappers. Linux distributions that use *xinetd* typically place configurations for individual servers in files located in */etc/xinetd.d*; the Telnet server's file (typically called *telnet* or *telnetd*) looks like this:

```
service telnet
{
    disable      = no
    socket_type  = stream
    protocol     = tcp
    wait         = no
    user         = root
    group        = root
    server       = /usr/sbin/in.telnetd
    server_args  =
}
```

Many systems disable Telnet by default in the super server configuration files. In the case of *inetd*, the line defining the Telnet server is commented out by placing a hash mark (#) at the start of the line. To use Telnet, you must remove that character. In *xinetd*, the disable = yes option disables the server; this line must be changed to read disable = no to activate the server.

Whether you launch the server via *inetd* or *xinetd*, you can add a few options that modify the server's behavior. In the case of *inetd*, you place these options at the end of the Telnet server's configuration line; for *xinetd*, you place them on the server_args line, which you may need to add to the configuration file. Some of the more common and useful Telnet server options include:

-h Telnet normally sends a *banner* to clients, announcing some basic information about the system, which is likely to include your distribution and kernel version number. The -h option disables the display of this banner.

-U This option causes the server to block connections from computers whose IP addresses can't be resolved to hostnames. This can slightly improve your security if you're certain that all legitimate clients should have hostnames that can be obtained from their IP addresses.

-L *program-file*

Ordinarily, Telnet calls the standard Linux *login* program to authenticate users. This option enables you to substitute another program, which might be handy if you have special authentication needs or want to use Telnet for some specialized non-login purpose. For example, you can have the server launch a specialized network diagnostic tool rather than give users conventional login access.

This list of options isn't complete, and, in fact, the options may vary from one Telnet server to another, so you may want to consult your local documentation for details on other options. Many installations work well with no Telnet server options, but to improve security slightly, you might want to use -h and, if it won't cause problems for legitimate users, -U.

Once you've finished configuring your super server, you must restart the super server or force it to reload its configuration. In most cases, passing the restart or reload option to your super server's SysV startup script will do the trick:

```
# /etc/init.d/xinetd reload
```

Thereafter, the system should be accessible via Telnet. If you have problems logging in, consult the server's log files; chances are the super server or the Telnet server will log error messages concerning login failures or an inability to launch the Telnet server.

Telnet Server Security Concerns

As you may be tired of hearing by now, Telnet's main flaw is its lack of security features—in particular, its lack of encryption. This limitation has implications you should understand, but there are also ways to add encryption. Another security concern with any remote-access protocol is controlling the computers that can connect to the server. Because Telnet is typically run from a super server, you can use its features, or those of tools that the super server calls, to control remote access.

Encryption

The basic Telnet provides no encryption features. This means that all data transferred between the client and the server (in *both* directions) is unencrypted. This flaw is most important for passwords—although you don't see your password echoed on the screen, it can be easily retrieved should your Telnet session be intercepted. This risk is very serious for ordinary user accounts and completely unacceptable for *root* logins.

Because of the risks of password interception, most Linux distributions configure themselves to forbid direct *root* logins via Telnet.

Even if login password interception isn't an issue, Telnet's unencrypted nature can be a problem during login sessions. If you read a sensitive email in a Telnet session, use *su* to acquire *root* privileges, or use SSH from your Telnet session to another computer, you'll be sending sensitive data in the clear.

Various methods of adding encryption to Telnet have been developed. Typically, the Telnet protocol is extended with an encryption layer. The Kerberized version of Telnet, described in Chapter 9, is one somewhat common example. Another approach is to encrypt Telnet traffic with the Secure Sockets Layer (SSL) library. The result is packaged with some distributions as *telnet-ssl* or a similar variant. A third approach is to *tunnel* Telnet through an encrypting protocol, such as SSH. The disadvantage to all of these approaches is that it requires extra software on both the client and the server, and this software is not as common as is Telnet. In fact, with the SSH tunneling approach, chances are you wouldn't need to use Telnet at all, because SSH is a perfectly good text-mode login tool in its own right.

Controlling access by IP address

Because of Telnet's poor security, if you use it you should employ your super server's or firewall's access control tools to limit who may access the server. For instance, you might want to restrict access to the server to computers on your own local subnet, or perhaps even to just those computers that absolutely need to use Telnet.

In *xinetd*, which is fast becoming the most common Linux super server, you can limit remote access by adding options to a server's control file in */etc/xinetd.d*:

only_from

> This option sets a list of hostnames, IP addresses, or address/netmask pairs that are permitted to access the server. All other computers are denied access.

no_access

> This option takes addresses much like only_from, but it specifies systems that should *not* be given access. For Telnet, only_from is likely to be the more useful tool, but you might use no_access to create exceptions to a range of addresses granted access with only_from.

bind

> This option tells the server to bind to one interface only. This feature is most useful on routers and other computers with multiple network interfaces; you can bind Telnet to a secure local interface but not to the interface that's accessible from the Internet. You might also use it to bind exclusively to the localhost (127.0.0.1) interface or to an interface that's used by an emulator, to enable the emulated OS

to contact Linux. This parameter takes the IP address of the interface to which you want to bind as an option.

access_times

This option controls access by time rather than by IP address; you specify a time range in the form *hh:mm-hh:mm*, where each *hh* is an hour in 24-hour format (between 00 and 23) and *mm* is the minute.

As an example, you might use the `bind` and `only_from` parameters to restrict access to computers on the 192.168.7.0/24 network, if the computer in question has the address 192.168.7.27:

```
bind      = 192.168.7.27
only_from = 192.168.7.0/24
```

 Depending on the network settings, the `bind` and `only_from` settings may seem redundant; however, they actually perform slightly different tasks. The `bind` option binds to a physical network card, so if a computer's traffic is being routed in an unusual way or if it's spoofing an address, `bind` won't be fooled. In this context, `only_from` might be redundant, or it might not, if traffic from other networks should be arriving on that port. In any event, layered security, in which multiple checks of the same basic restriction are performed, can help improve a system's overall security.

Windows Remote-Login Tools

If Windows systems are to interact with Linux systems via text-mode tools, you must locate matching Windows clients to Linux servers or locate Windows servers for Linux clients. The first task is considerably easier and likely to be more productive than the second; although text-mode Windows login servers do exist, they aren't nearly as useful as Linux remote text-mode login servers because Windows was never designed with this sort of operation in mind.

Locating Client Software

Windows client software for both Telnet and SSH protocols is fairly easy to find. In fact, all versions of Windows that support TCP/IP networking ship with a Telnet client. Type **TELNET** in a DOS prompt window or select the Telnet item from the Start menu to launch this client.

If you're not satisfied with the features of the standard Windows Telnet server or if you want to use SSH to access your Linux system, you'll need to look elsewhere. One excellent resource is the Free SSH web site's Windows page, *http://freessh.org/windows.html*, which lists Windows SSH clients and servers, of both the free and the pay variety. Many of these SSH clients can also handle Telnet and other protocols, so they're well worth investigating.

As an example of a Windows text-mode login client, consider PuTTY (*http://www. chiark.greenend.org.uk/~sgtatham/putty/*). This program can handle *rlogin*, Telnet, and SSH protocols. When you first launch it, you'll see a PuTTY Configuration dialog box, as shown in Figure 10-1. To open a basic SSH session, type the hostname or IP address of the server in the Host Name (or IP Address) field, check that the Protocol item is set to SSH, and then click Open. The first time you connect, the system will notify you that the server's host key is not cached. This is normal for an initial connection, so click Yes to accept the key. The system will then prompt you for a username and password in the access window and, if you enter them correctly, you'll be in and able to use the remote system.

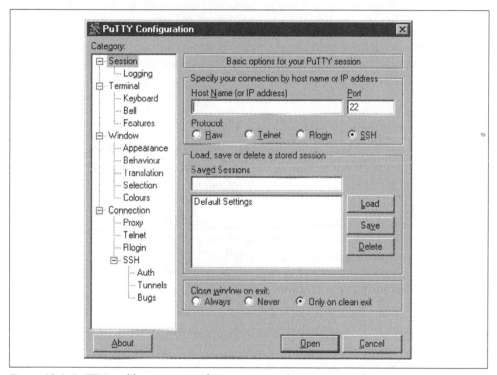

Figure 10-1. PuTTY enables you to specify many options for your remote login sessions

For more advanced uses, you can adjust various options by clicking their categories in the list in the Category field of the PuTTY Configuration dialog box. If you regularly use particular settings (including connections to specific servers), you can make the adjustments you want, type a session name in the Saved Sessions field, and click Save to save your settings. Thereafter, double-clicking on the session name launches a session with those settings.

Windows Telnet and SSH Servers

Windows, unlike Linux, was not designed with remote text-mode use in mind. Although Windows has DOS—a text-mode OS—in its history, Windows simply never embraced the notion of remote text-mode access in the way Linux has. Furthermore, Windows is tied more tightly to its GUI for both common user programs and system administration than is Linux, so using it from a text-mode login will tie your hands in terms of the tasks you can accomplish.

These caveats aside, remote text-mode access tools for Windows *are* available. Because these tools are of limited utility, I don't describe them in great detail, but they do deserve a few pointers. A few of the available servers include:

Cygwin OpenSSH
> The Cygwin package includes an OpenSSH server, whose setup and basic operation is documented at *http://tech.erdelynet.com/cygwin-sshd.html*. This configuration provides access to a Windows system using the Cygwin environment, which resembles a Unix environment but enables you to run many text-mode DOS and Windows programs.

OpenSSH for Windows
> This package borrows from Cygwin but doesn't install a full Cygwin environment. As a result, when you log into the server, you'll see a DOS-style C:\> prompt. You can learn more at *http://sshwindows.sourceforge.net/*.

Georgia Softworks Telnet and SSH
> Georgia Softworks (*http://www.georgiasoftworks.com*) sells a commercial Telnet server for Windows and a commercial SSH server for Windows. These packages provide unusually good terminal emulation; that is, they do a better job than most at enabling you to run text-mode programs that require extensive cursor control, such as text-mode editors.

As noted earlier, the Free SSH site's Windows page (*http://freessh.org/windows.html*) provides pointers to Windows SSH servers as well as SSH clients, so you can consult it for links to more servers. As a general rule, the free offerings are scarce, but several commercial products are available.

One of the difficulties in using a text-mode Windows remote-access tool manifests itself when you try to run programs that move the cursor around the screen in an arbitrary way, such as text editors. Under Linux, a set of libraries between programs and the screen display handle the translation for any number of display types—a text-mode console, an *xterm* window, a remote Telnet session, and so on. (In fact, some Windows Telnet and SSH clients provide options that influence how they interact with these libraries by changing their *terminal emulation* mode, which can improve their ability to handle features such as colored text.) Windows lacks these libraries, so the remote-access server must either implement these translations themselves or ignore the issue. The former is a difficult task, so many servers ignore the issue. The result is an inability to run text-mode programs that do more than display text in a simple linear fashion. For instance, typing **EDIT** in an OpenSSH for Windows session effectively hangs the session.

Despite these limitations, text-mode login tools for Windows can be handy in some situations; you can run simple tools and scripts that don't rely on GUI components or the more advanced text-mode features. If you have a specific use in mind for the access, you might be able to track down or write a program to do a job, thus saving considerable bandwidth (and, hence, time) that might otherwise be required to use a GUI login tool. You can also use an SSH server as a way to establish encrypted connections to other servers running on the Windows machine, by using SSH's port-forwarding capabilities.

Summary

Remote text-mode logins have been around for a long time, and they remain useful tools, particularly for accessing Linux systems. Ordinary users can use text-mode logins to perform various tasks, but they may be more important as remote administrative tools, enabling you to handle tasks at a distance that would otherwise be tedious or require your physical presence. Telnet has long been a popular remote login protocol, but SSH has eclipsed it, at least in security-conscious circles, because of SSH's support for encryption. Although Telnet variants with encryption are available, they're harder to find than SSH. For the most part, remote text-mode access tools are best used to access Linux from clients that can run just about any OS, but text-mode login servers for Windows are also available. These tools are much more limited in their utility, however, because of the more GUI-centric nature of Windows user programs and system administration tools.

CHAPTER 11

Running GUI Programs Remotely

Text-mode logins, as described in Chapter 10, can be handy tools for using or administering a Linux system remotely; however, they're rather limited. Many programs—particularly user-friendly tools to perform common tasks such as word processing—require the use of a graphical user interface (GUI). Such tools can't be used via a text-mode login alone, although as this chapter describes, using such a tool can be *part* of an overall remote GUI access plan. If you want to run GUI word processors, web browsers, graphics editors, and other programs remotely, you must use remote GUI access tools. These tools are most important as user access tools because most users today expect GUI environments. They can help provide relatively seamless access to multiple systems from a single keyboard and screen, or they can be part of a thin client configuration, as described in Chapter 12. Remote GUI access can also be used for system administration, either to run GUI administration frontends or to run text-mode programs in *xterm* or similar windows. (In the latter case, though, a simpler solution is usually to access the system via a text-mode login protocol.)

The features, requirements, and potential uses of GUI login tools are somewhat different from those of text-mode login tools, so these factors require some explanation, and this chapter begins with this topic. This chapter then moves on to the traditional Linux remote access tool, the X Window System (or X for short), which Linux also uses to manage its local GUI display. Next up is information on a popular alternative, Virtual Network Computing (VNC), which can be used to access either Linux or Windows systems remotely.

What Can GUI Logins Do?

GUI logins can be used for the same broad classes of purposes as text-mode logins, as described in Chapter 10—to run user programs remotely or to administer the computer. Because GUI logins are, well, *GUI*, you can run a wider range of programs using them than you can with a text-mode program. This includes GUI word processors, graphics editors, web browsers, and more. Programs that work best when they can display arbitrary fonts and graphics will work best with (or even require) GUI login tools. Because Windows programs are more likely to require GUI access than are Linux programs, GUI login tools are particularly important if you want to run Windows remotely.

GUI login tools' advantages come at a price, though: increased network bandwidth consumption, which translates into lower speed. You can use a text-mode login tool quite comfortably over a dialup link or an overloaded local network, but a GUI tool used in the same environment might be painfully slow. Details do differ, though, depending on the tool and the programs you use.

Several GUI access protocols are available today. In the Linux world, X and the *Remote Frame Buffer* protocol (most commonly implemented by VNC) are the most popular remote-access tools, and these are the two tools that are described in this chapter. An interesting variant is the NoMachine (*http://www.nomachine.com*) NX Server and NX Client. The NX Server is built around X, while the NX client can connect to other systems using the NX, X, or RFB protocols, as well as protocols that are more common in the Windows world.

 Remote X access involves a lot of back-and-forth transfers, but X delivers some types of data using few bytes. VNC, by contrast, requires more bandwidth but fewer transactions. Thus, X is likely to perform best on low-latency connections, whereas VNC performs best on high-bandwidth connections. Tunneling, encryption, compression, and other options can influence both protocols' performance, though. If speed is a problem, you may need to experiment with both protocols.

Both X and VNC are a bit odd as network protocols go, but in different ways. X reverses the usual client/server relationship, as described in the next section. VNC is frequently run as a user process rather than as a conventional all-users server, as described in the section "Configuring a Linux VNC Server." Both oddities have implications for how you use the protocols. At their simplest, they require users to log in using a text-mode protocol before a direct GUI connection can be made. Ways to eliminate this requirement exist for both protocols, but these require extra configuration, which can be intimidating to those unfamiliar with the tasks at hand.

Unfortunately, neither X nor VNC encrypts data by default, so both protocols, by themselves, are risky ways to access a computer. (VNC does encrypt initial password exchanges, though.) One common solution to this problem is to use the SSH protocol to *tunnel* the GUI protocol—that is, to use an SSH connection as a carrier for the GUI connection, thus encrypting the GUI traffic. Alternatively, you can use a full-fledged virtual private network (VPN) to encrypt traffic. Precisely how to handle such encryption schemes is different for X and VNC, though.

Using Remote X Access

X is Linux's native GUI system, but unlike the Windows or Mac OS GUIs, X was designed with network access in mind; user programs communicate with the X server using network protocols, even when the computer isn't connected to a network. This feature makes remote X access easy—at least, in theory. In practice, you must still select an X server (if you're using a non-Linux/Unix system to access your Linux computer) and know enough about X to initiate the connection. In fact, several methods of initiating that connection exist, and some require special configuration. Most notably, you may want to configure a remote X login server, which is separate from the X server itself, to accept logins. Finally, using X in a Windows/Linux environment presents its own unique challenges.

The X Client/Server Model

One unusual detail about using X is the way the client and server roles are assigned. Many people think of servers as powerful computers (or the programs they run) that sit in machine rooms away from users, and clients as being computers (or the programs they run) at which individual users sit. Although this description is often true, it's not actually a definition of what makes a client a client or a server a server; rather, clients initiate network transfers and servers respond to those requests. In the case of X, the client is the computer or program that does data processing (a word processor, for instance), and the server is the computer or program that provides human input/output for the client. In other words, X reverses the usual configuration; users sit at X server computers and use them to run programs on X client computers. To make sense of this arrangement, think of it from the application program's point of view. To an X-based word processor, the keyboard and screen are just I/O devices, like a network file share or a network printer. The application program initiates contact with the keyboard and screen (via the X server) in order to do its work. The fact that a human sits at the X server computer is unimportant.

 Because application programs are the X clients, X can't, by itself, be used as a tool for accessing Windows systems remotely. Most Windows programs aren't written as X clients but instead use calls to the Windows GUI environment. Some exceptions to this rule do exist, but they're mostly ports of Unix programs to Windows. Overall, X is a useful tool for running Unix or Linux programs from another computer, which can run Unix, Linux, Mac OS, Windows, or various other operating systems.

When using a single Linux computer, this unusual relationship seldom causes a problem; after all, the client and server computers in this case are one and the same. In network arrangements, though, the odd relationship can become confusing. For instance, to use a Linux computer from a Windows computer, you must obtain an X

---

server for *Windows*. More importantly, the fact that the client (on the remote computer) initiates the connection with the server (on the user's local computer) complicates matters. Specifically, the user on the server computer needs a way to signal the client program to begin running and to contact the X server. You can accomplish this task several ways; for example, you can use a remote text-mode login tool or a protocol designed specifically for this purpose. These options are described later in this chapter.

The reversal of client/server roles can have implications on your overall network design. Specifically, many networks use firewalls or Network Address Translation (NAT) tools to isolate desktop systems from the outside world. Users of such systems can often use Telnet, SSH, or other text-mode protocols to reach outside servers, but these tools may need to be reconfigured to permit *incoming* connections to the X servers running on users' desktop computers. Precisely how to accomplish this task varies greatly from one firewall or router to another, so you'll have to consult its documentation (or your network administrator) for advice. X servers typically run on TCP/IP port 6000, though, so that's the one you'll have to unblock or forward appropriately.

X Server Options

If you want to use Linux as an X server for another Linux or Unix system, you'll probably use the standard X server that ships with your Linux distribution. Until 2004, this server was almost always XFree86 (*http://www.xfree86.org*), which as I write is at Version 4.4.0. The release of this version of the server also saw some subtle changes in the server's license, and many open source advocates became alarmed because they believed the changes would make distribution of XFree86 in typical Linux distributions difficult. For this reason, 2004 saw a mad rush of Linux distributions to locate another X server, and the easy winner in this contest has been X.org's X11 (*http://www.x.org/*). Its first real release, numbered 6.7.0, is a fork of the XFree86 3.3.99 code (the last version released under a license that Linux distribution maintainers found acceptable).

XFree86 and X.org-X11 aren't the only X servers for Linux. Xi Graphics' commercial Accelerated-X (*http://www.xig.com*) is also available. For the most part, there's little reason to use this server; however, you might find that it supports an exotic feature not supported by XFree86 or X.org-X11, or you might have a video card for which Accelerated-X provides superior support. Thus, if you have unusual needs or if your distribution's X server just doesn't seem to work very well, you might want to investigate Accelerated-X.

A trickier decision involves locating an X server for Windows. Quite a few exist, ranging from open source products to extremely expensive commercial offerings. A company that produces one of the lower-cost X servers maintains a list of options at *http://www.microimages.com/mix/prices.htm* but without direct links to its competitors. Here are some highlights:

XFree86
> This package, although primarily intended for Unix-like systems, has been ported to Windows. Check *http://x.cygwin.com* for details. This package, like many ports of Unix-like tools to Windows, is associated with the Cygwin project. One of XFree86's big advantages is that it's free.

MI/X
> MicroImage's MI/X (*http://www.microimages.com/mix/*) are the lowest-cost of the commercial X servers, at $25 per user, or less for site licenses. This server used to be quite spartan, but it's improved substantially over the past few versions.

Xmanager
> Netsarang's Xmanager (*http://www.netsarang.com/products/xmanager.html*) is a bit pricier than MI/X, but at $69 for a single-user license, it's still fairly inexpensive. In my experience, it works well with most Linux software.

X-Win32 and X-Win64
> Starnet produces a server called X-Win32 (*http://www.starnet.com/products/*), which sells for $225 in single-user quantities. A 64-bit version for 64-bit versions of Windows is also available, but at a higher price ($325). This server works well, in my experience.

Exceed
> Hummingbird's Exceed (*http://www.hcl.com/products/nc/exceed/*) is marketed for large enterprises; I've seen it used in universities and other large installations. No single-user price is available on the company's web site.

Generally speaking, as you move up the price scale, the number of features provided by the X server software also goes up. For instance, X-Win32 provides OpenGL support, which is missing from many lower-cost packages. XFree86 is an exception to this rule; it provides features comparable to or better than those of many of the lower-priced commercial X servers. In any event, if you plan to deploy Windows X servers widely or in any critical roles, you should probably evaluate at least two or three of them. Many publishers make evaluation versions of their X servers available at no cost, typically with a time-limited license, so you should be able to test several without making a huge monetary investment.

Initiating a Connection from a Text-Mode Login

As noted earlier, one of the challenges in using X is initiating the initial connection between the X client and the X server. One approach for doing this is to use a text-mode login protocol, such as Telnet or SSH, to initiate a connection from the user's desktop computer to a remote system, then use that text-mode connection to launch X programs. For instance, suppose you're sitting at the computer called *earth* and you want to run programs on *pluto*. If both systems run Linux or Unix, you can do so as follows:

1. Start an X server on *earth*. One may already be running, but if not, and if the X server is properly configured, typing **startx** from a text-mode login should accomplish this task.

2. Open an *xterm* or other command-prompt window on *earth*.

3. Configure the *earth*'s X server to accept connections from *pluto*. You can do this by typing **xhost +pluto**. This command tells the local X server to accept all connections from *pluto*.

4. Using Telnet, SSH, or some other remote-access protocol, log into *pluto*. For instance, you might type **ssh pluto**. Answer any login prompts you receive.

5. Using your remote login session, set the DISPLAY environment variable to point to your X server. This variable includes both the hostname and the X session number, which is the same as the X server's TCP/IP port number minus 6000— that is, it's usually 0. If you use *bash*, type **export DISPLAY=earth:0**.

6. Run X programs by typing their names; for instance, type **kmail** to launch the KMail program.

7. When you're done using remote programs, shut them all down and, in an *xterm* window that's not linked to *pluto*, type **xhost -pluto**. This command removes *pluto*'s right to access your local X server, reducing the odds that another user of *pluto* can wreak havoc with your display.

This procedure works well but is a bit tedious. You can take some steps to simplify matters, such as creating a script with a simple name or a command shell alias to simplify typing the awkward *xhost* commands and setting the DISPLAY variable. If you use SSH for the text-mode connection, you may also be able to simplify things by omitting Steps 3 and 5, and the *xhost* command in step 7. This process is described in more detail later, in the section "Encrypting X by SSH Tunneling."

 Do *not* set the DISPLAY variable in a startup script unless you always use the computer from the same X server. The DISPLAY variable is used even if you're accessing Linux locally, so setting it in a script that always executes may make it impossible for you to use X locally.

Windows X Server Concerns

The preceding procedure will work with Windows X servers; however, most of these servers have few or no access restrictions by default. Therefore, there's no need to type the *xhost* commands in Steps 3 and 7. Many Windows X servers also provide ways to combine several steps automatically, which enables you to click a link to log into a remote server and launch a program you specify (such as an *xterm*) automatically. For instance, Figure 11-1 shows the dialog box Xmanager displays when you launch it via its Xstart program. Enter the relevant login information, including the command you want to run, and click Run. Xmanager then executes a series of steps that have an effect similar to those described earlier. The default command for Xmanager is to launch an *xterm* window, using the -display option to have the *xterm* window, and all the programs you launch from it, run on your Windows X server.

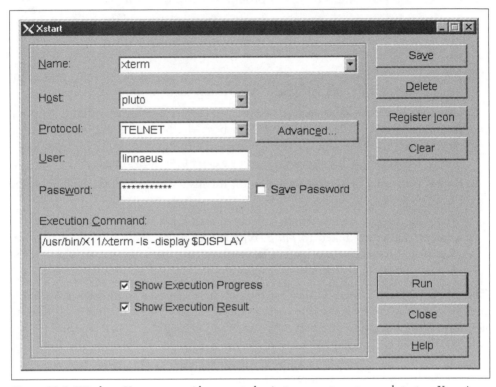

Figure 11-1. Windows X servers provide a way to log in to a remote system and start an X session

X servers can run in one of two basic modes: *rooted* or *rootless*. A rooted X server displays everything in its own window, as illustrated by Figure 11-2, which shows a rooted display on a Linux system running the XFce desktop environment with an *xterm* window and the KDE Control Panel running. This approach is useful if you want to run an entire Linux desktop environment remotely but don't want that environment to take over your local computer's desktop.

A rootless X server displays individual windows from remote applications side-by-side with local windows, as illustrated by Figure 11-3, which shows the same Linux and Windows programs as in Figure 11-2, with the exception of the XFce desktop environment programs. This approach may be easier to manage because you can place local and remote windows more flexibly. Note, for instance, that the KDE Control Panel is sized more comfortably in the rooted display, and local and remote

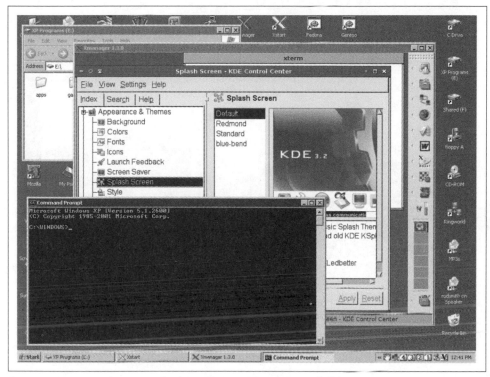

Figure 11-2. A rooted X server display contains an entire Linux desktop environment

programs can be layered any way you like. On the other hand, a rootless display requires you to launch programs via an *xterm* window or some other tool that doesn't take over the whole screen, because your Linux desktop environment can't run without interfering with your Windows desktop. Many Windows X servers let you choose to run in rooted or rootless mode, so check your documentation to learn how to select the one you want. Sometimes the programs use other terms, such as *single window* for rooted and *multiple window* for rootless displays.

If you use a rooted X server, you'll have to start a window manager or desktop environment as soon as you log in. You can start GNOME or KDE by typing **startgnome** or **startkde** in your initial *xterm* window. Slimmer window managers, such as IceWM or Blackbox, can also be started by typing their names. In fact, you might be able to launch your preferred window manager or desktop environment by providing its name to your X server's startup tool. Remember, however, to also set the DISPLAY environment variable or pass options to the desktop environment or window manager to have it access the correct display! (Consult your preferred environment's documentation to learn how to do this.)

Figure 11-3. A rootless display lets you freely intermix Linux and Windows programs but makes it awkward to run a Linux desktop environment

Simplifying Remote X Logins with XDMCP

One way to simplify the remote X login process is to use a program that implements the X Display Manager Control Protocol (XDMCP). This protocol is essentially a way for an X server to initiate a login connection with a remote computer, enabling an X server user to launch programs on a remote system. Three XDMCP programs are common in Linux: the original X Display Manager (XDM), the KDE Display Manager (KDM), and the GNOME Display Manager (GDM). Of these, XDM provides the fewest features, but all should work for remote logins.

XDMCP basics

One peculiarity of XDMCP is that it's used by default for local X logins as well as remote logins. All major Linux distributions run an XDMCP program whenever they're configured to boot directly into X. The default configuration, though, is to block external access requests. Thus, your task in configuring an XDMCP server is to figure out which one your system uses and reconfigure it to accept remote access, rather than install, configure, and start an entirely new server. (Of course, you can change which server you use by default, if you don't like your standard one.)

Tracking down the XDMCP server your distribution uses can be tricky. One way to start is to type **ps ax | grep [xkg]dm** after you've configured your system to boot into a GUI login mode. This command should return information on running *xdm*, *kdm*, or *gdm* processes, which will help you locate the correct configuration files.

Most Linux distributions start the XDMCP server when configured to run in a particular runlevel—typically runlevel 5. Thus, you can tell the system whether to run this server by changing your runlevel, as in **telinit 5**. A few distributions, such as Debian and Gentoo, don't use the runlevel to set the XDMCP server's running status; they use a SysV startup script that's active (or not active) in all runlevels, at least by default. You can locate this script and use normal SysV script handling tools to enable or disable your XDMCP server.

You also need to tell your system which XDMCP server to run. Unfortunately, there's no standardization on this point, although most distributions use a variable that's set in a configuration file. For instance, Red Hat, Fedora, and Mandrake use the */etc/sysconfig/desktop* file; Gentoo uses */etc/rc.conf*; and SuSE uses the */etc/sysconfig/displaymanager* file. In all these cases, you can change the default XDMCP server by setting the DISPLAYMANAGER variable. Depending on the distribution, you may need to set this variable to the name of the XDMCP server, as in KDM, or to the associated desktop environment name, as in KDE. Most distributions work with either notation, be sure to read any applicable comments in the configuration files.

Some distributions use another approach to setting the XDMCP server: they call the server directly in a startup script. Debian uses the */etc/X11/default-display-manager* file, and Slackware uses */etc/rc.d/rc.4*. In Debian, this file contains the complete path to your preferred XDMCP server program. The default Slackware script checks for the presence of several XDMCP servers in sequence and launches the first one it finds. To change the server your system launches, you must change the order of these checks or uninstall the servers you don't want to use.

Configuring XDM

XDM is the oldest and least feature-laden of the common XDMCP servers. It provides a simple login prompt for a username and password, with no other user-accessible options. Because most desktop users expect to be able to easily shut down their computers, most distributions have moved away from XDM to KDM or GDM, both of which provide options to display buttons to shut down or restart a computer as part of the XDMCP login display. Nonetheless, XDM configuration is important because KDM borrows some XDM configuration file features.

The primary XDM configuration file is */etc/X11/xdm/xdm-config*. Most lines in this file set options you shouldn't need to adjust. To configure an XDM server to accept remote accesses, though, look for a line like the following, which is usually near the end of the file:

```
DisplayManager.requestPort: 0
```

This line tells XDM not to listen on a regular port. The result is that your local X server can use the XDM server for login authentication, but remote systems can't. To enable remote servers to connect to the XDM server, either change the port number from 0 to 177, which is the default XDMCP port, or comment the line out entirely, which has the same effect.

This isn't the only change you need to make, though. You must also tell XDM what types of services it's to offer. To do this, you need to edit another file: */etc/X11/xdm/ Xaccess*. This file controls what clients can use the server and in what ways. A typical configuration should have lines like this:

```
*
* CHOOSER BROADCAST
```

The default configurations often have these lines, but they're likely to be commented out by hash marks (#) at the start of the line, and they may be separated by intervening comment lines explaining their purpose. In brief, the first line tells the system to accept logins from any computer, and the second line tells the system to provide a list of available local computers to any computer that asks for one. To improve security, you can specify computers or groups of computers rather than use asterisks (*) on these lines. For instance, the following configuration restricts access to computers in the *pangaea.edu* domain:

```
*.pangaea.edu
*.pangaea.edu CHOOSER BROADCAST
```

Finally, recall that the XDMCP server provides local login access by default. In fact, launching this server typically forces X to start, and this is how most distributions start X: they start the XDMCP server. What if you want to provide remote X login service but not run X locally, though? You can do this by editing the */etc/X11/xdm/ Xservers* file, which typically contains a line like this:

```
:0 local /usr/X11R6/bin/X -nolisten tcp -br vt7
```

Details vary from one system to another, but the line is almost certain to begin with :0 local. Whatever the precise form of this line, you can comment it out by placing a hash mark at the start of the line. This action forces XDM to accept remote accesses without starting X whenever it starts.

 The -nolisten tcp option causes X to not accept connections from other systems. This configuration improves security for a desktop system that shouldn't be accessed remotely, but it's detrimental for systems that should be remotely accessible. If you want to leave X running by default but enable remote logins, you should ensure that this option is *not* present in your */etc/X11/xdm/Xservers* file.

Once you've made your changes, you have to restart the XDM server to implement your changes. Precisely how you do this varies from one distribution to another, but typically, you can change to a text-only runlevel and then back to your GUI login runlevel. For instance, typing **telinit 3; telinit 5** accomplishes the job on many distributions. Some distributions, such as Debian and Gentoo, use the SysV startup scripts to shut down the XDM server and then restart it.

Configuring KDM

KDM's configuration is modeled after that of XDM, so if you want to configure KDM, you should begin by reading the previous section on XDM configuration. Most KDM installations, however, change the names and locations of some configuration files. In particular, many use *kde-config* rather than *xdm-config*. KDE configuration files may also reside in odd places, such as */opt/kde3/bin* or */usr/bin*. The *Xaccess* and *Xservers* files may also reside in an out-of-the-way place, such as */opt/kde3/share/config/kdm* or */etc/kde/kdm*.

 You can use your distribution's package management tools to help locate the KDM configuration files. For instance, on an RPM system, you can type **whereis kdm** to locate the *kdm* binary, then use *rpm*'s -qlf option set **rpm -qlf /opt/kde3/bin/kdm | grep Xaccess** to query the location of that file and find the *Xaccess* file, making the necessary change to the path to *kdm* on your system, of course.

To support KDM's additional features compared to XDM, extra configuration files are required. The most important of these is *kdmrc*, which is likely to be stored in the same location as the *Xaccess* file. Use your package management system or the *find* or *locate* command if you can't find it. This file is broken into sections with labels in square brackets, such as [Xdmcp]. It's this section you may need to edit; look for the Enable and Port lines. These tell the system whether to enable externally accessible XDMCP functions and on what port to offer them. In effect, these lines duplicate the purpose of the line in *xdm-config* for XDM. (For safety, make changes to both files.) You should edit these lines so that they look like this:

```
Enable=true
Port=177
```

Once you've reconfigured KDM in this way, you must restart it, much as you'd restart XDM if you were using it.

Configuring GDM

GDM uses its own unique configuration file, *gdm.conf*, which usually appears in */etc/X11/gdm*. This file is similar in format to KDM's *kdmrc*, but GDM doesn't use the XDM-style configuration files, so you can ignore the XDM configuration information presented earlier; *gdm.conf* handles everything. To enable GDM to accept remote logins, activate its server features in its [xmdcp] section, much as you do in KDM's *kdmrc*:

```
Enable=true
Port=177
```

These lines may be separated by other lines containing comments and even other configuration options. If you want to use GDM for remote logins only and not have it start a local X server, locate the [servers] section, which should have a line such as:

```
0=Standard
```

This line tells GDM to manage the first X display. If you comment out this option by placing a hash mark at the start of the line, GDM won't start an X server when it's run.

Unfortunately, GDM doesn't provide an easy way to restrict access to the server akin to XDM's *Xaccess* file; it's open either to everybody or to nobody. For this reason, GDM is best used only on well-secured local networks. If you want to use GDM on a system that's exposed to the Internet at large, you may want to use a firewall to block access to the server's UDP port 177 from unauthorized systems.

GDM provides a GUI configuration tool that enables you to set many of its options, including enabling XDMCP. To use this tool, type **gdmsetup** in an *xterm* or similar command prompt window or select the GDM configuration tool (often called Login Screen) from your desktop environment's menu system. The result should resemble Figure 11-4. The XDMCP tab contains the options for XDMCP. Be sure the Enable XDMCP box is checked.

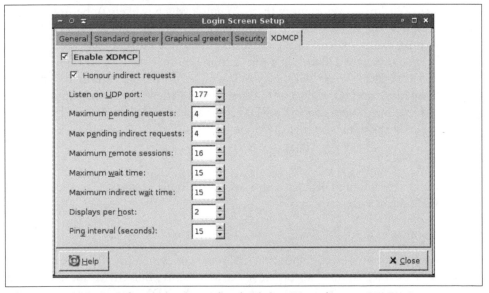

Figure 11-4. GDM provides a GUI setup utility that helps you configure a GDM server

Configuring an XDMCP client

XDMCP server configuration is, naturally, only half the story. Once your XDMCP server is running, you must configure a client. These clients are actually X servers.

The X server contacts the XDMCP client to start an X session. When it's successful, the remote system then sets its DISPLAY environment variable and runs its X login scripts. The result is typically an X session running on your local computer.

Precisely how you configure an XDMCP client depends on the X server. Windows X servers typically provide a configuration utility that lets you point the X server to an XDMCP server. For instance, Figure 11-5 shows the Xconfig program for Xmanager.

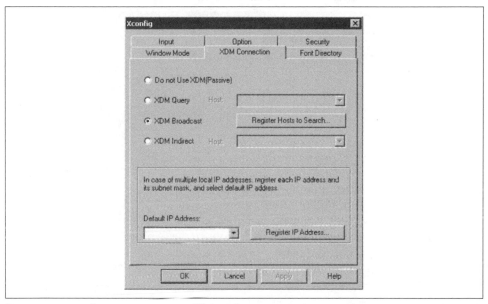

Figure 11-5. Windows X servers typically provide ways to perform XDMCP queries on startup

The XDM Connection tab in Xconfig provides the means to handle XDMCP queries. In addition to the option not to use XDMCP, three modes of operation are typically available:

Query

This option connects directly to a single XDMCP server, which you must specify. If you use an X server to connect to a single system, this can be a good option.

Broadcast

An XDM broadcast should locate all the appropriately configured XDMCP servers on your local network. You can also usually add off-network systems (by clicking "Register Hosts to Search..." in Figure 11-5), in which case your X server queries them, as well. The result, when you launch your X server, is an XDMCP chooser display similar to the one shown in Figure 11-6. You pick one of the systems, and click Connect to log in to it.

Indirect

An indirect use of XDMCP works much like a broadcast, but the task of performing the broadcast is handed off to a remote XDMCP server. This feature can be handy if you want to access a remote network; rather than enter each potential hostname or IP address in a broadcast list, you enter a single remote XDMCP server name in the indirect field and let it do the work.

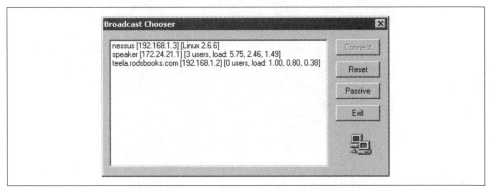

Figure 11-6. An XDMCP chooser enables you to pick which system to use

You can use a Linux system and its X server as a GUI terminal for another computer. To do so, however, you must pass options to the X program when you start it. These options are -query *host.name*, -broadcast, and -indirect *host.name*, to perform queries, broadcasts, or indirect broadcasts, respectively. For instance, with X *not* running, the following command performs an indirect connection, presenting a list of available systems:

$ /usr/X11R6/bin/X -indirect mars.pangaea.edu

One notable difference between Linux and Windows X servers is that Linux X servers (XFree86 and X.org-X11) don't present a chooser if you perform a broadcast query; instead, Linux X servers connect directly to the first XDMCP server that responds. This feature makes indirect connections more desirable under Linux, at least most of the time.

 Chapter 12 describes how to use old computers running Linux as dedicated X servers for more powerful Linux systems. This approach can be a useful way to squeeze extra life out of elderly computers.

Because an XDMCP-mediated login runs the user's normal startup scripts, it usually starts a full desktop environment. This desktop environment is likely to overlay a Windows desktop if a Windows X server is configured to use a rootless configuration. Alternatively, you can alter the X login scripts to provide an option to not start a full desktop environment.

Encrypting X by SSH Tunneling

One of the big drawbacks to X is that it provides no way to encrypt your data. Thus, raw X sessions are risky choices for performing tasks with sensitive data, including system administration tasks. One way around this problem is to tunnel the X connection through SSH. Fortunately, this task is fairly easy to do, and it provides an excellent level of encryption. It does require specific configuration options on both the client and the server, however.

Advantages and Disadvantages of X SSH Tunneling

By and large, SSH tunneling is a great boon for using X. Its main advantage is its encryption, but it has other pluses, as well:

Compression

> SSH supports data compression as well as encryption. Using these features can improve the speed of X sessions, depending on the speed of the two computers' CPUs and their CPU loads. (See the upcoming list of drawbacks for more on this issue.) This feature is most likely to be important on slow network links.

Simplified sign-ons

> The procedure for initiating the connection using the remote text-mode login protocol, described earlier, is awkward. Using SSH tunneling actually simplifies this procedure, although the underlying connection model is actually more complex.

Simplified firewall requirements

> Because a tunneled X connection is carried over an SSH link, you don't need to be concerned with working around firewall limitations for X alone. If you can establish an SSH connection between a user's desktop computer and a remote server, the X connection can be tunneled through any intervening firewalls. (Firewalls on the X client and server might still remain obstacles if they're extremely tight.)

Tunneling X through SSH isn't without its drawbacks:

CPU time and speed

> The encryption and decryption processes take a certain amount of CPU time on both systems. This fact can slow down connections, particularly if one or both systems has a weak CPU. This factor can sometimes be mitigated by use of SSH's compression features, which can improve data throughput, but the compression itself will consume CPU time. Ultimately, the speed consequences of using SSH tunneling are uncertain; you'll have to test it on your own network to know.

Support

Using SSH for tunneling means that you'll need to run an SSH server on your X client computer and an SSH client on your X server system. This may complicate your software installation, particularly if you wouldn't ordinarily be installing SSH clients on your X server (that is, desktop) systems. Furthermore, not all SSH clients support tunneling X connections, although most do.

Extra configuration and debugging

Even when you'd ordinarily install the necessary SSH software for purposes other than tunneling X, you must configure both the client and server to handle the job. This task shouldn't be a difficult one, but doing it on dozens or hundreds of systems could be tedious. If something doesn't work, tracking down the source of the problem will become more tedious than it would be without SSH in the picture.

Lack of XDMCP support

Tunneling X connections over a standard text-mode login session is fairly easy, but adding XDMCP to the mix is not. If you want to provide remote system selection akin to that provided by an XDMCP chooser (Figure 11-6), your best bet is to write a simple program or to use an X server that can do the job via an integrated SSH client.

Overall, tunneling X over SSH is worth doing; these disadvantages are minor compared to the advantages, particularly in encryption. In fact, if you want to use X between computers on the Internet at large, I wouldn't recommend doing it in any way that doesn't provide encryption, and SSH is one of the simpler ways of providing encryption to X connections.

SSH Server Options

Chapter 10 provides information on configuring SSH to accept remote text-mode logins. If you've not already read that chapter and don't know how to configure SSH, you should read up on the topic. The assumption hereafter is that you have a working SSH server and can log into it from the system you intend to use as an X server.

On the SSH server computer, you should examine the */etc/ssh/sshd_config* file. (Be sure to examine the correct file and not the similarly named *ssh_config* file, which configures the SSH client.) This file contains an option that's critical for tunneling X:

```
X11Forwarding yes
```

The default setting for this option is no, so unless you explicitly set it to yes, your SSH server will refuse to forward X connections. If this option needs to be altered, you should do so and then restart or reload your SSH server.

SSH Client Options and Use

In the Linux OpenSSH client, the */etc/ssh/ssh_config* file controls the client options. This file contains an option that's analogous to the SSH server's X forwarding option:

```
ForwardX11 yes
```

This option defaults to *no*, which blocks X tunneling. To enable this feature by default, you must change the setting in the main SSH client configuration file. Unlike the server option, individual users can override this default with command-line options to the *ssh* command: the -x option disables X forwarding, and -X enables it. (Note that these options differ only in case.)

Using X forwarding is fairly straightforward: from an X session, a user can employ SSH to log in to a remote system and then immediately launch X programs, without typing extra commands:

```
$ ssh -X linnaeus@pluto
Password:
Last login: Mon Dec 27 11:24:49 2004 from venus.pangaea.edu
Have a lot of fun...
linnaeus@pluto:~> xeyes
```

The elaborate procedure of setting the DISPLAY environment variable and setting permissions on the local X server becomes unnecessary; more precisely, the X client and server handle these tasks transparently to the user. Programs run on the remote system are displayed on the local X server just as if a more traditional unencrypted X connection had been established. Of course, if X isn't already running locally, it must be started first.

 This particular example uses the -X option, which means that it will work whether or not the local SSH client is configured to tunnel X. This option may be omitted if you've configured your local X client to do so. The remote SSH server must be configured to tunnel X in either case, though.

What about Windows, though? The procedure is basically the same for it, but configuration details may differ. In particular, you should check your preferred SSH client's configuration options for one that enables X forwarding. For instance, Figure 11-7 shows the relevant option for the PuTTY SSH client in Windows. You must check the "Enable X11 forwarding" option and, if necessary, adjust the "X display location" field (the default is fine in most cases).

Some Windows X servers include integrated SSH clients. These systems can be used to establish encrypted SSH sessions that tunnel X automatically, much as they can establish links using Telnet or other unencrypted login protocols. Thus, you may want to check your Windows X server for SSH support before using a separate SSH client.

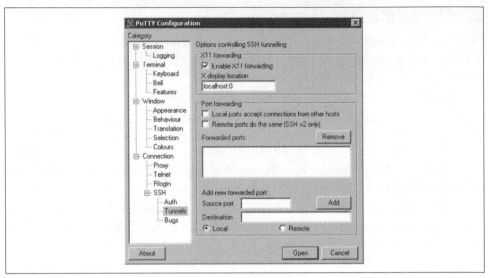

Figure 11-7. *Windows SSH clients typically provide a GUI menu option to enable X forwarding*

If you're not sure whether your encryption is encrypted, one quick check is to type **echo $DISPLAY** in an *xterm* window that uses the connection. If the result reads localhost:10.0, you're almost certainly using a tunneled SSH connection. This response indicates that programs are connecting to their local computer on the tenth X port, which is the one that the SSH server sets up for its tunneling. If the result of typing this command is *your.host.name*:0.0, and *your.host.name* is your X server's hostname, it means that your connection isn't encrypted.

VNC Configuration and Use

X enables remote users to access a Linux system, but it's not the only tool for doing so. VNC can also function as a remote login tool, with a different set of advantages and disadvantages compared to X. One big plus of VNC is that it can provide remote access to Windows, as well, so you can log into Windows from Linux, Windows, or other OSs. Of course, configuring the server is just part of the job; you must know how to handle VNC clients. Fortunately, this task is fairly straightforward.

VNC runs a client on the computer at which the user sits and a server on the remote computer. Thus, VNC's client/server terminology is more familiar to most people than is the X terminology.

VNC Versions

One of the earliest versions of VNC was released by AT&T. That version is no longer maintained or hosted by AT&T, but it's available under the name RealVNC from *http://www.realvnc.com*. Binary versions of RealVNC are available for Windows, Linux, Solaris, and HP-UX, with source code available that will compile for other Unix-like OSs. Many Linux distributions ship with RealVNC.

Another VNC variant is available under the name *TightVNC*, from *http://www.tightvnc.com*. This VNC implementation is notable because it includes some improved compression algorithms, which can improve VNC's speed. TightVNC is available in binary form for Windows and Linux, with source code for other Unix-like systems also available. Many Linux distributions ship with TightVNC in addition to or instead of RealVNC.

If your network houses more unusual operating systems (including some that aren't particularly exotic, such as Mac OS X), you may want to consult *http://www.uk.research.att.com/archive/vnc/platforms.html*. This page contains links to VNC implementations for a variety of operating systems.

One other VNC implementation deserves mention: KDE. This Linux desktop environment provides support for VNC's RFB protocol independent of a separate VNC server. This implementation is described later in this chapter.

Configuring a Linux VNC Server

VNC servers for Linux are plentiful, and some can be configured in diverse ways. Before delving into server details, though, you should understand something of how X and VNC interact because using VNC doesn't mean that you're not using X. Linux GUI programs still expect to connect to an X server, so VNC provides one. Beyond that, several options for running VNC (or other RFB server software) exist, including traditional VNC server launches, linking VNC to an XDMCP login server, and KDE's built-in tools.

X and VNC interactions

From a user's perspective, using VNC can seem simpler than at least some methods of using X for remote access; however, VNC actually complicates the internal workings of the system. Figure 11-8 illustrates the relationship between VNC and X. The VNC server is actually two servers in one: it's a server for the RFB protocol and a server for X. The X client program connects to the VNC server as if it were a local X server. The VNC server then creates a bitmap for display, much as a local X server would, but instead of sending that bitmap to a local screen, it's sent to the VNC client. This VNC client does double client duty because it's also a client for the local X server. The VNC client delivers the bitmap to the X server, which displays it on the screen. Similar interactions occur, but in the opposite direction, for delivering keypresses and mouse movements from the user to the target X program on the remote system.

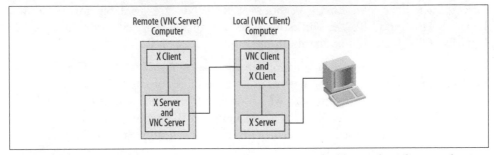

Figure 11-8. On a Linux-to-Linux connection, VNC serves as a double translator between the X client and server

 Because Windows doesn't use a client/server model for its windowing system, Figure 11-8 is not entirely accurate when a Windows system is involved. In the case of a Windows VNC client, the VNC client delivers data to the Windows display subsystem, but it's not a client/server relationship in quite the way it is under Linux. A Windows VNC server must intercept display output using various programming tricks, rather than interface in an approved and clean way as an X server allows.

VNC was designed to provide whole-screen displays to its clients. For this reason, it delivers an entire remote desktop, much like to an X server that runs in rooted mode (as in Figure 11-2). VNC has no equivalent to X's rootless display.

VNC delivers entire bitmaps from the server to the client. By contrast, an X client can and often does deliver shorthand descriptions of operations, which the X server interprets locally. This difference means that VNC must frequently deliver more data across the network than does X, but X's transactions involve more back-and-forth exchanges. These characteristics give rise to the differing performance limitations of the two protocols, with VNC degrading on low-bandwidth networks and X degrading on high-latency networks.

Traditional user VNC server sessions

To use a regular VNC server, such as RealVNC or TightVNC, you must first install it. You may want to check your distribution's package list to see if it includes a VNC server (probably under a name like *tightvnc* or *vnc-server*). If you can't find a VNC package for your distribution, check the RealVNC and TightVNC web sites. These have source code and binaries in various formats, such as tarballs and RPMs. Note that some VNC packages split off the VNC client from the VNC server, whereas others include everything in a single package.

Once you've installed the VNC server, it's time to configure it. You must do this as an ordinary user—specifically, the one who will be using the server:

1. Create a ~/.vnc directory in your home directory to hold VNC configuration files.

2. Create a new VNC password by typing **vncpasswd**. By default, VNC doesn't use the Linux password database, so each user must set a VNC-specific password.

3. Run the server by typing **vncserver**. The system should respond with a message like this:

```
New 'pluto:0 (linnaeus)' desktop is pluto:0

Creating default startup script /home/linnaeus/.vnc/xstartup
Starting applications specified in /home/linnaeus/.vnc/xstartup
Log file is /home/linnaeus/.vnc/nessus:6.log
```

At this point, the VNC server is running on VNC port 0 (indicated by the :0 trailing the machine name—pluto in the preceding example). Be sure to remember this port number because it's necessary for connecting to the VNC server! The VNC port number, like an X port number, is relative to a larger number—5900, in the case of VNC—so VNC port 0 is TCP port 5900. You should be able to connect to the server using the VNC port number in a client, as described in the section "Using a VNC Client."

When you first start the VNC server, it creates a default startup script in ~/.vnc/ xstartup. This script is equivalent to a normal X startup script; it launches applications when the VNC X server starts. The basic configuration, though, is to launch an extremely primitive window manager called *twm*. If you're used to another desktop environment or window manager, you should edit this file to change the reference to *twm* to something else, such as *startkde* to start KDE or *icewm* to launch IceWM.

The *vncserver* command is actually a script that calls the real VNC server program, *Xvnc*. If you want to make systemwide changes to VNC's defaults, you must edit the *vncserver* script. Ordinarily, you'll do this as *root*, although you can copy the script to your home directory as an ordinary user and edit it yourself, if you prefer. Options you may want to adjust include:

The new user startup script
   The startup script written by *vncserver* is contained within it, typically identified as defaultXStartup or something similar. You can edit this script as you see fit; however, this change will affect only new VNC users, not existing ones.

The font path
   Unfortunately, VNC is very sensitive to the *font path*—the list of directories in which it searches for fonts. This is identified by the -fp parameter to *Xvnc*, so if you want to change the font path, you should search for that string and make changes to any variables or *Xvnc* calls that specify it. The -fp parameter takes a comma-separated list of directories as its option. You may want to try using the font path specified in your */etc/X11/XF86Config* or */etc/X11/xorg.conf* file, although these files specify the font path in a multiline format rather than as a comma-separated list. Including empty or invalid directories on your font path is

likely to cause the VNC server to crash, so if in doubt, start with a shortened font path and add entries to make it work as you like.

Virtual screen size

VNC presents a virtual screen in which it creates your Linux desktop. You can adjust the size of this virtual screen with the -geometry option to *Xvnc*, so look for the line in the *vncserver* script that sets this option. This is usually set in a variable called geometry near the start of the script.

Color depth

If you want to have VNC deliver more or fewer colors, you can set the color depth option, which is passed to *Xvnc* via the -geometry parameter. Most *vncserver* scripts set this value with the depth variable near the start of the script.

Once you as an ordinary user are finished with VNC, you can shut it down by passing the -kill :*session-number* option to *vncserver*. For instance, **vncserver -kill :0** kills VNC session number 0.

Linking VNC to an XDMCP server

The usual mode of VNC's operation is peculiar by Linux server standards. Instead of connecting to the server using a fixed port and entering a username and password to gain entry, you must log in using a text-mode tool or run the server while you're at the console, then connect using a port number that you must remember and enter a password (but no username). This approach certainly works, but it can be a bit awkward if arbitrary users should have access to the VNC server. To work around this problem and create a more typical Linux-style login experience, you can tie VNC to an XDMCP server. The result is that, when users connect to the VNC server, they'll be greeted by a GUI login screen that's similar to the one they see when logging in at the console or via an XDMCP-enabled remote X server.

Before proceeding, check the earlier section "Simplifying Remote X Logins with XDMCP." You should configure your XDMCP server to accept remote connections, with one possible exception: you can use *Xaccess* rules or firewall rules to restrict XDMCP access to the local computer itself. Both the XDMCP server and the VNC server will be running on the same computer, and the XDMCP server only needs to accept connections from the VNC server. You can configure the XDMCP server to be more promiscuous in the connections it accepts, but if this isn't necessary, it can be a bit of a security risk, particularly if the computer is accessible to the world at large, and you use firewall rules or super server security settings to restrict access to the VNC server.

Once you've configured the XDMCP server, you should edit your */etc/services* file. This file gives names to various TCP and UDP ports. You should add entries for any ports you want to assign to VNC. The names you use are arbitrary, but vnc or something related to it is a logical choice. Note that you can use just one port or many ports. Using many ports lets you run multiple VNC servers with different options—

for instance, to run servers with different virtual screen resolutions for the benefit of clients with different screen resolutions. For example, suppose you intend to run VNC with 760×530 and 950×700 resolutions. First, create two entries in */etc/ services*:

```
vnc-760x530    5900/tcp
vnc-950x700    5901/tcp
```

This configuration assigns TCP ports 5900 and 5901 to VNC, using names that describe the intended uses for these ports as supporting different resolutions.

Once this is done, edit your super server configuration to call the *Xvnc* server. This call must include several parameters that are normally handled by the *vncserver* script, such as -geometry, -depth, and -fp. Other options that may be necessary include:

:*session-num*

This option specifies the X session number; each unique X session needs its own session number. Note that this is an *X* session number, not a VNC session number. If your system normally runs a local X server, begin with :1. You can also begin with :0 if no conventional local X server ever runs on the system. Some systems work best if you omit the X session number, enabling VNC to pick one dynamically.

-ac

This option disables access controls in TightVNC—that is, the initial password request. Because XDMCP handles this task, disabling the initial VNC password request is desirable. Some VNC versions don't need or support this option, though; they use the -SecurityTypes option instead or disable access controls as a side effect of other settings necessary for this configuration.

-SecurityTypes=none

This option is RealVNC's equivalent of TightVNC's -ac option.

-once

Ordinarily, a VNC server runs until killed; even if you disconnect from the server, it continues to run. This option causes the server to terminate after a connection is lost. Its behavior is desirable when VNC is used with XDMCP because it better implements the traditional Linux login/logoff procedures.

-inetd

This option tells *Xvnc* that it's running from a super server.

-query localhost

This option speaks to the VNC server's X server side; it tells the server to contact a specific computer for an XDMCP login. In this case, the server contacted is localhost, which should work well. You can use 127.0.0.1 or your computer's external IP address or hostname if you prefer. (Using localhost or 127.0.0.1 may result in slightly better performance, though.)

To produce a *xinetd* configuration incorporating these elements, create the file */etc/xinetd.d/vnc*. This file should have one or more entries like this:

```
service vnc-760x530
{
    disable     = no
    socket_type = stream
    protocol    = tcp
    wait        = no
    user        = nobody
    server      = /usr/bin/Xvnc
    server_args = :1 -inetd -query localhost -geometry 760x530 \
                      -depth 24 -ac -once \
                      -fp /usr/share/fonts/misc/,/usr/share/fonts/100dpi/
}
```

 The large number of arguments passed to *Xvnc* dictates splitting them across three lines in this book; however, they should all be entered on a single line in reality. Backslash characters (\) denote continued lines here but should not be entered in your real configuration files.

You may need to experiment with the -ac and -SecurityType parameters to get this to work. Your font path is also likely to be longer than the one shown here. Some distributions, such as Fedora, provide a font server for local use, which can greatly shorten the font path entry, but the entry is likely to read unix/:7100.

After restarting your super server, the VNC server should become available to VNC clients, as described in the section "Using a VNC Client." You'll notice several differences in how VNC behaves, though:

- Multiple users can log into a single VNC port.
- Users don't need to explicitly configure their VNC sessions.
- Users' VNC logins produce their standard desktop environments, as set by X system defaults and users' own options.
- Sessions are destroyed when users log out; they must save open files or their unsaved work will be lost.
- Users don't enter VNC passwords, but they have to enter a password at the XDMCP login prompt.
- If you set up multiple VNC ports to accept logins with different parameters, the VNC session number controls access to the options you set. For instance, connecting to *pluto:0* could yield a 760×530 display, whereas connecting to *pluto:1* can produce a 950×700 display.

Overall, linking VNC to an XDMCP server can be an excellent way to provide remote GUI logins to a Linux system. This approach follows typical expectations for GUI logins and works much like accessing Linux via a rooted X server using XDMCP. VNC client software is inexpensive and easier to configure than X servers, though, which can simplify your overall configuration and education efforts, even if linking VNC with XDMCP is a bit more work.

 One downside to this approach is that usernames and passwords sent to the XDMCP server are unencrypted. (Ordinary VNC passwords are encrypted, although the rest of the session data is not.) Given that most VNC data isn't encrypted, this isn't a huge difference, but it is worth noting and may make a difference in your plans, particularly if you want to use VNC across the Internet.

KDE's VNC features

KDE is unusual in that it supports the VNC protocol, RFB. You can access KDE's options from the KDE Control Center (type **kcontrol** in an *xterm* window or locate the Control Center option in the KDE menu system). The options in question are visible in the Desktop Sharing area within the Internet & Network option set, as shown in Figure 11-9. (Specific KDE implementations vary somewhat in their names for these options; for instance, some use Network rather than Internet & Network.) KDE's Desktop Sharing system works more like VNC under Windows than under Linux: it shares an existing login session, rather than create a new session. The intent is that it be used as a collaborative tool, to enable users to create demonstrations and presentations for other users at remote locations. For this reason, it emphasizes use by invitation: click Create & Manage Invitations to create a time-limited password, which you can give to another user in some appropriate way, such as over the phone. (You can also email invitations directly, but this makes them susceptible to network sniffing.)

KDE also supports "uninvited" connections, which are essentially time-unlimited invitations. This tool isn't likely to be useful for providing yourself with remote access, though, because KDE displays a dialog box on its local display whenever a connection attempt is made. If you don't accept the connection, the remote system is refused access. Thus, remotely accessing the system via KDE's VNC features requires that somebody be present at the console when a connection attempt is made.

Configuring a Windows VNC Server

One of VNC's advantages over X is that you can use VNC to remotely control a Windows computer. Windows wasn't designed with multiuser access in mind, however, so instead of running a server that creates a virtual session unrelated to anything displayed on the console screen, VNC under Windows copies what's shown on the computer's main display to the client. This is similar to the approach taken by KDE with its integrated VNC support, although some details differ. This can be a good way to control your own single-user machine when you're away from it, but it obviously won't do if two users want to share a single computer; each user's actions would battle the other's.

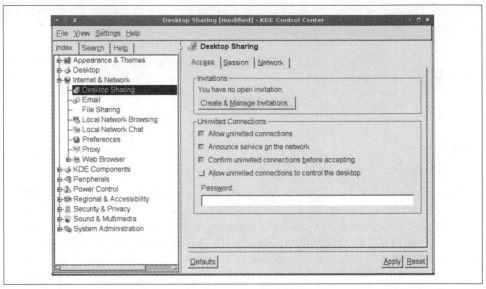

Figure 11-9. KDE's VNC support enables you to share an existing KDE login session

You can obtain VNC for Windows from the RealVNC and TightVNC web sites. This chapter uses TightVNC for Windows 1.2.9 as a reference. The program comes as a Windows self-installing archive, so you can double-click it to launch an installer, which is typical of this class of program in Windows. You'll be asked if you want to install the client, the server, or both (the default is to install both). If you install the server on a Windows NT/200x/XP system, at the end of the process, you're asked if you want to register TightVNC as a Windows service. Doing so launches TightVNC when Windows starts, so you can access it remotely before any user has logged in. This can be a handy way to provide multiple users access to the computer, but only one at a time. If you don't want to provide this sort of access, TightVNC will launch only after you explicitly run it. (You can also place a link to the TightVNC server in a user's *Startup* folder, in which case it runs as soon as the user logs in.)

When you first launch the VNC server, it presents the WinVNC: Current User Properties dialog box shown in Figure 11-10. This dialog box enables you to set various options, some of which are equivalent to Linux VNC options and some of which are Windows-specific. The most important of these options is to set the password for VNC access, so enter that immediately. When you've set the options you want to use, click OK to launch the server. You should notice a small VNC icon appear in the task bar on the bottom of your screen; double-click it to change your VNC server's options.

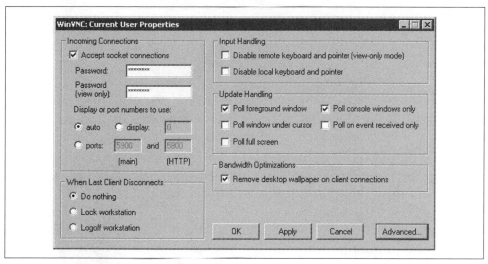

Figure 11-10. The Windows VNC server uses a GUI tool to set options that are set via command-line switches in Linux

Using a VNC Client

VNC client operation is fairly straightforward. In Linux, you use the *vncviewer* program. If you type the command name alone, it presents a GUI prompt for the VNC server. Alternatively, you can pass the server name on the command line. In either case, you can include the VNC session number, as in **vncviewer pluto:0**. If you don't include the session number, the default is 0. This default works well for most Windows VNC servers and for the first VNC server launched on a Linux system.

Under Windows, you can launch the VNC client by selecting it from the Windows Start menu. The result is a GUI prompt for the VNC server, similar to the one the Linux VNC client presents. As with that prompt, you may need to enter a session number if the server runs more than one VNC server.

With either OS client, after you enter the server's name, the client tries to connect. If it succeeds, the client immediately prompts for a password if the session is password-protected; however, if you've configured a Linux VNC server to interface to an XDMCP server as described earlier, you'll see no VNC-specific password prompt. Instead, you'll see a Linux XDMCP login screen, as shown in Figure 11-11, which shows a Windows VNC client connected to an XDMCP-enabled Linux VNC server. You can then log in as if you were at the console. Thereafter, no matter the type of the server, you can use the system more or less as if you were sitting at the remote computer.

Figure 11-11. VNC can present a close replica of the remote computer's display, potentially including a GUI login screen

 Some Windows configurations require you to press Ctrl-Alt-Del to log in. To do so from a Linux VNC client, press F8 to obtain a menu of special keystrokes and options. Windows VNC clients provide similar options from their windows' menus.

VNC isn't without its flaws. Here are some problems and quirks you may notice when using the server:

- Overall system responsiveness may seem sluggish, particularly if you're using a slow or overburdened network or if your display is quite dynamic.

- When connecting to Windows servers, parts of the display may not update in a timely fashion. This is a consequence of VNC's imperfect interfacing to the Windows display system. Linux servers tend to be better about displaying screen updates as they should appear.

- Keyboard mapping may be imperfect, particularly when connecting to or from systems with odd keyboards. Some Macintosh keys may not map sensibly, for instance, if you connect to or from a Mac OS system.

- Colors may appear strange. Unfortunately, VNC clients and servers don't always handle colors in a perfect manner. Changing the server's color depth can often improve matters.

Encrypting VNC Connections

VNC's lack of encryption can be a serious drawback. Fortunately, it's one that can be corrected with the help of additional software—namely, SSH. Using SSH to encrypt VNC can be more complex than using SSH to encrypt X, though. Configuration begins on the VNC server computer, which must run an SSH server in addition to the SSH server. The SSH server must be configured to accept tunneled TCP connections:

```
AllowTcpForwarding yes
```

This option, which should appear in the */etc/ssh/sshd_config* file, is the default, so chances are you won't need to change it. Once it's set, SSH is configured to accept forwarded connections, and the server-side configuration is done.

The simplest way to use a tunneled connection is to employ the -via option to Tight-VNC's *vncviewer* command in Linux. This option takes the name of an SSH server that forwards the traffic to the ultimate target system. For full point-to-point encryption, this system would be the same as the VNC server:

```
$ vncviewer -via pluto.pangaea.edu pluto.pangaea.edu:0
```

The result will be a prompt for your SSH password on the remote system followed by an ordinary VNC login. Unfortunately, this approach isn't available in the Windows version of TightVNC or in either version of RealVNC. For these systems, you must set up an explicit SSH tunnel using the SSH client package on the client computer. You do this by using several options to the *ssh*:

```
$ ssh -N -f -L 5902:pluto.pangaea.edu:5900 proxy.pangaea.edu
```

This command tells the SSH client to set up a mapping from the localhost port 5902 to *pluto.pangaea.edu*'s port 5900, using *proxy.pangaea.edu* as the system that passes on the data. (Ordinarily, you'd want to use a single hostname for both the proxy and the target system; I've specified two names here just to make it easier to identify what's doing what. Likewise for the port numbers; chances are you'd use the same one on both systems, although you might use different numbers if your local port 5900 is occupied.) Once you type this command, you're prompted for a password and then the link is established. To use this link, you can run any VNC client, but you must link to your localhost address on the VNC port specified in the *ssh*, minus 5900:

```
$ vncviewer localhost:2
```

When combined with the preceding *ssh*, this command links to *pluto.pangaea.edu*'s port 5900 (VNC port 0), using *proxy.pangaea.edu* as the SSH proxy. This might be useful if your main concern is with snooping on intermediate systems, and you trust the security of the connection between *proxy.pangaea.edu* and *pluto.pangaea.edu*. You can also specify the same computer as both systems, though, provided you can run both an SSH and a VNC server on that computer.

This approach works with Windows clients and servers as well, although of course some details do differ. In the case of a Windows VNC server, you need to install and configure an SSH server, as described in Chapter 10. Precisely where you'll find the option to enable TCP forwarding varies from one server to another, so consult your documentation. Likewise, Windows SSH client configuration for this task varies from one client to another. Typically, you must enter the source and destination ports in a special configuration screen, such as the one shown in Figure 11-12 for PuTTY. In PuTTY, after entering the information in the Source Port and Destination fields as shown, you click the Add button to add forwarding, then initiate an ordinary SSH session to the VNC server or the SSH server you intend to use as a proxy. Thereafter, connecting to the localhost address on the specified port with your VNC client forwards the connection.

Figure 11-12. Windows SSH clients typically enable you to enter port forwarding instructions in a special configuration menu

Running Windows Programs from Linux

If you are willing to make a monetary investment that will enable your Linux clients to run Windows applications, there are two popular and related methods to consider. Both methods run a Windows desktop session on a server that you connect to and control from a Linux desktop running the appropriate client software. This is similar to VNC on Windows as described in the previous section, but one of the major differences is that multiple Linux desktops, possibly several hundred, can connect to a single Windows server at a time. This is a perfect setup when you want to deploy Linux desktops but still need the ability to run one or more Windows programs in their native form. Nearly all programs should run flawlessly because they really are running on a Windows computer; it's simply their display output that's shown on the Linux machine. However, processor or memory-intensive applications should not be run in this fashion because a single program consuming most of the system's resources may ruin the experience for the users.

The minimum requirement for this kind of setup is a Windows server, preferably Windows Server 2003, that has Terminal Services enabled. Windows 2000 also has this ability built-in, but Windows NT requires the special Terminal Server version. On the Linux side, you can use a program called *rdesktop*, which speaks Microsoft's Remote Desktop Protocol (RDP), to connect to the Windows server and run a desktop session. Just like VNC, these sessions can run at full screen or inside a program window. It is possible to cut, copy, or paste text between the remote Window desktop and the local Linux desktop, but you can't drag and drop files. Beyond the cost for a Windows server and server license, you have to purchase a Terminal Services Client Access License for each user or machine that will connect to the Windows server. The *rdesktop* program isn't supported by anyone other than the open source community, so if you have problems using it, Microsoft won't help you. This is one reason you might want to consider the second method.

The second most popular way to run Windows applications on Linux uses a third-party application called Citrix Metaframe that runs on top of Windows Terminal Services. This program provides additional features not found in regular Terminal Services, such as concurrent licensing, server pooling, and a native Linux client that uses Citrix's thin client protocol known as ICA. Citrix licensing fees are on top of the ones that already exist for the first solution, but if the extra features are needed, the price is easily justified.

Setting up either server is beyond the scope of this book. However, if you want a quick test to see how well this works, you can use *rdesktop* to connect to a Windows XP Professional computer. Microsoft includes support for one remote desktop connection in Windows XP Professional to enable administrators to make a remote GUI connection for troubleshooting purposes. In most cases, this service is already running on the computer, and you simply need to install *rdesktop* on your Linux client and run a command, such as: **rdesktop -g 800x600 *IP address*** (where *IP address* is replaced with the actual address of the Windows computer) to connect to the Windows computer.

Summary

Remote GUI logins can be a useful tool for enabling users to run complex GUI programs remotely and even for system administration. Windows benefits the most from remote GUI system administration, because text-mode Linux tools are usually sufficient. Two tools are particularly important in cross-platform remote GUI logins: X and VNC. X is Linux's native GUI tool and is a very useful way to access a Linux system from another Linux system or from a Windows system. VNC is a cross-platform tool that can enable Linux or Windows clients to access either Linux or Windows servers. (Other operating systems are also supported.) One problem with both X and VNC is that they don't encrypt data by default, with the exception of VNC passwords. One way around this limitation is to employ SSH as a tunneling protocol. This process works most easily with X, but, with a bit of effort, it can also be used with VNC.

## CHAPTER 12

Linux Thin Client Configurations

Chapter 11 presented information on using GUI remote login protocols—namely, the X Window System and Virtual Network Computing—to control one computer from another one. This technique can be handy in many situations, as described in Chapter 11. One specific application of this technique deserves elaboration, though: *thin client computing*. In a thin client environment, one computer (the thin client) is configured with a minimal OS installation and is dependent on another computer (the server) to handle most computing tasks, aside from input/output. This approach to computing can greatly simplify system administration by centralizing most administration tasks on a single larger server. It also enables you to extend the life of aging computers; even a 486 system might make an acceptable thin client! It does require a server that's powerful enough to handle multiple simultaneous logins, though. Thin clients are best used by workers who need to run a handful of low-resource applications. You don't need to use thin clients for *everybody*; you can mix thin clients with more conventional desktop systems.

 You can use Linux as a thin client OS, on the server side, or both. Windows systems can function as servers, although Windows needs special software to handle multiple simultaneous users.

This chapter begins with an overview of thin client computing—what it is and when you might want to use it. Next up is a look at the hardware you'll need to deploy a thin-client network, including the thin clients themselves, their servers, and the network infrastructure requirements. The next topic is configuring Linux as a thin client, which builds on the VNC client and X server topics in Chapter 11. Finally, this chapter looks at how to configure a Linux system as a server for Linux or non-Linux thin client workstations.

The Role of Thin Client Computing

Thin client computing can be a great way to stretch limited computing budgets and simplify system administration headaches. It's not the best solution to all problems, though. Deciding when to use thin client computing requires understanding the different forms it can take and the advantages and disadvantages of these forms.

Types of Thin Client Computing

In practice, the term *thin client computing* covers a range of configurations, from extremely simple thin clients that use powerful remote login servers to much more capable thin clients with substantial onboard software that uses remote login servers for file storage and software not provided on the thin client. In fact, it can sometimes be difficult to draw the line between thin client configurations and traditional desktop systems that use remote login servers for occasional uses or specialized tasks. Different people can draw this line in different places or by using different definitions. For instance, one common definition uses the presence or absence of a hard disk on the client as a deciding feature: if a system has no hard disk, it's a thin client. Not all thin client definitions include this feature, though.

In practice, thin client computing is essentially a return to an older model of computing that was common in the 1960s through the 1980s, in which *dumb terminals* were the primary means of accessing the mainframes and minicomputers of the day. Typically, employees, students, or other users would use the dumb terminals (which provided text-only displays) from their desks or from public computing environments. After the advent of X for Unix, some dumb terminals were replaced by *X terminals*, which were essentially dumb terminals capable of running an X server. In fact, X terminals are still available today and can make excellent thin clients for Linux systems.

 An X terminal runs an X server, but in the language of the thin client world, the X terminal is a thin client. This is yet more confusing fallout from the peculiar client/server relationship in X, as described in Chapter 11.

Although you can use old-style dumb terminals (or computers that run terminal emulators to stand in for dumb terminals) with Linux, modern thin client computing relies on GUI remote login tools to run GUI programs. Chapter 11 describes two protocols that are commonly used in thin client computing, but the range of possible protocols is actually wider than that:

The X Window System
> X can make an excellent thin client protocol when accessing Linux (or other Unix-like OSs). You can run Linux and X on older or stripped-down systems or

use dedicated X terminals as thin clients. You can't easily use X to access Windows servers, though, except in limited ways.

VNC

VNC, or the Remote Frame Buffer (RFB), as the protocol is more properly known, is a useful thin client tool. Linux can function as a VNC server or client, enabling you to reuse old computers. You can also run a VNC server on Windows systems to provide remote access, although VNC doesn't provide multiuser access to Windows. (Using VNC to access Linux isn't so limited.) Some dedicated thin client appliances support VNC, so it can provide remote access to Linux from such thin clients.

RDP

The Remote Desktop Protocol is Microsoft's favored thin client protocol and is supported by Microsoft's Terminal Server software package. Linux RDP client packages are available, such as *rdesktop* (*http://www.rdesktop.org*) that lets you configure a Linux system as a thin client for a Microsoft server.

ICA

The Independent Computing Architecture protocol is favored by Citrix, which provides tools to access Microsoft Windows servers using thin clients that support the ICA protocol. Citrix (*http://www.citrix.com*) provides a free ICA client for Linux, so Linux can function as a good ICA thin client OS.

Typically, to provide remote access to Linux systems, you'll use X or VNC. To access Windows systems, VNC, RDP, or ICA will work, although only the latter two protocols support multiuser access. (Technically, changes to the underlying OS enable multiuser access; the protocols simply connect to that new feature.) Thus, RDP and ICA are the protocols of choice for thin clients accessing Windows servers.

When to Use Thin Client Computing

This chapter has already alluded to some of the advantages of thin client computing, namely hardware cost savings. This isn't the only reason to use this approach, though. Here are some common advantages of thin client computing:

Hardware cost

By recycling old computers as thin clients or buying new stripped-down computers or dedicated thin clients, you can reduce your expenditures on new desktop systems and upgrades to desktop computers.

Reliability

Thin clients, being much simpler than conventional desktop systems, are less likely to break down, all other things being equal. This can reduce the need for tedious hardware troubleshooting sessions.

Reduced noise and power consumption

Particularly if you use dedicated thin client hardware or old computers without hard disks, thin clients are likely to be quieter and consume less power than full desktop computers. This also results in less heat, which can help lower air conditioning bills. One partial exception to this rule is if you reuse old CRT monitors rather than buy new LCD monitors. CRT monitors consume a lot of power compared to new LCD monitors, replacing CRTs with LCDs can further reduce your power consumption.

Decoupling users from hardware

In a thin client environment, any user can use any thin client computer. Users see their own desktop environments and their own files, no matter which thin client is used. This feature can be great in public computing centers or when you want to upgrade hardware or move users between offices.

Administrative effort

Administering a single login server computer and dozens of thin clients is typically simpler than administering dozens of desktop computers.

Security

In some sense, this advantage is a corollary of the last one. Simple thin client computers are less likely to become infected by worms or otherwise compromised than are typical desktop systems. This advantage is particularly great if the thin clients are simple dedicated units with their OSs in ROMs or if they can boot from files stored on a network server. If you use Linux systems with their own hard disks as thin clients, an intruder might be more likely to gain access to and modify the clients. Thin clients can also benefit by the fact that it's seldom necessary to give them public IP addresses; they can reside on entirely private subnets that link *only* to your local servers and to each other. This can be even more secure than a conventional desktop behind a network address translation (NAT) router, because the thin clients can't initiate outside connections (say, because of a viral infection).

Ultimately, most of these advantages boil down to cost, either for hardware or for labor in maintaining all of a site's computers. These advantages are offset by disadvantages, though, some of which are in the same areas as the advantages:

Hardware cost

The cost benefit on the client is at least partially offset by the fact that you'll need to invest more in the server or servers that users will access. The login server must typically be substantially more powerful than individual workstations, although precisely how much more powerful depends on your site's computing needs. Light uses, such as word processing, may need a server scaled to the needs of a typical user plus a small increment in RAM and CPU speed for each additional user. CPU- or RAM-intensive tasks such as running scientific simulations may not work well at all with a centralized approach unless you invest in a *very* powerful server. As a general rule of thumb, a high-end IA-32 system (say, one that sells for about $3,000) can usually support about 30 users.

Reliability

Although thin clients are likely to be more reliable than individual desktop systems, this approach is essentially one of putting all your eggs in one basket. If the login server computer or your main network infrastructure fails, no user will be able to do any work. For this reason, you should be particularly careful in buying or building a login server for a thin client environment; buy the most reliable hardware possible, and whenever possible, employ reliability-improving tools, such as a Redundant Array of Independent Disks (RAID) array. Keep backups of your data and have backup hardware on hand so that if a critical server hardware component fails, you can quickly replace it. Using server clusters or having redundant servers can also be useful techniques to improve reliability. Also, if you use old PCs as thin clients, their reliability advantage over new desktop systems may evaporate, but the thin clients are cheap and easy to replace should they break.

Local devices

Using some types of local hardware devices, such as sound cards, scanners, and CD-ROM drives, can become tricky in a thin client environment. Solutions to these problems do exist, but they often require extra configuration to work well. For instance, you might need to configure a thin client computer as a file server to give users access to a local CD-ROM drive.

Thin clients can be deployed in any number of environments, from two-user small offices to academic or corporate sites with thousands of users. Depending on the type of work being done and the server's speed, a single server can support anywhere from a handful of concurrent users to several dozen; thus, large sites are likely to have multiple servers.

The thin client approach tends to work best with applications that are relatively undemanding in terms of the CPU and display. CPU-heavy tasks such as raytracing or scientific simulations work best when all users have their own CPUs, and graphics-intensive tasks, such as watching real-time video, make huge demands on network infrastructure when deployed on thin clients. Tasks that are better suited for thin client environments include word processing, light spreadsheet use (so long as spreadsheets aren't doing extremely lengthy computations), reading email, web browsing, using a corporate database, and other basically textual tasks. These jobs require users to read for long periods of time, and much of the interaction involves typing, which changes the onscreen display slowly.

Hardware Requirements

One of the advantages of thin client computing is that it minimizes the hardware requirements, at least for the computers at which users actually sit. The server hardware, though, must be heavy duty, at least if it's to support more than a few users. Thus, you must evaluate your hardware requirements very differently for the two sides of the thin client/server coin. You must also consider the hardware that connects these two sides of the coin, because a deficiency in your network infrastructure will severely degrade a thin client network.

Server Requirements

The trickiest part of determining your thin client network's hardware needs is in deciding what sort of hardware to use on the server. This task is made extremely difficult by the fact that it varies so much depending on the type of work done at your site. Different programs make different demands on memory and CPU time, and these demands scale differently to multiuser loads.

The scaling question is an important one. For instance, suppose you've determined, through experimentation, that a desktop system needs a 2-GHz Pentium 4 CPU, 512 MB of RAM, and a 60-GB hard disk to operate comfortably for a typical user. An obvious, but probably wrong, extrapolation would be that a 10-user server would need a 20-GHz Pentium 4 CPU, 5 GB of RAM, and a 600-GB hard disk—10 times the single desktop system's values. (Of course, some of these specifications, such as a 20-GHz Pentium 4 CPU, can't be met!) Most desktop computer CPUs are idle most of the time; processing user keystrokes and mouse clicks as they use a word processor, web browser, or most other user applications takes little CPU time. Likewise, a great deal of RAM is consumed by the OS kernel and other overhead items that's not duplicated in a multiuser environment. In addition, shared libraries can greatly reduce the memory footprint of adding new users when they all run more or less the same programs. Similar comments apply to disk space. Depending on the applications used, a 10-user system might need only a 3-GHz CPU, 1 GB of RAM, and 120 GB of disk space to provide performance comparable to a 2-GHz CPU/512-MB RAM/60-GB disk single-user desktop system, or it might need something more powerful.

Beyond a certain point (typically about two or three dozen users), scaling a single server becomes impractical. Thus, if you need to serve several dozen to thousands of users, you should look into multiserver configurations. In this configuration, load balancing can become an important issue, but this topic is beyond the scope of this book.

In early 2005, desktop users can still usually work quite well with single-CPU Intel Architecture 32 (IA-32) systems. In any but the smallest thin client configurations, though, your server should have more CPU power, and is likely to benefit from a shift to a multi-CPU or 64-bit system. Of these two features, multiple CPUs are likely

Determining Hardware Requirements

To evaluate your hardware needs, try judging a desktop system's performance with just one user running typical programs. Note the subjective performance level, and also use tools such as Linux's *uptime* or *top* to measure CPU load and *free* to measure memory use. (Be sure to read from the `-/+ buffers/cache:` line in *free*'s output; the `Mem:` line includes buffers and caches, and so normally shows very little free memory.) You can then use a remote access protocol (ideally the one you intend to use) to add users and have them use the system normally. Repeat your measurements, and note how system resource requirements go up and performance goes down. In this way, you should be able to estimate the amount of CPU power and RAM you need for a multiuser system. Disk space is likely to be easier to estimate: the multiuser disk space needs are isolated to users' own data files, so you can use tools such as Linux's *du* to see how large existing users' home directories are.

to be more important than 64-bit CPUs. The latter are most likely to be necessary if the total memory exceeds 4 GB; unless they use special tricks, IA-32 systems are limited to 4 GB of RAM. Although 64-bit multi-CPU systems tend to be expensive, each one can serve quite a few users, which greatly reduces the per-user cost.

The login server systems for thin clients also need fast and robust disk subsystems. In the past, this has usually meant RAID arrays based on SCSI drives, and indeed SCSI RAID systems are still a good, if expensive, choice for this role. Recently, though, SATA RAID hardware has become common, and such systems often at least approach the performance of SCSI RAID systems, although they tend to produce higher CPU loads, so SCSI still beats out SATA.

 Many motherboards include SATA controllers that claim to be RAID-enabled; however, most or all of these are actually fairly ordinary non-RAID controllers with minimal BIOS hooks and drivers that enable RAID functionality in software. Linux also provides software RAID drivers, but for the best possible performance, particularly at RAID levels 4 and 5, which provide error correction features for improved reliability, you need a true hardware RAID driver with support for the server's OS.

Of course, the login server needs the best available network hardware. Most systems sold today include gigabit Ethernet. To do any good, though, the gigabit Ethernet or other high-speed network connector must either be matched with equivalent hardware on the clients or fed via a switch or router that can combine slower client feeds into a faster link to the server.

Client Requirements

The requirements of the thin client depend to some extent on your site's needs. For instance, you might need extra-large displays, clients that can handle multiple protocols, or clients with their own built-in web browsers. Much of the appeal of thin client computing, though, is that the thin clients themselves are commodities; you can reuse old PCs as thin clients, buy dedicated thin client hardware, or both. You can replace one thin client with another one (even a very different one) with little impact on its user's ability to work.

If you intend to recycle old PCs as thin clients, the basic needs are fairly minimal: the computer must be functional and have some form of network connection. In theory, even an RS-232 serial port for using the Point-to-Point Protocol (PPP) will do, but in practice, Ethernet or some other network protocol is needed. The computer must have a working monitor, keyboard, and mouse. If you intend to run Linux on the system, it must have an 80386 or better CPU and sufficient RAM for your distribution. In practice, a fast 80486 or slow Pentium-class CPU and 16 MB or even 32 MB of RAM is likely to be desirable. Older computers are unlikely to have speedy video hardware by today's standards, but most should suffice for simple GUI programs. The biggest problem with old video hardware is the amount of RAM they hold, which influences the maximum display sizes (in pixels) and color depths they support, as summarized in Table 12-1. You can use older Macintoshes or other computers with CPUs other than those in the IA-32 line, but some of the Linux distributions that work best as thin clients are designed exclusively for IA-32, so your configuration task is likely to be harder with these computers.

Table 12-1. Video RAM and supported video modes

Resolution	8-bit (256 colors)	16-bit (65,536 colors)	24-bit (16,777,216 colors)	32-bit (4 billion colors)
640 × 480	300 KB	600 KB	900 KB	1.2 MB
600 × 800	469 KB	938 KB	1.4 MB	1.8 MB
1024 × 768	768 KB	1.5 MB	2.3 MB	3.0 MB
1280 × 1024	1.3 MB	2.5 MB	3.8 MB	5.0 MB
1600 × 1200	1.8 MB	3.7 MB	5.5 MB	7.3 MB

Both dedicated thin clients and those built from old computers may require some hardware replacements, such as upgraded monitors, video cards, and mice. Mice are particularly worthwhile upgrades because many GUI Linux programs assume the user has a three-button mouse. They can work with two-button mice using a *chord* (pressing both buttons simultaneously) as a stand-in for the middle (third) button, but this is a bit awkward.

If you intend to purchase dedicated thin clients, you should study their specifications very closely. Many thin clients are intended for use solely with Windows, using RDP or ICA. Such clients won't work with Linux servers; for that, the thin client should support either X or VNC. If the client will be used with both Linux and Windows servers, be sure it supports all the necessary protocols.

To operate as fully diskless systems, many thin clients must have network cards with ROMs that support booting from the network. Such configurations also require you to configure a system to respond to the boot requests and deliver appropriate files to the thin client. (This topic is described in more detail later, in the section "Linux as a Server for Thin Clients.") If you're trying to recycle older PCs, you may therefore need to use a local boot disk (a floppy disk, CD-ROM drive, or even a hard disk) or replace network cards that don't enable you to boot from the network.

Network Hardware Requirements

Because thin client computing requires transferring large amounts of data, you must pay careful attention to your network infrastructure. An outdated network will likely perform so poorly as to make a thin client configuration impractical, even if everything else is done right.

Generally speaking, on a network of up to a dozen or so users, you must have a 100-Mbps local network that uses switches. Up to a few dozen, a similar configuration will work, but you should upgrade the server's network card to support gigabit Ethernet and use a switch that can handle the gigabit/100-Mbps interface.

If your network hosts more than a few dozen users, you may need to upgrade it further or segment it in some way. (Such a network will also probably require multiple servers.)

No matter the details of your network hardware, you should attend to its reliability and monitor its performance. Flaky old network cables, overheated switches, and other problems can cause degraded performance or complete loss of connectivity. If you're considering switching an existing network to a thin client model, you might need to look into replacing some or all of your network infrastructure to deal with the increased demand. On the other hand, a fairly recent network may be up to the requirements just fine. You'll have to evaluate your network hardware yourself.

Linux as a Server for Thin Clients

Thin clients rely on servers to do any good. Most obviously, this reliance is on the login servers themselves. Chapter 11 describes two such servers, XDMCP (for use with X) and VNC. For the most part, the configurations described in that chapter work well with thin clients, although there are a few caveats. Thin clients booted from the network also rely on DHCP and TFTP, so knowing how to configure these two servers is important.

Linux Distribution Selection and Configuration

In principle, you can use any mainstream Linux distribution as a login server for thin clients. Distributions that are geared toward desktop use, such as Mandrake and Xandros, can provide lots of eye candy and be very friendly to users, but these features may generate more in the way of video (and hence network) activity than you'd like, because they might use lots of animation and demand large or color-intensive displays. Thus, you might prefer starting with a distribution that provides less fluff, such as Debian, Gentoo, or Slackware, and build it up to the point that you want and no further. This can help you control network and server load.

For the most part, you can configure a Linux login server for thin clients just as you'd configure any other desktop system. Appendix B describes some of the issues involved in such a configuration. When planning this configuration, remember that the video display involves a network access, so features such as animated icons will consume network bandwidth. Because thin clients may be running on small or low-bit-depth displays, you may also need to test your applications on such systems, and perhaps adjust their default configurations.

XDMCP and VNC Options

Fortunately, very little needs to be done to XDMCP and VNC configurations to support thin clients. The configurations described in Chapter 11 should work fine with X terminals and thin clients that support VNC.

For XDMCP, though, one feature you may want to be sure you support is indirect accesses. Some X terminal thin clients can't present a list of available servers by themselves; they need the help of an XDMCP server that's configured to provide this list. This can be accomplished on the XDM and KDM servers by editing the *Xaccess* file to include an appropriate line:

```
* CHOOSER BROADCAST
```

You can also specify a pattern of hostnames for the asterisk (*), which lets only specified computers receive the server list. In GDM, the equivalent configuration can be found in the *gdm.conf* file, which is usually in */etc/X11/gdm*:

```
HonorIndirect=true
```

This line should appear in the [xdmcp] section of the file. In either case, you must then configure your thin client to make an indirect query of the XDMCP server that supports indirect lookups.

Of course, all this is necessary only if you want your users to be able to use more than one computer from their thin clients. If each thin client should connect to precisely one system, you can configure it to make a direct connection to the remote system and be done with it.

If you're running VNC on the Linux system to enable remote logins via thin clients, chances are you'll want to link VNC to an XDMCP server. This configuration enables users to type their usernames and passwords when logging in, rather than logging in via a text-mode protocol, running a VNC server, and then connecting to a specified port. Linking VNC to XDMCP is described in Chapter 11, so consult it for details.

DHCP Configuration

Thin clients are generally much simpler to configure if you use DHCP to help configure them, particularly if you want the thin client to download its OS from a TFTP server. DHCP configuration is described in more detail in Chapter 15, so if you're not already familiar with DHCP configuration, consult that chapter.

 Many thin clients actually use a protocol known as BootP for automatic configuration via a BootP server. DHCP provides a superset of BootP functionality, though, and common DHCP servers can configure BootP clients. Thus, I describe DHCP configuration using the common Linux DHCP server. This configuration should work with clients that use BootP.

In addition to the common options described in Chapter 15, you may want to add more options for the benefit of thin clients:

`allow booting`
This global option enables support for clients that boot remotely.

`allow bootp`
This global option adds support for BootP, which is necessary for some thin clients.

`option x-display-manager server.name`
This option delivers the name of the XDMCP server for the network. Some X terminals use this information to locate an XDMCP server, but not all do so. This option is important only if you're using X as a remote GUI access tool.

`option tftp-server-name "server.name"`
You can tell thin clients where to go to find their boot files with this option, which takes the hostname of the Trivial File Transfer Protocol (TFTP) server as an option.

`next-server server.name`
This option normally appears within a parameter block for a group of servers. It has an effect similar to that of the `tftp-server-name` option, and you should normally give it the same hostname or IP address as a value.

filename "*/path/to/file*"

    This option also typically appears in a group with other options. It specifies the filename that a server is to download from the TFTP server. For Preboot Execution Environment (PXE)-enabled PXES clients, this should often be */pxes/pxelinux.0*, which is essentially a PXE boot loader. For EtherBoot clients, it should be the filename of the network bootable image you specified when you enabled this support when configuring PXES. In either case, this filename is specified relative to any chroot environment used by the TFTP server, if the TFTP server is run that way. For dedicated thin clients, consult their documentation; they may come with a floppy disk or CD-ROM with files that the TFTP server should deliver, and this parameter will do the job.

Consider Example 12-1, which shows a short but typical configuration for enabling network booting. Many of these options are described in Chapter 15, so consult it for details. This listing points to an XDMCP server and a TFTP server in the opening lines. It also creates a group with options for PXE-bootable hosts, including an additional pointer to the TFTP server and a reference to the file that's to be delivered to the clients. (To use EtherBoot rather than PXE, change the filename to point to an appropriate *.nbi* file.) Two specific clients are defined in this group; you can create other groups with other options. This might be handy if your thin clients have different needs, in terms of features such as default resolutions or even the OSs they run. You can mix Linux-based PXES clients with dedicated X terminals, for instance, by creating separate groups for each set of systems and identifying individual clients by their hardware Ethernet addresses.

Example 12-1. Sample /etc/dhcpd.conf file to support booting thin clients

```
allow booting;
allow bootp;

# Standard configuration directives...
option domain-name "example.com";
option domain-name-servers ns1.example.com, ns2.example.com;
option routers 172.24.21.1;
#option resource-location-servers server.your.domain;
#option font-servers server.your.domain;
option x-display-manager xdmcp.example.com;
option tftp-server-name "tftp.example.com";

max-lease-time 120;
default-lease-time 120;

subnet 172.24.21.0 netmask 255.255.255.0 {
}

# Options for PXE-bootable hosts
group {
    next-server tftp.example.com;
    server-name "dhcp.example.com";
```

```
    filename "/pxes/pxelinux.0";
    get-lease-hostnames true;
    use-host-decl-names on;

    host thin1 {
        hardware ethernet 00:0C:76:96:A3:73;
        fixed-address 172.24.21.101;
    }

    host thin2 {
        hardware ethernet 00:80:C6:F9:3B:BA;
        fixed-address 172.24.21.102;
    }
}
```

TFTP Configuration

Configuring your DHCP server to deliver information to clients is only part of the job. To do any good, clients must be able to download Linux files from a server. The TFTP protocol was designed for this task; it's a very simple file transfer protocol that's useful for clients with minimal software, such as systems that haven't yet fully booted.

 Despite the similarity in names, TFTP is not closely related to FTP. Most importantly, an FTP server can't handle requests from TFTP clients; you *must* install a TFTP server.

Most Linux distributions ship with a TFTP server, typically in a package called *tftp*. This server is usually launched through a super server such as *inetd* or *xinetd*. A typical *xinetd* configuration, stored in */etc/xinetd.d/tftp*, looks like this:

```
    service tftp
    {
      socket_type  = dgram
      protocol     = udp
      wait         = yes
      user         = root
      server       = /usr/sbin/in.tftpd
      server_args  = -s /tftpboot
      disable      = no
    }
```

This configuration is fairly typical of *xinetd*-launched servers that use UDP. If your distribution uses *xinetd*, chances are it ships with such a configuration file, but it may be disabled by default; you must change disable = yes to disable = no.

This example also passes an argument to the TFTP server: -s /tftpboot. This option tells the TFTP server to use the chroot( ) system call, which "locks" the running program in the specified directory, making the server treat that directory as if it were the root directory for the system. This is a useful security feature, and it has implications for file access and naming; all files served by the TFTP server must reside in the specified directory tree, and references to files omit the name of the chroot directory. For instance, the file */tftpboot/pxes/pxelinux.0* is referred to as */pxes/pxelinux.0* in client configurations. Because boot clients receive their filenames from a DHCP server, this means you must use these truncated filenames in DHCP server configurations.

 In theory, you should be able to install and run the TFTP server on any computer on your network. Unfortunately, some thin clients seem to assume that the DHCP and TFTP servers are one and the same. Thus, if you have problems getting some thin clients to boot, you may want to consolidate both functions on a single computer.

Linux as a Thin Client

Because of its low cost and flexibility, Linux can make an excellent thin client OS. You can load Linux on computers that aren't powerful enough to run the latest software, configure Linux to run appropriate thin client software, and the computer can then access more powerful Linux, Windows, or other computers.

In many respects, the simplest thin client configuration is to use a traditional Linux distribution or a dedicated thin client package to run Linux as a thin client, using a basically traditional hardware configuration, including a local hard disk or at least a CD-ROM drive. Perhaps the most appealing way of doing the job is to use a dedicated thin client distribution, which provides you with precisely the tools you need—no more and no less—to use Linux as a thin client. However you do it, you can run Linux without a hard disk using a bootable Ethernet card and configuring a system to deliver Linux OS files to computers that boot with such a card.

Distribution Selection and Installation

Your first choice is what distribution to use on the thin client computers. The needs of a thin client are such that a good desktop or server distribution may not be the best choice for a thin client. Many popular distributions, such as Fedora, Mandrake, and SuSE, install many unnecessary desktop or server applications that, in fact, may be undesirable on a dedicated thin client. These distributions also often require a lot of disk space or memory—features that may be lacking on the older computers you want to convert to thin client status.

Among mainstream Linux distributions, those that install small standard package sets by default are likely to be the best choices for thin client use. For instance, Debian, Gentoo, and Slackware can all be installed in well under 1 GB of disk space, omitting such large packages as GNOME, KDE, Mozilla, and OpenOffice.org. Even if users will ultimately run these packages, they'll probably be run from the server, not on the thin client. Slimmer Linux installations are likely to lack a few components you need, at least in their minimal installations. Most notably, you'll probably have to install an X server (XFree86 or X.org-X11). Depending on the protocols used by your server, you may also need to install a thin client package, such as a VNC client.

Another option, and one that's arguably superior even to the slimmed-down mainstream distribution option, is to use a distribution that's dedicated to thin client use. Notable in this regard are the PXES (*http://pxes.sourceforge.net*), LTSP (*http://www. ltsp.org*), and ThinStation (*http://thinstation.sourceforge.net*) distributions. These are distributions that support the PXE system, which is a way for computers to boot over a network from a remote server. These distributions are useful tools if you want to divest yourself of a local hard disk, as described in the section "Booting a Thin Client from the Network," but you can also install these thin client distributions directly on a local hard disk or on a CD-ROM to use on computers with network cards that don't support direct network boots.

Configuring PXES

Because PXES is designed explicitly for thin client use, this section describes it in more detail. You can download PXES in several forms from its web site. The CD-R image (*.iso*) file is a quick way to get started, particularly for testing its operation. This image file, though, is very generic; it runs in 800 × 600 mode by default and may not take proper advantage of your network's resources. To best use PXES, you should download the *pxes-base* and *pxesconfig* packages, both of which are available in RPM and tarball forms. You can then create a PXES image that's customized for your needs and can be booted from a hard disk, from a CD-R, or from the network. This section uses PXES Version 0.8-9 as an example; if you use another version, it may differ slightly from what's described here.

 Before you can use PXES (or any other thin client), you need to have a remote login server configured. Chapter 11 describes this topic for Linux systems. Some configurations also require you to run a TFTP server to deliver OS files to the PXES thin clients. (The TFTP server can run on the same computer as the remote login server, or it can be on another system.) The basics of TFTP configuration are described in the earlier section "TFTP Configuration."

Once you've downloaded the base and configuration packages, install them on an existing Linux distribution. (This system doesn't need to be the same as your ultimate login server; it's just a platform for customizing the PXES client files.) You can then use the configuration utility to enter details of your network's configuration and create a custom PXES image, which you can then burn to a CD-R, place on a hard disk, or deliver to thin clients via TFTP. The configuration tool uses a wizard to guide you through the configuration steps:

1. Create an entry in your */etc/fstab* file for a special loopback device the configuration tool can use to create a small RAM disk that will hold the PXES distribution:

```
/tmp/pxes.initrd  /tmp/pxes  ext2  loop,noauto,user,owner  0 0
```

2. As *root*, type **pxesconfig** to launch the utility. The first screen of the PXES configuration wizard should appear.

3. Click Next in the wizard's window. The result should resemble Figure 12-1.

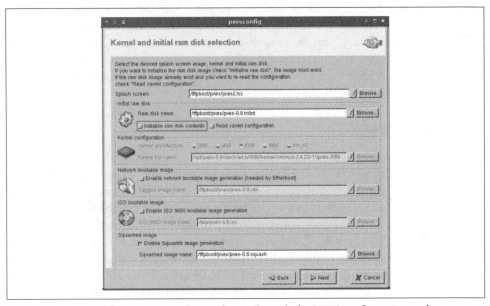

Figure 12-1. pxesconfig uses a wizard to guide you through the PXES configuration tools

4. Select the "Initialize ram disk contents" item in the "Initial ram disk" area of the window. The program will warn you that the current RAM disk's contents will be destroyed. However, because the package doesn't ship with a default RAM disk, nothing is destroyed unless you've already run the program. This action makes a few more options available.

5. If you want to use a kernel other than the default provided with the package, specify it on the Kernel File Name line. Chances are the default kernel will work fine. Be sure to note the location of the kernel and the other files specified on this page of the wizard.

6. Check one or both of the "Enable network bootable image generation" or "Enable ISO 9660 bootable image generation" options if you want to use Ether-Boot for network booting or a CD-R disc for booting thin clients using local CD-R drives. I recommend you check both options, simply so you'll have both

in case you ever want them. The ISO-9660 image is particularly handy for testing PXES without having to rely on your TFTP server, the client's ability to boot from the network, and so on.

7. Click Next. The result is a screen for specifying various hardware characteristics, as shown in Figure 12-2. Chances are you can leave all these options alone, and PXES will autodetect the hardware, but if you know what hardware your clients use, you can enter appropriate values.

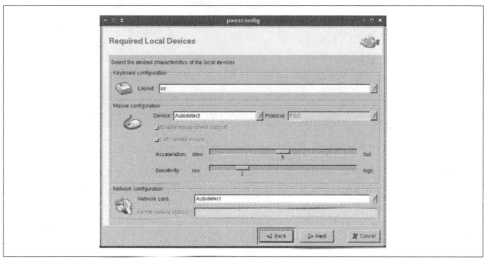

Figure 12-2. PXES can autodetect most hardware types

8. Click Next to configure local hardware, as shown in Figure 12-3. For initial testing, you may want to leave these options disabled; however, if you want to give your users access to their local hardware, enabling these options will be necessary in the long run.

9. Click Next. The PXES configuration wizard gives you a choice of types of protocols to support. You can specify multiple options, such as an X session using an XDMCP server as well as ICA. One of the selected protocols must be the default. The local X session option provides a minimal local X session, from which you can launch additional sessions. This can be handy if users need to access multiple remote systems simultaneously.

 Some features are grayed out by default. These require the installation of extra software, some of which is commercial. Consult the PXES documentation for information on these protocols.

10. Click Next to configure assorted X options, as shown in Figure 12-4. The default options usually work, but the defaults also support only 800×600 displays. If your thin clients can do better than this, you may want to change this option.

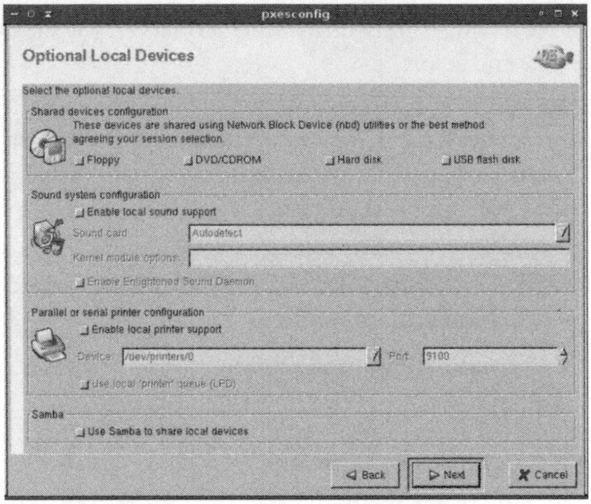

Figure 12-3. PXES can grant login servers access to the thin client's devices

When connecting to modern Linux systems, XFree86 4.x often works better than XFree86 3.3.6, as well. If you know the capabilities of your thin client's monitor (in terms of horizontal and vertical refresh rates), enter the correct values. If you don't do this, you may not be able to use the monitor in your preferred resolution.

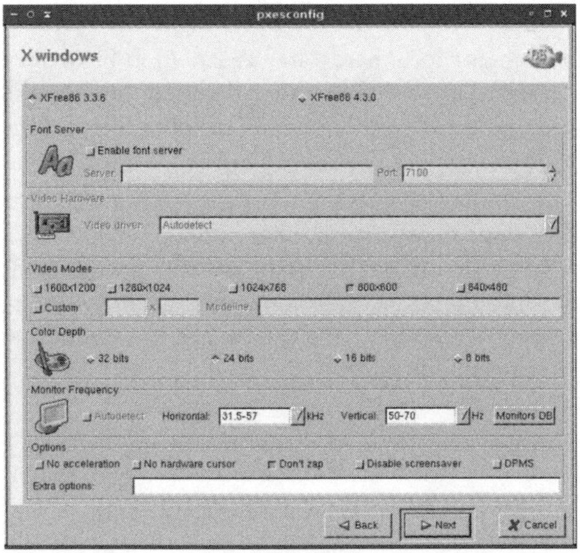

Figure 12-4. PXES lets you specify Linux-like options for your thin client's video card and monitor

11. Click Next, and the wizard displays a brief summary of your configuration.

12. Click Next. At this point, the configuration options diverge depending on the protocol options you selected earlier. For instance, if you chose to support XDMCP, the tool asks you to enter XDMCP options, as described for XDMCP clients in Chapter 11. You may run through several such screens, one for each protocol.

13. After entering information on your protocols, the configuration tool presents general configuration options. You can have it delay starting X or connecting to remote servers, run a local Telnet server for administrative purposes, and enable the use of per-client configuration files (which can be handy if your thin clients vary substantially in their hardware or other features).

14. Click Next, and the system informs you that configuration is complete and is about to be saved.

15. Click Finish to finalize the configuration. The system presents a status dialog box as it prepares an initial RAM disk image and performs various other tasks. When this dialog box reports that configuration is complete, dismiss it, and *pxesconfig* terminates.

The result of all this processing is one or more files you can use to boot a Linux-based thin client:

The kernel file
> Although it's delivered with PXES rather than generated by it, you should note the location of the kernel file, particularly if you want to perform a direct network boot of the thin client.

pxes-0.8.initrd
> This file, located in */tftpboot/pxes* by default, holds the initial RAM disk image, which is a tiny but complete bootable Linux filesystem that's passed to thin clients in one way or another.

pxes-0.8.squash
> This file is a compressed read-only filesystem image that's equivalent to the *initrd* image. Its advantage is that it's usually smaller than an *initrd* image. It's usually stored in */tftpboot/pxes* by default.

pxes-0.8.nbi
> This file is generated only if you select the network bootable image option. It's stored in */tftpboot/pxes* by default and is necessary for some types of network boots.

pxes-0.8.iso
> This file, stored in */tmp* by default, is a CD-R image file and is created only if you chose the ISO image option when configuring PXES. You should burn it to CD-R if you intend to boot your thin client using a CD-ROM drive.

Testing Your PXES Image

Now that you've created a PXES system, it's time to use it. One good way to test it is to use the CD-R image file. Using a Linux program such as *cdrecord* or a GUI front-end such as X-CD-Roast, burn the image file to a CD-R disc. (Alternatively, you can transfer the image file to a Windows, Mac OS, or other computer and use its CD-R drive.) You can then place the CD-R you've created in the CD-ROM drive of a computer that's configured to boot from its CD-ROM drive and boot the computer. Testing in this way eliminates the possibility of errors in certain network-specific servers and configurations, such as TFTP. If the CD-R boot works, you can move on to a network configuration and be sure that any problems you encounter there are network-related, rather than problems with the basic PXES configuration.

When booting a PXES image, you're greeted by a boot prompt that asks you what protocol you want to use. Type the number associated with the protocol (such as **2** for XDMCP), followed by the Enter key. If you just press the Enter key, PXES boots and runs the default protocol you selected when configuring the system. Once you select the protocol, you'll see typical Linux kernel boot messages scroll by.

After a few seconds of kernel messages, the system will be booted. Depending on your configuration options for the protocol you selected, you may now be asked for certain details, such as the hostname of the remote system you want to use. After you enter this information, or if you entered this information in the configuration phase, the screen will clear and you'll see either a system-selection screen (similar to the XDMCP chooser shown earlier in Figure 11-6) or a GUI login screen for the computer you've contacted. You should now be able to log in and use the computer as if you were sitting at its console.

If you pick the screen option when booting PXES or if you chose Local X Windows Session as your default option and run this default, PXES boots into a simple Linux desktop with a handful of icons along the left edge of the screen for initiating various types of connections. When launched, these tools can open connections to other computers in their own windows, as shown in Figure 12-5. This figure shows an indirect XDMCP login session and, in front of that, a VNC session open to a Linux system that's configured to interface to its own local XDMCP server.

When you're done with a PXES session, log out of the remote system as you normally would. Usually, PXES will then redisplay your login or system-selection menu, enabling you to begin again. If you want to shut off the computer, simply flip its power switch. Unlike normal disk-based Linux systems, a PXES thin client doesn't need to be shut down with a special command. Although it's got a local filesystem, it's a temporary one in a RAM disk, and it will be recreated from the boot medium the next time PXES boots. Thus, you needn't be concerned about corrupting the local PXES computer's filesystem.

Figure 12-5. PXES can display separate windows on different remote systems

Booting a Thin Client from the Network

PXES is a great tool; however, using it by booting off of a CD-R isn't optimal. After all, much of the appeal of PXES is being able to use it with diskless workstations that can boot automatically from the network, and relying on CD-Rs—which can be lost or damaged, as well as the CD-ROM drives to read them—reduces the appeal of PXES.

As already noted, the *PXE* part of the *PXES* name refers to a network boot protocol. This protocol is promoted by Intel as a way to boot diskless workstations; however, PXES uses it to enable network boots of a Linux-based thin client. You should consult the documentation for your thin client's motherboard to determine if it's PXE-enabled. If it is, enable the PXE boot option in the BIOS to boot the system from the network. This option also requires a supported Ethernet card; consult your motherboard's documentation to learn what works.

 Some motherboards' PXE support requires you to press a key, such as F12, at a specific point in the boot process. This can be tricky to do because it's easy to miss this point. You might even prefer using a floppy-assisted boot rather than rely on such an unintuitive network boot feature.

If your computer isn't PXE-enabled, you may still be able to boot from the network, but you'll need a network card that supports network boots in its own BIOS. Many low-cost cards sold today lack this support, so you may need to replace the card. Sometimes you can add an EPROM chip to the card to add this support; check the EtherBoot project (*http://www.etherboot.org*) for information on doing this. If your system supports EtherBoot, you need to enable that support when you configure

PXES, as described earlier, and specify the EtherBoot files when you configure your DHCP server, as described in the earlier section "DHCP Configuration."

As a last resort, you may be able to boot *partially* from the network, by employing a boot floppy that contains the minimal code necessary to have the network card continue the boot process from the network. One way to accomplish this goal is to use the universal boot floppy that's distributed as part of Thinstation (*http://thinstation. sourceforge.net*). This floppy disk includes boot code that's compatible with Ether-Boot; when you boot from the floppy, it continues the boot process as if your network had an EtherBoot-compatible network card.

However it's done on the client side, the client relies on two servers to obtain information and an OS: a DHCP server and a TFTP server. These servers may be your remote login server, but they need not be; you can use some other computer to fill these roles.

Summary

By keeping the computers most people use simple and placing most programs on remote GUI login servers, you can reduce your overall computing costs and reduce your total administrative effort. Using such thin clients does impose certain needs, though; although the thin client computers themselves can be simple, they require more powerful login servers and better network infrastructure than you'd otherwise need. Linux can play a role in thin client computing as an operating system with which you can turn outdated desktop systems into thin clients, as the server the end users log into, or both.

## PART V

Additional Server Programs

Previous parts of this book have focused on coherent collections of topics, such as file sharing servers or login servers. This section, though, examines a few networking "stragglers"—servers that aren't easily grouped together with similar tools. Chapter 13 covers mail servers, using the Simple Mail Transfer Protocol (SMTP), the Post Office Protocol (POP), and the Internet Message Access Protocol (IMAP). Chapter 14 describes using Linux as a backup server—a system that's used to back up other computers on a network. Finally, Chapter 15 describes several miscellaneous servers—specifically, a Dynamic Host Configuration Protocol (DHCP) server, Domain Name System (DNS) servers, and Network Time Protocol (NTP) servers.

Many of the servers and protocols described in this part of the book are themselves quite complex, and entire books have been written about most of them. Thus, these servers and protocols are in no way trivial or unimportant. The intent of this part of the book is to introduce the basics of configuring the servers described and to illustrate where such servers can fit in a network. You should be able to get any of these servers working in a basic way after reading the relevant chapter, but for more advanced configurations, you may need to consult server-specific documentation.

## CHAPTER 13

Configuring Mail Servers

Email is a particularly important part of most networks' functioning. Many businesses rely on email for both internal and external communications. Naturally, then, Linux can function as an email server—a computer that receives, stores, and forwards email for end users. As part of this function, a Linux mail server can filter out spam and worms from email, thus reducing both nuisance factors and security threats. Linux's advantages as a mail server over Windows include the low costs of the server and of add-on filters for spam and worms, as well as Linux's reliability and immunity to the Windows-based worms that are such a problem today. Even if you already run a Microsoft Exchange email server, Linux can be an excellent supplement to this server, providing filtering features that might require paying extra to obtain in Windows.

This chapter begins with a look at common email protocols and some common server software to implement them on Linux. Most of the chapter is devoted to basic configuration of the sendmail and Postfix servers, as well as to additional servers that can be used to deliver mail to clients. Filtering mail for spam, worms, and viruses requires its own coverage, as does a tool that can help users integrate mail delivered to outside ISPs into their own local mail systems.

Linux Mail Server Options

Before delving into the process of configuring mail servers, you should understand the role of mail servers on a network. The most basic issue is the distinction between *push* and *pull* protocols, which differ in whether the sender or the recipient initiates the transfer. Depending on your needs, you might want to configure a push server or a server that runs both push and pull protocols. You should also know what options are available for both push and pull server programs. On a Windows-dominated network, you may already have a Microsoft Exchange server, so knowing how to fit a Linux server into this existing configuration is important. Finally, running a mail server is not risk-free; they can be abused in various ways, and understanding a bit about the threats will enable you to plan your installation to minimize the risks.

Push Mail Versus Pull Mail Protocols

The most common email protocol today is SMTP, which is an example of a push mail protocol—the sender initiates the data transfer. Typically, a user runs a mail client (also known as a *mail user agent*, or MUA) to send the mail to the SMTP server (which is also referred to as a *mail transfer agent*, or MTA). The SMTP server then delivers the message to other servers, which then send it on until it reaches its destination. This chain can run for an arbitrary length.

Traditionally, users have had login accounts on the mail server computer and have used mail readers on the computer itself. This configuration, though, requires either mail delivery using SMTP to users' desktop computers or login accounts for all users on a central mail server. Both options are a bit awkward, so a second class of mail server protocols exists: pull mail protocols. These protocols enable the client to retrieve (pull) the mail from the server. If an SMTP server that's the ultimate destination for a message runs a pull mail server, a user on a desktop computer can run a mail reader that supports the pull mail protocol to read mail directly from the desktop computer, as illustrated in Figure 13-1. Two pull mail protocols are common today: POP and IMAP. (The differences are described in more detail shortly.)

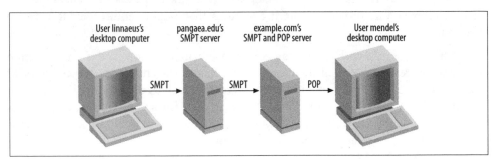

Figure 13-1. A pull mail server enables users to read mail using mail clients on their local computers

Of these two pull mail protocols POP is the simpler one. It provides a single storage area for each user's messages; users then download the messages and immediately delete them from the server. (Mail readers typically delete the messages automatically.) Users can then create local folders on their desktop computers using the email clients and store their messages that way. IMAP, on the other hand, supports mail folders on the mail server computer, as well as more sophisticated options for retrieving *parts* of messages. IMAP, isn't quite as well supported as POP, but its ability to store messages in folders on the server helps when users frequently use multiple computers.

As a practical matter, most networks now use POP, IMAP, or a similar protocol (such as Microsoft's MAPI) for the final leg of email delivery. If you want to use Linux as a pull mail server, you certainly can; several POP and IMAP servers are available for Linux and are described in a later section. These servers can work with Linux, Windows, and other clients. If you're not sure whether to use POP or IMAP, you can install and use servers for both protocols; however, each user should probably use just one protocol. Mixing them can cause confusion; for example, messages disappear from an IMAP inbox after a POP client has been used.

Linux SMTP Server Options

Quite a few SMTP servers are available for Linux; however, four servers are the most popular and readily available. These servers differ in their design philosophies, mail storage formats (mbox or maildir, described in more detail shortly), ease of configuration, popularity, and other features:

Exim

> This server, headquartered at *http://www.exim.org*, uses a *monolithic* design: one program does most of the work. It supports both mbox and maildir storage formats, with mbox being the default. This is the default server on Debian GNU/ Linux and some of its derivatives.

Postfix

> This server is a *modular* mail server, meaning that various subtasks of mail delivery are handled by separate programs. In theory, this makes it easier to write a server that's free of security-related bugs. Postfix supports mbox and maildir formats, with mbox being the default. Some distributions, including Mandrake and SuSE, now use Postfix as the default mail server. You can learn more at *http:// www.postfix.org*.

qmail

> This server uses an unusual license that's not *quite* open source: binary redistribution is prohibited unless certain conditions are met. Thus, *qmail* isn't the default mail server for any major Linux distribution. This server supports both mbox and maildir email storage formats, with maildir being the default. Like Postfix, *qmail* uses a modular design. Overall, it's the least compatible with sendmail, which makes it harder to replace sendmail with *qmail* than to replace sendmail with Postfix or Exim; but *qmail* has a devoted band of followers.

Sendmail

> The most popular mail server for years has been sendmail (*http://www.sendmail. org*), which uses a monolithic design and supports the mbox mail storage format. In the 1990s, sendmail acquired a bad reputation for security problems, but such problems have become much rarer since the late 1990s. The main sendmail configuration file format is confusing at best, so most administrators use a metalanguage, known as *m4*, to create configuration files, but even the *m4*

configuration files aren't as easy to handle as the files for most other Linux mail servers.

Throughout the 1990s, sendmail ran on a majority of the mail servers in existence, according to most studies of the issue. More recently, though, sendmail has declined in popularity, while others (Exim, Postfix, *qmail*, and others, including Windows mail servers) have risen in popularity. Despite this decline, sendmail remains a very popular (perhaps still the single most popular) mail server program on large mail server computers. For this reason, sendmail configuration is described later in this chapter. Because it's becoming popular as the default server on many Linux distributions, this chapter also describes Postfix configuration. Although Exim and qmail are both perfectly good mail servers, they aren't described in this chapter, in order to keep the chapter's size manageable. If your Linux system is already running one of these servers, you can either try to find equivalent options to those described here or you can replace your current server with Postfix or sendmail. Most Linux distributions ship with at least two or three SMTP servers, or at least make them available in an online file repository. You can also check the mail servers' web sites for links to versions for your distribution.

The preceding descriptions referred to the local mail storage formats supported by each server. The mbox format uses a single file, to which email messages are appended. Each user has a mailbox, typically somewhere in the */var* directory tree, to which the server adds messages as they arrive. The maildir format, on the other hand, stores messages as individual files in a directory. Users' incoming messages may be stored in subdirectories of users' home directories. Each format has its adherents, but your primary consideration should be compatibility. Local mail clients and pull mail servers must be able to read messages in the appropriate format. Some programs are limited in their capabilities, which can dictate your choice of options for the SMTP server, or even completely rule out an SMTP server. If you're building a mail system from scratch, you might want to assemble a list of software you want to use, based on features and recommendations from others, then pick the file format based on what your collection of software supports. If you wish to replace an existing SMTP server program, the simplest approach is to pick one that supports whatever format you're currently using.

Linux POP and IMAP Server Options

Just as with SMTP, several POP and IMAP servers are available for Linux. Some packages support only one protocol, but many support both. Many of the servers are limited to just one mailbox format, though, and some of the IMAP servers use their own format for folders other than the inbox. On the whole, you may need to hunt a bit to find the server that best suits your needs.

Courier

This server, located at *http://www.courier-mta.org*, is a complete mail server package, including support for SMTP, POP, IMAP, and other protocols. Although the full Courier package isn't one of the "big four" SMTP servers, the POP/IMAP component (available separately from *http://www.courier-mta.org/imap/*) is moderately popular. It provides access to mail stored in maildir format but not mbox.

Cyrus IMAP

Although *IMAP* is part of this popular server's name, it supports both POP and IMAP. Cyrus IMAP stores POP mail in mbox format but uses its own format for IMAP folders. This server provides more options than some and emphasizes encrypted authentication protocols using its own password database. You can learn more at *http://asg.web.cmu.edu/cyrus/imapd/*.

Dovecot

This server, headquartered at *http://dovecot.org*, is a fairly recent entry to the POP and IMAP server field, but it's rapidly becoming a popular server. It supports both protocols, as well as both mbox and maildir file formats. The Dovecot documentation indicates that it was written with security as a primary focus. This server provides more options than many POP and IMAP servers, so it's worth investigating if you have unusual needs.

nupop

This server was designed for environments hosting a large number of users; it aims to operate as efficiently as possible. It supports POP but not IMAP and maildir but not mbox. Check *http://nupop.nuvox.net* for more information.

popa3d

Security, reliability, standards compliance, and performance are the primary goals of *popa3d*, which is a POP server headquartered at *http://www.openwall.com/popa3d/*. It's designed to support mbox mail files, but a patch that provides maildir support is available on its web site.

qmail-pop3d

This program is part of the *qmail* package (*http://www.qmail.org*). As such, it's most often used with *qmail* and employs the maildir format that's the default for *qmail*. This is a POP-only server.

QPopper

Despite the Q in their name, this server is unrelated to *qmail*. Versions prior to 4.0 were commercial servers, but as of Version 4.0, the server is open source. It's a POP-only server that works with the mbox mail format. Check *http://www.eudora.com/qpopper/* for more information.

UW IMAP

The University of Washington IMAP server (*http://www.washington.edu/imap/*) has long been the default POP and IMAP server in Linux. This server, which uses the mbox format, is easy to get running but provides few options to fine-tune its operation.

Most of these servers use normal Linux authentication mechanisms, such as Linux's PAM (described in more detail in Appendix A), although some provide options for using or must use some other authentication mechanism. Broadly speaking, UW IMAP is usually the simplest server to configure, and it's usually adequate for small sites, particularly if you want to use POP rather than IMAP. (IMAP use with UW IMAP may be complicated if users also have shell access, because the server hard-codes the location of IMAP folders in the user's home directory, which can be awkward. This isn't a problem if users don't have shell access to the server, though.) Dovecot has recently been gaining in popularity and is worth investigating if you find UW IMAP too limiting. Any of the other servers may also be good choices for particular uses—for example, if you only want to use POP or if you want to provide access to maildir-format mailboxes. This chapter describes running UW IMAP later, in the section "Configuring POP and IMAP Servers."

Mail Security Concerns

Mail servers, like all servers, are potential security risks. In fact, mail servers—and particularly SMTP servers—can be more vulnerable than you might at first think, because they must perform some operations as *root*. For instance, when storing mail, the server needs to be able to write to arbitrary users' mail queues, which are owned by their respective users. This means that mail servers must run as *root*, and the complexity of modern SMTP servers means that bugs in the code can give clever intruders access. This is why modular mail servers are, theoretically and all other things being equal, potentially safer than monolithic servers. By isolating tasks that must be run as *root* to separate programs, other mail server programs can run as non-*root* users, reducing the risk that a bug will lead to a system compromise.

That said, recent versions of the monolithic Exim and sendmail servers don't have bad security reputations. I can't promise that you won't encounter problems if you use one of them, but the risk isn't unmanageable for most sites.

In recent years, another email security concern has come to dominate the news: worms and viruses. (Most of these are technically worms by most definitions, but the term *virus* is frequently applied to them all.) An email worm is a piece of code sent via email that, when run, replicates and sends copies of itself to others, usually via email. Typically, such worms are sent as attachments that appear innocuous. They also might rummage through victims' address books to locate new addresses, so recipients may trust the worms because they know the apparent senders.

Worms have become a serious threat; outbreaks have become fairly frequent, and the sheer number of worms being sent requires extra storage capacity, faster CPUs, and better network connections on mail servers than would otherwise be required.

When a new worm is released and spreads rapidly, the demands placed on all these resources spike, often beyond the capacity of the hardware to cope with the problem.

Another security issue with email is that SMTP servers send their mail without encryption. This doesn't pose a direct security threat to the mail server computer, but it does mean that email can be intercepted and read if any system between the source and the destination is compromised. For this reason, sensitive data such as passwords and credit-card numbers shouldn't be sent via email. One approach to fixing this problem is to equip mail clients with encryption tools such as the GNU Privacy Guard (GPG; *http://www.gnupg.org*). Two GPG-equipped systems can send encrypted messages to each other, although the SMTP protocol itself remains unencrypted.

Configuring Sendmail

Sendmail has long been the most common SMTP server. Although its popularity has dropped somewhat in recent years, it remains the dominant mail server on the Internet at large and is the standard mail server installed in many Linux distributions, including Fedora, Red Hat, and Slackware.

To configure sendmail, you must first know where to find its configuration files, understand their formats, and know how to create and modify these files. These tasks are trickier in sendmail than in most other mail servers, which is one of sendmail's big drawbacks compared to other popular Linux mail servers, especially for new mail administrators. This chapter looks at three particularly important areas of sendmail configuration: address options, relay options, and antispam options.

 Sendmail is an extremely complex server, so this chapter can only begin to scratch its surface. If you need to do more with sendmail than is described here, you should consult its own documentation or a book on sendmail, such as O'Reilly's *sendmail* or *sendmail Cookbook*.

Sendmail Configuration Files

The main sendmail configuration file is called *sendmail.cf*, and it's usually located in */etc*, */etc/mail*, or some other subdirectory of */etc*. Unfortunately, this file is very difficult to edit directly because the configuration options are numerous and have formats that are fairly obtuse. For this reason, few people even attempt to edit this file directly. Instead, they use the *m4* utility to create a *sendmail.cf* file from a file with a simpler format.

In order to use the *m4* utility, though, it must be installed on your system. What's more, the utility relies on a series of support files, which may be installed from yet another package. In Fedora and Red Hat, for instance, you must install the *sendmail-cf* package. Look for the *m4* package on your distribution medium, and also look for any likely sendmail *m4* configuration packages. (They're likely to include *sendmail* in the package names.)

The *m4* tool converts a file with a name that typically ends in *.mc* into sendmail's *sendmail.cf*. Unfortunately, the precise name used varies from one distribution to another. For instance, in Fedora and Red Hat, it's */etc/mail/sendmail.mc*, whereas in Slackware it's */usr/share/sendmail/cf/cf/sendmail-slackware.mc*. To perform the conversion, you use the *m4* command, piping the *.mc* file into this command and redirecting output to the desired file:

```
# m4 < /etc/mail/sendmail.mc > /etc/mail/sendmail.cf
```

 This command overwrites the existing */etc/mail/sendmail.cf* file. For safety, you should back up this file by copying it to another location before running this command.

Once you've rebuilt the configuration file, you must restart sendmail. In most cases, this can by done by passing a `restart` or `reload` argument to the sendmail SysV startup script:

```
# /etc/rc.d/init.d/sendmail restart
```

Alternatively, you can use *kill* to send a `SIGHUP` signal to the *sendmail* process. This procedure can be less disruptive than completely restarting sendmail, and so it may be preferable.

Before you do this, however, you must make changes to your sendmail *.mc* file. Compared to the *.cf* file, the *.mc* file is simple and comprehensible. Most options are set in parentheses using a `define` or `FEATURE` keyword:

```
define(`SMART_HOST',`smtp.pangaea.edu')
FEATURE(always_add_domain)
```

Additional option names exist, but these two account for many of the sendmail features. The parameters passed to these options are sometimes enclosed in single quotes, but unlike most configuration files, the opening and closing quote characters are different: The opening quote is actually a backtick (`` ` ``), located to the left of the 1 key on most keyboards. The closing quote is an ordinary single quote character ('), located to the right of the semicolon (;) key on most keyboards.

The sendmail *.mc* file uses the string dnl to denote a comment. Many sample configurations include quite a few options that are commented out by placing this string at the start of the line. Sometimes a hash mark (#) also appears on the line, but this character isn't an actual comment character; it's just there for the benefit of users who are accustomed to seeing a hash mark used as a comment marker.

In addition to the main sendmail *.cf* and *.mc* files, other files serve to hold ancillary data:

access.db
    This binary file is created by the *makemap* utility from a plaintext file that often has the same name with a different or no filename extension. This file controls

which computers may interact with the sendmail server and in what ways. This information is particularly critical for sendmail relay configurations, as described shortly.

aliases.db

> This file is a binary file created by *makemap* or *newaliases*. (Passing the -bi option to *sendmail* also does the job.) This file defines *aliases*—that is, mappings of email addresses onto other email addresses. For instance, most distributions set up an alias of *postmaster* to *root*, so that *root* receives mail addressed to *postmaster*.

These files usually appear in */etc/mail* or sometimes in */etc*. If you examine the *.mc* configuration file, you'll probably find references to these files. Chances are you shouldn't modify these references, although you may want to adjust the files' contents, particularly if you need to adjust your relay configurations.

Sendmail Address Options

In a basic sendmail configuration, the most important settings relate to ports and addressing. Some distributions ship sendmail configured to bind only to the localhost (127.0.0.1) address. The result is that the server can be accessed only from the local computer. This can be a good configuration if you're running a desktop system that shouldn't accept outside SMTP connections, but for a mail server, you probably don't want this restriction. Check the sendmail *.mc* file for a line like this:

```
DAEMON_OPTIONS(`Port=smtp,Addr=127.0.0.1, Name=MTA')dnl
```

If this line is present, and you want the server to accept outside connections, add dnl to the start of the line to comment out this option. If you don't see a line like this, you don't need to make any changes.

Another address-related option is to set the server's hostname. Frequently, the server has a specific hostname, such as *smtp.pangaea.edu*, but you want mail from your users to use your domain name only, such as *linnaeus@pangaea.edu*, rather than *linnaeus@smtp.pangaea.edu*. Frequently, mail clients can set this address; however, if you find that some of your outgoing mail sets an incorrect domain or includes a hostname in the address, you can have sendmail change this by including the following lines in the *.mc* file:

```
MASQUERADE_AS(`pangaea.edu')
FEATURE(masquerade_envelope)
```

Of course, you'd change pangaea.edu in the first line to your own domain name. The first line tells sendmail what should appear to the right of the at sign (@) in email addresses if users' mail clients don't specify an address. The FEATURE(masquerade_envelope) line takes this a step further, by masquerading the address provided in email headers, which are normally invisible to users. If you don't use these options, sendmail assumes that its hostname is as set on the computer (as determined by the gethostbyname( ) system call), but sendmail won't adjust the address in outgoing email.

 An important part of the email addressing scheme is setting the *mail exchanger* (MX) entry in your domain's DNS record. This record tells sending mail servers the name of your domain's mail server computer, so that mail addressed to *linnaeus@pangaea.edu* is sent to *smtp. pangaea.edu*. Chapter 15 describes DNS configuration, including setting the MX record.

Sendmail Relay Options

An important part of any SMTP server configuration is setting mail relay options. A mail server can function as a relay (that is, accept mail that's destined for another location) or use a relay (that is, send outgoing mail by way of a server other than the ultimate destination). Setting these options so that sendmail does what you need it to do without doing too much can be tricky sometimes.

 If a mail server accepts relays from systems or users who shouldn't be able to use it for this purpose, the server is known as an *open relay*. Such mail servers are easily abused by spammers, so open relay configurations should be avoided at all costs.

Configuring sendmail to relay mail

Sendmail is frequently employed as a mail relay server for a network. That is, you configure mail clients to send all outgoing mail via the Linux sendmail server. Out of the box, though, recent versions of sendmail refuse such relay attempts as an antispam precaution. You can loosen this configuration using any of several options, specified within a FEATURE specification:

relay_entire_domain
> This option tells sendmail to perform a DNS lookup on a sending computer's IP address and to accept relay attempts if the resulting hostname is within your domain. This is a quick and easy way to enable relaying, but it can be abused; spammers can modify their own networks' DNS servers to provide a reverse lookup in your domain, thus tricking your system into accepting undesirable relays.

relay_local_from
> If you use this option, sendmail accepts any mail for relay so long as the From: address in the message is in sendmail's local domain. This address is very easily forged, though, and so is a poor option in most cases.

relay_based_on_MX

This option is another DNS-based rule. It tells sendmail to accept mail for relaying if the mail is destined for a domain that lists the sendmail server in its MX record.

relay_hosts_only

With this option, sendmail looks up the sending system in a database (described shortly); if the specific computer that's attempting to relay mail is listed in the database, the mail is accepted.

access_db

This option is similar to relay_hosts_only, but it employs a more flexible interpretation of data in the database, enabling you to list entire domains. Many default sendmail configurations use this option by default, albeit with an empty initial database.

 Another relay option is promiscuous_relay, but this option should *never* be used. It tells sendmail to accept *all* relay attempts. This configuration is effectively an invitation to spammers to abuse your system.

As an example, suppose you want to use the access_db method. You might then include a line like the following in your sendmail *.mc* file:

```
FEATURE(`access_db')
```

Some configurations add more options within the parentheses—say, to specify the method of encoding data and the access database filename (normally */etc/mail/ access.db*). The access_db and relay_hosts_only options are the safest ways to configure mail relays, and they both use the same *access.db* configuration file. This file is a binary database file that's built from a text-mode file, typically called *access*. This text-mode file consists of lines that take the following format:

```
host.specification   CODE
```

In addition to these lines, the file may contain additional modifiers, as well as comments that begin with hash marks (#). The *host.specification* takes the form of IP addresses, IP address groups (specified by incomplete IP addresses, as in 192.168.24 for the 192.168.24.0/24 network), hostnames, domain names, or email addresses. If you use relay_hosts_only, though, specifications must match individual computers, not groups of computers. The CODE tells sendmail what to do with mail from the specified computers:

OK   Sendmail should accept mail for local delivery from the specified host.

RELAY

Sendmail relays mail that originates from or is addressed to the specified host.

REJECT

The server should refuse any message from the specified host using a 5*xx* code. Many senders generate a bounce message in response to such a code.

DISCARD

The server should accept and then discard any message from the specified host; no bounce message is generated.

As an example of an *access* file, consider the following:

```
localhost.localdomain    RELAY
localhost                RELAY
127.0.0.1                RELAY
spammer@abigisp.net      DISCARD
iamspam.biz              REJECT
192.168.24               RELAY
```

The first three lines tell sendmail to relay mail that's generated locally (on the local-host address, using any of three common names for that system). Such lines are common in default sendmail configurations. The next line tells the system to quietly discard mail from *spammer@abigisp.net*; but this rule has no effect on mail from other users of *abigisp.net*. The fifth line rejects (refuses with a bounce message) mail from the *iamspam.biz* domain. The last line authorizes sendmail to relay mail that originates from the 192.168.24.0/24 address range, which is presumably the server's own local network.

Once you've created an *access* file, you must convert that file to binary form using the *makemap* command:

```
# makemap hash /etc/mail/access.db < /etc/mail/access
```

Many distributions include an appropriate command as part of their sendmail startup scripts, so you may not need to explicitly enter this command.

Configuring sendmail to use a relay

Mail relaying involves at least three systems: the source, the destination, and the relay. The destination requires no special configuration, and the last section described the relay itself. On the source side, though, sendmail can require special configuration. Sometimes, the source computer doesn't run sendmail at all; a source might be a desktop system running a mail client. You can, though, use sendmail as a mail source. For instance, the source system might be a Linux computer that runs programs that assume the local computer is running sendmail and that therefore try to send mail using the server. Another configuration is to have a Linux computer serve as both a relay and a source for another relay. For instance, you might want a Linux server to handle mail for your local network but to relay it through an ISP's mail server. In either case, you must configure sendmail to use another computer as a relay.

By default, sendmail looks up the recipient's address via DNS and attempts to deliver the mail directly. If you configure sendmail to use a relay, as described here, it bypasses this attempt, and instead delivers the mail to the specified relay system.

Most distributions' default sendmail configurations don't use a relay. You can add one to the mix by adding one or more lines to your *.mc* configuration file:

```
define(`LOCAL_RELAY', `outgoing.mail.relay')
define(`MAIL_HUB', `outgoing.mail.relay')
define(`SMART_HOST', `outgoing.mail.relay')
```

The first line applies to outgoing mail that lacks a domain or machine name (for instance, mail addressed to *ben*); the second applies to mail addressed to users on the computer on which sendmail is running (for instance, *ben@armonica.pangaea.edu*, where sendmail is running on *armonica.pangaea.edu*); and the third applies to mail addressed to all other systems.

A somewhat simpler way to implement relaying is to use another line:

```
FEATURE(`nullclient', `outgoing.mail.relay')
```

This line, however, is intended for use in otherwise nearly empty configuration files. Only the FEATURE(`nocanonify') option should be used with it.

In all these cases, you must adjust the *outgoing.mail.relay* to point to the server you want to use as a relay.

Configuring sendmail to forward mail

Particularly when your domain has multiple mail servers or is connected to multiple networks, you may need to configure the system to forward mail in different ways depending on its source or destination. For instance, consider the "gatekeeper" Linux mail server in Figure 13-2. The intent of a configuration like this is to use Linux to provide useful preliminary processing on incoming mail, such as spam filtering and directing email to the correct internal mail server. This server can also pass mail between the two internal servers and filter outgoing mail.

Typically, the Linux SMTP server is listed as the domain's MX server, so external systems will deliver mail to it. Likewise, the internal mail servers, and perhaps individual client systems, can deliver outgoing mail to the Linux server. The trick is to configure the Linux server to deliver mail correctly, without getting into an infinite loop. For instance, you don't want the server to attempt to deliver mail for your domain back to itself, because this creates an infinite loop. One solution is to use a feature known as a *mailer table*. This can be activated with a line like this in the sendmail *.mc* file:

```
FEATURE(`mailertable')
```

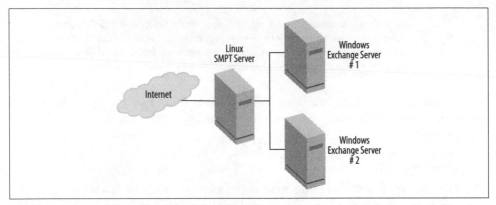

Figure 13-2. Linux can serve as a gatekeeper for one or more other mail servers

This entry may include additional options, such as a pointer to the mailer table database file (typically */etc/mail/mailertable.db*). Check your *.mc* file for the default entry, if it exists. As with many other sendmail files, this one relies on a text-mode file that's converted into a binary database file. The text-mode *mailertable* file contains entries like this:

```
.subnet1.pangaea.edu  smtp:exchange1.pangaea.edu
.subnet2.pangaea.edu  procmail:/etc/procmailrcs/exchange2
```

This configuration tells the server to deliver mail addressed to any computer in the *subnet1.pangaea.edu* subdomain to *exchange1.pangaea.edu* using SMTP and to deliver mail addressed to any computer in the *subnet2.pangaea.edu* subdomain using Procmail and the */etc/procmailrcs/exchange2* Procmail rule set. The first line results in a simple forwarding and so may not be extremely useful; you can just set up your DNS MX record to point directly to that computer. The second line, though, enables you to employ Procmail, which can be used as an interface to spam filters and other tools, on mail passed through the server. Procmail is described in more detail later in this chapter, in the section "Using Procmail."

Configuring Postfix

Postfix is an alternative to sendmail that ships with most major Linux distributions, although many of them don't install it by default. If your distribution doesn't ship with Postfix but you want to try it, check the Postfix home page (*http://www.postfix.org*) for source code download links. You might be able to install a binary package intended for another distribution, but chances are you'll need to modify or replace the SysV startup scripts.

As with sendmail, configuring Postfix for your network requires understanding the main Postfix configuration files. You can then set the main Postfix options, including those relating to addressing, relaying, and spam control.

Postfix is a very complex server, so this chapter can present only the basics of its configuration. For more information, consult the documentation at the Postfix web site or a book on the subject, such as *Postfix: The Definitive Guide* (O'Reilly).

Postfix Configuration Files

Linux Postfix binary packages typically store configuration files in */etc/postfix*. The main configuration file in this directory is *main.cf*, which controls the overall Postfix configuration. This file consists of comments, which are denoted by lines beginning with hash marks (#) and option lines of the form:

```
variable = value
```

The *variable* is typically a descriptive name, such as relayhost to set the hostname of another SMTP server that's to act as a mail relay. The *value* can be a hostname, IP address, filename, or other string. Sometimes a *value* can have multiple components, separated by commas. A *value* can also refer to an earlier *variable* by name: precede the earlier *variable* name by a dollar sign ($), as in myorigin = $mydomain to set the myorigin variable to be identical to mydomain.

The default *main.cf* file is extremely well commented, so you can learn a great deal about the configuration and how you can change it by reading the comments. Further information, including information on obscure options not mentioned in the default comments, can be found in the online Postfix documentation.

After making changes to *main.cf*, you should tell Postfix about those changes. The simplest way to do this is to type **postfix reload**.

In addition to the *main.cf* file, Postfix relies on several other configuration files. Most of these are binary database file with filenames ending in *.db*. These files are similar in purpose to sendmail's database files; they control username aliases, relay host mapping, and so on. Like the sendmail files, the Postfix database files are generated from plain-text files that typically take the same name as the database file but without the *.db* extension. Some of these files are described in upcoming sections.

Postfix Address Options

The Postfix address options begin with setting the server's name. As with sendmail, Postfix uses gethostbyname() to determine the computer's hostname and sets the hostname it reports to other systems appropriately. You can override this feature by setting myhostname:

```
myhostname = smtp.pangaea.edu
```

Two related options are mydomain and myorigin. The first of these sets the server's Internet domain; it defaults to the value of $myhostname minus its first component, as in pangaea.edu if $myhostname is smtp.pangaea.edu. The myorigin variable sets the hostname that Postfix appends to email addresses that don't specify a hostname. The default value is $mydomain, but you can change this to $myhostname or any other value, as appropriate.

If you want to force outgoing mail to have a particular return hostname, you can use the masquerade_domains option. You pass a domain name to this option, and hostnames within that domain are stripped down to the domain portion. For instance, if you set this option to pangaea.edu, and a user sends mail that has a return address of *linnaeus@gingko.pangaea.edu*, Postfix changes the outgoing address to *linnaeus@pangaea.edu*. This can be a handy option for coping with clients that insist on adding their own hostnames to outgoing mail. Mail with return addresses outside of the *pangaea.edu* domain are unaffected by this line, though. The masquerade_classes option affects the precise parts of the mail that are affected. You can set this to one or more of envelope_sender (the sender in the mail envelope), header_sender (the sender in the mail header), and header_recipient (the recipient in the mail header, typically used to strip hostnames from incoming mail). Typically, one or both of the first two options is used.

Still more complete address rewriting can be accomplished with the help of a file called *sender_canonical*. You specify the use of this file with the sender_canonical_maps option in *main.cf*:

```
sender_canonical_maps = hash:/etc/postfix/sender_canonical
```

You then edit the *sender_canonical* file so that each line holds an original email address or address fragment followed by the address or matching fragment you want substituted:

```
FETCHMAIL-DAEMON@localhost postmaster@pangaea.edu
@mandragora.example.com @pangaea.edu
```

These lines tell Postfix to replace *FETCHMAIL-DAEMON@localhost* with *postmaster@pangaea.edu* and to change any address at *mandragora.example.com* with the matching address at *pangaea.edu*. Once you've edited this file, type **postmap sender_canonical**. This command creates a *sender_canonical.db* file from the text-mode *sender_canonical* file.

When receiving mail, Postfix uses the mydestination variable to determine what addresses it's to treat as local. Mail addressed to any user at any of the $mydestination addresses is passed to local users; mail addressed to other addresses is relayed to that address, assuming relaying is authorized. You can set multiple hostnames for mydestination by separating them with commas, as in:

```
mydestination = $myhostname, localhost.$mydomain, mail.pangaea.edu
```

Postfix Relay Options

Most default Postfix configurations relay mail from the local network and deliver mail directly to the destination server without using an outgoing relay. Thus, if you want to fine-tune your relay configuration or use an outgoing mail relay system, you must adjust your Postfix configuration. You may also want to make changes if you want Postfix to deliver incoming mail to other servers, such as to Microsoft Exchange servers, using Postfix as a spam filter, mail sorter, or in some role other than the final destination system.

Configuring Postfix to relay mail

The default Postfix configuration relays mail under certain limited circumstances:

- The sender is on one of the $mynetworks networks. This defaults to the IP subnet on which the computer resides, but you can change it by setting mynetworks to a list of IP address ranges or by pointing to a file that holds this information. Alternatively, you can change mynetworks_style. This variable defaults to subnet, which sets the default behavior; however, you can set it to host, which causes Postfix to trust only the local machine. Setting mynetworks_style to class causes Postfix to trust the computers on the same class A, B, or C subnet on which it resides, which often (but not always) results in the same behavior as setting it to subnet.

- The sender is in one of the domains specified by relay_domains. This variable defaults to $mydestination.

- The sender is attempting to relay mail to a computer in $relay_domains or to a computer on the $mynetworks networks.

Overall, these defaults are laxer than those of sendmail. If you don't want your computer to relay mail at all, you should restrict these settings:

```
mynetworks = 127.0.0.0/8
relay_domains = smtp.pangaea.edu
```

The first line tells Postfix to relay only mail from the localhost address. The second sets the relay domain to the server's hostname (you should adjust it for your system, of course). A configuration that relays for some computers and networks, but not quite the default set, is also possible; for instance:

```
mynetworks = 127.0.0.0/8, 172.24.0.0/16, 192.168.24.0/24
relay_domains = $mydestination, pangaea.edu
```

This configuration tells Postfix to relay mail for two subnets by IP address, for the local domain ($mydestination), and for the *pangaea.edu* domain.

Configuring Postfix to use a relay

If Postfix should send mail through another computer as a relay, you should use the relayhost option to do the job. This option accepts a hostname as an option; Postfix sends mail through that system. Alternatively, you can provide a domain name if that domain's MX record points to an appropriate server. For instance, suppose you want to relay mail through *relay.pangaea.edu*:

```
relayhost = relay.pangaea.edu
```

 If you're in the same domain as the outgoing mail relay and if your domain's MX record points to the server you want to use, you can use $mydomain as the value of this option. Doing so has the advantage of adjusting automatically should you change your mail relay; Postfix can track the change using the MX record in your DNS server.

If your local DNS server is unreliable or if you use non-DNS methods of local name resolution, you may want to include the disable_dns_lookups = yes option. Ordinarily, Postfix uses DNS in preference to other name resolution methods; disabling this causes Postfix to use whatever name resolution methods are defined locally, such as your */etc/hosts* file.

Configuring Postfix to forward mail

Postfix, like sendmail, can serve as a system that forwards incoming mail to its final destination. (Figure 13-2 illustrates this configuration.) The most basic method of configuring such a system is to use what Postfix refers to as a *transport map*. You point to a file containing this map with the transport_maps option:

```
transport_maps = hash:/etc/postfix/transport
```

Such a line may already be present in your default configuration, so check for it before adding it. As with other Postfix references to outside databases, this one uses a text-mode file (*/etc/postfix/transport*) that's used to create a binary database with a similar name (*/etc/postfix/transport.db*). The plaintext file has a format that's similar to sendmail's *mailertable*. For instance, you can have Postfix deliver messages addressed to users in the *subnet1.pangaea.edu* subdomain to *exchange1.pangaea.edu* and use Procmail with the */etc/procmailrcs/exchange2* configuration file for addresses in the *subnet2.pangaea.edu* subdomain with a configuration like the following:

```
.subnet1.pangaea.edu   smtp:exchange1.pangaea.edu
subnet1.pangaea.edu    smtp:exchange1.pangaea.edu
.subnet2.pangaea.edu   procmail:/etc/procmailrcs/exchange2
subnet2.pangaea.edu    procmail:/etc/procmailrcs/exchange2
```

This configuration actually includes two lines for each subdomain. The lines with names that begin with dots (*.subnet1.pangaea.edu* and *.subnet2.pangaea.edu*) handle mail explicitly addressed to systems within the subdomain. The lines with names that lack leading dots handle mail addressed to the subdomain itself (such as *ben@subnet1.pangaea.edu*).

Configuring POP and IMAP Servers

SMTP servers tend to attract a lot of attention; after all, Internet mail delivery runs mostly over SMTP. Still, pull mail protocols—POP and IMAP—are just as important in many situations. Typically, users configure their desktop computers' email clients to contact POP or IMAP servers in order to read their incoming mail. Knowing how to handle these servers' configurations is therefore quite important. In the simplest cases, this requires launching the servers and setting authentication options. Most sophisticated servers provide additional options, though.

Launching POP and IMAP Servers

POP and IMAP servers vary in how they're launched. For the popular and simple UW IMAP, the typical method of launching and controlling the server is via a super server. (This method doesn't scale up very well, though, so for a busy server system, you might want to look into launching the server via a SysV startup script, or even running a server that uses this configuration by default.) On distributions that use *xinetd* as the super server, the UW IMAP package typically ships with one or more files in */etc/xinetd.d*. Typically, each file starts the server to handle a single protocol (POP or IMAP, sometimes with variants for different protocol versions or to add encryption). A typical entry looks like this:

```
service imap
{
   socket_type = stream
   protocol    = tcp
   wait        = no
   user        = root
   server      = /usr/sbin/imapd
   disable     = yes
}
```

Most distributions disable most or all of the servers by default, by setting the `disable = yes` option. To enable the server, you must delete this line or change it to read `disable = no`. You must then restart *xinetd*, typically by typing **/etc/init.d/xinetd restart** or something similar. Thereafter, *xinetd* responds to incoming requests for the protocols you've enabled. If you want the server to respond to multiple protocols, you must be sure to enable them all.

If your distribution uses *inetd* as a super server, you may need to add one line to */etc/inetd.conf* for each protocol you want to use. These lines set the same options that you'd set in the *xinetd* configuration:

```
imap stream tcp nowait root /usr/sbin/tcpd imapd
```

This example uses *tcpd* (that is, TCP Wrappers) to manage the server. You can therefore use the TCP Wrappers configuration files, */etc/hosts.allow* and */etc/hosts.deny*, to provide access restrictions based on IP addresses. (You can enable similar restrictions using *xinetd*'s built-in features if you use it as your super server.)

Some POP and IMAP servers, such as Dovecot, are more commonly launched via their own SysV startup scripts. To launch such servers on a one-time basis, you typically pass the start option to their startup scripts:

```
# /etc/init.d/dovecot start
```

To configure the server to start automatically when you boot the computer, you must set up your SysV links appropriately. Many distributions provide tools to help with this task, such as *chkconfig* (used by Fedora, Mandrake, and SuSE, among others) or *rc-update* (used by Gentoo). Consult distribution-specific documentation for more information on these tools.

Setting Authentication Options

The UW IMAP server provides no authentication options, in the sense of command-line arguments or configuration file entries, that affect authentication. (In fact, UW IMAP has no main configuration file.) UW IMAP, though, does use the Linux PAM system for authentication. As such, you can edit the IMAP PAM configuration files to change how IMAP authenticates users. Typical UW IMAP installations actually provide two PAM files, one for POP and one for IMAP: */etc/pam.d/pop* and */etc/pam.d/ imap*. Thus, you can use different authentication options for POP as for IMAP. Some POP and IMAP servers call their PAM configuration files something else; for instance, Dovecot uses */etc/pam.d/dovecot*, which controls both POP and IMAP access.

If your server uses the local Linux password database for POP and IMAP authentication, the default UW IMAP PAM configuration files should work fine. If you want to use another authentication tool, though, such as an NT domain controller or a Kerberos server, you need to modify the PAM configuration files. This topic is described in detail in Appendix A.

 Using Kerberos, or any other encrypted network authentication tool, via a PAM configuration encrypts the authentication between the POP or IMAP server and the authentication database, but not between the POP or IMAP server and its client. If you want to encrypt the authentication between the POP or IMAP server and its client, you must either tunnel the protocol in some way (say, via SSH) or use a server and client that support an encrypted exchange natively. The encrypted versions of POP and IMAP are commonly referred to as POPS and IMAPS, respectively.

More sophisticated POP and IMAP servers, including Cyrus IMAP and Dovecot, support their own authentication tools instead of or in addition to PAM. These servers often include configuration options to enable the authentication methods you want to use, so consult their documentation for details.

Additional Options on Advanced Servers

UW IMAP is easy to set up and configure, but it's inflexible; you can't change features such as where it looks for IMAP folders except by editing the source code and recompiling it. Using more sophisticated servers is, of course, an option; however, doing so opens up many additional options, some of which can be tricky to configure. As an example, consider Dovecot (*http://www.dovecot.org*), which is rising rapidly in popularity. This server uses the */etc/dovecot.conf* configuration file to hold options, which take the form:

```
option = value
```

For the most part, the default options work well; however, you might want to peruse the file or the Dovecot documentation to learn about its configurable features. As with many Linux configuration files, *dovecot.conf* uses hash marks (#) as comment characters, and the default file is well commented.

Dovecot provides options relating to protocol support (protocols, which takes one or more values such as imap and pop), SSL options, an option to disable cleartext authentication (disable_plaintext_auth), the default mailbox format to use (default_mail_env), options to enable special authentication methods, and so on.

Scanning for Spam, Worms, and Viruses

Unwanted email is arguably the worst problem facing email administration today. Two types of unwanted email are common: spam and worms/viruses. Spam is unsolicited bulk email, usually commercial in nature. Most spam markets worthless body-enhancement products, questionable financial advice, and so on but is more of a nuisance than a threat—at least, if you ignore the substantial network bandwidth that spam consumes. Worms and viruses, on the other hand, are malicious computer code that, if executed on an unprotected computer, can spread and cause damage. Despite the fact that spam is quite different from worms or viruses in their intent, the two classes of junk email can be combated in similar ways.

The distinction between worms and viruses is a tricky one to define and depends on who you ask. Thus, I don't try to distinguish the two types of menaces in this chapter, and hereafter I use the word *worm* to refer to both types of program. Sometimes I refer to "spam-fighting tools" or the like. Such tools can often be used to fight worms, as well, but such phrases omit this detail for brevity's sake.

Dealing with spam and worms requires first knowing a bit about the types of approaches to dealing with the problem. One of the tools that can be used to directly combat spam and worms is Procmail, so I describe it shortly. Procmail can also be used to invoke other spam-fighting tools. SpamAssassin and Bogofilter are two such antispam tools. Finally, as a site policy issue, you may want to place suspicious attachments in a special holding area until you can examine them.

An Antispam and Antivirus Tool Rundown

Spam and viruses are difficult to detect. This is particularly true of spam, because spam identification is somewhat subjective: one person's spam may be another person's desirable commercial communication. The line between worms and non-worms is clearer, but worms can also be difficult to distinguish between legitimate email attachments, particularly in some environments (for instance, if you have a legitimate business reason to send or receive executable files). For this reason, the number of spam-fighting tools available is quite large. Indeed, the number of *approaches* to fighting spam and worms is large. Here are some general methods:

Blackhole lists

> This approach, described in the earlier sections on sendmail and Postfix, relies on central authorities maintaining databases of IP addresses from which messages shouldn't be accepted or should be accepted only with caution. Typically, these databases are updated frequently, based on spam reports from their users. This method is best implemented in receiving SMTP servers because they receive direct connections from the sending systems and therefore aren't easily tricked into believing the message originated from a false IP address. (Headers are easily forged, so the originating IP address can be obfuscated by clever spammers if another system does this check.) Note that this approach doesn't test the message's content; it's based solely on the IP address and so is susceptible to false alarms should an address send both spam and nonspam messages.

Distributed hashes

> Some network databases work on more than the originating IP address; they store hashes of entire spam messages. When your server receives a message, it can hash the message (minus its headers) and query a network server for the presence of this hash. If it's present, it means that somebody else has received an identical message and entered it as spam in the hash database. This approach is a potentially powerful one, but it can be easily "poisoned" with respect to legitimate mailing lists; that is, individuals can classify mailing list messages as spam, which can then cause these legitimate messages to be misclassified as spam. You can work around this problem by creating a "white list" (see entry later in this list) of addresses that aren't tested against a distributed hash system.

Simple pattern matches

Examining the message's content is the most reliable way to identify spam. The simplest type of examination relies on simple pattern matches. For instance, you might decide that any message containing the word *Viagra* is spam, and discard it. This approach can be implemented in either the SMTP server or in add-on software, such as Procmail. It has the disadvantage of great potential for false alarms, particularly if your rules are too broad. For instance, if you discard all messages containing the word *Viagra*, you may catch a lot of spam, but you'll also discard legitimate email to people who are actually corresponding with others (perhaps their doctors) about this drug. Maintaining a good set of pattern match rules can also be quite time-consuming, although some packages, such as SpamAssassin, aim to minimize this problem by providing frequent updates to a general rule set.

White lists

A *white list* is a list of addresses or keywords that trigger automatic acceptance of a message. They're frequently used with simple pattern matches or other spam-catching tools in order to minimize the risk of discarding important messages. Typically, you add your regular correspondents to your white list, and their messages get through even if another rule would reject them. They're usually implemented using the same tools that can perform simple pattern match rejections.

Challenge-response tests

A challenge-response system is a variant on white lists. When a message arrives from a source other than one that's on the white list, the recipient automatically sends a challenge to the message source. This challenge is a message asking the sender to perform some action to prove that the message isn't spam, such as to respond with a keyword. Automated spamming systems can't cope with this request, but humans can. Once a response is received, the original message is delivered, and the sender is usually added to the white list. This method of spam fighting can be quite effective, but it can generate more traffic and, because they must respond to challenges, places an extra burden on those who send mail. A poor implementation can also result in a continuous loop of challenges to challenges, should two systems use similar systems that don't exempt challenges to their own challenges.

Statistical tests

A spam-catching tool that emerged on the scene in 2002 involves statistical tests (often called *Bayesian tests*, after Bayes' Rule, a statistical principle they employ). These tests use a database of words, word pairs, and other message features. Typically, you feed the software a sample of spam and another sample of nonspam, and the software adds up the number of times a word appears in each category. For instance, *Viagra* might appear 50 times in spam and once in nonspam, whereas *Linux* might appear 50 times in nonspam and once in spam. If a message with the word *Viagra* is analyzed, then, a statistical filter will give it a high probability of being spam. The analysis is typically based on many words, though, so a single word isn't likely to "poison" an analysis, as can happen with simple pattern matches. One statistical spam filter, Bogofilter, is described in more detail later. Some tools, such as SpamAssassin, employ statistical tests as part of their overall operation.

These same tools can detect worms, although some worm-detection tools rely on an analysis of the binary file that's attached to the message rather than English words in the message body. (Some worms can also be reliably identified by their message texts.)

Some tools are hard to classify in just one way. For instance, Procmail directly implements pattern-matching tests but can call other tools that use other methods. The upcoming sections describe Procmail, SpamAssassin, and Bogofilter in more detail.

Sendmail Antispam Options

One way to deal with spam and worms is to use SMTP server features. One of these features in sendmail has already been described: the *access.db* file, in conjunction with the FEATURE(`access_db') option in your sendmail *.mc* file. You can block mail from sites known to send nothing but spam using this technique. Unfortunately, the world of spam is a fast-changing one, so by the time you add a hostname or address to this list, chances are the spammer will have started using another. The sheer quantity of spam also makes this approach an awkward one. Nonetheless, you can use this method for some particularly persistent offenders.

Another spam-fighting approach is to use a *blackhole list*, which is a frequently updated list of sites that are known or suspected spam sources or that shouldn't be sending email directly. Blackhole lists work as services, much like DNS: your mail server queries the blackhole list with the IP address of a connecting server that's trying to initiate a connection, and the blackhole list server returns a value that indicates the sender's status. To use a blackhole list, you enter a line like the following in your sendmail *.mc* file:

```
FEATURE(`dnsbl', `relays.ordb.org', `"550 Email rejected due to sending server
misconfiguration - see http://www.ordb.org/faq/\#why_rejected"')
```

This line tells sendmail to use the blackhole list at *relays.ordb.org* and to include a message with a URL in bounced emails. (This enables senders to check the messages, should nonspam messages be bounced.) Of course, this raises a question: how do you know *which* blackhole list to use? Many are available. You may want to peruse *http://www.declude.com/Articles.asp?ID=97* or *http://www.moensted.dk/spam/* for pointers to more than 100 blackhole databases with varying criteria for inclusion and other features. Some are free; others require you to pay for the privilege of using them. If you like, you can include multiple blackhole list definitions, each on its own line.

More sophisticated spam-fighting techniques require additional software. In particular, you can add Procmail to the mix to filter on keywords or to call other programs to check your incoming email in various ways. This topic is covered in a later section. If the sendmail server is an intermediary system, you may want to call Procmail as part of the forwarding configuration, as described earlier, in the section "Configuring sendmail to forward mail."

Postfix Antispam Options

Postfix provides a number of antispam options, some of them are quite sophisticated. In addition, you can use Procmail as a delivery agent to call external programs or perform checks Postfix alone can't handle.

One of the simpler Postfix antispam configurations is to use a blackhole list. One *main.cf* option enables this feature:

```
smtpd_client_restrictions = reject_rbl_client relays.ordb.org
```

The smtpd_client_restrictions option tells Postfix when to reject mail. The reject_rbl_client value corresponds to a positive lookup in the blackhole list database specified after this value (*relays.ordb.org* in this example). Postfix can use the same blackhole lists as sendmail; consult *http://www.declude.com/Articles.asp?ID=97* or *http://www.moensted.dk/spam/* for pointers to more than 100 blackhole databases. Other values can be added to this line, separated by commas, to reject mail from systems that don't have matching DNS A records for their PTR records (reject_unknown_client), to check an external database for rejection rules (check_client_access *type:table*), and so on. Consult the Postfix documentation for details.

> Prior to Version 2.0, Postfix used a pair of options to achieve the effect described here. Specifically, maps_rbl_domains contained a comma-separated list of blackhole list servers; these were used only if the reject_maps_rbl option was passed to smtpd_client_restrictions.

Spam and worms can often be identified by the presence of strings in message headers or bodies. For instance, you might know from experience that any message with a subject of earn $$$ is spam and can be discarded. Postfix includes several options that check message headers and bodies for such content:

header_checks
: This option points to a file that contains checks that are applied to message headers—the parts of a message that contain the subject, the return address, etc. Typically, you'll check headers for suspicious email subjects, senders, and perhaps recipients.

mime_header_checks
: Increasingly, email messages use Multipurpose Internet Mail Extension (MIME) to encode special formatting and nontextual data. MIME extensions are also

loved by spammers and worm authors because they can deliver text that's harder to identify as spam or malicious computer code. You can use this option to point to a file that matches suspicious MIME headers. This option is available in Postfix 2.0 and later, and defaults to $header_checks.

nested_header_checks
Users and programs sometimes attach one email message to another. To search such attached messages' headers, you can use this option, which is available only in Postfix 2.0 and later, and defaults to $header_checks.

body_checks
This option searches email messages' bodies—the parts of the message that users read, as opposed to the headers. Scanning message bodies can be a good way to identify worms and spam. This option is available only in Postfix 2.0 and later.

All of these options take an external filename, along with a code for the file's format, as an option. This file is typically a plain-text file or a database file that's derived from a plain-text file. The resulting entry in *main.cf* looks something like this:

```
header_checks = pcre:/etc/postfix/header_checks
```

The pcre code stands for *Perl compatible regular expression*. Alternatively, you can employ regexp to use non-Perl regular expressions. In either case, lines in the original text file take the specified form followed by one of the following action codes:

DISCARD *optional text*
Accepts the message for delivery but quietly rejects it. If *optional text* is present, enter it in the mail logs; otherwise, log a generic message.

DUNNO
Moves on to the next input line. This option is synonymous with OK.

FILTER *transport:destination*
Passes the message through the external content filter, as specified by the *transport* method (smtp, procmail, and so on) and *destination* (a hostname or filename, typically). The filter receives the message only after Postfix has examined all the message's lines, so the message can be rejected before the filter is called.

HOLD
Places the message in the *hold queue*, which is a sort of limbo in which the message is neither delivered nor discarded. A system administrator can examine the hold queue using the *postcat* command and release messages from the queue or destroy them using *postsuper*.

IGNORE
Ignores the current line of input and moves to the next one.

PREPEND *text*

> Places the specified *text* at the start of the input line. This can flag lines for further spam processing.

REDIRECT *user@domain*

> Sends the message to the specified user rather than the recipient specified by the mail's envelope. This feature can be used to forward mail for users who have moved elsewhere, as an alternative method of forwarding mail to internal servers, and in other ways. However, many potential uses of this action are better achieved through other means.

REJECT *optional text*

> Rejects delivery of the message. If you specify *optional text*, it's passed to the sender; if not, a generic error message is delivered to the sender.

WARN *optional text*

> Logs a warning with the specified *optional text* in the mail log file. This action is intended primarily for testing new rules before implementing them.

Many of these action codes are available only in Postfix 2.0, 2.1, or later. As an example of their use, consider the following entries:

```
### Subject headers indicative of spam
/^Subject: ADV:/ REJECT
/^Subject: Accept Credit Cards/ DISCARD
### Additional header checks
/^(From|Received):.*iamspam\.biz/ REJECT
/^From: spammer@abigisp\.net/ FILTER procmail:/etc/procmailrcs/maybespam
```

This set of rules rejects mail with a subject header of ADV: or with from or received headers that include the string iamspam.biz. It also discards mail with a subject header of Accept Credit Cards and passes mail from *spammer@abigisp.net* through a Procmail filter, */etc/procmailrcs/maybespam*. This filter presumably performs additional checks that are too complex for Postfix to handle by itself.

In addition to its own checks, Postfix can send mail through Procmail for processing. In fact, using Procmail is usually the default. If in doubt, check your *main.cf* file for a line like the following:

```
mailbox_command = /usr/bin/procmail
```

When called in this way, Procmail is used for final message delivery. You can call it in other ways, such as in a FILTER action in a header check. Broadly speaking, Procmail is a more powerful way of looking for suspicious patterns in email than Postfix's own rules. Procmail can also be customized on a user-by-user basis, which is harder with Postfix's rules. Thus, you may prefer to use Procmail alone, rather than use Postfix's pattern matching tools. The main advantage of Postfix's rules is that they can be used to reject messages before they're fully received. In particular, if a header check causes a message to be rejected, Postfix refuses delivery before many bytes are transferred. This feature can help conserve bandwidth, at least if you can devise rules that correctly identify large spams or worms from their headers alone. Procmail delivery rules, by contrast, operate only after the mail server has accepted the mail for delivery. Unfortunately, spammers and worm writers have become very good at disguising their unwanted emails' headers, so you may have no choice but to accept the entire email in order to properly identify it. The topic of spam and worm control is covered in more detail later in this chapter.

Using Procmail

Procmail is a very powerful mail processing tool. It does far more than spam filtering; it can redirect mail based on nonspam criteria, sort mail into folders, copy messages for archival purposes, pass mail through arbitrary external programs, and more. Still, one of Procmail's main applications is as a spam-fighting tool; you can use its native pattern-matching features to discard mail or shunt it into a suspected spam folder. You can also pass messages to external programs for tests that Procmail can't handle by itself.

Using Procmail requires calling it in some way. Typically, you do so by configuring your SMTP server to call Procmail as part of its mail delivery process. You can then move on to Procmail configuration. To configure Procmail you need to understand the Procmail configuration file format and be able to create Procmail *recipes*, which are the rules used to direct mail in Procmail.

Calling Procmail

The first step in Procmail use is to ensure that your mail system uses it. Most Linux SMTP server configurations use Procmail by default, so you may not need to change anything about your basic SMTP configuration to use Procmail. If you're in doubt, though, or if you want to fine-tune the configuration, you can check some settings:

Sendmail

You should set three options in the sendmail *.mc* file to use Procmail. The first of these is:

```
define(`PROCMAIL_MAILER_PATH', `/usr/bin/procmail')
```

This tells sendmail where to find the Procmail binary. (Some configurations put this option in another configuration file, but you can override it in your sendmail *.mc* file if you need to do so.) The remaining options are `FEATURE(`local_procmail')` and `MAILER(procmail)`, which collectively tell sendmail to use Procmail for local deliveries. As described in the earlier section "Configuring Postfix to forward mail," you can also call Procmail in other ways, such as in a forwarding configuration.

Postfix

To call Procmail as part of the Postfix delivery rules, you must tell Postfix to use the Procmail binary as part of its delivery system: `mailbox_command = /usr/bin/`

procmail. As described in an earlier section, you can also tell Postfix to use Procmail in mail forwarding configurations.

The Procmail configuration file

Procmail can use one or more of several configuration files:

/etc/procmailrc

This file is the global Procmail configuration file. It's called as *root* to process all the mail that the SMTP server handles. For spam-control purposes, you use this file to apply rules you want to use on *all* the email that's delivered to your local users. Typically, this means you use it to apply rules that are very unlikely to result in false alarms.

~/.procmailrc

Individual users can create *.procmailrc* files in their home directories. These files have the same format as */etc/procmailrc*, but they're applied only to email directed to specific users. This enables users to apply their own customized Procmail rules. Alternatively, you can provide some standard configuration files in specific locations and allow users to create symbolic links to those files to achieve preset effects.

Other configuration files

Some methods of calling Procmail, such as those that use Procmail as part of mail forwarding schemes, enable you to pass the name of a configuration file to Procmail. Sometimes these reside in a directory such as */etc/procmailrcs*, but that location is arbitrary.

 Procmail runs as the user who calls it, although when it's called as *root*, it can drop its privileges under some circumstances. A rule that works well in *~/.procmailrc* (when Procmail is called as the end user) may not work well when placed in */etc/procmailrc* (when Procmail is called as *root*), or vice versa. Typically, you must be more careful about file permissions when calling Procmail as *root*, because writing to or creating a file (such as a mail folder) as *root* can make that file inaccessible to ordinary users, such as the mail's intended recipient.

Whatever its name, a Procmail configuration file consists of three parts: comments (denoted by hash marks), environment variable assignments (similar to those in *bash*, such as MAILDIR = $HOME/Mail), and recipes (described next). The bulk of most Procmail configuration files consists of its recipes.

Creating Procmail recipes

Procmail recipes consist of three parts: the identification line, the conditions, and the action. The idea is that the action is initiated when the conditions are met. For instance, a condition might be that the string Viagra appear in the message body, and the action might be that the message is sent to */dev/null*—that is, that the message be discarded. The form of the recipe is as follows:

```
:0 [flags] [:[lockfile]]
[conditions]
action
```

The identification line always begins with :0; that's just the convention. The *flags* are described shortly; they specify where Procmail looks for condition matches, how it matches, and so on. The *lockfile* is a file that controls access to a mail file. If a file is locked, Procmail defers operating on it. Normally, a single colon (:) is sufficient, but you can specify the filename, if necessary. The *conditions* are technically optional, but in practice, most recipes have at least one condition line. (A recipe with no *conditions* lines matches all mail messages.) Including multiple conditions causes Procmail to require all of them to match before an *action* line is implemented. Precisely one *action* is required for each recipe.

Procmail's default behavior is to match *conditions* against message headers in a case-insensitive way. Several *flags* are available to change how Procmail handles these matches, though. Here are the more common:

H   This value does matches on message headers, which is the default.

B   This value does matches on message bodies.

D   This value does a case-sensitive pattern match, as opposed to the normal case-insensitive match.

c   Ordinarily, if a recipe matches, it's passed to the *action*, which may discard it, alter it, or otherwise make the original inaccessible. This option causes the *action* to act on a "carbon copy" of the original message, which is useful if you want to, for example, send a duplicate copy of a message to another account or mail folder.

w   This value causes Procmail to wait for the *action* to complete. If the *action* fails, Procmail leaves the message in the queue for other recipes.

W   This option is similar to w, but it suppresses error messages.

f   This option pipes a message through another program, treating that program as a filter.

The Procmail recipe *conditions* can look like Greek to the uninitiated. Each begins with an asterisk (*), followed by a *regular expression*. At its simplest, a regular expression is simply a string that must match exactly. For instance, the regular expression Viagra matches the word *Viagra* in the input. Many characters have special meanings, though, such as:

^   A caret symbol indicates the start of a line; for instance, ^Viagra denotes the string *Viagra*, but only at the start of a line. Many *conditions* begin with a caret.

$ This character signifies the end of a line.

. A period matches any single character except for an end-of-line character. For instance, h.t matches *hat*, *hut*, *hot*, or any other similar string.

x* This string (where *x* is any single character) matches any number of *x* characters, including none. This is often combined with a dot (.), as in .*, to match any arbitrary group of characters.

x+ This expression works much like *x**, but matches any occurrence of one or more *x* characters, rather than 0 or more.

x? This string matches zero or one *x* characters.

(*string1*|*string2*)
This expression matches one of two strings by separating them by a vertical bar within parentheses. This principle can be extended to more than two strings, as well.

(*string*)*
This expression matches zero or more instances of the specified *string*.

[*chars*]
Placing characters within square brackets causes Procmail to match any one of the enclosed characters. For instance, [abcz] matches any one of the characters a, b, c, or z. You can specify a range of characters by using a dash, as in [c-j] to indicate any letter between c and j.

\ The backslash character removes the special meaning from the subsequent character. For instance, to match a dot, you enter \. in the *conditions*.

! This character appears only at the start of a *conditions* line and reverses its meaning; that is, if the regular expression matches, the recipe does *not* match.

? Like !, this character appears only at the start of a *conditions* line. It tells Procmail to use the exit code of the specified program.

Regular expressions can be extremely complex, so you may need to consult the Procmail manpage or another source of information on regular expressions to learn more. The next section provides some examples.

Finally, each Procmail recipe ends with an *action*. Each *action* can take any of several forms:

A *filename*
An *action* that takes the form of a filename indicates that the message is to be stored in the specified file, which is treated as an mbox mail folder.

A *subdirectory name*
A filename that ends in a slash (/) is interpreted as a subdirectory name, in which case Procmail stores the message in this subdirectory in maildir format.

! An exclamation mark denotes a list of email addresses to which the message should be forwarded. This can be useful for setting up individual mail forwarding to another system.

| Procmail treats a vertical bar as a pipe character, much like *bash*. Its presence at the start of an *action* tells Procmail to pass the message to an external program for further processing.

{ You can nest multiple tests by using a left curly brace as the *action* line; subsequent lines, until a right curly brace (}), constitute one or more additional recipes that are used only if the initial recipe matches. You can use this feature to control whether or not to perform certain tests; for instance, to perform spam checks only if mail doesn't come from certain addresses (that is, to implement a white list).

Because Procmail supports just one *action* per recipe, you may need to create an external script if you want to perform some complex action. Be sure your external script reads the entire message. If it doesn't, Procmail may send the message through additional recipes, which can result in duplicate deliveries.

Examples of Procmail recipes

Example 13-1 shows a sample Procmail recipe file intended for use by individuals. (When used by the system, some file ownership issues can arise. This problem can be avoided by adding a DROPPRIVS = yes line to the start of the file.) This example illustrates several useful techniques:

Nesting
> The first rule contains two nested subrules, the intent being to exclude mail from two regular correspondents from spam checks, which are nested. The nested rules are indented to set them off, but this indentation isn't required.

Spam checks
> The two spam-check rules look for strings that are indicative of spam. The first searches message bodies for the string 301 followed by 0 or more characters, followed by S, 0 or more characters, and 1618. This string is found in some spams that reference a failed piece of U.S. legislation, S.1618, which dealt with spam. The legislation failed years ago, but spam still references it, as if to legitimize itself. The second spam check looks for a string in subject headers that identifies messages encoded using a system that's common for certain Asian languages. Most non-Asian users seldom or never receive nonspam mail with such subject headers, but a lot of spam uses them.

Flags
> Several rules use flags to search the text of messages or to create carbon copies.

Mail sorting
> The spam messages are "sorted" to */dev/null*, which effectively discards the messages. The last rule saves mail from a mailing list (identified by a unique "to" header) into the *genetics-list* mbox mail folder in the $MAILDIR subdirectory, which is identified on the first line of the recipe file.

Example 13-1. Sample Procmail recipe file

```
MAILDIR = $HOME/Mail

# Do some spam checks, but exclude anything from good addresses
:0
*! ^From:.*(goodguy@pangaea\.edu|linnaeus@example\.com)
{
  :0 B
  * ^.*301.*S.*1618
  /dev/null

  :0
  * ^Subject:.*=\?big5\?*
  /dev/null
}

# Forward mail from goodguy@pangaea.edu with "peas" in the
# subject line to mendel@luna.edu
:0 c
* ^From:.*goodguy@pangaea\.edu
* ^Subject:.*peas
! mendel@luna.edu

# Shunt mail from a genetics mailing list into its own folder
:0:
* ^To:.*genetics@mailer\.example\.org
$MAILDIR/genetics-list
```

One of the major problems with using Procmail alone as a spam-control tool is that creating and maintaining a set of Procmail rules can be quite labor-intensive. This is particularly true because spam and worms are constantly changing, so a good set of rules for today may be inadequate tomorrow. You may want to search for a ready-made set of Procmail recipes, such as SpamBouncer (*http://www.spambouncer.org*) or the Sample Procmail Recipes with Comments (*http://handsonhowto.com/pmail102.html*). The first of these is specifically intended as an antispam tool, whereas the second is a practical teaching tool. If you periodically check back with such pages and update your filters, you can keep a reasonably up-to-date Procmail antispam configuration. On the other hand, rules created by somebody else are more likely to miss spam or, worse, falsely identify nonspam as spam.

 Before deploying a new Procmail recipe, or especially an extensive set of recipe changes, try testing it on a small scale. You can create a test account, place your new recipe in its *.procmailrc* file, and send test messages—both spam and nonspam—to that account.

Using SpamAssassin

SpamAssassin (*http://spamassassin.apache.org*) is an antispam tool based on a large number of tests. Each test changes the *score* of the message. SpamAssassin doesn't actually delete messages; instead, it adds headers identifying likely spam as such. The idea is that you'll call SpamAssassin from Procmail, a mail server, or a mail reader and use it to detect the SpamAssassin spam report and delete or redirect messages based on that report.

 SpamAssassin has grown into quite a large tool. In fact, it's complex enough that it's spawned its very own book: *SpamAssassin* (O'Reilly). If you need to perform complex tasks or configure SpamAssassin as part of a mail server for a large site, it's worthwhile to read this or other SpamAssassin-specific documentation.

SpamAssassin basics

The SpamAssassin software comes with most major distributions, so installing it from your distribution medium is usually the simplest course of action. If you can't find SpamAssassin with your distribution, go to the main SpamAssassin site, and download it. SpamAssassin is actually a Perl script and relies on several Perl modules, so you may need to install additional packages that hold these modules.

Once SpamAssassin is installed, you should test its operation by manually feeding it a few spam and nonspam messages. You do this by redirecting a message in a file into the *spamassassin* command. Adding the -t option adds an extra report to the end of the output, which appears on the screen:

```
$ spamassassin -t < message.txt
```

The *message.txt* file should contain a complete message, including full headers. Most mail readers have an option to save messages to disk with full headers so use that option to get your samples. The SpamAssassin output includes two additions to the message. The first addition appears at the end of the message headers, and constitutes SpamAssassin's report, as intended for subsequent mail processing tools, such as Procmail or an email reader. For a nonspam message, this addition is likely to resemble the following:

```
X-Spam-Checker-Version: SpamAssassin 3.0.0-g3.0.0 (2004-09-13) on mail.example.com
X-Spam-Level:
X-Spam-Status: No, score=0.1 required=5.0 tests=RCVD_IN_SORBS autolearn=unavailable
        version=3.0.0-g3.0.0
```

The first line simply identifies the version of SpamAssassin and the computer on which it's running. The second line holds the spam level, which is expressed as a number of asterisks (*). Because this is an innocuous nonspam message, no asterisks are displayed; however, some nonspam messages will have a small number of asterisks (five is the typical cutoff point for spam, although you can use something else if you like). The third line, which typically extends across multiple lines, summarizes the tests that raised alarms. In this case, the total spam score is 0.1 (hits=0.1). That 0.1 value came from the RCVD_IN_SORBS test, which isn't explained at this point. The -t option to *spamassassin*, though, adds extra lines at the end of the message:

```
Content analysis details:   (0.1 points, 5.0 required)

 pts rule name              description
---- ----------------------  --------------------------------------------------
 0.1 RCVD_IN_SORBS           RBL: SORBS: sender is listed in SORBS
                             [172.24.98.102 listed in dnsbl.sorbs.net]
```

This text identifies the RCVD_IN_SORBS flag as meaning that the sender address is listed in the SORBS blackhole list. This information can help you understand what Spam-Assassin is doing right (or wrong), but it's not provided in normal operation. You can, of course, consult the SpamAssassin documentation to learn more about specific tests.

When you test a spam message, the spam headers added to the message are likely to report more serious problems:

```
X-Spam-Flag: YES
X-Spam-Checker-Version: SpamAssassin 3.0.0-g3.0.0 (2004-09-13) on mail.example.com
X-Spam-Level: ******
X-Spam-Status: Yes, hits=6.8 required=5.0 tests=FORGED_MUA_OUTLOOK,
        FORGED_OUTLOOK_TAGS,HTML_40_50,HTML_FONTCOLOR_UNSAFE,HTML_MESSAGE,
        HTML_TAG_EXISTS_TBODY,RCVD_IN_BL_SPAMCOP_NET,RCVD_IN_DSBL,
        RCVD_IN_SORBS autolearn=spam version=3.0.0-g3.0.0
```

This output includes one header line that's not present in the nonspam output: X-Spam-Flag: YES. You can search for this line using a Procmail recipe, as described shortly, to detect spam after messages have been processed with SpamAssassin. The X-Spam-Level header shows six stars, corresponding to the 6.8 hit rating reported in the X-Spam-Status line. This line also shows quite a few hits on individual spam tests. These are reported in greater detail at the end of the message if you use the -t option to *spamassassin*.

You should run several spam and several nonspam messages through SpamAssassin. You should verify that none of the nonspam messages are rejected and that a significant number of spams are rejected. SpamAssassin might not detect all of your spams, though. You can take the time to fine tune its operation by changing the points assigned to individual rules or by enabling its auto-learning feature, which enables it to update its rules on the fly. You can also combine SpamAssassin with other tools, such as your own custom Procmail filters.

Calling SpamAssassin from Procmail

You can call SpamAssassin in various ways. One is to use Procmail for local mail delivery. (Calling SpamAssassin as part of a mail gateway system is described next.) Add the following recipes to the start of your Procmail configuration file to call Spam-Assassin and sort suspected spam into two folders, *almost-certainly-spam* and *probably-spam*:

```
:0fw
* < 256000
| spamassassin
```

```
:0:
* ^X-Spam-Level: \*\*\*\*\*\*\*\*\*\*\*\*\*\*
almost-certainly-spam

:0:
* ^X-Spam-Status: Yes
probably-spam

:0
* ^^rom[ ]
{
  LOG="*** Dropped F off From_ header! Fixing up. "

  :0 fhw
  | sed -e '1s/^/F/'
}
```

These rules are taken from the *procmail.example* file that ships with SpamAssassin. That file also includes several comments that describe its rules. In short, the first recipe passes messages that are smaller than 256,000 bytes through SpamAssassin, which adds its headers to the messages. (Larger messages are almost certainly not spam, although they can contain worms. SpamAssassin doesn't cope well with very large messages, hence this size limitation.) The second recipe dumps messages with a spam score of 15 or higher into the *almost-certainly-spam* folder, while the third recipe places messages that are flagged as spam but that weren't caught by the second recipe into the *probably-spam* folder. The final recipe fixes a Procmail bug that can cause the leading F in the From: to be dropped. (This bug has been fixed, but it's included in case you're running an old version of Procmail.)

Of course, you can change these rules if you like. For instance, you can send suspected spam to */dev/null*, but doing so means that if any such messages really *aren't* spam, you won't be able to retrieve them. Placing suspected spam in folders means that you can open those folders and recover any misclassified messages.

Calling SpamAssassin from sendmail

Calling SpamAssassin from Procmail is fine for local mail delivery, but it doesn't work well for a mail server that should operate as a spam filter for another server, such as a Microsoft Exchange server. For this configuration, you need a way to call SpamAssassin more directly as part of the mail relay process; the MIMEDefang tool (*http://www.mimedefang.org*) can do so. Although a complete description of MIME-Defang and the sendmail features it uses is beyond the scope of this book, a brief description should get you started.

The key to the process is to use the sendmail INPUT_MAIL_FILTER configuration line to call MIMEDefang, which in turn is configured to pass incoming messages through SpamAssassin and take actions accordingly. A full sendmail *.mc* file that implements these features appears in Example 13-2.

Example 13-2. Sample sendmail configuration with SpamAssassin

```
divert(-1)
#
# Spam-checking gateway configuration
#
divert(0)dnl
VERSIONID(`Spam-checking gateway')
OSTYPE(linux)dnl
DOMAIN(generic)dnl
FEATURE(virtusertable)dnl
FEATURE(mailertable)dnl
FEATURE(access_db)dnl
FEATURE(always_add_domain)dnl
FEATURE(nouucp,`reject')dnl
FEATURE(`relay_based_on_MX')dnl
define(`confDEF_USER_ID',``8:12'')dnl
define(`confPRIVACY_FLAGS', \
   `goaway,noreceipts,restrictmailq,restrictqrun,noetrn')dnl
define(`confTO_QUEUERETURN',`7d')dnl
define(`confTO_QUEUEWARN_NORMAL',`1h')dnl
define(`confMAX_DAEMON_CHILDREN',`60')dnl
define(`confMAX_MESSAGE_SIZE',`10000000')dnl
define(`confMAX_CONNECTION_RATE_THROTTLE',`10')dnl
define(`confMAX_RCPTS_PER_MESSAGE',`500')dnl
INPUT_MAIL_FILTER(`mimedefang',`S=unix:/var/spool/MIMEDefang/mimedefang.sock, \
   F=T, T=S:60s;R:60s;E:5m')dnl
MAILER(smtp)dnl
MAILER(local)dnl
MAILER(procmail)dnl
```

 A couple of lines in Example 13-2 are very long; they're denoted by trailing backslashes (\) at the end of the first line, but should be entered on single lines without the backslashes.

This configuration also requires you to set up the sendmail mailer table file (typically */etc/mail/mailertable*) that was described earlier. It must include a line that points the system to an internal server that will receive the spam-filtered messages:

```
pangaea.edu    esmtp:internal.pangaea.edu
```

In addition to the sendmail configuration, you must configure MIMEDefang. This tool requires three directories, */var/spool/MIMEDefang*, */var/spool/MD-Quarantine*, and */var/spool/MD-Bayes*. Assign ownership of these directories to the account used to run MIMEDefang (typically *defang*). Once this is done, edit *mimedefang-filter* (usually stored in */usr/local/etc/mimedefang*). Set the $AdminAddress, $AdminName, and $DaemonAddress lines to point to your local postmaster's email address, the postmaster's name (often your domain's name and Postmaster), and the email address used in messages MIMEDefang generates. You should also set the $SALocalTestsOnly item to 0 or 1 to forbid or allow SpamAssassin to use network-based tests.

Configure the internal server computer (*internal.pangaea.edu* in this example) to accept mail only from the spam-filtering gateway or from this system and any local systems that should be able to relay outgoing mail. This server shouldn't accept mail directly from the outside. Certainly it shouldn't be listed as an MX server in your domain's DNS configuration; only the spam-filtering mail gateway should be listed in this capacity.

Using Bogofilter

Unlike SpamAssassin, which combines many different spam-fighting tools in one system, Bogofilter (*http://bogofilter.sourceforge.net*) takes a single approach to spam fighting. It's an implementation of a statistical spam filter. As such, it requires training on a corpus of both spam and nonspam messages before it can work. Thus, you may need to save your spam for a few days before you can effectively use Bogofilter.

 SpamAssassin can use a statistical filter as part of its rule set. To do so, you must give it sample messages to train it, using its *sa-learn* command. Consult this command's manpage for details; the training process is similar to that for Bogofilter, although the command details differ.

Bogofilter can be installed like most other packages; check your distribution to see if a version is available with it. If not, go to the project's home page, and download a binary or source code version from there. Like SpamAssassin, Bogofilter is called from Procmail or a mail reader program. Before you do that, though, you must train Bogofilter.

The training procedure requires examples of both spam and nonspam messages—the more, the better. (A collection of several thousand messages is not excessive, but Bogofilter can do some good with just a few dozen.) Ideally, these messages should be typical of spam and nonspam messages that *you* receive; you want Bogofilter to learn to differentiate your spam from your nonspam. Although you can find spam collections on the Internet, using them for Bogofilter training can cause problems, because other people may receive different types of spam, or because you might not classify everything in such collections as spam. The simplest way to train Bogofilter is to place all your spam messages in one file and all your nonspam messages in another file, both of which should be in mbox format. In subsequent examples, I refer to these as *spam.mbox* and *nonspam.mbox*, respectively.

Conceptually, the simplest way to train Bogofilter is to pass the spam and nonspam messages through the *bogofilter* command using the -s and -n options, respectively:

```
$ bogofilter -s < spam.mbox
$ bogofilter -n < nonspam.mbox
```

These commands create a database file, *~/.bogofilter/wordlist.db*, which contains all the words contained in all the messages, along with counts of how often they appear in spam and nonspam messages. When Bogofilter later encounters a spam, it can then use these classifications to estimate the probability that a message is spam or nonspam.

 Because the Bogofilter database file is stored in the user's home directory, you should create the Bogofilter database file by running the program as that user. This user can conceivably be *root*, but for security reasons, it's best if you find a way to run Bogofilter as a non-*root* user. If necessary, you can create an initial database, place the mail classification call to *bogofilter* in users' individual *~/.procmailrc* files, and modify the global configuration to use the global word files in addition to individual users' word lists.

Another approach to Bogofilter training is to use a training script, such as *bogominitrain.pl* or *randomtrain*. These scripts might or might not be shipped with a distribution-provided Bogofilter package. If they're not on your system, consult the main Bogofilter site. These scripts perform more sophisticated training; namely, they use the *bogofilter* command to classify each message and perform training only if the message isn't classified correctly by Bogofilter. If necessary, this process is repeated until Bogofilter classifies every message correctly. The result tends to be smaller databases, and often more accurate results, but initial training takes longer. Consult the documentation that comes with the training script for details. Typically, you pass the script the names of both the spam and the nonspam files, and perhaps additional parameters:

```
$ bogominitrain.pl -fnv ~/.bogofilter nonspam.mbox spam.mbox '-o 0.9,0.3'
```

This example passes the location of the word list, the nonspam and spam files, and classification parameters (described in more detail shortly).

Whatever training method you use, you should also examine, and perhaps modify, the Bogofilter configuration file. By default, */etc/bogofilter.cf* provides systemwide defaults, but individual users can override these by creating a configuration file called *~/.bogofilter.cf* (this filename can be set in */etc/bogofilter.cf*). Options in this file are well commented, so perusing it will give you some idea of what you can change. Some options you may want to modify include:

bogofilter_dir

> This option points to the word list directory. Changing it is one way ordinary users can access a global word list; however, doing so may make it impossible for individuals to change that word list.

ignore_case

> Ordinarily, Bogofilter pays attention to case; Viagra is distinct from viagra. You can set ignore_case=yes to have Bogofilter convert all words to lowercase,

though. This can help overcome attempts to confuse antispam tools by mixing up case in words, but it can also reduce Bogofilter's sensitivity to strings for which case can be important.

algorithm

Bogofilter can use several different algorithms for determining the *spamicity* of a message (that is, the probability that a message is spam). These algorithms are graham, robinson, and fisher. The default is fisher, which generates a three-way classification: spam, nonspam, or unsure.

ham_cutoff

This option sets the maximum spamicity score (between 0.0 and 1.0) that's needed to classify a message as nonspam. A value of 0.10 is typical and usually works well.

spam_cutoff

This option sets the minimum spamicity score (between 0.0 and 1.0) that's required for a spam classification. A value of 0.95 is typical and usually works well.

Once you've set these values and trained Bogofilter, you should test its operation by passing spam and nonspam messages through the *bogofilter* command. Ideally, you should use messages that you held back from the training so that you can judge how Bogofilter handles messages it's never seen. Use the -v option to have the program generate a verbose report of the input messages, which you redirect as input:

```
$ bogofilter < message.txt
X-Bogosity: Yes, tests=bogofilter, spamicity=1.000000, version=0.16.4
```

This result shows a classification of the message as spam (X-Bogosity: Yes), with a very high spamicity score (1.000000). A nonspam message is likely to generate a much lower score:

```
$ bogofilter < message.txt
X-Bogosity: No, tests=bogofilter, spamicity=0.000000, version=0.16.4
```

Because of its three-way output, Bogofilter can also tell you that it's unsure of the status of the message:

```
$ bogofilter < message.txt
X-Bogosity: Unsure, tests=bogofilter, spamicity=0.500008, version=0.16.4
```

If you find that Bogofilter isn't classifying your messages correctly, you should revisit your training procedures. Perhaps you didn't classify enough messages or delivered them with the wrong parameters (confusing spam and nonspam messages, for instance). Note that a classification of "unsure" works like a nonspam classification in most respects, so you shouldn't be too concerned if some of your nonspam messages are classified in this way, unless the spamicity ratings are very close to the spam cutoff point. If you have classification problems, you might also consider fine-tuning the Bogofilter cutoff criteria (ham_cutoff and spam_cutoff). You can increase or decrease these values, but with certain risks; if you make either the nonspam or spam category too large, you'll risk misclassifying messages.

 Numerically, the largest range of spamicity values is above the ham_cutoff value but below the spam_cutoff value. Thus, you might expect that most messages will end up classified as "unsure." In practice, though, most messages achieve very high (close to 1.0) or very low (close to 0.0) spamicity ratings.

With Bogofilter now correctly classifying at least most of your messages, it's time to integrate it into your mail delivery system. One way to do this is by calling Bogofilter in Procmail. The following Procmail recipe will do this:

```
:0HB:
* ? bogofilter -u -l
probably-spam
```

This recipe passes the message through the *bogofilter* command. The -u option tells Bogofilter to automatically add messages that it classifies as spam or nonspam to the appropriate word lists. This option is both potentially useful and potentially dangerous; it's useful because it can help keep your spam database updated, but it's dangerous because if Bogofilter misclassifies a message, that misclassification can lead to more misclassifications. (If a message is classified as "unsure," it won't be added to the database.) The -l option logs Bogofilter activity. This recipe stores spam messages in the *probably-spam* folder; nonspam messages go on for normal delivery.

If you use the -u option, and Bogofilter misclassifies a message, you should correct the problem. You can do this with the -N and -S options, which undo previous registrations of a message as nonspam and spam, respectively. You can combine these options with -s and -n to reregister the messages correctly. For instance, if Bogofilter has registered a message as nonspam but in fact it's spam, you can extract the message to a file (complete with its headers) and type the following command:

```
$ bogofilter -Ns < message.spam
```

To test that it's worked correctly, pass the message through *bogofilter* again, using -v rather than -Ns; Bogofilter should now classify the message as spam, or at least give it a much higher spamicity score. (Register it again with **bogofilter -s** to strengthen Bogofilter's tendency to classify the message as spam, if desired.) Use -Sn rather than -Ns to undo an incorrect classification of a nonspam message as spam.

Discarding or Quarantining Suspicious Attachments

The vast majority of email worms released over the years have been written for Windows systems. Any of the antispam tools described here can be used to locate and deal with worms. Using a Linux system for this task ensures that the mail server itself can't become infected, even through gross negligence. (At least, assuming Windows worms are in play; theoretically, Linux worms could be written to take advantage of flaws in Linux software.)

The threat of Windows worms is such that many sites have taken drastic measures to protect themselves: they reject all mail carrying certain types of attachments, or even all email attachments. The reasoning is that nobody has a valid reason to email, say, Windows *.exe* executables, so any such executable must be a worm. The validity of such reasoning is uncertain, but it may be so close to the truth for certain sites that discarding or quarantining messages with such attachments may be worthwhile. Example 13-3 shows a couple of Procmail recipes that discard certain suspicious messages.

Example 13-3. Procmail recipes to discard suspicious attachments

```
:0 B
* ^Content-Type: audio/x-(wav|midi);
/dev/null

:0
* ^Content-Type: multipart/(mixed|alternate|alternative|related)
{
  :0 B
  * ^.*name=.*\.(bat|com|exe|pif|scr|vbs|zip)
  /dev/null
}
```

The first of these rules discards everything with a `Content-Type` line of `audio/x-wav` or `audio/x-midi`. Theoretically, these lines identify certain types of audio files, which might be legitimate attachments in some environments; however, in practice, worms often try to masquerade as these file types. The second rule looks for any of several content types in the header and, if found, searches for a line that includes `name=` followed by any of several filename extensions. Some of these, such as *.bat*, *.com*, and *.exe*, identify Windows executables. Others don't, but again, Windows worms frequently try to masquerade as files of these types.

Unfortunately, rules such as these are likely to produce false alarms. The second rule is particularly overzealous because it discards messages with attached Zip files. You can, of course, eliminate some of these filename extensions, but that reduces the effectiveness of the tests. Alternatively, you can enclose the test in a white-list test to enable trusted senders to deliver mail containing these attachments. Another option is to rename attachments rather than discard them; for instance, rename a *.zip* file to *.zip.txt*. This enables users to access the files, but makes it harder for worms that are named in this way to do harm automatically.

These rules, as shown in Example 13-3, are also potentially deleterious because they discard the messages by sending them to */dev/null*. Placing the messages in a folder to hold suspected worms might be a good alternative. Users can then open the messages only with extreme caution. If you place these rules in a systemwide Procmail configuration file, you can even send the suspect messages to a mail folder that only *root* can read.

Supplementing a Microsoft Exchange Server

Linux can fit into a network's email picture in any of several ways. One obvious way is to function as your domain's primary mail server, handling SMTP and, if you desire, POP or IMAP. Used in this way, the Linux mail server will most likely communicate with Windows desktop systems as POP or IMAP clients. This configuration can work quite well, but many Windows networks already have a Microsoft Exchange mail server. At first glance, there seems to be little reason to deploy a Linux mail server if you already have a working Microsoft Exchange server. Sometimes, though, a Linux server can be used to help an Exchange server.

Microsoft Exchange provides features that are most readily used by Microsoft email clients, and that aren't fully replicated by non-Microsoft servers. Thus, depending on your needs, a Linux server might not be an adequate replacement for an Exchange server. Some projects are underway to change this. Specifically, the SuSE Linux Openexchange Server (SLOX; *http://www.suse.de/en/business/products/openexchange/*), Kroupware (*http://kroupware.org*), and the Open Source Exchange Replacement (OSER; *http://www.thewybles.com/oser/*) are projects intended to replace the Exchange server, while *otlkon* (*http://otlkcon.sourceforge.net*) aims to provide Linux client features. Note that these projects aren't quite drop-in replacements or aren't yet finished. Thus, Linux can't yet replace an Exchange server, but Linux can supplement one.

A Linux mail server is commonly used as an additional link in the email chain, appearing just before the Microsoft Exchange server, as shown in Figure 13-3. Placed in this way, the Linux mail server functions as a filter, similar to a firewall. Using tools designed to detect and remove spam and worms (as described in the section "Scanning for Spam, Worms, and Viruses"), the Linux system can keep these unwanted messages from ever reaching the Exchange server. This can be preferable to filtering them out on the Exchange server because it reduces the load on the Exchange server, improving performance, particularly for entirely local actions. Another advantage of this configuration is that you can use strong packet-filter firewall rules on the Exchange server, protecting it from all outside access attempts. You can also use a Linux system to determine which of several internal servers should receive any given email; for instance, you can direct email according to the username to either of two or three servers, each of which handles only some of your site's local users.

Configuring a Linux mail server this way isn't greatly different from configuring it as a domain's only mail server. The main difference is that the system forwards all the

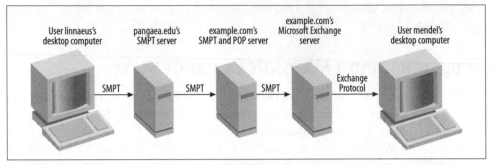

Figure 13-3. A Linux mail server can fit into an existing Exchange network as an email filter system

mail it receives; it treats few or no messages as local. This is done by setting the server's mail relay options, as described in an earlier section.

 A Linux mail server configured this way can protect you from spam and worms that originate outside your network. If you send your outgoing mail through the Linux mail server, it can also protect outside systems from worms that might get loose on your local network. Local mail that's handled exclusively by the Exchange server won't be examined, however, unless you configure Exchange to send even local mail via the Linux server, which increases the network load between those two systems. Thus, if a worm breaks loose on your local network, it can still spread quickly to other computers.

Using Fetchmail

A prototypical chain of mail delivery uses SMTP from the sender through to the recipient's mail server, and optionally uses POP or IMAP from the final mail server to the user's desktop system. Sometimes, though, it's desirable to use POP or IMAP earlier in the chain. For such situations, a program called Fetchmail comes to the rescue; this program enables you to pull mail from a POP or IMAP server and inject it into your local mail queue; from there it can be delivered to the same or another computer.

Before installing and using Fetchmail, you should understand precisely why it exists and how it can be used. Although it's a popular and useful tool, it's not for everybody, so attempting to use it unnecessarily can be a waste of time. If you're sure you want to use it, you must understand Fetchmail's configuration file format. Once it's configured, you can use it, which involves running it as a daemon, running it at scheduled times, or running it as part of a larger task.

The Role of Fetchmail

If you own or work for a small business, you might contract with an outside company to host your domain. This domain hosting ISP runs a server that houses your web pages and probably provides another server that can receive your domain's email. Typically, domain hosting ISPs allow you to connect to their email servers with POP or IMAP to retrieve your mail. You might be content to read your mail more or less directly like this, in which case you don't need to run any email server at all. On the other hand, you might want to perform additional processing, such as handling your own spam filtering, sorting mail for multiple users into different accounts, supporting IMAP when your domain hosting ISP provides only POP, integrating mail from multiple ISPs, or integrating mail from the Internet with your local network's mail. Individuals with small home networks often have similar needs, even if they don't have their own domains. In all these cases, what you need is a way to pull mail from the ISP's server using POP or IMAP and make it available via your own POP or IMAP server. You might even send the mail from one server to another via SMTP. This configuration is outlined in Figure 13-4. In the figure, your (*example.com*'s) mail server uses Fetchmail to retrieve mail from the *abigisp.net* mail server using POP. Local computers can then retrieve the mail using IMAP.

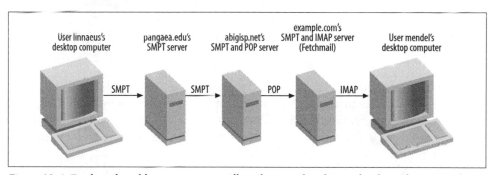

Figure 13-4. Fetchmail enables you to use a pull mail protocol earlier in the chain than normal

Because pull mail protocols are initiated by the receiving end, Fetchmail has no way to know when mail is waiting for it to pick up. For this reason, Fetchmail typically *polls* the remote server; that is, Fetchmail checks for new mail at a regular interval. This can be done either by running Fetchmail as a daemon with a built-in polling interval or by calling Fetchmail in a regular process, such as in a *cron* job. Alternatively, you can call Fetchmail as part of a regular or irregular process. For instance, if you use a dial-up Internet connection, you can call Fetchmail as part of a connection script. This gives you access to all your accumulated mail as soon as you connect.

Configuring Fetchmail

The Fetchmail configuration file is located in the user's home directory and is called *.fetchmailrc* by default (there is no global Fetchmail configuration file). As with many files, this one uses hash marks (#) to denote comments. Aside from comments, the file begins with a number of set directives, which set various global options. Some of the more important of these options are summarized in Table 13-1.

Table 13-1. Common Fetchmail global directives

Directive name	Possible options	Description
postmaster	Local username	Username to which error messages are sent. This user may also receive failed deliveries as a last resort.
bouncemail	–	Tells Fetchmail to send bounce messages to the apparent sender of the message. This practice can be risky because spammers and worms usually forge the return addresses, sometimes to the addresses of legitimate but innocent individuals.
no bouncemail	–	Tells Fetchmail to send bounce messages to the address set with postmaster, rather than to the apparent sender.
syslog	–	Logs Fetchmail activities through the local *syslog* daemon.
logfile	Filename	Logs Fetchmail activities to the specified file.
daemon	Time in seconds	Causes Fetchmail to run in daemon mode, in which it loads but doesn't exit. Fetchmail then checks for new mail at the specified interval.

The global options are just the start of Fetchmail configuration, though. The heart of the configuration lies in the account specifications. Each begins with the keyword poll and defines everything Fetchmail needs to know about an account in order to retrieve mail from it and direct it to an appropriate local or remote address. Broadly speaking, the poll lines take the following form:

    poll server.hostname server-options user-options

The *server.hostname* is, of course, the server's hostname. The *server-options* and *user-options* both consist of multiple options, which tell Fetchmail how to interact with the server and give Fetchmail information on the accounts (both the remote server's account and how Fetchmail is to deliver the mail locally). Tables 13-2 and 13-3 summarize the most common options for these two parts of the poll specifications.

Table 13-2. Common Fetchmail server options

Option name	Possible values	Description
proto or protocol	Protocol name	The name of the protocol Fetchmail should use to communicate with the server. Common values are POP3 and IMAP, but Fetchmail supports several other protocols, as well.

Table 13-2. Common Fetchmail server options (continued)

Option name	Possible values	Description
interface	Interface name/ IP address/netmask triplet	An interface that must be active before Fetchmail attempts to connect to a server. For instance, ppp0/192.168.99.0/24 means that the system must have a PPP connection on the 192.168.99.0/24 network before it attempts a connection. This is most useful for dial-up users.
monitor	Interface name	Fetchmail monitors the specified interface (such as ppp0 or eth1) and attempts a connection only if there's been activity on that interface since the last polling interval. This option works only in daemon mode. It's most useful to prevent activity that might unnecessarily activate a dial-on-demand connection.
interval	Integer	Causes checks to occur only at some polling intervals. For instance, setting interval 4 causes Fetchmail to check the site only every fourth polling period (as set by the global daemon value). This is useful if you want to poll multiple remote servers, but with different frequencies.

Table 13-3. Common Fetchmail user options

Option name	Possible values	Description
user or username	Username	A username on the remote server, unless the username is followed by here, in which case it's the local username to which fetched mail is delivered.
pass or password	Password	The password used to access the remote server.
ssl	–	Enables an SSL connection to the remote server. This option isn't universally supported, but if your server supports it, using SSL can improve security.
sslcert	Filename	The file in which an SSL certificate is stored.
sslkey	Filename	The file in which an SSL key is stored.
is or to	Username	Links the remote account information with the local account information.
here	–	This keyword follows a local username to identify it as local.
smtphost	Hostname	The hostname of the server to which Fetchmail sends mail it receives. The default is localhost, which is usually fine if you want to read mail or run your own pull mail server on the same computer.
keep	–	Tells Fetchmail to leave mail on the remote server after fetching it. The default is to delete fetched mail. This option is mostly useful when testing or debugging or new or changed configuration.
fetchall	–	Retrieves all messages on the remote server, even if Fetchmail has already fetched them. Used with keep, this can result in duplicate messages.
forcecr	–	Technically, email messages should have lines that end in carriage return/line feed (CR/LF) pairs; however, in practice, many messages have only the LF. Some mail servers, such as *qmail*, react badly to this deviation from the norm, and this option corrects this problem.
preconnect	Local command	A program that's run before each connection. This can bring up a network connection, run a program to delete spam from the remote server, or perform any other task you want done just before retrieving mail.

The poll specification can be quite long. Typically, it's split across two or more lines, with the second and subsequent lines indented. No line-continuation characters are required.

In addition to the options shown in Tables 13-2 and 13-3, Fetchmail accepts some more exotic options; consult its manpage for details. Certain keywords, such as and, has, options, wants, and with, are ignored by Fetchmail. These keywords can help you parse the meaning of a poll statement. Most option values can be enclosed in quote marks, but this isn't usually required unless the value contains an embedded space. Overall, although the Fetchmail poll options may seem confusing when listed in tables, in practice they're designed to be easy to parse. When strung together, they read almost like an English sentence, as shown in Example 13-4.

Example 13-4. Sample .fetchmailrc file

```
set postmaster "linnaeus"
set no bouncemail
set syslog

poll pop.abigisp.net with proto POP3
    user "mendel" there with password "p7Tu$ioP" is gregor here
    options fetchall forcecr preconnect "mailfilter"

poll mail.asmallisp.org with proto IMAP
    user "karl" there with password "QhIO4a-23Ybz" is linnaeus here
    options forcecr smtphost mail.example.com
```

 One of Fetchmail's weaknesses is that it requires you to store your remote email passwords in plain text in its configuration file. Be sure the configuration file has 0600 or 0400 (rw------- or r--------) permissions. If the file is readable to other users, Fetchmail refuses to act on the configuration file.

This configuration shown in Example 13-4 retrieves mail from two sources: the *mendel* account on *pop.abigisp.net* and the *karl* account on *mail.asmallisp.org*. Mail from each account is directed to a different user. The second poll statement also directs mail to a specific server (*mail.example.com*), which might or might not be the same server on which Fetchmail is running.

If you want to fetch mail from multiple remote accounts or for multiple users, you can use a single Fetchmail configuration, as shown in Example 13-4; by calling Fetchmail from multiple accounts, with one configuration per account; or by creating separate configurations and calling them from a single account by passing special options to Fetchmail to have it consult a nonstandard configuration file for all but one account. The account used to run Fetchmail doesn't need to be related to those that receive the local mail; for instance, *linnaeus* can run Fetchmail, which might deliver mail to the *gregor* account.

Although Fetchmail relies on a text-mode configuration file, you can use a GUI tool to help you configure Fetchmail. Type **fetchmailconf** in an *xterm* or other command-line window to run this program, which guides you through setting the Fetchmail options. This configuration tool is often installed separately from Fetchmail, though, so you may need to locate it on your distribution's installation media.

Running Fetchmail

The simplest way to run Fetchmail is to call it by name from the command line:

```
$ fetchmail -k
```

If all goes well, Fetchmail retrieves mail and inserts it into your local mail queue (or delivers it to another system, if you've so configured it). For testing purposes, you may want to add the -k option, which has the same effect as the keep user option. This way, if your configuration is incorrect, and Fetchmail loses your mail, you can recover it from the remote server.

For ordinary use, you should probably run Fetchmail constantly (in daemon mode) or run it periodically. To run the server in daemon mode, ensure that your *.fetchmailrc* file has a set daemon *interval* line. You can then run Fetchmail at system startup via a SysV or local startup script. Typically, you'll want to run the program as a non-*root* user, which you can do via the *su* command in your startup script:

```
su -c '/usr/bin/fetchmail -f /home/karl/.fetchmailrc' karl
```

This command runs Fetchmail as *karl*, when typed as *root* or entered into a startup script that's run as *root*. This command also illustrates the use of -f, which enables you to specify a configuration file.

If you want to run Fetchmail as part of a network connection procedure, such as that used to initiate a PPP connection, you can place a similar command in your network connection script. If you initiate the connection as an ordinary user, though, you might not need to use *su*; just call *fetchmail* as an ordinary user.

Another way to run Fetchmail is via a *cron* job. On most Linux systems, the *cron* process is a daemon that launches programs that should be run on a periodic basis. These *cron* jobs are controlled via a *crontab*, which is a file that's registered with the *cron* daemon as a way to run programs on a regular basis. Example 13-5 shows a sample *crontab* that runs Fetchmail on a regular basis.

Example 13-5. Sample crontab file for running Fetchmail

```
SHELL=/bin/bash
PATH=/sbin:/bin:/usr/sbin:/usr/bin
```

Example 13-5. Sample crontab file for running Fetchmail (continued)

```
MAILTO=karl
HOME=/home/karl

16,36,56 7-20 * * * /usr/bin/fetchmail > /dev/null
```

The first few lines of the *crontab* file set environment variables, much as they're set in *bash* scripts. The final line in Example 13-5 tells *cron* to run the */usr/bin/fetchmail > /dev/null* command at a specific time. The time format is five space-separated fields: the minute, the hour, the day of the month, the month, and the day of the week. An asterisk (*) sets a field to match any value. You can separate multiple values with commas or use a dash (-) to specify a range of values. Thus, Example 13-5 tells *cron* to run Fetchmail the 16th, 36th, and 56th minute of every hour between 7:16 A.M. and 20:56 (that is, 8:56 P.M.) on every day of every month. The program's output is redirected to */dev/null*; if it weren't, the user who registers this *cron* job would receive an email with Fetchmail's output every time it runs.

 Be sure that the *.fetchmailrc* file doesn't contain a set daemon line if you call Fetchmail via a *cron* job. If it does, the first time Fetchmail is run, it daemonizes and prevents subsequent runs from succeeding.

To register the *crontab* file, you must use the *crontab*. In the simplest case, you can log in as the user who you want to run Fetchmail and issue the following command:

```
$ crontab crontab
```

This assumes you've called the *crontab* file *crontab*; if you've called it something else, you'll need to change the filename passed to the *crontab* command.

 If the user who's to run Fetchmail already has a *crontab* file, you should modify it to add the call to *fetchmail*. If you type **crontab crontab**, the new *crontab* file replaces the old one.

If you create a new non-login account to run Fetchmail, you can use the *root* account to enter a *crontab* file for this user. Call the *crontab* file something distinctive, and use the -u option to *crontab* to tell the program what user's *crontab* you're entering:

```
# crontab -u fmail crontab-fmail
```

This command enters the *crontab-fmail* file as the *crontab* for the *fmail* user. The result is that Fetchmail will run as this user, which can be a very low-privilege user. Be sure the user exists and has a home directory, or at least can read a configuration file you specify with the -f option to *fetchmail* in the *crontab-fmail* file.

Summary

Email is extremely important for most individuals and businesses today, and Linux can function as part of your network's email system. You can use a Linux SMTP server, such as sendmail or Postfix, to handle incoming mail instead of or in addition to a Microsoft Exchange server, and you can use a Linux POP or IMAP server to deliver mail to Windows, Mac OS, Linux, and other clients. One of the ways you can employ a Linux mail server is as a screening system for spam and worms. You can do this whether Linux is your sole mail server or it's just part of a larger mail solution. Finally, a tool called Fetchmail enables you to retrieve mail from a remote pull mail server and deliver it using your own pull mail server or deliver it via SMTP to another server.

## CHAPTER 14

Network Backups

Data storage technologies are imperfect. For this reason, it's wise to invest a small amount of time, effort, and expense in backing up your data, rather than risk spending crippling amounts of time, effort, and expense on recreating your data from scratch. If your primary data storage device dies, you'll have your backup, which can greatly reduce the recovery time. In a small office, backups may be performed without using the network—say, by using a portable tape backup unit and backing up each system directly. On a larger network, though, network backup tools can prove beneficial, and Linux can play a role in such systems. Linux can fit into the backup picture by providing an inexpensive platform to handle this task, along with tools of varying sophistication that can back up Linux, Unix, and Windows systems. Of course, backing up Linux itself (and other nonbackup Linux servers) is also important. Some Windows tools can do this, or you can use a Linux backup server to help out.

To begin this chapter, you should understand something of network backup strategies, such as what hardware is available, what types of backups are best suited to which situations, and so on. You must also understand how to back up a Linux system *without* using any network connections. This task is helpful in protecting the backup computer itself, and the skills involved transfer to some types of network backups. This chapter then looks at two specific network backup tools: Samba and the Advanced Maryland Automatic Network Disk Archiver (AMANDA).

Backup Strategies

To the uninitiated, computer backup can be an intimidating topic, filled with its own list of things that must be learned. These include backup hardware, complete and incremental backups, local and network backups, and client- versus server-initiated network backups. These topics all require at least minimal description before you can make an informed decision about how to set up a network backup system.

Backup Hardware

The first choice you must make when putting together a network backup solution is what type of hardware to use. The choices can be baffling because there are so many. If you want to use Linux with an existing backup device, you must consider Linux's compatibility with your hardware. In any event, backup hardware falls into several broad classes, each of which has many specific models and subtypes:

Tapes
Tape backup has historically been the most common form of backup medium, due largely to the low cost per gigabyte of tapes, their high capacities, and the fact that they're highly portable, which is a boon for storing some of your back-ups off-site. Tape, though, is an inconvenient backup medium because of its *sequential-access* nature, meaning that data must be read or written sequentially; you can't randomly seek to and read a particular file, as you can with disks and other *random-access* media. The price advantage of tapes is less advantageous in recent years, as hard disk prices have plummeted. Tape is less reliable than many other media; finding that a tape has lost some or all of its data is a sadly common occurrence. Tape is unusual because most mid-range and high-end tape drives provide built-in data compression features. In fact, manufacturers often advertise their typical capacities when using compression. Be sure to remember this fact when comparing tapes to other backup media.

Optical media
Optical media include CD-R, CD-RW, and various recordable DVD formats. These media have the advantages of being extremely common and inexpensive, but their capacities (even of DVDs) are low, at least for full network backups. Nonetheless, optical media can be important for backing up individual projects or for creating basic desktop system recovery disks.

Removable disks
This category includes floppy disks, magneto-optical (MO) disks, Zip disks, Jaz disks, and similar devices. These devices use technologies similar to those of hard disks (MO disks are a cross between magnetic disk and optical technologies, though), but individual disks can be removed from their drives for storage or transport to other computers with compatible drives. As computer backup tools, however, they're poor choices because the media are expensive and usually low in capacity. These disks work well for backing up individual users' files or specific projects.

Removable hard disks
A variant on the removable disk idea is to place a hard disk in a special housing that enables it to be easily removed. This can be either an external disk that connects to the computer using SCSI, IEEE-1394, or USB-2.0 connectors, or an internal disk with a special mounting bay. Removable hard disks have the advantage of fast random access and, increasingly, low cost. Hard disks are fairly

delicate, though, so they aren't good for routine transport between sites; the risk of a shock causing damage is too great.

Of these broad classes, tape is still the medium of choice for backing up entire networks, but the initial cost can be high. A high-capacity single-tape drive can cost over $1,000, and a *tape changer*, which automatically changes several tapes, enabling you to treat several as one, is even more expensive. However, high-end tape formats, use tape media that are relatively inexpensive—typically about $1 per gigabyte, uncompressed. Individual tape capacities range from 4 GB to 160 GB uncompressed, for current models.

Removable hard disks have fallen in price enough that they're now competitive with tape, particularly for small sites. A typical removable disk system costs about $100, with extra trays going for another $50 or so. You'll need one tray for each hard disk you use, which is likely to raise the price for the media (tray plus disk) to $1 per gigabyte or thereabouts, at least in early 2005. Hard disk capacities, of course, compete with those of tapes.

Removable disks (other than hard disks) and optical media simply lack the capacity to be used for full network backups, or even for full backups of individual servers or desktop systems. You might still want to use them as part of your backup plan, however. For instance, if your desktop systems hold an OS but little or no user data (that is, if you store user data on a server), you can create CD-R or recordable DVD backups of your OS installations when you first set the systems up or when you perform major OS upgrades, then omit these computers from your normal backup schedules. If your OS installations are small enough, they might fit (with compression) on a single CD-R, and almost certainly on a recordable DVD. Because most desktop systems have CD-ROM drives, and many now have DVD-ROM drives, you can restore these backups without using the network, which greatly simplifies the restore process. You could also use this approach in conjunction with selective network backups of user data directories (such as */home* on a Linux desktop system) to protect data stored on users' desktop systems.

If you elect to use tapes for some or all of your backup needs, you must choose a tape format. Quite a few exist, with varying capacities, prices, and speed. Table 14-1 summarizes some of the more common tape formats. Prices in this table were taken from Internet retailers in late summer 2004; they may change by the time you read this. Also, existing tape formats are often extended to support higher capacities, and new formats are periodically introduced. Thus, you may find something better suited to your needs than anything described here. Table 14-1 summarizes drives that are currently on the market and tapes for these drives; tapes for lower-capacity variants of these units are still available and may cost less than indicated here. This table also shows prices for single-tape units; changers for many of these formats are also available, but cost more.

Table 14-1. Common tape formats

Drive type	Drive price	Media price	Uncompressed capacity	Speed
Travan	$250–550	$30–50	10–20 GB	0.6–2 MB/s
DAT/DDS	$400–1,200	$5–30	4–20 GB	1.5–5 MB/s
8mm	$800–4,000	$8–90	7–60 GB	3–12 MB/s
VXA	$600–1,300	$30–100	33–80 GB	3–6 MB/s
AIT	$800–3,800	$75–120	35–100 GB	3–12 MB/s
DLT and SuperDLT	$800–4,700	$50–170	80–160 GB	3–16 MB/s

One more consideration in your choice of backup hardware is how the hardware interacts with software. Removable disks and removable hard disks can be accessed like internal hard disks, by creating a filesystem on the disk and copying files to the disk. You can also compress files and store them in carrier archives, such as tarballs. Tapes must be accessed using special tape device files, which provide sequential access to the drive. Typically, files are backed up using a carrier archive file. Optical media are usually written using a special program, such as *cdrecord*, which writes the entire disc's contents at once. The disc usually holds a filesystem, though, so that it can be read as if it were an ordinary magnetic disk. Some software enables more direct read/write access to the drive, but it is still relatively new in Linux and may not be suitable for backup purposes. In all cases, using a carrier archive file can help preserve file permissions, time stamps, and so on, even if the carrier file isn't a strict requirement.

Complete Versus Incremental Backups

One of the difficult questions you must answer when designing a backup solution is *how much* to back up. Most computers hold gigabytes of data, but only some of that data changes frequently. For instance, most executable program files change infrequently. Even many user data files can go unchanged for extended periods of time. Thus, if you can identify the changed files and update them without updating unchanged files, you can save considerable time (and backup media space) on your backups. Doing this is called an *incremental backup*, which contrasts with a *complete backup* or *full backup*, in which every file is backed up.

Incremental backups sound like a great idea, but they do have a drawback: they complicate restores. Suppose for the sake of argument that you perform a complete backup on Monday and an incremental backup every day thereafter. If the hard disk dies on Friday, you need to restore Monday's full backup followed by either every intervening incremental backup or the last one, depending on whether the incremental backups copy files that have changed since the last backup of any type or just the last full backup. What's more, your restored system will have files that might have been intentionally deleted during the week. This can cause serious problems if the system sees heavy turnover in large files, such as if users routinely create and then quickly destroy large multimedia files. (Some backup packages can spot such deletions and handle them automatically, but not all backup software can do this.) These problems become more severe the longer you go between full backups.

Generally speaking, using a small number of incremental backups between full backups can be a great time-saver. For instance, on critical systems that see lots of activity, you might perform a weekly full backup and a daily incremental backup. A less busy or less critical system might manage with monthly full backups and weekly incremental backups.

Given these examples, you may be wondering just how often you need to perform backups. There's no easy answer to this question because it depends on your own needs. You should ask yourself how much trouble a complete system failure would cause and design a backup schedule from there. For instance, if losing a single day's work would be a major hassle, that system should be backed up daily; however, if losing even a week's worth of data would not be a major inconvenience, weekly or even less frequent backups might suffice. The answer to this question, of course, can vary from one system to another; a major file server might need daily backups, whereas desktop computers might need much less frequent backups, or even none at all if they just hold stock OS installations.

Local Versus Network Backups

Much of the preceding description has assumed that individual computers are being backed up. You can certainly back up computers one by one, equipping each one with its own backup hardware or using portable backup hardware that you can move between computers. This is likely to be tedious and expensive, though. When it comes to users' desktop systems, getting them to perform backups can be difficult. One solution to these problems is to perform network backups. These use network protocols to transfer data from the system being backed up (the *backup client*) to the computer that holds the backup hardware (the *backup server*).

The main advantages of performing network backups are reduced hardware cost and the potential for simplified backup administration. This second advantage has a corollary: because backups are likely to be less tedious, they're more likely to be done. On the other hand, network backups have certain disadvantages: they can consume a great deal of network bandwidth, they require larger backup storage devices than do individual backups, they require careful planning so as to operate smoothly, and they may require overcoming cross-platform differences (such as Linux versus Windows filename conventions).

Overall, network backups are worth doing on all but the smallest networks—or at least, on any network with more than a tiny number of computers that are worth backing up. Typically, your first priority will be your servers, followed by workstations on which users store their data files. You may want to create your own priority list, though; knowing what's most important on your own network will help you plan what hardware to buy and what software will best back up the data.

The backup server computer itself can be fairly unassuming, aside from its backup device and a decent network connection. The computer most likely won't be running any RAM-intensive programs. (Some high-end backup software uses large RAM buffers, however.) If you compress your backups, the CPU might need to be adequate to back up the data, but this task won't strain a CPU unless you've paired it with much more modern network and data storage systems. You might be tempted to equip a major file server with the backup hardware and make it your backup server, and this does have the advantage of simplifying the backup of this important server. On the other hand, it also imposes an extra load on the file server, both in terms of CPU (particularly if you use it to compress data) and network bandwidth. This might be acceptable if you expect to be able to fully complete backups in off hours, but if you expect your backups to occur partly when the network is in use, you might want to use a dedicated backup server. Also, a backup server may have increased vulnerability to certain types of attack, so placing it on its own computer can have security implications compared to having a file server do double duty.

Client- Versus Server-Initiated Backups

When doing network backups, one critical detail is which system controls the backup process: the backup server or the backup client. Both approaches have several consequences:

Scheduling
> When the backup server initiates the backup process, it can do so in a way that makes scheduling sense for the network as a whole, and you can specify this schedule from a single computer (namely, the backup server). When the backup client initiates the process, by contrast, scheduling can become difficult, because the possibility of conflicts increases dramatically. This is particularly true if backups are performed on an as-needed basis rather than being strictly scheduled.

Computer availability
> When the backup server initiates the backup process, the backup clients must be turned on and available for backup whenever the server does its job. This might be a hassle when backing up desktop computers, which are often powered down at night or over the weekend. When the backup clients initiate the process, though, the server must be available at all times, or at least at scheduled backup times. Because this requirement is placed on just one computer, it's usually less onerous.

Security
> When the backup server initiates the backup, the backup client computers must all run a server to respond to backup requests. This server is a potential security risk, making the backup clients vulnerable to outside intrusion. When the

backup client initiates the backup, by contrast, it means that the backup server must run a server program. Again, this is a potential security risk, but it applies to just one computer. (The client's files must typically be accessed using a program running as *root* or its equivalent, but this program need not respond to outside accesses, and therefore needn't be as much of a security risk.) Thus, server-initiated backups can be more of a risk to your network as a whole, particularly if the server software used for backups isn't something you'd otherwise run. (Some backup methods, however, use protocols, such as SMB/CIFS, that you might use even if you didn't perform network backups.)

 Network backups use the terms *client* and *server* in an unusual way. Typically, the backup server is the computer that houses the backup hardware, and the backup client is the computer that holds data to be backed up. When the backup client initiates the backup, the client/server relationship is as you'd expect; however, when the backup server initiates the backup, the backup client runs network server software, and the backup server runs network client software. This relationship can be confusing if you're unfamiliar with the terminology.

Both client- and server-initiated backups have their uses. Broadly speaking, client-initiated backups work best on small networks with few users and irregular backup schedules, such as in a business with half a dozen employees. As the number of computers grows, though, the scheduling hassles of client-initiated backups become virtually impossible to manage, so server-initiated backups become preferable. You might also prefer server-initiated backups even on a small network because of software features of specific packages or for other reasons; don't feel compelled to use a client-initiated backup strategy on a small network.

Backup Pitfalls

Backups don't always proceed as planned. Worse, *restores* don't always work the way you expect, and a backup is useless if you can't restore it. Some common problems, particularly in cross-platform network backups, include:

Network bandwidth consumption
  Backing up over the network necessarily consumes a certain amount of bandwidth. Ideally, you should schedule backups during off hours to minimize the impact of this activity on day-to-day work.

Metadata support
  Every filesystem supports its own types of *metadata* (data about files, such as file creation times and permissions), and not all backup tools support all the metadata you need. This issue comes up again later in this chapter.

In-use files

Sometimes it's not possible to read a file that's in use by another program, or a file's backup may be corrupted if it was being modified at the moment of the backup. This can cause problems with such Windows files as the Registry, the Outlook mail file, and files used by Microsoft Exchange. One radical solution is to shut down the system and boot it into a secondary OS installation (of the same OS or of another one) for backup, but this is a disruptive process. Some program-specific solutions exist, such as creating backups of the affected files from the programs that create them. These backups should then be handled by the backup software and can be restored to the main files if it becomes necessary.

Restore glitches

No matter what backup solution you choose, you should perform periodic tests of your ability to restore data, simply to ensure that it can be done. Unused and untested procedures have a tendency to "rot" as you upgrade software, rendering a formerly working procedure inoperable.

Unfortunately, backup pitfalls can be very site-specific because they often involve details of your own network, the systems you're backing up, your backup hardware, and the programs you use (both for backup and on the systems being backed up). You may need to rely on testing and experience to discover these problems, then try to find a solution on the Web or in some other way. This is why testing your backups is so critically important; it's far better to discover problems before you need to restore data than after such a restore is needed!

Backing Up the Linux System

The backup server itself should be backed up, which constitutes a local backup procedure. Certain Linux network backup tools also resemble the local backup procedures. For these reasons, you should understand how to perform a local backup. This involves knowing what backup packages are available and how to use at least one. (I describe the *tar* command, which is often used when backing up to disk and tape media.) Because optical media are particularly complex, I also describe them in more detail. Finally, no backup is complete unless you can restore data from it, so I describe how to do this.

A Rundown of Linux Backup Packages

Backing up a computer is essentially a matter of copying files. Backup, though, presents certain unique challenges that aren't present in many other file-copying operations. One of these is the preservation of file metadata. Some file copying techniques lose some types of metadata, but backup tools tend to preserve more metadata. Another unique backup challenge is use of tapes, CD-R drives, and other unusual media used for backups. Most Linux backup packages are either designed for use with tapes as well as or instead of disk files, or they use additional programs to help store the data on the backup media. Finally, backup media are often of limited capacity, so a method of compression is desirable. Some Linux backup tools include compression algorithms, but others rely on additional programs, such as *gzip* or *bzip2*, to compress a backup archive file before sending it to the backup medium.

Numerous programs can be used for backing up a Linux system. Some of the more popular of these include:

tar
> This program, which is a standard part of all major Linux distributions, is a simple but popular backup tool. It's described in more detail in the next section. This program performs backups and restores on a file-by-file basis, placing all files in a carrier file. It's also frequently used to create *tarballs*, which are disk-based archives of files that can be moved across a network, placed on removable media, and so on. Tarballs are commonly used to distribute program source and executable files.

cpio
> The *cpio* program is conceptually similar to *tar*, in that it's a file-by-file backup tool that creates an archive file. This file can be compressed or copied to a backup medium.

dump
> The *dump* program is another file-by-file copying program; however, *dump* is tied to a specific filesystem, such as ext2fs or XFS. It reads filesystem data structures at a lower level than *tar* or *cpio*, and can therefore back up files in a slightly less intrusive way. Unfortunately, versions of *dump* are not available for all filesystems; in 2004, only ext2fs/ext3fs and XFS have *dump* programs, of common Linux filesystems. Worse, with 2.4.x and later kernels, *dump* may not work reliably, so it shouldn't be used. (See *http://lwn.net/2001/0503/a/lt-dump.php3* for a mailing list message from Linus Torvalds on this subject.) To restore data backed up using *dump*, you must use a separate *restore* program.

Partition Image
> This program works at a still lower level than *dump*; instead of backing up individual files, it backs up disk sectors that are marked as being used. This method of operation means that Partition Image is tied to the filesystem you use. As of Version 0.6.4, stable filesystems are ext2fs/ext3fs, ReiserFS, JFS, XFS, FAT, and HPFS. UFS and HFS are considered beta, while NTFS support is marked as *experimental*. This package can only back up and restore an entire partition, which makes it most useful for creating images of just-installed desktop systems and the like, rather than backups from which individual files might need to be retrieved in the future. You can learn more at *http://www.partimage.org*.

cp Although the Linux file copy command, *cp*, is seldom considered a backup tool, it can be used in this capacity, particularly with removable disk and removable hard disk media. Using the -a parameter performs a recursive copy that pre-serves most file metadata. Because *cp* performs a file-by-file copy without using a carrier file, it's most useful for backing up relatively limited numbers of files to removable disks.

BRU

The Backup and Recovery Utility is a commercial backup tool for Linux and other Unix-like systems. It includes compression and provides easier file restore opera-tions than are available from most open source backup programs. It also ships with a GUI, although you can use command-line tools, as well. Check *http://www.bru.com* for details.

Veritas

Veritas (*http://www.veritas.com*) offers a line of commercial network-enabled backup products for Linux, Windows, and other platforms.

Legato

Legato (*http://www.legato.com*), like Veritas, offers commercial network backup products for Linux, Windows, and other platforms.

Most of these programs store data in archive files. In Linux, tape drives are accessed as files, so you can use these programs to back up data directly to tape. You can also apply compression by using *gzip*, *bzip2*, or a similar tool to the archive file. Most of these programs provide a means to do so automatically by adding a special com-mand-line parameter.

These programs can all be used to back up a single computer, although with certain additions, they can be used for network backups. (The upcoming sections describe some of these capabilities.) In addition, some network-centric backup programs are available. One of these is described in a later section, "Backing Up with AMANDA."

Using tar for Tape and Disk Backups

All major Linux distributions ship with a version of *tar* that's part of the GNU's Not Unix (GNU) project. This version of *tar* is similar to commercial versions of *tar* that ship with commercial versions of Unix, but a few commands differ slightly. GNU *tar* can read most other *tar* archives, but the reverse isn't usually true.

GNU *tar* takes precisely one function and any number of options as arguments, along with a list of files or directories. The available functions are described in Table 14-2, while Table 14-3 shows the most common *tar* options. Some options also take their own arguments, as detailed in Table 14-3.

Table 14-2. Available tar functions

Function	Abbreviation	Description
--create	c	Creates an archive.
--concatenate	A	Links together two tarballs.

Table 14-2. Available tar functions (continued)

Function	Abbreviation	Description
`--append`	`r`	Adds files to the end of an existing archive.
`--diff` or `--compare`	`d`	Finds differences between files on disk and those in an archive.
`--list`	`t`	Displays the contents of an archive.
`--extract` or `--get`	`x`	Extracts files from an archive.
`--delete`	–	Deletes files from an archive (can't be used on archives stored on tape).

Table 14-3. Common tar options

Option	Abbreviation	Description
`--directory` *dir*	`C`	Performs operations in the specified directory (*dir*) rather than in the current directory.
`--file` [*host*:]*file*	`f`	Creates or uses the specified archive *file*. If the *host* is specified, *tar* uses the *file* on that system.
`--listed-incremental` *file*	`g`	Causes *tar* to perform an incremental backup, using *file* as a list of files from the last backup.
`--one-file-system`	`l`	Restricts the backup to a single filesystem (disk partition or other device).
`--multi-volume`	`M`	Performs a backup across multiple media.
`--tape-length` *length*	`L`	Used with `--multi-volume`; specifies the length of each individual tape, in kilobytes.
`--same-permissions`	`p`	Preserves all possible file metadata.
`--absolute-paths`	`P`	Stores filenames with their leading slashes (/) or other directory indicators.
`--verbose`	`v`	Lists filenames as they're stored or extracted. When used with the function `--list`, adds ownership, time stamp, and file size information.
`--verify`	`W`	Verifies newly created archives (similar to running `--diff` on a second pass).
`--exclude` *file*	–	Prevents *file* from being backed up or restored.
`--exclude-from` *file*	`X`	Prevents files listed in *file* from being backed up or restored.
`--gzip` or `--gunzip`	`z`	Uses *gzip* to process the archive.
`--bzip2`	`j`	Uses *bzip2* to process the archive.

In use, you specify the function, one or more options, and any required arguments, including a pointer to the directories or files you want to back up:

```
# tar --create --verbose --one-file-system --file /dev/st0 /home / /usr
```

You can state the same command more succinctly using abbreviations:

```
# tar cvlf /dev/st0 / /home /usr
```

Some non-GNU versions of *tar* require a dash (-) before the abbreviated functions and options, as in **tar -cvlf**. GNU *tar* can work with or without the dash.

For system backup purposes, *tar* is ordinarily run as *root*, because only *root* is guaranteed read access to all ordinary files. You may also need *root* privileges to write to your backup device. Non-*root* users can run *tar* to create tarballs in their own directories or to back up files to a backup medium if they have write privileges to the device.

This command looks simple enough, even if it's fairly long in the nonabbreviated form. It does deserve some explanations, though:

Archive filename

This command uses */dev/st0* as the archive's filename. This filename corresponds to a rewinding SCSI tape device, which automatically rewinds after every operation. A nonrewinding SCSI tape device, which might be used when packing multiple archives on a single tape in an incremental backup scheme, is */dev/nst0*. ATA tape devices use the device filenames */dev/ht0* and */dev/nht0* for rewinding and non-rewinding devices, respectively. If you back up to a removable hard disk, you can use a similar command, but you specify a partition on the disk (such as */dev/hde5*) or a filename on a mounted disk filesystem (such as */mnt/backup/05-05-backup.tar*).

Compression

This example command didn't include the --gzip or --bzip2 options. The idea is that the tape device probably provides its own compression. When backing up to a disk backup device, chances are you'd enable compression.

Because tape backups are less reliable than some other media, using compression with tape can be risky. This is particularly true of *tar*'s --gzip and --bzip2 options, which compress an entire archive in such a way that a read error can make all subsequent data unrecoverable. Tape drives' built-in compression usually causes fewer problems when recovering subsequent data from a corrupt archive.

Limiting backups

The --one-file-system option prevents backup of data from partitions that aren't explicitly listed as backup targets. This option is often used as a means of preventing backup of mounted removable media and the */proc* filesystem, which holds pseudo-files that could cause real problems when restored. Alternatively, you could use --exclude or --exclude-from to explicitly exclude such directories from being backed up.

Backup order

The order of the directories in the backup command is potentially important. This example backs up the */home* directory first, followed by root (/) and */usr*.

Because tape is a sequential-access medium, restores must read all preceding data, which means that you want the directories with files that are most likely to need recovery to appear first. In this example, the idea is that users might accidentally delete files and request their recovery, so you want those files to be first in the archive. You might have other priorities depending on your needs, though.

The preceding tar command creates a full backup—or at least, a full backup of the specified directories. Each backup uses the --listed-incremental option to point to a log file. On the first backup, this file is empty or nonexistent, which results in a full backup. For subsequent backups, you have two choices:

- After the full backup, you can copy the log file to a backup location. After each backup except for the first, you then copy the copied file over the log file. The end result is that each incremental backup will be done relative to the original full backup. These backups will grow in size as time goes on and changes accumulate, but they'll be relatively simple to restore because you'll only need to deal with the full backup and the latest incremental backup.

- You can issue precisely the same command every time without changing the log file. The result is that every backup will be an incremental backup relative to the last incremental backup. This backup style is sometimes called a *differential backup*. On average, each differential backup will be the same size as the others, but restoring data may require accessing multiple backups.

A backup solution that uses *tar* is likely to rely on scripts you write yourself for your specific need. A simple backup script might contain nothing more than a single call to *tar* with appropriate parameters to perform a full backup of your system. A more complete script might include housekeeping commands, such as commands to copy log files for incremental backups or to use *mt* to skip over intervening backups on a tape, as described in the sidebar "Controlling the Tape Device." A still more complete script can accept parameters to specify a full or incremental backup or to set other site-specific options. Backup scripts like this may be called from *cron* jobs in order to perform backups on a regular basis. Of course, you must be sure that the correct tape is in the drive!

Backing Up to Optical Media

Optical media pose certain special challenges. Where you can use *tar*, *cpio*, or most other backup programs to create archive files on disk partitions or to store archives on tape, direct read/write access to optical media requires the use of special programs, such as *cdrecord* or *cdrdao*. These programs ship with all major Linux distributions, but integrating them into your backup plans requires extra effort.

Tools to provide disk-like direct read/write access to optical media have been making slow inroads in the Linux world. GUI desktop environments often provide such access via their file managers, for instance. Such tools are still difficult or impossible to use as full backup solutions, although of course you can drag-and-drop individual files and directories to the media in this way. This can be a good way to back up individual project files or the like, but not an entire computer.

Several approaches to optical media backups exist:

Backup archive direct to media

The first approach to using optical media is to treat these media much like a tape: store a tarball (or other archive file) directly to the optical medium.

Typically, you'll create a tarball on disk and then use *cdrecord* to copy it to the optical disc, or you can pipe the output of *tar* directly to *cdrecord*. This approach has the drawback that non-Unix OSs may have a hard time reading the backup. On the other hand, instructions for doing tape backups and restores need relatively few changes. Restores work precisely as they do for tapes, except that you specify a CD-ROM device's filename rather than a tape device's filename, and *mt* isn't used.

Backup archive on carrier filesystem

A variant on the preceding approach is to store tarballs (or other archive files) on a filesystem, which is recorded to the optical disc. To do this, you create a tarball on disk, create an ISO-9660 filesystem containing that tarball using *mkisofs*, and then record the ISO-9660 filesystem to the optical disc using *cdrecord*. (You can pipe some of these operations together or use GUI tools, such as X-CD-Roast, to help with some parts of the job.) This approach is more complex initially, but it makes the archive easier to access from non-Linux systems. You can also include text files (perhaps including an index of files in the tarball) or other explanatory materials in the disc's filesystem, which can make access easier. Because most people and OSs expect optical discs to have ISO-9660 or other filesystems, this approach is less likely to cause confusion when accessing the media in the future.

Backup files on optical filesystem

The final backup method is to store files directly on an optical disc's ISO-9660 filesystem. To do this, you use normal CD-R creation tools, such as *mkisofs* and *cdrecord*, or GUI frontends to these tools, such as X-CD-Roast. This approach makes recovery of arbitrary files relatively easy; you can mount the disc and access the files just as you would the original files on the hard disk. The drawback is that you'll lose some file metadata. (Precisely how much you lose depends on the options you choose.)

 If you back up files directly to an optical disc's filesystem, use the -R option to *mkisofs*, rather than -r. Using the uppercase version of this option preserves more file metadata, including write permission bits. This is most important for performing system backups; for backing up smaller sets of data, using -r may be preferable, particularly if you don't know who'll be reading the data. Using -J or -hfs to generate Joliet or HFS filesystems won't hurt, but they won't provide any real benefit, either, at least not if Linux is to read the backup. If non-Linux systems will read the data, using one or both of these options may be helpful.

Generally speaking, storing backups in a carrier archive on an optical disc's own filesystem is the best way to perform system backups to these media. For backing up project files or the like, though, storing them directly on the optical disc's filesystem, without a carrier file, is often the best way to proceed; this enables the quickest access to the individual files.

To perform a backup using a carrier archive inside a filesystem, you must run *tar*, *mkisofs*, and *cdrecord* in sequence:

```
# tar cvzlf /tmp/bu/backup.tgz / /home /usr
# mkisofs -r -o /tmp/backup.iso /tmp/bu
# cdrecord dev=0,6,0 speed=8 /tmp/backup.iso
```

These commands presuppose that the temporary backup directory (*/tmp/bu*) exists and holds no extraneous files. (You could store files there that describe the backup, if you like.) You might also want to make adjustments for your specific needs, such as changing the SCSI device ID (dev=0,6,0) or speed (speed=8) passed to *cdrecord* to suit your hardware.

> The optical recorder specification passed to *cdrecord* is peculiar. The form shown in the preceding example is used for SCSI devices and takes the form *bus,target,LUN*, where *bus* is the SCSI bus (typically, the SCSI adapter number), *target* is the SCSI ID number of the drive, and *LUN* is the logical unit number (LUN), which is typically 0. Through the 2.4.x Linux kernel, even ATAPI optical drives were accessed as SCSI devices, using the kernel's ATA SCSI emulation layer. With the 2.6.x and later kernels, though, you can access ATAPI drives directly, using a Linux device file as the device specification, as in dev=/dev/hdc.

After running these commands, you'll have two temporary files on your hard disk: the tarball and the ISO-9660 image file. Remember to delete them both. If you like, you can pipe the last two commands together to bypass the creation of the ISO-9660 image file:

```
# mkisofs -r /tmp/bu | cdrecord dev=0,6,0 speed=8 -
```

Be sure to include that trailing dash (-) because it tells *cdrecord* to accept the previous command's output as its input.

Restoring Data Locally

No backup will do you any good unless you can restore the data. Broadly speaking, data restores fall into two categories:

Partial restores

In a partial restore, you need to restore only a few files to a system that's basically functional. The files could be user datafiles or system files, but they're not critical to the basic functioning of the computer or its backup and restore software. To perform a partial restore, you can basically run the backup process in reverse, although specifying the precise files can be tricky, as described shortly.

Full restores

In a full restore, you need to restore all of a computer's files. These are typically necessary when a hard disk fails completely, when a computer is stolen, or when you intentionally replace one computer with a new one. Full restores are much trickier than partial restores because you need some way to run the restore software on a computer that holds no OS. Thus, you must carefully plan how to perform your full restore *before* the need arises. Attempting to plan the restore when a server has crashed, and your boss is demanding it be restored immediately, is stress-inducing and will result in wasted time as you try to work out a solution.

To begin planning a restore, start with some deliberate partial restores. Try backing up a test directory and then restoring it using the backup software's restore feature (such as *tar*'s --extract function). A trickier variant is restoring just some of the files. In the case of *tar*, you must specify the files or directories to be restored, much as you specify the files or directories you want to back up:

```
# tar xvlf /dev/st0 home/linnaeus/gingko/biloba.txt
```

This command extracts the file *home/linnaeus/gingko/biloba.txt* from the backup archive to its original location. You can as easily specify a directory or a set of individual files. A couple of details of this command require elaboration, though:

- The leading slash (/) in the file specification is missing. This is because *tar* normally omits this feature of the filename. If you provide a leading slash but they aren't recorded in the archive, *tar* will fail to restore the file. This can be a time-consuming mistake to make because *tar* can take minutes or hours to scan the entire archive before finishing, with no file restored.

- Because *tar* restores files using the filenames recorded in the archive, and because the leading slash is normally missing, files are restored relative to the current directory. Thus, in most cases, you must execute the restore command from the root (/) directory to restore them to their correct locations. Alternatively, you can restore the files to a temporary location and then move them elsewhere.

A tricky part about partial restores, particularly with simple programs such as *tar*, is in specifying the file that's to be restored. If you mistype the filename, *tar* won't restore it and won't provide any helpful error messages. This can be particularly frustrating if you don't know the exact filename.

 If you perform incremental backups, you can use the incremental backup log to scan files for a precise match to a given filename. Even if you don't perform incremental backups, you can pipe the output of *tar* using the --verbose option to a file and use it to help locate files. If you have only a vague notion of what the correct filename is and have no record of it, you can use the --list function to *tar* to create a file list similar to what might be produced at backup. This can, however, take as long to complete as a full backup.

In principle, full restores work just like partial restores, except that you don't provide a file specification, which lead *tar* to restore everything in its backup. (You can exclude some individual files or directories if you like, though.) The tricky part is in running Linux on a computer whose OS has been wiped out in some way. Several ways of handling this chicken-and-egg problem exist:

Emergency disk

> You can create an emergency disk that enables you to boot a minimal Linux system and direct the restore process much as if you were running a partial restore. You can either prepare your own emergency disk system or locate one on the Internet. Several options for the latter exist, ranging from floppy-based systems to Linux systems that boot from CD-ROM. Examples include Tom's Root/Boot (a. k.a. `tomsrtbt`, *http://www.toms.net/rb/*), a floppy-based system; ZipSlack (*http://www.slackware.com/zipslack/*), a variant of Slackware designed to fit on a 100-MB Zip disk; and Knoppix (*http://www.knoppix.org/*), a Debian variant that boots from a CD-R. Many other variants exist, as well; a web search on keywords that are important to you may turn up helpful pointers. If you have specific needs, such as an ability to restore using particular software, be sure that your needs are met by the option you pick, or create your own custom variant that includes the software you need.

Emergency OS installation

> Some administrators like to create a minimal emergency OS installation alongside the regular OS installation. This practice enables you to boot the emergency installation in case of a serious problem with the main installation. This practice requires extra planning beforehand, though, and it won't help in case of a complete hard disk failure, system theft, or other catastrophic problems. It can, however, be a helpful approach in case of massive filesystem corruption or other problems that don't damage the emergency system.

Partial OS bootstrap

> You can reinstall the core OS files and use this system to restore your main system. When doing a truly full restore, this practice works best if you reinstall your OS as a secondary OS, much like an emergency OS installation; trying to restore a backup over a working OS is an iffy proposition because you might be left with a bizarre mish-mash of files. Alternatively, you can reinstall the OS and all its files, and then perform a partial restore of user files alone. This approach works well if you want to upgrade to a newer version of your distribution or to another distribution, but it's likely to entail additional effort in reconfiguring your new OS installation.

Second computer assist

> You can enlist the aid of another computer in your restore procedures. Place a new hard disk and a backup device in an existing Linux system and use that system to restore your failed system's files to the new hard disk. You can then move the new hard disk to the target computer and reboot it into the restored OS. This

approach is conceptually similar to using an emergency OS or an emergency disk, but it uses an entirely separate computer as a key component. Juggling the physical disks can be tedious, though, and you may run into problems related to the way the two computers handle the disk's cylinder/head/sector (CHS) geometry; if they don't match, some disk utilities will complain.

In all these cases, one particular challenge is in restoring the system to a bootable state. The safest way to proceed is usually to place a copy of the restored system's kernel on a floppy disk or a small FAT partition and use a utility such as *LOADLIN.EXE* (a DOS program to boot Linux) to boot the kernel. This should get you into a working Linux system, from where you can reinstall the Linux Loader (LILO) or the Grand Unified Boot Loader (GRUB) to boot Linux normally. Most Linux distributions provide GUI utilities to help with these tasks, or you can reinstall the boot loader by using command-line tools. LILO can be reinstalled by typing `lilo`, although if you've changed your partition layout, you may need to edit */etc/lilo.conf* first. Similarly, typing `grub-install` often installs GRUB, although in some cases you may need to edit */boot/grub/grub.conf* or */boot/grub/boot.lst* or use the *grub* utility to install it with special options. Consult the LILO or GRUB documentation if you have problems.

Backing Up with Samba

One of the conceptually simplest network backup tools is Samba, the network file and printer sharing program described in Part II. Using Samba enables you to back up Windows computers using either client- or server-initiated backup procedures. You can also perform client-initiated backups of Linux and other non-Windows computers using Samba, although server-initiated backups of Linux systems are tedious when done with Samba.

Before proceeding further, you should understand the basic features and uses of Samba backups. These determine the advantages and disadvantages of using Samba as part of the backup picture. This chapter also presents two basic Samba backup scenarios: using a backup share for client-initiated backups and using *smbtar* for server-initiated backups.

 The following pages presuppose at least some familiarity with Samba basics. If you know little about Samba, you should read Part II or at least Chapters 3 and 4.

Pluses and Minuses of Samba Backups

Samba is a Linux implementation of the SMB/CIFS protocol—the default file-sharing protocol for Windows. Although Samba is frequently considered a server package, it includes client tools. Thus, Samba can be used as part of either a client-initiated (using Samba server tools) or a server-initiated (using Samba client tools) network backup design.

SMB/CIFS supports common Windows filesystem metadata, but it provides limited support for Unix-style ownership, permissions, and other metadata. Thus, SMB/CIFS can be a good way to back up files from Windows systems while preserving metadata, but SMB/CIFS is a poor way to back up Linux or Unix systems. If you transfer data in a carrier file, though, such as creating a tarball on a Linux system and then using SMB/CIFS to copy the tarball across the network and onto a backup device, SMB/CIFS provides no inherent problems relating to preservation of file metadata; that information is stored within the tarball. Such a backup approach is best handled in a client-initiated backup procedure, though, which is why Samba and SMB/CIFS make a poor choice for backing up Linux systems using server-initiated backup methods.

Although SMB/CIFS supports Windows filesystem metadata, Linux doesn't. Samba provides ways to map most important Windows filesystem metadata onto Linux filesystem metadata that Windows can't use. Thus, if you use Samba with identical configurations on backup and restore, chances are you won't lose any important filesystem metadata when restoring data. One exception to this rule is certain advanced NTFS features, such as multiple data streams and (depending on your Samba server's options) support for ownership and ACLs. Thus, you may lose some metadata when backing up a Windows system that uses NTFS in a server-initiated backup or even in some types of client-initiated backup. However, client-initiated backups that use Windows-specific backup software can preserve these metadata.

Another problem with SMB/CIFS backups is that restoring data to the backup client can be tricky, particularly in the case of a complete restore. This topic is covered in more detail later, in the section "Restoring Data with Samba."

On the plus side, support for SMB/CIFS is free in both Windows and Linux. Thus, implementing a Samba-based backup solution can be inexpensive, particularly if you're willing to invest some time in creating appropriate backup scripts. In fact, Samba ships with a tool that's specifically designed with backup in mind: *smbtar*, which is described shortly.

Because of Samba's support for FAT-style metadata, Samba can be a good way to back up all the data from systems that continue to use FAT. Even some Windows NT/200x/XP systems use FAT, and many of those that use NTFS don't rely heavily on NTFS-specific metadata. Thus, you may be able to back up such systems, or at least their user data, without risking undue loss of file metadata on restore.

Using a Samba Backup Share

The first approach to backup using Samba is to create a special Samba share for the purpose. This Samba share is then accessed from the backup client in a client-initiated backup scenario. Typically, the share accepts files (either directly or in a carrier archive, such as a tarball) and then copies them to a backup device.

Creating a backup share

Broadly speaking, you can design a backup share in any of three ways:

- The share may point directly to the backup device. This approach works only with removable disk or removable hard disk media; you can't point a Samba share directly at an optical disc or tape device. Typically, users then copy their files, either raw or in a compressed carrier archive, to the backup device. The share often includes mechanisms to automatically mount and unmount the backup device, as described shortly.

- The share points to a holding area in which users copy their files. When the connection is terminated, Samba runs a script that backs up the share using *tar*, *cpio*, *cdrecord*, or other Linux backup tools.

- The share accepts a prepared carrier archive from the backup client and copies it to a backup medium. This approach handles any metadata the client's backup tools can handle, so Samba's metadata limitations aren't an issue.

From a Samba perspective, the simplest type of backup share is the first: create an ordinary file share that points to your removable disk's mount point. The removable disk can use any common Linux filesystem. You can even use FAT if you think the disk might be read directly by Windows or some other OS in the future, but ironically, using FAT will cause some Windows metadata—such as archive, hidden, and system bits—to be lost. The tricky part of this type of backup share is mounting and unmounting it. One approach is to use Samba's preexec and postexec configuration parameters. These reside in the *smb.conf* file's share definition and point to commands that Samba executes when the user connects to or disconnects from, respectively, the share. For instance, a complete backup share might look like this:

```
[backup]
    comment = Direct-Access Backup Share
    directory = /home/samba/backup
    max connections = 1
    read only = No
    preexec = mount /home/samba/backup
    postexec = umount /home/samba/backup
```

The preexec parameter mounts a removable medium to */home/samba/backup*. This mount point must be properly defined in */etc/fstab*, though. The postexec parameter reverses this process. The max connections = 1 option limits the connections to a single user, which can help avoid problems that might be caused should two users try to use the backup share simultaneously. To the user, the share looks just like any other; it's accessed from Network Neighborhood or My Network Places on a Windows system just like any other share, and it accepts files that are copied there in the Windows file manager or in any other way. Users will presumably insert and remove disks themselves, though, or perhaps ask somebody in physical proximity to the server to do so for them.

 One problem with this approach is that Windows systems frequently don't terminate their connections to the server in a timely manner. Thus, the postexec command may not execute until several minutes, or even hours, after activity ceases. Logging out of the Windows session usually terminates it on Windows NT/200x/XP clients, but Windows 9x/Me clients may need to be rebooted. Another approach is to use the global Samba deadtime parameter, which tells Samba how many minutes of inactivity to accept before disconnecting a client. For instance, deadtime = 5 ensures that inactive connections are terminated in five minutes.

A similar approach can be used to back up to tape or to optical media, except that the preexec and postexec options are likely to do more:

```
preexec = rm -r /home/samba/backup/*
postexec = tar cvlC /home/samba/backup --file /dev/st0 ./
```

These options, used in place of those shown earlier, cause Samba to back up the contents of the backup directory when the user disconnects. (As with a mounted share, Samba may wait a while before doing this, because Windows clients often don't disconnect immediately.) The preexec option tells Samba to delete all the files in the backup directory. This ensures that two consecutive users' backups don't collide.

Perhaps the most flexible type of client-initiated Samba backup, though, uses a *printer* share, odd as that may sound. The idea is to use a Samba printer share option, print command, to have Samba execute a command that can operate on a single file sent by the client. Typically, this single file is a tarball, Zip file, or other archive file. The print command copies the file to the backup device. For instance, consider this share definition:

```
[print-bu]
    comment = Pseudo-Printer Backup Share
    directory = /var/spool/samba
    max connections = 1
    printable = Yes
    print command = dd if=%s of=/dev/st0; rm %s
```

This share uses *dd* to copy the received file, whatever it is (the %s Samba variable refers to the received print file) to /dev/st0. A more complex command stores the received file on an optical disc using *mkisofs* and *cdrecord*, or even uncompresses a tarball and creates a CD-R from its contents. One important point to note about this share is that its print command ends in rm %s. Removing the received print file is vitally important; Samba printer shares don't do so automatically, so if you fail to remove the print file, your backup server's disk will soon overflow with old backup jobs.

If you want to create a very complex print command, try writing a script to do the job and then call the script. This enables you to perform arbitrarily complex actions, while keeping your *smb.conf* file's share definitions readable.

Using a backup share

The tricky part to using a pseudo-printer backup share comes on the client. You must create a backup archive using local tools and then copy them to the server. For instance, you can use *tar* for Windows (see *http://unxutils.sourceforge.net* or *http://www.cygwin.com* for a couple of sources) to do the job:

```
C:\> TAR -cvf D:\BACKUP.TAR C:\
C:\> COPY D:\BACKUP.TAR \\BUSERVER\PRINT-BU
C:\> DEL D:\BACKUP.TAR
```

This series of commands, typed at a DOS prompt, backs up the client's *C:* drive to the *PRINT-BU* share on the *BUSERVER* server. This specific set of commands uses *D:* as a temporary storage area; you may need to change this detail for your own system. Of course, many variants on this approach are possible. For instance, you can use a Zip utility or a dedicated Windows backup tool to create the archive that's copied to the backup server. You can also perform more-or-less the same task using Linux tools, in order to back up a Linux server; however, you'll use the Linux *smbclient* program to copy a file, rather than the Windows *COPY* command. If you send a file in tarball form and if Samba dumps it directly to tape, the result will be indistinguishable from creating a backup using a tape drive that's directly connected to the backup client.

You can enter commands to back up a Windows system into a Windows batch file. Thereafter, running that batch file backs up the client. To make the process even more user-friendly, you can create a desktop object that points to the batch file. Call it *Backup* or something similar, and users should have no trouble double-clicking it to back up their computers.

All of these client-initiated Samba backup methods do have certain limitations, in addition to those described earlier for client-initiated backups. Most notably, they all require that the Samba server have enough disk space to temporarily hold a complete backup. This disk space must be available in the directory used for the backup share. For removable disk backups, this isn't a very special requirement; the disk space needed must reside on the backup medium itself. For other methods, though, the server must be able to temporarily hold the entire archive before copying it to an external medium. If your backup plan involves manipulating files, such as storing a set of backup files on an optical disc, you may need more space for the temporary files you create in this process.

Using smbtar for Backups

The *smbtar* program is a script that comes with Samba. It combines the Samba *smbclient* program and the standard *tar* utility to read files from an SMB/CIFS server and store them in a tarball or on a tape. As such, it can be a good way to perform a server-initiated backup using SMB/CIFS. To do so, you must first configure your backup clients to share files (that is, to be file servers). Once this is done, you can actually employ *smbtar* to do the backup.

 Because SMB/CIFS provides limited support for Linux file metadata, server-initiated SMB/CIFS backups of Linux systems are unlikely to work well, except perhaps for partial backups of user data files, particularly on a Samba server. For this reason, this chapter assumes that such backups use Windows backup clients.

Configuring Windows clients to share files

To perform a server-initiated backup via SMB/CIFS, you must configure the backup client as a file server. On Windows systems, this task requires installing and activating the SMB/CIFS software, although it's not called that in the Windows network tools. A typical procedure, for Windows XP, is as follows:

1. Open the Windows Control Panel.
2. Double-click the Network Connections icon. This displays a window of the same name. (This icon is called Network and Dial-Up Connections in Windows 200x.)
3. In the new window, right-click the Local Area Connection icon. This produces a pop-up menu; select Properties in this menu. The result is the Local Area Connection Properties dialog box shown in Figure 14-1.
4. If the protocol list includes an item called File and Printer Sharing for Microsoft Networks, skip ahead to Step #8.
5. Click the Install button to bring up a dialog box called Select Network Component Type.
6. Pick the Service item and click Add in the Select Network Component Type dialog box. This should produce the Select Network Service dialog box.
7. In the Select Network Service dialog box, pick the File and Printer Sharing for Microsoft Networks item, and then click OK. This action will install SMB/CIFS server support on the computer.
8. In the Local Area Connection Properties dialog box, verify that the File and Printer Sharing for Microsoft Networks item is checked. Click OK in this dialog box to dismiss it.

Adding SMB/CIFS server support is only part of the job; you must also define shares that the backup server will access. To do so, follow these steps.

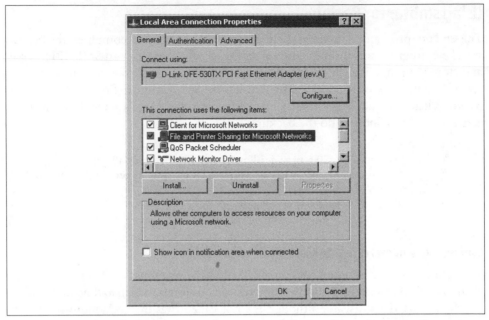

Figure 14-1. Windows displays the protocols it supports in the Local Area Connection Properties dialog box

1. Open the My Computer folder on the desktop.

2. Locate the icon for the drive you want to back up, and right-click it to produce a context menu. Select the Sharing and Security item from this menu. (This item may be called Sharing or something else on some versions of Windows.) This action brings up a Properties dialog box with a Sharing tab selected.

3. In Windows XP, the Sharing tab displays a warning that sharing an entire drive can be a security risk. Click this notice to view the real configuration tab, as shown in Figure 14-2.

4. Check the "Share this folder on the network" button and enter a name for the share in the "Share name" field. This interface is somewhat different in Windows 200x and Windows 9x/Me. In Windows 200x, you must click the New Share button to enter a share name.

5. Windows XP allows you to enable or disable write access to the share via the "Allow network users to change my files" button. Windows 9x/Me provides two fields for passwords for read-only and read/write access. A backup share can ordinarily be read-only, although you will have to enable read/write access when you want to restore data.

6. To start sharing the drive, click OK.

Unfortunately, every major release of Windows has changed these user interfaces slightly. The preceding description is based largely on Windows XP. Windows 9x/Me

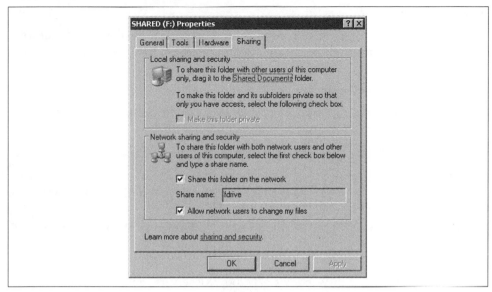

Figure 14-2. The Properties dialog box for a disk or directory enables sharing via SMB/CIFS

is different. Most importantly, the Network icon in the Control Panel brings up a Network dialog box that's similar to the Local Area Connection Properties dialog box (see Figure 14-1).

For Windows XP Professional and Windows 200x systems, you use a local username and password to access the share. For improved security, you might want to create a special backup account that provides read access to all the files you want to back up, but that's not used for ordinary local access. Windows 9x/Me systems use share-level security; i.e., a password without a username provides access to the shares. You enter the password when creating the share, as just noted. From the Linux backup server, you can enter a dummy username; it's ignored by the Windows 9x/Me file server.

Windows XP Home, which ships on many new computers, provides *no password* to protect its shares. This configuration makes Windows XP Home a very risky version of Windows to back up using server-initiated backups. If possible, upgrade such computers to Windows XP Professional or Windows 200x to obtain password-based share protections. If this isn't possible, you should at least use a strong firewall to limit access to TCP ports 139 and 445, so that only the backup server and other authorized systems can access the SMB/CIFS file servers on Windows XP Home systems.

Some versions of Windows require you to reboot at some point during this procedure, typically after installing the SMB/CIFS server software but before configuring shares.

Backing up with smbtar

Once you've configured a Windows system as a backup client (that is, a file server), you can try using *smbtar* on the backup server to perform backups. This command's basic syntax is:

```
smbtar [options] [filenames]
```

The *smbtar* command accepts quite a few *options*, but the most important are:

-s *server*
: You pass the name of the file server (that is, the backup client) with this option.

-x *share*
: You must tell *smbclient* what share to back up with this option. If you omit it, the program looks for a share called *BACKUP*.

-v
: You can have *smbtar* provide more verbose information about its actions with this option.

-u *username*
: When connecting with Windows NT/200x/XP servers, *smbtar* must pass a username to the file server with this parameter.

-p *password*
: Unless the backup share requires no password (a risky configuration), you must deliver one with the -p parameter.

-a
: Microsoft filesystems provide an *archive bit*, which is cleared when files have been backed up and set when they're modified. This can be helpful in performing incremental backups. If you use this option, *smbtar* clears the archive bit when backing up files.

-i
: This option performs an incremental backup by backing up only those files on which the archive bit is set.

-N *filename*
: This option implements a different type of incremental backup system, in which *smbtar* backs up only files that are newer than the specified *filename*, which is ordinarily a backup log file from the previous backup.

-t *tape*
: You should pass a filename to *smbtar* with this option. The filename can be a tape device, such as */dev/st0*, or a regular file.

-r
: By default, *smbtar* backs up files from the remote share. This option reverses the process and causes the program to restore files.

As an example, consider this command:

```
$ smbtar -s GINGKO -x CDRIVE -u redwood -p Y#iWT7td -t /dev/st0
```

This command backs up the *CDRIVE* share on the *GINGKO* server, using the *redwood* account and the password *Y#iWT7td*, and storing the backup on */dev/st0* (a

SCSI tape device). You may also add filenames to the end of the *smbtar* command line. Doing so backs up the specified files or directories without backing up other files.

Server-initiated backups using *smbtar* can certainly be convenient, particularly when you want to back up an entire network of computers from a central location. Typically, you'll write a script to back up one computer per night on a small network, or perhaps do several each night on a larger network. Of course, you'll need to ensure that the backup clients are turned on at the scheduled backup times. This backup method is also limited in the types of metadata it can handle. Because *smbtar* doesn't understand some of the more sophisticated NTFS features, such as ownership and multiple data streams, it might not be a suitable tool for performing complete backups of Windows NT/200x/XP systems. Nonetheless, *smbtar* may be adequate for backing up user datafiles on Windows workstations, and it can even perform full backups of Windows computers that run off of FAT filesystems.

Restoring Data with Samba

Restoring data over the network introduces an extra component in the equation: the backup client must be able to accept the data transfer. Precisely how this happens depends on how you backed up the data:

Client-initiated removable disk backups
> When using removable disks as if they were ordinary file shares, files can be restored by inserting the original backup medium and using drag-and-drop operations to restore files. This practice requires no special extra configuration on the client or the server, except for full restores (as described shortly).

Client-initiated two-stage backups
> When the backup server processes data in some way, such as bundling data into a tarball and storing it on tape, a restore operation can be tricky. You may need to extract the data to a special data-restore share on the backup server and then copy it to the client. Alternatively, you may be able to configure the backup client as for a server-initiated backup and use *smbtar* or similar tools to perform the restore.

Server-initiated backups
> In a server-initiated backup scenario, restores can be done very much like the initial backups, but you must specify the restore option (-r) to *smbtar* to do the work. You must also ensure that the backup client's file server accepts full read/write access to the share, at least when the restore operation is in progress. (If you like, you can disable read/write access once the restore is done.)

With some backup methods, you can restore data without using of a network. For instance, if you back up to an optical disc, and if the backup client has an optical reader that can read the backup, you can restore the data locally. In some cases, you can even move the backup drive to the backup client to perform a local restore without involving the network. This is most likely to be helpful when performing full restores.

With the exception of two-stage backups, partial network restores usually aren't much more work than similar restores would be on a local backup. The real trouble occurs when a full restore is necessary. With these, many of the same problems described earlier with reference to full local restores apply (see the section "Restoring Data Locally"). The difference is that instead of having access to local backup software on the emergency system, you must have access to network tools—your SMB/CIFS client or server software.

 When restoring a Windows system to a FAT disk, you can use a Linux emergency disk if your backup archive can be read by Linux. This usually works well, although there may be some minor changes to file-name case. Also, short filenames are occasionally restored differently by Linux than by Windows, which can sometimes cause problems if configuration files refer to files by their short filenames.

Once you've restored data to a Windows system, you may need to take special steps to ensure that it's bootable. For Windows 9x/Me, you can do this from an emergency boot floppy created from the same version of the OS. Boot from the floppy, and use the *FDISK* program to mark the boot partition as bootable. You should then type **SYS C:** to restore a boot loader to the partition's boot sector. With Windows NT/200x/XP, boot from an emergency disk or the Windows installation CD, and select the system repair options. These should detect the lack of boot sectors and correct the problem.

Backing Up with AMANDA

Samba can be an effective part of a network backup solution, but it's got its limitations. Most importantly, it can be difficult to schedule backups, particularly on larger networks; you must add each machine individually to a network backup schedule. One solution to this problem is AMANDA, which was designed to automate the tape backup process as much as possible, while also providing tools to simplify the restore process. AMANDA serves as a "wrapper" around several other tools, and as such requires extra configuration. Once it's configured, though, AMANDA simplifies the day-to-day administration of a backup plan.

To begin using AMANDA, you should first understand its principles of operation: what can it do and how does it do it? Three types of configuration are then relevant: the AMANDA backup server, Linux backup clients, and Windows backup clients. Once you've configured all your systems, you can proceed to using AMANDA for both backups and restores.

AMANDA Principles

AMANDA was designed as a network-centric backup solution, in the sense that it's designed to treat a network as a single entity that's to be backed up. This contrasts with *tar* or even *smbtar*, which treat backups on a computer-by-computer basis. Of course, you must still tell AMANDA about the individual computers that are to be backed up, but you needn't be concerned with details such as scheduling when each system is backed up. Instead, let AMANDA work out those details, based on information you provide it concerning how often you want to complete a backup and what your network bandwidth is. Of course, you must ensure that backup clients are accessible to the backup server at the scheduled times. Because you may not know what those times are, it's best to make the backup clients accessible at all times.

AMANDA performs backups using two types of network protocols: its own unique tools and SMB/CIFS. AMANDA uses its own protocols to back up other Linux or Unix systems; these systems run *tar* or *dump* locally and transfer data to the AMANDA server. For Windows systems, AMANDA uses *smbclient* to transfer data using SMB/CIFS. In both cases, the backup clients must run server software and respond as servers. The AMANDA backup server, though, also runs server software, for the benefit of client-initiated restores. This configuration means that AMANDA can be trickier to configure than most backup server systems. Once configured, though, the backup procedure can be highly automated, and partial restores can be simpler, as well.

 AMANDA hardcodes some values in its executables. Thus, mixing AMANDA client and server packages for different Linux distributions may not work very well. If your site has multiple Linux distributions, or Linux and other Unix-like systems, you may need to compile AMANDA locally to get these systems to interoperate. Pay particular attention to the --with-user and --with-group options, which set the AMANDA user and group. In theory, a low-priority backup user should work, but in practice, you may need to run it as *root* to back up all files on the backup clients. This isn't a concern for networks with a Linux AMANDA backup server and Windows backup clients; because the Windows backup clients run SMB/CIFS servers rather than AMANDA servers, no special coordination is necessary.

AMANDA's normal mode of operation is to first copy data from the backup client to a holding area on the backup server's hard disk and then copy this data to the backup tape. (AMANDA was designed with tape backups in mind and can't be used with other backup media.) AMANDA therefore works best with a large local hard disk, or at least something that's large enough to hold a substantial chunk of a day's backup. If your local hard disk is smaller than this, AMANDA will perform the backup in bursts, pulling as much data as it can from the client, backing it up to

tape, pulling more from the client, and so on. This process is likely to be less efficient than retrieving a full backup and then spooling it all to tape.

Configuring an AMANDA Server

The bulk of the effort in AMANDA configuration is on the backup server side. Tasks
include running the server programs for client-initiated restores, setting general
AMANDA options, preparing tapes, and defining backup sets.

AMANDA server programs

The AMANDA backup server computer doesn't need to run any server programs for
ordinary backup operations, but it does need to run two server programs to handle
client-initiated restores: *amandaidx* and *amidxtape*. These programs are typically run
from a super server (*inetd* or *xinetd*). If your distribution uses *xinetd*, and you install
AMANDA from a package provided by your distribution, it may include one to three
files in */etc/xinetd.d* to handle the servers—both the servers for the backup server system and the server for the backup clients. (This third server is described in the section "Linux AMANDA Client Configuration.") If these files aren't present, you can
create one or two files to do the job. These files should contain entries like these:

```
service amandaidx
{
    socket_type  = stream
    protocol     = tcp
    wait         = no
    user         = amanda
    group        = disk
    server       = /usr/lib/amanda/amindexd
    disable      = no
}

service amidxtape
{
    socket_type  = stream
    protocol     = tcp
    wait         = no
    user         = amanda
    group        = disk
    server       = /usr/lib/amanda/amidxtaped
    disable      = no
}
```

These entries tell *xinetd* to handle the servers. You may need to adjust some items for
your system; pay particular attention to the user and group entries, which should
match the values used when the servers were compiled. (Consult your binary package's distribution if you installed a binary package.) You might also need to adjust
the path to the server. If your package includes *xinetd* configuration files, you

shouldn't need to adjust these features, but you may need to change the disable lines, as these usually ship set to yes, which disables the servers.

 The user who runs AMANDA on the backup server must have read/write access to the backup device files.

If your distribution uses *inetd* rather than *xinetd*, you must create entries in */etc/inetd.conf* to handle these two servers:

```
amandaidx  stream  tcp  nowait  amanda.disk  amindexd  amindexd
amidxtape  stream  tcp  nowait  amanda.disk  amidxtaped  amidxtaped
```

In addition to the *inetd* or *xinetd* configuration files themselves, you should check your */etc/services* file to be sure that port numbers are registered under the names used in your super server registration:

```
amandaidx  10082/tcp
amidxtape  10083/tcp
```

Once you've made these changes, restart or reload your super server. You can typically do this using a SysV startup script by typing **/etc/init.d/xinetd restart** or something similar. Consult your distribution's documentation if you have problems.

Setting AMANDA options

AMANDA uses two main configuration files, each stored under */etc/amanda* or subdirectories of that directory:

amanda.conf
> This file holds the main AMANDA configuration options. This file sets site-wide options.

disklist
> This file specifies the computers that are to be backed up and the partitions on those computers that you want to back up. It's covered in more detail in the section "Defining dump types and backup sets."

In theory, these files can reside in */etc/amanda*, or sometimes in */etc*, */usr/local/etc*, or a similar location. In practice, it's common to define multiple sets of configuration files, each of which resides in a subdirectory named after its purpose. For instance, you might use a directory called */etc/amanda/daily* for daily backups and */etc/amanda/archive* for long-term archival backups. You can then perform radically different types of backups by running AMANDA with appropriate options to use the configuration files you specify. Many AMANDA configurations provide a sample *amanda.conf* file in the */etc/amanda/example* directory. You can copy this file to a new directory you create and modify it to suit your purpose.

Most *amanda.conf* options consist of a keyword followed by one or more options, such as netusage 800 Kbps to tell AMANDA that it may use up to 800 Kbps of network bandwidth. Some configuration options, though, require multiple lines. These use an opening curly brace ({) to mark the beginning of the block of lines that apply to an option and a closing curly brace (}) to mark the end of the block.

You can leave most of the options alone in a typical example configuration file. Here are some of the options you might need to adjust:

org
> This option sets a name that appears in reports, so it's not critical for basic functioning, but you might as well set it.

mailto
> Specify usernames or email addresses using this option, and AMANDA will send reports on its activities to those addresses.

dumpuser
> AMANDA runs backups as the user you specify with this option. If it's unspecified, it uses a compile-time option that's specified via the --with-user option when building the program.

netusage
> This option specifies the maximum amount of network bandwidth that AMANDA can expect to have available to it.

dumpcycle
> You tell AMANDA how long you want a full network backup to take with this option. Typically, you specify a value in days or weeks, such as 5 days or 2 weeks.

runspercycle
> This option sets the number of times that AMANDA expects its *amdump* program, which does most of the real work, to run in each dump cycle. Setting this value equal to the number of days in dumpcycle results in an expectation of one run per day, while setting it to a higher or lower value results in multiple runs per day or less than one run per day. (The *amdump* program is actually run by *cron*; this option just tells AMANDA what to expect for planning purposes.)

tapecycle
> This option specifies the number of tapes used in a dump cycle. Ordinarily, it's the same as runspercycle plus a few for error handling; in case a tape goes bad and can't be used, you want AMANDA to be able to recover relatively gracefully.

runtapes
> You can tell AMANDA to use multiple tapes per run by specifying the number with this option. The default value is 1, which is usually desirable.

tapedev
> You tell AMANDA what tape device to use with this option. AMANDA expects to use nonrewinding tape devices, so be sure to point to one.

tapetype

> To plan its backups, AMANDA must know several key things about your tape backup device. You therefore specify the tape type with this option, which refers to definitions that appear later in the *amanda.conf* file. (Search for define tapetype to find this list.) If you don't see your tape device in the list, you'll need to either locate one on the Internet (check the AMANDA home page, and click the *Tape Type* link) or generate one yourself. To do the latter, you'll need the *tapetype* utility, which comes with the AMANDA source code but isn't built by default. Type **make tapetype** in the source code directory to build it. You should then insert a tape that holds no important data and type **./tapetype -f /dev/ device** to test the tape accessible from /dev/*device*. This operation erases all data on the tape and will probably take several hours. If your tape device supports hardware compression, you may be able to increase the reported tape length by the compression ratio (typically about 2), but if you then try to back up data that's not easily compressed, AMANDA may run out of space on the tape, which will cause problems.

labelstr

> When preparing tapes, as described in the next section, you give each tape a name. You must provide a regular expression describing the form of this label; AMANDA will use only tapes that match this label. This helps prevent accidental erasure of tapes if you insert the wrong one in the tape drive.

Another important option is the description of holding disks. You can define one or more holding areas, and each definition spans multiple lines, as in:

```
holdingdisk hd1 {
    comment "primary holding area"
    directory "/var/spool/amanda"
    use -500 MB
    chunksize 2000 MB
}
```

The comment is a comment for human use, and the directory specifies the location of the holding area. The use line is optional; when it's present, it specifies how much space may be used in this area. A negative use value tells AMANDA how much disk space to leave free; this example causes AMANDA to leave at least 500 MB available. The chunksize line is also optional, and it specifies the maximum size of individual files that are temporarily stored in the holding area. This feature can be useful on some older filesystems or 2.2.x kernels, which have file size limits of about 2 GB. A negative chunksize value tells AMANDA to attempt to pass files larger than the absolute value of the specified size directly to the tape device, which saves disk space but may result in slower operation, depending on your hardware.

Preparing tapes

AMANDA labels every tape that it uses, then keeps track of the tapes during the backup process. This arrangement enables AMANDA to tell you precisely what tape to insert in the drive when performing restores. To do any good, though, you must first label all the tapes you'll use for a backup set. To do this, use the *amlabel* command:

```
$ amlabel daily DailySet107
```

You must run this command as the user who will perform the backup. It takes the name of the backup configuration (that is, a subdirectory name within */etc/amanda*) and a label as options. In this example, the label is DailySet107. This label must match the regular expression specified on the labelstr line in *amanda.conf*, or AMANDA won't be able to use the tape.

Defining dump types and backup sets

In order to accommodate different computers' backup needs, AMANDA provides a number of *dump types* near the end of the *amanda.conf* file. These dump types are specified with the define dumptype option, as in:

```
define dumptype comp-user {
    global
    comment "Non-root partitions on reasonably fast machines"
    compress client fast
    program "GNUTAR"
    priority medium
}
```

Each named dump type is referenced in the *disklist* file to set assorted backup options, each of which appears on its own line within the dump type definition. Some of the options you might want to set include:

compress

> This option sets two options: whether compression occurs on the client or the server and the compression's speed/quality tradeoff (best, fast, or none).

exclude

> You can exclude individual files from backup using this option. Alternatively, exclude list enables you to pass a list of filenames that AMANDA will exclude from backup. AMANDA excludes no files by default.

holdingdisk

> Pass yes or no to this option to tell AMANDA whether to use a holding disk. The default value is yes.

index

> Pass yes or no to this option to tell AMANDA whether to store an index of files that are backed up. You might want to omit the index on disks that are likely to be restored only in a full restore as a measure for saving disk space. The default value is yes.

kencrypt

This option takes yes and no values, and controls whether AMANDA uses Kerberos encryption. Setting it to yes requires that your network use Kerberos, as described in Chapter 9. The default value is no.

program

Pass "DUMP" (including the quote marks) as this option's parameter to have it use *dump* for backups on the remote system; pass "GNUTAR" to have it use *tar*. Given the limitations of *dump*, routinely using program "GNUTAR" is often wise. The default is "DUMP" for AMANDA backup clients, but only "GNUTAR" is valid for Samba clients, so that's the default.

skip-incr

If this option is yes (the default is no), disks that use this dump type are skipped when performing incremental backups.

priority

This option accepts values of low, medium, and high, which describe the importance of the disk for the backup. In case of errors or insufficient disk space, disks with higher priorities are saved, at least in the holding area, in preference to disks with lower priorities. The default value is medium.

These and more options are described in comments in the *amanda.conf* file, so if you'd like to achieve some effect not described here, check that file's comments. The example configuration file includes many dump types, so chances are you can use those that are provided. Peruse them to learn more. You can then create a *disklist* file, which specifies the backup client computers, the directories you want to back up, and the dump types you want to use for each directory:

```
# Be sure to back up the backup server
buserver.example.org /      root-tar
buserver.example.org /var   root-tar
buserver.example.org /hold  holding-disk

# Back up a Linux client
buclient.example.org /      root-tar
buclient.example.org /home  user-tar

# Back up a Windows client
buserver.example.org //GINGKO/DRIVEC  user-tar
```

 The first set of entries in this example configuration backs up the backup server system. This means that the backup server must be configured as a backup client (as described in the next section), as well as being configured as a backup server.

For Linux or other Unix-like systems that run AMANDA software, you specify the hostname, a directory name, and a dump type. For Windows backup clients, you specify the backup server as the hostname and provide a hostname and share name in *//HOST/SHARE* format instead of a directory specification. AMANDA then uses Samba's *smbclient* to transfer the files. You must also create a password file, */etc/amandapass*, which holds share names along with usernames and passwords:

```
//GINGKO/DRIVEC  mypassword
//MAIZE/DRIVED   buuser%bupassword
```

This example sets a password alone for the *DRIVEC* share on *GINGKO*, and a username and password for the *DRIVED* share on *MAIZE*. Because this file contains unencrypted passwords, you should ensure that it's readable only to the backup user (and *root*, if the two aren't the same).

At this point, AMANDA is configured on the backup server; however, you must still configure it on any Linux clients and prepare Windows systems. Once this is done, you can actually begin using AMANDA for backups and restores.

Linux AMANDA Client Configuration

Linux AMANDA backup clients run a server program called *amandad*, which responds to commands from the backup server system. The *amandad* program is normally run from a super server. If you installed AMANDA from a distribution's package on a distribution that uses *xinetd*, it may have installed a file called */etc/xinetd.d/amanda* to handle this server. If you use *xinetd*, and this file isn't present, you'll have to create it:

```
service amanda
{
    socket_type  = dgram
    protocol     = udp
    wait         = yes
    user         = amanda
    group        = disk
    server       = /usr/lib/amanda/amandad
    disable      = no
}
```

As with the servers that are run on the AMANDA backup server computer, this one may need modification for your system. In particular, the user and group items may need adjustment. Be sure the specified user and group exist and have the necessary permissions to access the files you want backed up on the system. In practice, it's sometimes necessary to run the server as *root*, particularly if you want to back up files that only *root* may read. Even if your distribution provides a file to handle this server, you should check it and set disable = no; the default usually sets this value at yes, disabling the server.

If you use *inetd* as your super server, you must create an */etc/inetd.conf* entry for *amandad*:

```
amanda  dgram  udp  wait  amanda.disk  amandad  amandad
```

The server run on the AMANDA backup client, like all servers, is a potential security risk, particularly if it's run as *root*. A miscreant who manages to access the server can read files from the computer, potentially including sensitive files such as password databases. Be sure the port used by the server (UDP port 10080) is well protected by firewall rules.

You must also ensure that the server's port is defined in */etc/services*:

```
amanda   10080/udp
```

As a security measure, *amandad* uses an authorization file, *.amandahosts*, which is located in the home directory of the user who runs the server. This file contains the hostname of the backup server and the username of the user who runs the backup software on that system:

```
buserver.example.org amanda
```

The *amandad* server refuses to interact with *amandad* clients (that is, backup server systems) other than the one specified in this file. AMANDA doesn't use passwords for authentication, though.

Once all these features are set up, you should restart your super server. On most distributions, this can be done using SysV startup scripts, as in **/etc/init.d/xinetd restart**. Consult distribution-specific documentation for details.

Windows AMANDA Client Configuration

Because AMANDA uses SMB/CIFS to back up Windows systems, you needn't install or configure any special AMANDA software on these systems. Instead, configure them as you would for an SMB/CIFS backup using *smbclient*, as described earlier. Be sure to set the password for the backup user or share to the value you've set in the AMANDA backup server's */etc/amandapass* file.

Backing Up and Restoring Data with AMANDA

To run a backup via AMANDA, use the *amdump* command. This command has the following syntax:

```
amdump config [ host [ disk ] ]
```

Normally, you just pass it a *config* name, which should match one of the subdirectory names in */etc/amanda*. The *amdump* program then performs *part* of a network backup. The tool scans your configuration files to determine how many systems and disks it should back up over the course of a dump cycle. It can then perform an appropriate fraction of the full backup, the assumption being that the run you perform with this command is a regularly scheduled one. Of course, you must insert one of the tapes you prepared for this backup configuration in the tape drive before you issue this backup command.

Normally, you call *amdump* from *cron*. For instance, you might use a *crontab* entry like this to run *amdump* once every weeknight:

```
00 21 * * 1-5 /usr/sbin/amdump
```

You enter this line in the *~/crontab* file for the user who you want to perform the backup, then type **crontab -u *user* /home/*user*/crontab** as *root*, where *user* is the username in question. The result is that *cron* will run *amdump* at 21:00 (9:00 P.M.) every weekday (1-5 in the final date field corresponds to Monday through Friday). Depending on your network bandwidth, tape capacity, and so on, each run can take anywhere from a few minutes to several hours to complete. After each run, AMANDA will email a report of its activities to the address specified with the mailto option in *amanda.conf*, so you can use that information to verify AMANDA's correct operation.

Restoring from an AMANDA backup requires special tools on the backup client. (For Windows backup clients, though, you perform these steps on the backup server system.) In particular, the *amrecover* tool enables you to browse the backup database maintained by the backup server. This tool presents its own amrecover> prompt and accepts commands you type. You can select files to recover and then extract them all from the backup with a single command. Specific commands you're likely to use include:

sethost *hostname*
: Sets the name of the computer whose files you want to restore. The default is the localhost.

setdisk *diskname*
: Sets the name of the disk on which the files you want to restore were originally held. It must match a name set in *disklist*.

listdisk *diskname*
: Lists the contents of a disk.

setmode *mode*
: Tells *amrecover* how to extract files for SMB/CIFS operations. Setting *mode* to smb causes shares to be extracted directly to the SMB/CIFS backup client computer; setting *mode* to tar causes files to be extracted to the local system.

mode
: Displays the mode for extracting SMB/CIFS shares.

add *items*
: Adds the specified *items* (files or directories) to a restore set.

extract

> Begins the extraction process. To do any good, you must have added files to the restore set first. The tool prompts you to insert particular backup tapes, then recovers the data from those tapes.

In addition to these commands, *amrecover* accepts several more. Some of these, such as cd and ls, are similar to commands in *bash* or other common Linux shells; they enable you to move around the directories in the backup set and view files. Consult the *amrecover* manpage for more information.

As with local restores using *tar* or other tools, restores using *amrecover* are simplest if the systems involved are in more-or-less functional condition. To perform a full restore, you must have an emergency system working, as described in the section "Restoring Data Locally." This system must have a working version of the AMANDA backup client software running.

Summary

Backups are extremely useful insurance in case of hardware failure, major filesystem problems, system intrusion, or even user error. When these problems crop up, a backup can speed recovery of a working system. Unfortunately, backing up an entire network can be a tedious proposition. Fortunately, tools such as Samba and AMANDA can help simplify this process. Although they can take some time to set up, once they're configured, their day-to-day use is relatively straightforward, and they can pay off quite handsomely when problems occur that require data recovery from the backup.

## CHAPTER 15

Managing a Network with Linux

Linux can run several protocols that can provide important background functionality on networks. These protocols seldom make themselves obvious to users—except if the servers that manage them malfunction. Although most of them are major protocols in the sense that they provide many features and have even spawned entire books, they aren't tricky enough to configure to deserve entire chapters in this book. Therefore, I cover all of them in this chapter. These protocols are the Dynamic Host Configuration Protocol, which delivers IP addresses and other basic network configuration information to clients; the Domain Name System, which converts hostnames to IP addresses and vice versa; and the Network Time Protocol, which helps keep clocks synchronized on multiple computers.

Although all these protocols can be handled by Windows, doing so with Linux gives you all of Linux's advantages. The servers that handle these protocols are all small enough and require little enough in the way of CPU time, memory, and other resources that they can be run on a very modest Linux system—perhaps an old 80486 or Pentium system that's been retired. You can move one or more of these services onto such a Linux system, obviating the need to upgrade your software and hardware to enable the latest version of Windows to do the job.

Delivering IP Addresses with DHCP

Networks of all sizes use DHCP to simplify configuration of most computers on the network. A computer configured to use DHCP for basic network configuration tries to locate a DHCP server at startup and, if one is found, sets its basic network options to those specified by the DHCP server. This task may sound impossible because basic network configuration information is delivered via the network before the DHCP client is configured, but it is possible, and understanding the basics of how it's possible is the first order of business. Next up is an overview of DHCP configuration files. You can use DHCP to assign addresses either so that the same computer is or isn't guaranteed the same address on each boot, and understanding how to do both is important. Finally, knowing how to tell clients to use DHCP is critically important to this protocol's successful deployment.

The Role of DHCP

DHCP is an unusual protocol because it uses very low-level network protocols to help a computer "bootstrap" a more sophisticated configuration. When a DHCP client boots or starts its TCP/IP network stack, the client has no IP address, but it does have working hardware, and it can send data over the network wire. The DHCP client therefore sends a network broadcast with a query directed at any DHCP server that might be listening. Although the DHCP client has no IP address, it does have a working low-level hardware address, and the DHCP server is able to direct its reply to this address. The DHCP server's reply includes information on basic network settings—most importantly, the client's IP address and network mask, as well as the IP addresses of the subnet's router and the DNS servers the client should use. Additional information can be delivered, as well, such as the IP addresses of NBNS computers, but this information isn't delivered by all DHCP servers or used by all clients.

DHCP works by issuing *leases* on IP addresses. The idea is that, should the client crash or otherwise become inaccessible, the IP address will revert back to the pool of available addresses after a limited time. In this way, a DHCP server can continue delivering addresses from a fixed set of addresses. Clients can also give up their leases voluntarily—say, when they're shut down. Not all clients do this, though. Leases have fixed terms, and when a lease expires, a client must renew that lease. (Typically, clients attempt to renew their leases halfway through their terms. If the initial renewal attempt fails, subsequent attempts are made.)

Considered on the network as a whole, DHCP simplifies configuration. Instead of entering several IP addresses on each client (for the client itself, including its netmask, the router, DNS servers, and perhaps more), DHCP enables you to set a single option to use DHCP on each client. The details of IP address assignment can then be handled by the server, either automatically or by assigning one address to each computer. This centralized control has a certain appeal by itself, but it's also helpful because it reduces the risk of a typo causing problems, and it makes it easier to change your network's configuration. For instance, if you need to change your network's DNS server address for some reason, you can do so by implementing a change in the DHCP server configuration.

 Because DHCP works by providing leases of fixed length, changes to network features such as DNS and router IP addresses won't immediately propagate to all DHCP clients. Most clients should update their settings by half the DHCP lease time, though. You can adjust the lease time from the DHCP server.

Because DHCP can assign IP addresses arbitrarily to any computer that asks for one, it can be particularly handy on networks on which computers are frequently added and removed. For instance, if your office hosts a number of notebook computers that are frequently removed and taken on business trips, these computers might not have permanent IP address assignments. A DHCP server can assign addresses to them as they're used. Furthermore, if a notebook computer is used on two networks, and if both networks use DHCP, the notebook computer can adjust itself automatically to the settings needed by both networks.

 Although enabling DHCP to deliver IP addresses to any new computer it sees, and using notebook computers with any network's DHCP server are both useful procedures, they're also both potentially risky. If a new computer on your network is infected with a worm or virus, it might be able to spread locally, bypassing any firewall controls you have on your router. Likewise, a notebook computer can come under attack from worms or viruses if connected to a foreign network. To reduce risk in a security-conscious environment, you might configure DHCP to deliver IP addresses only to known computers. You can do so by referencing specific hardware addresses, as described in the section "Fixed address assignment."

In the Linux world, the Internet Software Consortium's (ISC; *http://www.isc.org*) DHCP server is the standard one. Most Linux distributions ship with this server under the package name *dhcpd* or *dhcp-server*. ISC also produces a DHCP client, which is frequently installed as *dhcpcd*. Other DHCP clients, such as *pump* and *dhcp-client*, are also available.

Kernel and Routing Requirements for DHCP

Because the DHCP server must communicate with clients that are not yet fully configured for TCP/IP, the server needs support for packet sockets. This is a way for programs to communicate over the network without using an intervening network protocol, such as TCP/IP. It's usually enabled by default, but if you've rebuilt your kernel yourself, you might want to check for it. In 2.6.x kernels, check Networking Support → Networking Options → Packet Socket. If this option isn't enabled, enable it and recompile your kernel. This option is also needed by some DHCP clients.

DHCP servers send their responses to clients using a broadcast address. This can be either a global broadcast (255.255.255.255) or a broadcast that reaches all the computers on a particular subnet (such as 172.24.255.255 to reach all the computers on the 172.24.0.0/16 subnet). Unfortunately, some DHCP clients (such as some versions of Windows) expect DHCP servers to deliver global broadcasts, but some Linux configurations convert global broadcasts into local broadcasts. The usual symptom of this problem is that some Windows clients (particularly Windows 9x/Me systems) can't obtain IP addresses via DHCP, but others (such as Linux clients) can. If this happens, try typing this command on the Linux DHCP server:

```
# route add -host 255.255.255.255 dev eth0
```

If the DHCP server is delivering addresses on a device other than eth0, change that part of the command appropriately. After making this change, try restarting an affected Windows system; it should now work. If so, add this line to a local Linux startup script or to the SysV startup script for your DHCP server.

 This *route* command adds an explicit route for traffic destined to 255.255.255.255; without it, Linux changes the IP address to conform to existing routes. You can check your existing routing table by typing **route -n**. After adding the route as just described, it should appear as the first entry in the routing table.

DHCP Configuration Files

The DHCP server's configuration file is */etc/dhcpd.conf*. Some package distributions include this file in this location, but some packages instead provide a sample file in another location. For instance, SuSE's *dhcp-server* package stores a sample file in */usr/share/doc/packages/dhcp-server/*. The ISC DHCP server also creates a file to track its leases, often called */var/lib/dhcp/dhcpd.leases*. You shouldn't need to adjust this file, although examining it can sometimes be a good way to check the server's operation.

 Don't confuse the DHCP server's *dhcpd.conf* file with *dhcpcd.conf*, which some DHCP *client* packages use as a configuration file!

Aside from comments, which are denoted by hash marks (#), *dhcpd.conf* contains two broad types of statements:

Parameters
> These are relatively simple statements that provide information for clients (such as a router's IP address) or that tell the server whether or how to do something (such as how long leases should be). Many parameters begin with the keyword option.

Declarations
> These statements describe the network topology, assign IP addresses to clients, or create a grouping of related parameters. Declarations often span multiple lines, in which case the grouped lines are denoted by curly braces ({ }).

Most *dhcpd.conf* files begin with a set of parameters and then move on to declarations. A simple network may contain just one declaration, which in turn contains multiple parameters. A more complex network might contain multiple declarations.

Assigning Addresses

The bulk of DHCP server configuration is in assigning IP addresses. A full configuration file, though, sets assorted other parameters, and it's best to consider them together. I therefore describe two complete configurations as examples: assigning dynamic IP addresses and assigning fixed IP addresses.

Dynamic address assignment

In a dynamic IP address assignment configuration, the DHCP server hands out IP addresses to any computer that asks for them but doesn't go to any great lengths to track computers and match them with the same IP address every time they boot. Thus, a single computer might receive four different IP addresses over the course of a week, depending on factors such as the lease time, the number of addresses available, the number of computers on the network, and how often the computer reboots or is shut down for an extended period.

 Even when a network uses dynamic IP addresses, a computer's IP address is unlikely to change unless the computer is shut down for an extended period of time, such that its lease expires and another computer grabs the address. Even when a computer reboots, it typically asks for its old address back, and will probably receive that address if the lease hasn't expired yet. When the computer stays up continuously, it renews its lease before the lease expires and so keeps the same IP address continuously.

Example 15-1 shows a typical *dhcpd.conf* file for assigning dynamic IP addresses. Although this example is simple, something like it should be adequate for many small networks or even simple large networks. Most lines in this file end in semicolons (;), and omitting that character is an easy way to create a nonfunctional configuration file, so be sure to check that detail. Multiline declarations, however, don't use a semicolon on lines that end in either an open or a close curly brace.

Example 15-1. Sample dynamic DHCP server configuration

```
allow bootp;
default-lease-time 86400;
max-lease-time 172800;
option subnet-mask 255.255.255.0;
option domain-name-servers 192.168.1.7, 172.24.21.7;
option domain-name "example.com";
option netbios-node-type 8;
option netbios-name-servers 192.168.1.7
option ntp-servers 192.168.1.7;
option x-display-manager 192.168.1.3;
option tftp-server-name "mango.example.com";
```

Example 15-1. Sample dynamic DHCP server configuration (continued)

```
subnet 192.168.1.0 netmask 255.255.255.0 {
    option routers 192.168.1.1;
    range 192.168.1.50 192.168.1.254;
}
```

This example begins with several lines that set assorted parameters. Most of these have fairly descriptive names, such as `default-lease-time` or `option subnet-mask`. However, some options require some elaboration:

`allow bootp`

> This option tells DHCP to respond to BootP requests, which are similar to DHCP requests but designed to be used by computers that boot off the network. Such configurations are often used with thin clients, as described in Chapter 12.

`default-lease-time`

> You set the default lease time, in seconds, with this option. The lease time is actually determined by negotiation between the client and the server, so you may end up delivering longer leases than you specify with this file, depending on the client's options.

`max-lease-time`

> This parameter sets the maximum lease time the server delivers. Even if the client requests a longer time, the server won't comply.

> When testing a DHCP configuration, or sometime before making important changes such as altering a router or NTP server IP address, you may want to reduce the `default-lease-time` and `max-lease-time` values to something short—possibly as short as a few minutes (say, 300—five minutes). This action reduces the amount of time that clients have invalid information, which can speed up DHCP testing. Using lease times in the range of several minutes to a few hours can be good on networks that see lots of coming and going, such as a network to which users frequently attach laptops for a few minutes at a time. Note that using short lease times will increase network traffic and load on the DHCP server. Setting lease times in the range of many hours or days (such as the 86400, or one day, default lease time in Example 15-1), is a better policy for a stable and working DHCP server on a network that sees few changes to its clients.

`option subnet-mask`

> As you might guess, this option sets the subnet mask (a.k.a. the network mask or netmask).

`option domain-name-servers`

> Point to your network's DNS servers with this option. You can specify multiple servers by separating their values with commas. Most clients accept up to three

DNS server addresses, but you can deliver fewer than this number if you like. Example 15-1 specifies DNS servers by IP address, but you can specify hostnames for the DHCP server to resolve when it starts up. (The DHCP server delivers IP addresses to clients in both cases.)

`option domain-name`

You can tell clients what domain name to use with this option. Not all clients use this information, but for those that do, it can be a handy feature.

`option netbios-node-type`

This option tells Windows clients how they should attempt to resolve names—whether to use a NBNS system, broadcast resolution, or both. A value of 8 tells the system to use an NBNS system if possible but to fall back on broadcast name resolution. Chapter 5 describes NBNS configuration in more detail.

`option netbios-name-servers`

This option is the NetBIOS equivalent of `option domain-name-servers` and works in a similar way. Linux clients ignore this information, though; it's useful only for Windows clients.

`option ntp-servers`

You can point clients at an NTP server with this option; however, many clients ignore this information. The upcoming section, "Keeping Clocks Synchronized with NTP," describes NTP in more detail.

`option x-display-manager`

This option can point certain X terminal thin clients at an XDMCP server, as described in Chapter 12. Some thin clients ignore this information, however.

`option tftp-server-name`

A TFTP server delivers files to computers, such as some thin clients, that boot off of the network. This option points such clients to the TFTP server.

`option routers`

Although Example 15-1 shows this option within a declaration block, it can appear outside such a block. It points the clients at the network's router (a.k.a. the gateway).

DHCP supports many additional parameters, but most of them are quite obscure. Consult the *dhcpd.conf* manpage or a book on DHCP for more information.

The core of the DHCP configuration, and the part that sets the dynamic addresses it can deliver, is the subnet declaration in Example 15-1. This declaration begins with a specification of the numeric subnet it serves—`192.168.1.0 netmask 255.255.255.0`. The curly braces then set off several lines that define features unique to this declaration. In Example 15-1, the declaration contains just two parameter lines, but you can add more. These lines override parameters set outside the declaration body or set new options. The key to defining a dynamic DHCP definition is the range parameter:

```
range 192.168.1.50 192.168.1.254;
```

This line tells *dhcpd* what IP addresses it may deliver. In this case, the range includes 205 addresses, from 192.168.1.50 through 192.168.1.254. The server won't deliver addresses outside of this range, even within the 192.168.1.0/255 subnet. Thus, you can assign IP addresses for some systems without using DHCP. For instance, the DHCP server itself typically has a static IP address. You might also want to give a router or other important server a static IP address outside the DHCP server's control.

Once you make changes to the DHCP server's configuration, you must restart the server. Typically, you do this using the server's SysV startup script, as in **/etc/init. d/dhcpd restart**. If the server isn't already running, you can start it the same way. Consult distribution-specific documentation if you need help with SysV startup scripts.

Fixed address assignment

The leap from dynamic IP address assignment to fixed address assignment is a matter of adding new declarations, one for each computer to which you want to assign a fixed address. These host declarations appear within the declaration for the dynamic subnet:

```
subnet 192.168.1.0 netmask 255.255.255.0 {
    option routers 192.168.1.1;
    range 192.168.1.50 192.168.1.254;

    host gingko {
        hardware ethernet 00:0C:76:96:A3:73;
        fixed-address 192.168.1.20;
    }
}
```

Each host declaration begins with a hostname (gingko in this case). This hostname may be passed to the client if you set the use-host-decl-names true parameter, but most clients ignore the name. The declaration then contains two lines. The first sets the client's media type (ethernet in this case, although token-ring is appropriate for Token Ring networks) and media access control (MAC) address, a.k.a. the hardware address. The DHCP server then knows to assign the specified fixed-address as the IP address whenever the computer with the specified MAC address requests an address.

 The IP address you specify with fixed-address must be *outside* the range specified with range but within the range determined by the subnet IP address and netmask declaration.

Of course, on a large network, managing all the computers' MAC and IP addresses can be tedious. For this reason, assigning fixed IP addresses in this way is best reserved for small networks or for a limited number of computers (say, important servers) on large networks. This type of configuration is also often used when configuring thin clients, which may need to be told on a client-by-client basis what files to use as a boot OS. This topic is described in Chapter 12.

One critical detail about this configuration is locating the target computer's MAC address. Several approaches to doing so exist:

Examining board markings

Some network card manufacturers mark the MAC address on their boards, usually by affixing a sticker. This can be a good way to get a MAC address if you're installing a card, but it can be inconvenient if the computer's already assembled and has the network card in it. Also, not all manufacturers label their cards this way.

Client configuration tools

Most clients enable you to view the MAC address in one way or another. On Linux and most other Unix-like clients, you can find the address using *ifconfig*, as in **ifconfig eth0**. The MAC address is called the HWaddr in the output. Typing **IPCONFIG /ALL** at a DOS prompt on Windows NT/200x/XP systems also displays this information, on a line labelled Physical Address. Windows 9x/Me systems provide a GUI tool, *WINIPCFG*, which delivers this information.

Using arp

You can give the client an IP address, either by configuring it statically or by using DHCP without a static IP address defined for the system. You can then use the Linux *arp* command to find the MAC address. For instance, **arp 192.168.1.78** finds the MAC address (and some other information) for 192.168.1.78. You may need to direct some other traffic at the computer first, though; using *ping* should do the job.

Examining DHCP logs

If you have the client obtain an IP address from the DHCP server's pool of dynamic addresses, you can then examine the */var/lib/dhcp/dhcpd.leases* file to locate the MAC address. This appears in a block named after the IP address given to the client. Similarly, the */var/log/messages* or other system logfile on the DHCP server usually records the MAC address of clients and the assigned IP address. These techniques are both simplest to use on a network with little DHCP activity, such as a small network. Locating the correct entry on a larger network can be trickier.

In all these cases, the exact form of the MAC address can vary. For inclusion in the *dhcpd.conf* file's host declaration, the address appears as a series of hexadecimal (base 16) numbers separated by colons (:). Some utilities may show the address in another form, such as separated by dashes. If necessary, make the change. For hexadecimal values between A and F, the DHCP server doesn't care about case. For instance, 5a is exactly equivalent to 5A.

Telling Clients to Use DHCP

Like any server, the ISC DHCP server is useful only if it has clients. These clients can be Windows, Linux, Mac OS, or just about any other system. The DHCP client sets its own basic TCP/IP features by consulting the DHCP server, so the DHCP client program must run before most other network-related programs on the client.

 A DHCP client can be a server for other protocols. For instance, you might use DHCP to assign an IP address to an SMB/CIFS file or printer server. Some servers work best with fixed IP addresses simply because this makes it easier to enter a name-to-IP-address mapping in your DNS server. For them, you can assign a fixed IP address to the server via DHCP, as just described.

To tell a computer to use a DHCP server, you must typically run the computer's basic network configuration tools. For instance, you can do this job on a Windows XP system that's already configured with a static IP address:

1. Open the Windows Control Panel.

2. Double-click the Network Connections icon in the Control Panel. This action opens a Network Connections window.

3. In the Network Connections window, right-click the Local Area Connection icon and select Properties from the resulting context menu. This action opens a Local Area Connection Properties dialog box.

4. In the Local Area Connection Properties dialog box, select the Internet Protocol (TCP/IP) item and click Properties. This action yields a dialog box called Internet Protocol (TCP/IP) Properties, as shown in Figure 15-1.

5. In the Internet Protocol (TCP/IP) Properties dialog box, click "Obtain an IP address automatically". If any are set, the values in the "Use the following IP address" fields should disappear.

6. If your DHCP server delivers DNS server addresses, click "Obtain DNS server address automatically". Any addresses you've set manually should disappear. (You can continue to set DNS server addresses manually, though, which can be handy if you want to use a nonstandard DNS server for some reason.)

7. Click OK. This should activate your changes. You then need to close the remaining open dialog boxes and network option windows.

In many cases, you'll configure the DHCP client when you first set up its networking features. For instance, you might double-click the Network Setup Wizard in Windows XP. This setup procedure will guide you through various network settings, but in all cases, you should be presented with a choice to use DHCP or to set the IP address manually, as in Figure 15-1. (Windows often doesn't use the term *DHCP*,

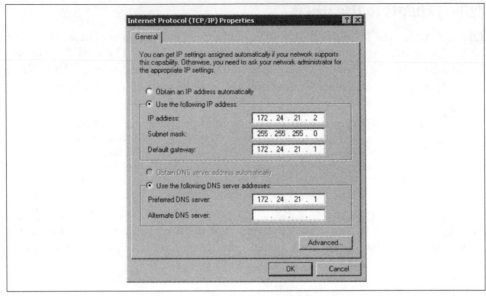

Figure 15-1. The TCP/IP Properties dialog box lets you set basic network features

though, instead referring to this option as "obtain IP address automatically," as in Figure 15-1, or something similar.)

Precise details vary from one operating system to another, as well. Most versions of Windows, Mac OS, and other GUI-oriented OSs provide a procedure similar to that just described for Windows XP, but many details differ. Consult the OS's documentation, or browse the system configuration options for ones relating to network configuration. Linux distributions with GUI system administration tools can usually be configured to use DHCP in much this way, as well. You can also do so using text-mode tools: install a DHCP client (usually in a package called *dhcpcd*, *dhcp-client*, or *pump*), and use *chkconfig* or other tools to enable this package in your default run-level. Consult distribution-specific documentation if you need help with this task.

Delivering Names with DNS

A second key network management tool is DNS. DNS servers fill two roles: enabling your local clients to convert names to IP addresses for local and remote computers, and enabling remote systems to find local computers that you choose (such as web or mail servers). One important question is whether you should even run a local DNS server; for many purposes, relying on outside servers makes a lot of sense. Sometimes, though, running a DNS server locally is very helpful. If you decide you want to run your own DNS server, you must be able to configure it. The basic DNS server configuration varies with the server software you select. BIND is the most popular Linux DNS server, and so it's described in this chapter. Once the basic configuration is set, you must create files that describe the computers on your network—their hostnames, IP addresses, and related characteristics. Finally, you must be able to tell clients to use the DNS servers you've configured.

Principles of DNS

DNS is, essentially, a global database of computer names. The huge size of the DNS database presents many challenges, including maintenance of the database and providing storage space for it. Both challenges are overcome by the fact that DNS is a *distributed* database; no one computer holds all the data in the DNS database. Instead, the DNS namespace is arranged hierarchically. At the top of the hierarchy are the *top-level domains* (TLDs), which appear at the end of a DNS hostname. Common examples include *.com*, *.edu*, and *.net*. These three TLDs are all examples of *generic TLDs* (gTLDs), which are (theoretically) not tied to specific nations. Another type of TLD is the *country code TLD* (ccTLD), which uses a two-digit country code as the TLD, such as *.us* for the United States or *.ru* for Russia.

Below the TLDs are the domain names that are so common, such as *oreilly.com* for O'Reilly Media or *upenn.edu* for the University of Pennsylvania. These domains can be further subdivided, such as *cis.upenn.edu* for the Computer and Information Science department at the University of Pennsylvania. At some point, individual computers can be specified, as in *www.oreilly.com* for the O'Reilly web server.

The beauty of DNS's distributed nature is that it ties into this hierarchy. At each level of the hierarchy, a single DNS server can reasonably hold data on all the domains or subdomains at that level. At the very top of this hierarchy, a set of computers known as the *root servers* maintain information on the TLDs. Each root server can field queries concerning TLDs; most importantly, the root servers can tell a client where to find DNS servers for the *.com*, *.ru*, and other TLDs. The client can then contact a TLD's DNS server for information on a specific domain, such as *oreilly.com*; the result is the address of the *oreilly.com* DNS servers. With this information in hand, the client can ask about a specific computer, such as *www.oreilly.com*.

The distributed DNS system therefore enables lookups in a huge address space relatively quickly. Although multiple queries may be needed, each one finishes rather rapidly. DNS also includes certain time-saving features. For instance, rather than have users' workstations perform the full *recursive lookup*, in which a name is queried starting with the root servers, a network can host a DNS server that does this job and caches the results. Thus, if two users on a network look up *www.oreilly.com* in quick succession, the local DNS server needn't perform a full recursive lookup for the second query; it simply retrieves the result of the original lookup from its cache and delivers that result. This characteristic is also a key to understanding the two main roles that a DNS server can play on your network:

- The DNS server can perform full recursive lookups for the benefit of your local computers, and also deliver information on local computers to other local computers. Running a DNS server this way doesn't require modifying your domain's registration with the outside world.

- The DNS server can hold information on your local network and deliver that information when queried by remote systems. This capability is extremely important for delivering the IP address of your externally accessible servers, such as your mail server. Although this chapter can help get you started running your own DNS server, you must consult your domain registrar to link your server to the global DNS system.

This chapter focuses on the first type of DNS configuration—that which is most useful to local computers. The principles described here also form the foundation for making changes that are accessible to the outside world, though.

You can assign one DNS server to be used by local computers and another for use by outside systems. In fact, you don't need to run both servers yourself. For instance, you might run your own local DNS server to help your computers perform DNS lookups, but rely on a domain registrar or a domain hosting provider to run DNS servers that hold information on your domain for the outside world.

Running a DNS server for the benefit of your local computers is most useful if your ISP doesn't provide one or if you want to deliver information that's unique to your private network. For instance, you might have a subnet behind a firewall that holds file servers, print servers, and pull mail servers to be used by other computers behind the firewall. Entering information on these systems in a globally accessible DNS server is unnecessary and can even give potential attackers information about your network, so running a DNS server behind the firewall can be a good way to provide local name resolution. This server can also handle full recursive lookups for the benefit of other local computers.

An alternative to DNS for local name resolution is to configure an NBNS system. Windows clients often use an NBNS system automatically if the DHCP server is configured to deliver the NBNS address, as described earlier in the section "Dynamic address assignment." You can also configure Linux systems to use NBNS, as described in Chapter 6. NBNS has certain advantages, such as simpler adaptation to dynamic IP addresses, but it's also got limitations, such as a lack of support for DNS domain information.

Basic Name Server Configuration

Running a name server involves two basic configuration tasks: setting up the name server itself (that is, the options it uses to control where it stores additional configuration files, how it should respond, and so on) and setting up the domains it handles. This section describes the first of these tasks, using the BIND software as an example. (If you use another server, such as *djbdns*, you need to read its documentation.) The second task is described in the next section.

The Berkeley Internet Name Domain (BIND) is distributed by the ISC (*http://www. isc.org*), which also distributes the most common Linux DHCP server. As with ISC's DHCP server, BIND is available with all major distributions, except for some very desktop-oriented ones; thus, you shouldn't need to download it from the ISC web site unless you have a specific reason to avoid your distribution's BIND package. Typically, the package name is *bind*.

Although the official name for this server package is BIND, the executable filename is *named*, and BIND configuration files are named after this—namely, the main configuration file is */etc/named.conf*. For a simple configuration, this file contains two broad classes of entries:

- Global options appear in a section called options. These include features such as a directory in which domain definitions exist, on what network interfaces the server should listen, and so on.

- Each domain or subdomain (that is, a *zone*) is briefly described in a zone section. This section sets only the broad outlines for a zone; the description of the zone's computers appears in zone configuration files, as described in the next section.

Example 15-2 shows a simple but usable */etc/named.conf* file. This file defines the basic settings for a BIND server handling the *example.com* domain. It includes an options section and four zone sections, which are described in more detail shortly. A DNS server for a network with multiple subnets or domains is likely to have additional zone sections.

Example 15-2. Sample /etc/named.conf file

```
options {
    directory "/var/named";
    listen-on{
        192.168.1.1;
        172.24.21.1;
    };
    forwarders {
        10.29.102.7;
        10.65.201.7;
    };
    forward first;
};
zone "." {
    type hint;
    file "named.ca";
};
```

Example 15-2. Sample /etc/named.conf file (continued)

```
zone "example.com" {
  type master;
  file "named.example.com";
};
zone "1.168.192.in-addr.arpa"{
  type master;
  file "named.192.168.1";
};
zone "0.0.127.in-addr.arpa"{
  type master;
  file "named.local";
};
```

The general format of the */etc/named.conf* file is similar to that of the ISC DHCP server. Most lines set individual options and end in semicolons (;). Other lines, though, begin or end blocks of options. The line that begins such a block ends in an open curly brace ({), and the line ending such a block ends in a close curly brace and a semicolon (};).

The options section in Example 15-2 sets several important global features of the server:

directory

> This may be the most important line in the options section; it sets the name of the directory in which BIND looks for zone definition files—that is, the files that define the mappings of hostnames to IP addresses and related domain features.

listen-on

> This optional subsection specifies one or more IP addresses on which BIND listens for queries. This feature can be handy if you run the server on a computer with multiple network interfaces but want to make the server available on only some of them.

forwarders

> This subsection is optional. If you use it, you can specify the IP addresses of one or more DNS servers that you want to handle DNS queries other than those for which your own server is the ultimate authority. Typically, you use this feature if your ISP offers DNS servers of its own. You can point BIND to your ISP's servers using this directive and, rather than perform a full recursive lookup itself, your server queries your ISP's servers and lets them perform the full recursive lookup. This can result in faster responses if your ISP's servers are working correctly, because they probably have better Internet connections than your own server. This option has no effect on lookups within your own domains (such as *example.com* in this example).

forward

> The forward option tells BIND when to use the DNS servers specified with the forwarders directive. The forward option takes either of two values: only or

first. The forward only directive tells BIND to use the servers listed in the forwarders section and its own zone files exclusively; BIND doesn't perform its own recursive lookup. The forward first directive, by contrast, tells BIND to attempt to use the servers specified by forwarders but to perform a full recursive lookup if those servers are unavailable. This option can improve reliability, but it can also slow the return of a failure code.

Many other directives can be placed within the options section, but the ones described here should be enough for many small configurations. Consult the documentation that came with BIND, or a book on the server, such as O'Reilly's *DNS and BIND*, for more information on these options.

If you want BIND to deliver information on your local network, the zone definitions are just as important as the options section. Each zone definition begins with the zone keyword followed by the name of the zone. Chances are your *named.conf* file will have three broad classes of zone definitions:

The root zone

The zone "." entry in Example 15-2 defines the root zone, which ultimately points BIND to the root DNS servers. This definition uses a type hint line, which is unique to the root zone definition.

Forward lookup zones

The only forward lookup zone in Example 15-2 is for the *example.com* domain. This type of entry specifies the domain or subdomain name as the zone name, and enables clients to pass a hostname to get an IP address. On the domain's primary DNS server, this zone will have a type master line in the zone definition. (Slave DNS servers can copy zone files from another DNS server and use a type slave definition; however, slave DNS server configuration is beyond the scope of this book.)

Reverse lookup zones

Frequently, DNS servers include zone definitions for *reverse lookups*, in which a client enters an IP address and receives back a hostname. Reverse lookups work much like forward lookups, but they require an unusual notation for the zone type. Specifically, reverse lookups use hostnames of the form *backwards-IP-address*.in-addr.arpa, where *backwards-IP-address* is an IP address fragment in reverse. For instance, Example 15-2 has two reverse lookup zones, named 1.168.192.in-addr.arpa and 0.0.127.in-addr.arpa. These correspond to the 192.168.1.0/24 and 127.0.0.0/24 network blocks, respectively—note that the order of the four bytes of the IP addresses are reversed. In both cases, the first byte of the reversed address (the final byte of the original) is omitted, which denotes the fact that these zones apply to networks with 255.255.255.0 netmasks. The reverse ordering of these names is confusing at first, but the reason is that the most- and least-significant portions of IP addresses and hostnames are reversed. A reverse lookup converts an IP address to a hostname in the special *in-addr.arpa* domain.

However, to define the individual hosts in this domain, the machine identifier portion (that is, the final byte of the address in a /24 netblock) must be the first part of the name in the *in-addr.arpa* domain, so the order of the IP address elements must be reversed. Example 15-2 defines two reverse lookup zones, one for the loopback address (127.0.0.0/24) and the other for the local network address (192.168.1.0/24).

 It's possible to omit a reverse lookup zone. In fact, if your DNS server will be serving names for IP addresses on the Internet as a whole and you don't control the entire netblock, you should omit the reverse lookup zone. You're responsible for handling forward lookups on your domain, but whoever controls the netblock (usually an ISP for small networks) is responsible for the reverse lookup. If you're configuring a DNS server for a small private network, though, you might want to include both forward and reverse lookups.

Once you've configured the basics in */etc/named.conf*, you might be tempted to restart the *named* server. You can do so in the usual way, such as by using a SysV startup script, however, you should probably wait until you've created appropriate domain configuration files, as described next.

Setting Up a Domain

Configuring the basics of the server's options is just the start of the process. In day-to-day operation, you're more likely to need to modify your zone definitions, which are stored in files in the directory specified with the `directory` keyword in the options section of the */etc/named.conf* file. Each zone has its own configuration file, which defines features of the zone as a whole and creates mappings of hostnames to IP addresses for each member of the zone.

Each type of zone definition in *named.conf* has its own variant style of zone definition file. The most fundamental of these is the root zone definition. Chances are your BIND configuration includes a default configuration that will work. Typically, the filename is *named.ca* or *db.cache*. If this file isn't present, or if it's very old, you should try to obtain a more up-to-date version. You can find the latest copy from *ftp://ftp.rs.internic.net/domain/db.cache*. Copy this file to the directory specified in your *named.conf* file, and name it as specified by the `file` option in that file's root zone definition (zone ".". Additional zone files are the forward and reverse zone files.

Configuring forward zone files

The second type of zone definition is for forward lookups—those that use an ordinary domain name in the zone line of *named.conf*. Use whatever filename you specify in *named.conf* for the file. Typically, this name is related to your domain's name, such as *named.example.com* for the *example.com* domain. Example 15-3 shows a sample forward lookup zone configuration file.

Example 15-3. A sample forward zone definition file

```
$ORIGIN .
$TTL 604800        ; 1 week
example.com    IN SOA  maize.example.com. linnaeus.example.com. (
                    2004102609 ; serial
                    28800      ; refresh (8 hours)
                    14400      ; retry (4 hours)
                    3600000    ; expire (5 weeks 6 days 16 hours)
                    86400      ; minimum TTL (1 day)
                    )
$ORIGIN example.com.
maize          IN A     192.168.1.1
gingko         IN A     192.168.1.2
mandragora     IN A     192.168.1.3
mandrake       IN CNAME mandragora

mail           IN A     10.23.186.78
www            IN A     172.24.217.102

@              IN NS    maize.example.com.
@              IN MX    10 mail.example.com.
```

The zone file begins with two lines that set some global parameters. The $ORIGIN . line should be present in your zone files unchanged. The $TTL 604800 line sets a default *time-to live* (TTL) value, which tells other servers how long, in seconds, they may cache entries obtained from your server. You may increase or decrease this value as you see fit.

The lines beginning with example.com and ending with a single close parenthesis ")" define the *start of authority* (SOA) record for this zone. This entry sets several important overall features for the zone:

Zone name

The zone name (example.com in this example) begins the SOA line. You should change it to match your own domain or subdomain name.

Entry class

The IN code defines the class of the entry. IN stands for *Internet*, and it's the most common SOA entry class and the only one described in this chapter.

Record type

The SOA code identifies this entry as creating an SOA record.

Master name server

The maize.example.com. entry in the SOA record identifies the zone's primary name server. Note that this hostname ends in a dot (.). Technically, all DNS hostnames end in a dot. Most user programs enable you to omit this dot, but you must include it when specifying a full hostname in the DNS configuration files.

Administrative email account

The linnaeus.example.com. entry, although it doesn't look like one, represents an email address for the person responsible for administering the domain. Replace the first dot with an at sign (@; to create linnaeus@example.com.) to generate an email address. As with other addresses, this one must end in a dot.

Timing information

The remaining information, beginning with the open parenthesis on the main SOA line and ending with the close parenthesis line, represents timing information for the data retrieved from this zone. This information is used mainly by other DNS servers. Values are a serial number (often set to the date followed by a code for the change number on the day), the interval for slaves to use between checks for updated information, the interval at which slaves should attempt transfers if the first one failed, the time after which a slave should expire and discard an entire zone if it's not been updated, and a minimum TTL value for remote DNS servers to cache information. The values shown in Example 15-3 are reasonable starting points. Note that most of these values are important only if you run multiple DNS servers, with one configured as a master and the rest as slaves.

Following the SOA record is a line that explicitly sets the $ORIGIN to your domain, including its trailing dot—example.com. in this case. Subsequent lines are similar in form to the SOA line, but they're simpler; most take the following form:

```
hostname IN code address
```

The *hostname* is the hostname in question, without a domain component. Some entries enable you to specify an at sign (@) as the *hostname*. This symbol stands in for the domain name and is used by certain *code* types, as described shortly. The IN component is invariant in these entries, at least as far as described in this chapter. The *code* is a code that stands for the entry type and is described in more detail shortly. Finally, the *address* is the address to associate with the *hostname*. In many cases, this is an IP address; but for some *code* types, it can be a hostname—either a hostname without a domain, which is interpreted as a hostname in the current domain or a hostname with domain component and trailing dot. The MX *code* is unique in that it includes a number before the address, as described shortly.

In defining a domain, you're likely to include several different types of *code*:

A   An A record defines an individual host in the domain. Use this to associate an IP address with a hostname.

CNAME

A CNAME record sets up an alias—a linkage of one name with another. CNAME records are often used when a single computer goes by multiple names, such as a single system that functions as both a web server and an FTP server, and that you want to be accessible by the names *www* and *ftp* for this reason. Alternatively, you can create multiple A records, but doing so requires you to change all the A records if you ever change the server's IP address; using CNAMEs for most records makes subsequent changes easier and less prone to error.

NS   A *name server* record identifies a DNS server for the domain. Normally, one NS record points to the computer you're configuring. Others may point to other DNS servers, such as slaves of a master server. The *hostname* on this line is either the domain name alone or an @ sign, and the *address* is the name of an A record—with or without the domain component.

MX   A *mail exchanger* record points to a domain's mail server. This record requires a priority number for each server listed; sending mail servers attempt to contact your mail servers in sequence, starting with the one with the lowest number and moving up from there. As with NS records, the *hostname* is either the domain name alone or an @ sign, and the *address* is the name of an A record.

PTR

Example 15-3 shows no *pointer* (PTR) records because they're unique to reverse lookup zone files. They use a pseudo-hostname based on an IP address as a *hostname*, and they list a regular hostname as the *address*. PTRs are described in more detail shortly.

Configuring reverse zone files

In some cases, you need to configure only forward lookups. For instance, your ISP might own your network block and so handle the reverse lookups, or you might simply not care about reverse lookups. (Some programs, though, perform reverse lookups and compare them to the forward lookups. If the two don't match, the programs terminate the connection or otherwise cause headaches. Thus, working reverse lookups can be more than just a convenience.) If you're in control of your network block, including if you're running in a private reserved address space, you can configure a reverse lookup zone. To do so, you must first specify a reverse lookup zone in the */etc/named.conf* file, as described earlier, in the section "Basic Name Server Configuration." You can then create a reverse lookup file in your zone file directory. This file is likely to be named after the zone, e.g., *named.192.168.1*. Example 15-4 shows an example of such a file.

Example 15-4. A sample reverse zone definition file

```
$TTL 1W
1.168.192.in-addr.arpa.   IN  SOA  maize.example.com.  linnaeus.example.com. (
                              2004102609 ; serial
                              28800      ; refresh
                              14400      ; retry
                              3600000    ; expire
```

Example 15-4. A sample reverse zone definition file (continued)

```
                              86400      ; default_ttl
                              )
1                        IN  PTR  maize.example.com.
2.1.168.192.in-addr.arpa. IN  PTR  gingko.example.com.
3.1.168.192.in-addr.arpa. IN  PTR  mandragora.example.com.

1.168.192.in-addr.arpa.   IN  NS   maize.example.com.
```

The reverse lookup file is very similar to the forward lookup file. Like the forward lookup file, it includes a $TTL directive. (Example 15-4 shows an alternative way of specifying the time, though, by including a one-letter abbreviation for the time unit—1W meaning one week.) This file also contains an SOA record, which takes the same form as the equivalent record in the forward zone definition file; the main difference is in the name of the domain. (You can use different specifics, such as refresh times or network administrator email address if you like, though.)

The bulk of the post-SOA entries in a reverse lookup file are PTR records, which tie an IP address (in the form of its reversed *in-addr.arpa* pseudo-hostname) to conventional hostnames. As with forward lookup files, you can abbreviate hostnames by omitting the domain portion of the name. In the case of reverse lookup files, though, the domain portion of the name is the reversed network portion of the address and *in-addr.arpa*. Thus, the reverse lookup for the 192.168.1.1 address in Example 15-4 is 1, referring to the final byte of the IP address. Example 15-4 doesn't use this convention for the remaining addresses. The looked-up names (maize.example.com., gingko.example.com., and so on in Example 15-4) may *not* be abbreviated by omitting their domain portions. You must also include the trailing dot after each of these names.

In addition to SOA and PTR records, reverse lookup zone files typically include one or more NS records, which point to the DNS servers that handle the network block. These might or might not be the same servers that handle forward lookups for the computers in that network block. Other record types, such as A, CNAME, and MX, are uncommon in reverse lookup files.

Running the server

Once you've set up your domain, you can start the server. Typically, this is done via a SysV startup script; typing **/etc/init.d/named start** or something similar usually does the job. To run the server permanently, you can use *chkconfig* or a similar tool to add the server to your default runlevel, or do the job manually by creating appropriate symbolic links yourself. Consult distribution-specific documentation if you need help with this job. Once the server has started, you may want to check the last few lines of your log files to see if the server has reported any problems. Typing **tail /var/log/messages** can do this.

If you restart the server, you may get an error message in your logs about the journal forward failed, and you might not be able to resolve names in a domain. This often happens if you change your BIND configuration while the server is running; it doesn't like that. The solution is to shut down *named*, delete the file whose name starts with the name of the zone configuration file but ends in *.jnl* in the directory that holds your zone configuration files, and restart *named*. A better practice is to make changes to your zone files only when *named* isn't running.

You can test your server's operation using the *host* command on the server or any other computer that has this tool. Type **host *name server*** to look up *name* using the specified *server*. If the computer pauses for several seconds and responds connection timed out, chances are the server has crashed on startup or you've specified the wrong *server*. (You may need to specify *server* as an IP address if the computer isn't configured to use that system for name resolution by default.) Other error messages typically denote problems with your DNS configuration; check your logfiles for clues. Be sure to test both forward and reverse DNS lookups.

Pointing Clients at the Name Server

Client configuration is, of course, critically important to DNS operation. If you want local workstations and servers to use your DNS server for name resolution, you must tell them to do so. If you use DHCP to assign IP addresses to these computers, the simplest way to configure them to use your DNS server is to adjust your DHCP configuration using the option domain-name-servers line in your DHCP configuration file, as described earlier, in the section "Dynamic address assignment." Once configured in this way, a DHCP server can deliver DNS server information to Windows, Linux, Mac OS, and other clients that use DHCP.

If you want to configure some or all of your computers using static IP addresses without using DHCP, you must configure these computers to use your DNS servers manually. Precisely how you do so varies from one OS to another, but most provide GUI tools that enable you to enter the DNS server addresses manually. Earlier, the section "Telling Clients to Use DHCP" described how to configure Windows XP to use DHCP. Part of this process provided an opportunity to tell Windows to use the DNS servers provided by the DHCP server or to use servers you specify. In particular, Figure 15-1 shows the relevant dialog box. Click "Use the following DNS server addresses," and enter up to two DNS server addresses to have Windows use them instead of those provided via DHCP or if you don't use DHCP at all. Similar tools exist in other versions of Windows and in other OSs.

Although you can enter DNS server addresses using GUI tools in most Linux distributions, Linux supports another method: the */etc/resolv.conf* file specifies DNS servers and the domains that Linux should attempt to search. This file is likely to be quite short:

```
domain example.com
search example.com,pangaea.edu
nameserver 192.168.1.1
nameserver 10.29.102.7
```

Each line has a specific purpose:

domain

This line tells the computer the domain to which it belongs. The main practical upshot is that names are searched for in this domain before they're searched in other domains or without the domain name.

search

This line enables you to tell the system to search domains instead of the one specified by domain. You can list up to six domains, separated by commas or spaces.

nameserver

You list DNS servers, one per line, using nameserver keywords. Linux supports up to three DNS servers; it tries each one in sequence until a lookup returns a definitive success code (a certain success or failure, as opposed to a failure of the server).

Whether the DNS client runs Linux, Windows, or some other OS, a DNS lookup normally uses a domain search list, even if the user specified a hostname with a domain. For instance, if you do a lookup on *mandragora.example.com* from within the *example.com* domain, the computer first tries a lookup on *mandragora.example.com.example.com*. If additional domains are in the search paths, similar lookups are performed on them, as in *mandragora.example.com.pangaea.edu*. When these lookups fail, the name resolver tries the lookup without appending any item from the search path. The assumption is that the user has entered a relative hostname without a domain component. You can block this initial, and probably erroneous, lookup by appending a dot, e.g., typing **mandragora.example.com.** rather than **mandragora.example.com** when entering the hostname. This trick works with most programs and protocols, but it might confuse some. In most cases, it's unnecessary; the extra lookup that fails is unlikely to take very long at all, so it does no real harm.

Keeping Clocks Synchronized with NTP

One of the frustrations of using a computer network is that the individual computer clocks can report different times. This fact can be a minor annoyance when, say, you seem to have jumped back in time by two minutes when switching computers. It can become more serious when programs that rely on time stamps see inconsistent times on files. A *make* utility, for instance, might fail to compile a file if it believes that file changed before the last compilation, when in fact it changed after the last compilation but the time stamps are off. Even more serious temporal problems result with tools such as Kerberos, which embed timestamps in some of their packets as a security measure. Depending on your Kerberos settings, logins can fail completely if two computers' clocks are inconsistent.

These problems can all be overcome using a protocol designed to keep computers' clocks synchronized. The most popular protocol to do this job is known as the Network Time Protocol, which is headquartered at *http://www.ntp.org*. Before proceeding with the details of NTP configuration, you should understand its basic operating principles; this will help you decide how to implement NTP. As with most protocols, you must then configure both servers and clients. The Linux NTP server, though, does double duty as both a server and a client. On the Windows side, you can use either a full NTP implementation or a built-in Windows command.

Principles of NTP

NTP can do more than simply keep your clocks synchronized on your local network: it's designed to help you keep all your computers' clocks set to an accurate time source. It does so by creating a hierarchy of NTP servers, most of which also function as clients to NTP servers that are closer to the ultimate time source—usually an atomic clock or a device that reads its time from one, such as a radio that receives signals from an atomic clock. This arrangement is illustrated in Figure 15-2.

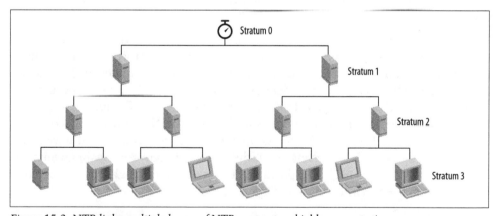

Figure 15-2. NTP links multiple layers of NTP servers to a highly accurate time source

The atomic clock or other time source is referred to as a *stratum 0* time source. The servers that communicate with this device are known as *stratum 1* servers; those that communicate with the stratum 1 servers are *stratum 2* servers, and so on. This arrangement provides a powerful exponential effect on the number of computers a single time source can serve. For instance, if each server has just 100 clients, a single stratum 1 server can have 10,000 stratum 3 and 1,000,000 stratum 4 clients. As the stratum level increases, the accuracy of the clocks decreases, but not by much; times are typically accurate to well under a second up to several stratums. (The exact values depend on factors such as the variability of transit times and how evenly divided the transit times are on each leg of the journey.)

At each step of the way, NTP works by measuring the time it takes for packets to traverse the network. For instance, if you send a packet to a computer, and it replies, you can measure the round-trip transit time. (You can use *ping* to do this in a crude way.) If the return packet includes a time stamp, you can use the time stamp and round-trip transit time to set your own clock to that of the remote server; you use the time stamp in the packet and half the transit time. NTP uses this principle at its core, although it's more sophisticated. For instance, a full NTP implementation runs as a daemon and checks its upstream time source on a periodic basis. It can use the data gleaned from these checks to adjust the rate at which its own clock "ticks," thus maintaining a more accurate time even between time checks. NTP can also refer to multiple upstream time sources, thus providing redundancy and enabling it to select the best time source.

In practice, you'll set up one computer as a master NTP server for your network. (You might set up more than one if your network is very large or is geographically diverse.) Your master NTP server refers to an upstream server to set its own clock; the rest of your computers set their clocks based on their own master NTP server. This configuration minimizes network traffic; you can set potentially thousands of computers' clocks using the external bandwidth required to set just one system's clock.

What computer should you use as your master NTP server? In practice, requirements are fairly minor. Compared to most other network protocols, NTP generates little network traffic and requires practically no disk space, aside from that needed for the OS itself. Therefore, it's common to piggyback NTP duties onto another server. On the other hand, you don't want to add master NTP duties to a server that's already overloaded, because delays in handling the NTP packets will be quite detrimental to the NTP server functions. In any event, the server should have ready network access to the Internet and to all the computers on your local network. Of course, like all servers, NTP is a potential security risk, although it's a minor one compared to servers that provide login or file access.

NTP Server Configuration

In Linux, an NTP server acts as both a client and a server. In fact, to maintain the most accurate time in Linux, you may want to install a full NTP server, even if it has no clients of its own; your NTP server will act only as a client.

All major Linux distributions ship with NTP servers, typically in packages called *ntp*, *xntp*, or a variant with a major version number appended, such as *ntp4*. The major

NTP configuration file is */etc/ntp.conf*. Most distributions ship *ntp.conf* files that should require few changes; you may only need to set an appropriate server. A few other options may need attention as well, though:

server

This line sets the hostname or IP address of an NTP server, as in server tick. pangaea.edu to tell NTP to refer to the NTP server on *tick.pangaea.edu*. You can also add various options to support authentication and other features, but, in most cases, these aren't needed. Picking a server is described in more detail shortly. One special case that deserves attention is setting server 127.127.1.0. This line tells NTP to use the local system clock. It may be included as a fallback position in case all other servers become unavailable.

fudge

Ordinarily, NTP automatically detects the stratum of the servers to which it communicates; it can then set its own stratum automatically. The fudge line enables you to force NTP to treat a server as belonging to another stratum. It's most often used in conjunction with the 127.127.1.0 address to force NTP to give the local NTP server a very high stratum number so that it's not used in preference to more accurate sources. For instance, fudge 127.127.1.0 stratum 10 tells NTP to treat the local clock as a stratum 10 server.

driftfile

You can specify a file in which NTP stores information on the hardware clock's drift. This information can help when you first start the server after it's been down for a while or in case your network access goes out. Using the drift file, NTP should be able to maintain your clock's accuracy much better than is possible using the computer's unmodified clock. You shouldn't need to adjust this entry unless you rearrange your directory structure in some unusual way.

broadcast

If your network hosts many systems that also run the full version of NTP, you can minimize local NTP-related network traffic by telling your main NTP server to periodically broadcast its time information, which then reaches all the clients, obviating the need for them to contact the server individually. To use this feature, specify the broadcast keyword followed by the computer's own IP address; it then broadcasts to the local network.

broadcastclient

The flip side of the broadcast feature is the configuration of the NTP broadcast clients. On these systems, you set broadcastclient yes to have NTP listen for broadcasts from other NTP servers, or broadcastclient no to have the server ignore such broadcasts.

One of the trickiest aspects of NTP configuration is in selecting an upstream NTP server. NTP server lists are maintained at *http://www.eecis.udel.edu/~mills/ntp/servers. html*; this list has links to both stratum 1 and stratum 2 servers, and it describes rules of etiquette for using the servers. You may be able to find other sources, as well. For instance, your ISP might operate an NTP server that you can use, or if you're setting up NTP for a single department in a much larger organization, your organization might run an NTP server. In most cases, you should contact the server's operator before connecting your own server, although some server operators provide blanket permission for certain people to use their NTP servers. (Lists of NTP servers often contain information on what types of permission should be obtained before using any given server.) You should try to pick a server that's close to you in network topology. For rough estimates of this measure, use *ping* to determine the round-trip transit time to potential servers, and use *traceroute* to measure the number of intervening systems. The lower the transit time and the fewer the intervening systems the better.

The higher you go in the NTP stratum hierarchy, the more accurate the times; however, NTP servers with low stratum numbers are few in number and shouldn't be used except by clients that themselves serve many clients. As a general rule of thumb, you shouldn't use a stratum 1 server unless your own server is itself delivering time to at least 100 clients. For smaller networks, use a stratum 2 or lower server; the accuracy of your time won't suffer much, and the variability within your network won't suffer at all, but you'll be helping to distribute the load on the NTP network as a whole.

You can specify multiple upstream NTP servers, but you can get by with just one. Using multiple servers provides redundancy and enables the NTP software to pick the best server from the lot automatically. On the other hand, using few servers reduces network load. Generally speaking, small networks can get by just fine with just one server, although you might want to try several at first to determine which works best. Large networks, or networks on which precision timekeeping is particularly important, may do well to use multiple upstream servers—typically, at least three to make it easier to pick the bad time keeper, if there is one.

Once you've entered one or more server lines in *ntp.conf* and made any other changes you like, you should start NTP. On most distributions, this can be done using a SysV startup script, e.g., by typing **/etc/init.d/ntpd start**. (The exact name of the SysV startup script varies; some omit the *d* from the end of the script name or add *x* to the start.) To run NTP regularly, use tools such as *chkconfig* to add the NTP startup script to your default runlevel. Consult distribution-specific documentation for help on this topic.

Once the NTP server is running, you can use the *ntpq* tool to monitor its operation. Type **ntpq** to run the program, and it replies with a ntpq> prompt. Type **peers** to obtain a list of upstream NTP servers and assorted statistics on them. In particular, note the value of the st column, which shows the upstream server's stratum. Initially, NTP polls the upstream servers frequently to determine which one is the most accurate. After a few minutes, it settles on one as its primary source and marks it with an asterisk (*) to the left of the server's hostname. Other servers that generate reasonable results receive a plus (+) mark in this position. Be wary of a server that's marked with an x to the left of its name; this is a *false ticker*, which is providing times that are inaccurate compared to the other servers.

To configure Linux NTP clients (which may run other servers, such as Samba), configure them just as you do your primary NTP server, but instead of pointing them at one or more external NTP servers, point them to your primary NTP server alone. Because these servers are all on the same network, the time for NTP packets to make their round trip will be tiny, and the NTP clients you configure will have times that are virtually identical to the time on your primary NTP server.

Configuring Windows Clients

In principle, Windows computers are no different from Linux computers when it comes to NTP. In practice, though, it may be easier to use a standard Windows command, *NET*, to set their clocks than to install a full NTP package. You can take the full approach if you prefer, though. This is most likely to be helpful on important servers or if you want the Windows system to function as an NTP server to other clients.

Using NET SET

The Windows *NET* command lets you set the Windows computer's clock. In Windows NT/200x/XP, you can use this command to set the clock using NTP with the /SETSNTP:*server* option, where *server* is the NTP server's name. For instance, to set the Windows system's clock to the time maintained by the *harrison.example.com* server, use this command:

```
C:\> NET TIME /SETSNTP:harrison.example.com
```

This command actually uses a simplified variant of the full NTP protocol, known as SNTP. This procedure should be good enough for most purposes. If the computer restarts on a regular basis, you can include a command like this in a batch file that runs when the computer starts. Placing it in the Windows *StartUp* folder can be a good choice, particularly on desktop computers; this ensures that the script is run on a regular basis. Another option is to place this call in a domain's network logon script.

Unfortunately, Windows 9x/Me doesn't accept the /SETSNTP option, so you can't set a Windows 9x/Me computer's clock using an NTP server in this way. You can, though, use a similar command to set the clock using part of the SMB/CIFS protocol suite:

```
C:\> NET TIME \\HARRISON /SET /YES
```

This command sets the computer's time to that maintained on *HARRISON*. If your main NTP server also runs Samba, this can be a good way to deliver the time to Windows 9x/Me clients. If your primary NTP server doesn't run Samba, but you do run

Samba on another computer, you can use this procedure to set the clock from the Samba server, which can use NTP to synchronize its clock to your main NTP server's clock. As with the /SETSNTP variant, you can include this command in a batch file you run from a *StartUp* folder or network logon script. Windows NT/200x/XP responds to this command as well, so if you want to simplify your configuration task, you can use this SMB/CIFS variant on all your Windows computers.

Windows NTP clients

Sometimes, only the "real thing" will do. Perhaps you want a Windows computer to function as an NTP server, or you want it to maintain highly accurate time without having to run *NET TIME* on a periodic basis. In such cases, running a full NTP package on Windows is an option. Even if you don't need a full NTP client/server package, you might want to track down an NTP client for Windows 9x/Me—say, if you don't use SMB/CIFS at all on your network but do want to set Windows 9x/Me systems' clocks.

The official NTP software package is available only for Unix and Unix-like systems. However, the NTP protocol has been implemented on many other OSs, either by porting the official package or by writing a new implementation. Microsoft's *NET TIME /SETSNTP* command is one implementation. Here are some others:

Automachron

> This is an SNTP client only, but it runs on all versions of Windows, making it a good choice for Windows 9x/Me clients. This program is free in the sense of no-cost, but it's not open source. Check its home page at *http://www.oneguycoding. com/automachron/* for more details.

NetTime

> This program, headquartered at *http://sourceforge.net/projects/nettime/*, is an open source SNTP client and server for all versions of Windows. This program can run as a service on Windows NT/200x/XP, meaning that it runs at all times, much like the NTP daemon in Linux. Development has officially been abandoned because of Microsoft's inclusion of SNTP support in recent versions of Windows, but NetTime can still be useful if you're running old versions of Windows.

NTP for Windows

> The Unix NTP code has been ported to Windows NT/200x/XP and is available, in both source and binary forms, from *http://www.eecis.udel.edu/~ntp/ntp_spool/ html/hints/winnt.html*. If nothing but a full NTP implementation for Windows will do, this package is well worth investigating. However, it doesn't run on Windows 9x/Me.

Summary

Linux can fill many unglamorous server roles on a network—roles that go largely unnoticed by users but that are vital to a network's normal functioning. A Linux DHCP server can help you automatically configure basic networking features of other computers; a Linux DNS server can convert between hostnames and IP addresses; and a Linux NTP server can help you keep your computers' clocks synchronized. Employing Linux in these roles can simplify your overall network administrative workload or improve your network's functionality.

Appendixes

What Chapters 7, 8, and 9 of this book have in common is that they deal with various ways to authenticate users on your network. All three also use Pluggable Authentication Modules (PAM). Rather than spread my PAM instructions throughout these three chapters, I felt it best to give you comprehensive instructions about PAM in a separate appendix. If you already know PAM, and can use the earlier chapters, you probably don't need to read this section.

I also briefly described using Linux as a desktop operating system in several places. Though this book isn't meant to give you thorough instruction in the deployment, maintenance, and use of a Linux desktop, I felt it prudent to include further information on this subject in Appendix B. This material is especially complementary to Chapters 11 and 12.

PART VI
Appendixes

APPENDIX A
Configuring PAM

Modern Linux distributions rely on the Pluggable Authentication Modules system for authentication. Part III of this book describes three network authentication tools, all of which can be used in conjunction with PAM to provide authentication for arbitrary servers and other programs that require authentication. In order to avoid duplicating content, therefore, this appendix describes PAM in detail; Part III provides a much briefer description of how PAM interacts with the relevant servers.

In order to get the most out of PAM, it helps to begin with some background—what PAM is, what it can do, why it's used, and so on. You must also understand the PAM configuration file format; PAM configuration involves editing one or more of these files. From there, knowing something about individual PAM modules, including both the standard ones and those described elsewhere in this book, will help you create an appropriate configuration. Finally, some examples of working PAM configurations will help you understand PAM and provide models you can adapt for your own use.

PAM Principles

In Linux's early days, every server or other tool that had to authenticate users did so by reading */etc/password*, the traditional Unix account file. This approach was easy to implement, but it had several problems. One of these was that the file, and hence the encrypted password, had to be readable by all users, making it vulnerable to cracking. Another problem is that changes to authentication methods, such as new password-encryption systems, required changes to all the programs that could authenticate users. This problem would result in a nightmarish tangle of upgrades should an administrator ever want to change the authentication system.

PAM is designed to solve these problems. PAM solves the problem of world readability of */etc/passwd* by implementing a system known as *shadow passwords*, in which passwords are moved out of */etc/passwd* and into a file that can be read only by *root*—typically */etc/shadow* on Linux systems. (Shadow passwords can be implemented without PAM, but today PAM is the tool that does it on all major Linux distributions.) PAM helps minimize the pain of changing authentication systems by working as a layer between the tools that authenticate users and the account database. Instead of accessing */etc/passwd* directly, programs consult PAM, which accesses */etc/passwd*. Thus, if the format of data in */etc/passwd* changes, individual servers don't need to be rewritten or even recompiled; only PAM must change. Indeed, PAM can be changed to support authentication systems that don't even consult */etc/passwd*. It's this feature of PAM that Winbind, LDAP authentication, and some Kerberos tools use. Rather than consult */etc/passwd*, PAM consults the appropriate network authentication tool.

 In addition to PAM, Linux relies on another software component, the Name Service Switch, for account information. Rather than authentication information, though, NSS provides more mundane information, such as a mapping of UIDs to usernames and the account's default shell. Like PAM, NSS is designed in a modular way and sits between applications that ask for this information and the actual account databases. Although you may think in terms of authentication, which is what PAM provides, this ancillary information is just as important, so you must configure NSS to link to your authentication system. The chapters on Winbind and LDAP describe configuring NSS to work with these tools, but Kerberos provides no NSS interface, which is a limitation of Kerberos if you want a network authentication system to handle all your account information.

In practice, PAM is a modular tool: it consults libraries to handle various parts of the authentication procedure. You tell PAM which libraries to consult with the help of the PAM configuration files, which are described in the next section. Thus, the overall authentication system, and its equivalent in pre-PAM days, are depicted in Figure A-1. PAM's modular nature is manifested in this figure by the fact that PAM is shown accessing three independent authentication tools—the */etc/passwd* file, an NT domain controller, and an LDAP server. A default configuration is likely to be simpler than this, but if you want to use a network authentication tool, chances are you'll leave the old-style */etc/passwd* authentication intact as a backup and to provide information for accounts you might not want to define using a centralized system, such as the *root* account.

In practice, PAM configuration is even more complex than Figure A-1 suggests, for three reasons:

- PAM provides management features beyond those related to account authentication. In particular, it supports authentication (verifying that users are who they claim to be), account management (checking for expired accounts, the right to use a particular server, and so on), session management (login and logout housekeeping), and password changes. Each management system must be configured

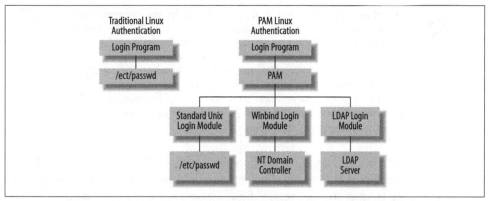

Figure A-1. PAM distances servers and other programs that require authentication from authentication implementations, increasing flexibility—and complexity

individually; for instance, the modules called in service of authentication may be different than those required for session management.

- A single act, such as logging in, may require multiple PAM modules. For instance, many PAM login configurations call a module called *pam_deny.so*, which explicitly denies access to the system if no earlier module has explicitly granted access. You can even tack on modules that aren't directly related to authentication, such as modules that display login notices.

- Each program that requires PAM's services may be configured individually. For instance, you might want to use one set of options for authenticating users for console logins and another for authenticating users to use the *su* command to change their effective UID numbers.

The PAM Configuration File Format

Configuring PAM means editing its configuration files. The format of these files is fairly simple, but these files use a number of options that aren't immediately obvious to the uninitiated. You must also know something about how the PAM configuration file works with multiple modules. These modules can also interact in unintuitive ways.

PAM Configuration Files and Fields

In order to implement its design goals, PAM uses one or more configuration files: either a file called */etc/pam.conf* or files in the */etc/pam.d* directory named after the particular systems they control. The */etc/pam.d* directory is more common in Linux; this approach enables packages to add files to the directory for their services, without having to modify */etc/pam.conf*.

When reconfiguring PAM, you can easily render your system unable to support logins. Thus, I recommend experimenting with one login server at a time, leaving yourself some way to log in should you create an inoperable system. For instance, experiment with the login service and leave the gdm or xdm service alone. Some distributions use the *pam_stack.so* module (described shortly) to control many login servers. With such a system, you may need to back up its original configuration file and leave a *root* session running to be sure you can undo any disastrous mistake without logging in anew.

The */etc/pam.conf* file entries are similar to the contents of files in */etc/pam.d*. The principle difference is that the */etc/pam.conf* entries begin with a service name field, which is missing from individual service files. The overall format for the lines in */etc/pam.d* files is:

```
management_group  control_flag  module  [options]
```

Each field has a specific meaning:

management_group

This field holds one of four keywords specifying the type of service it defines: auth for authentication, account for account management, session for session management, or password for password management. Most PAM configuration files have at least one line of each type.

control_flag

This field describes how PAM should react to the success or failure of a module. Possible values are requisite, required, sufficient, and optional. The meanings of these values are described in the next section. A more advanced syntax involves matching specific actions to the module's exact return value. This is flexible but tedious to configure (it involves 30 return codes and six possible actions), and so it isn't described in this book.

module

This field is a pointer to the module file itself, sometimes with its complete path. (If the path is missing, PAM checks its modules directory, which is usually */lib/security*.)

options

You can pass parameters to the module via the *options* field on the module definition line. Some options are highly module-specific, but others are recognized by many modules. Some of these options are described in the section "Standard PAM Modules."

This first field in the lines of *pam.conf*, which is missing from the */etc/pam.d* files in most Linux distributions, holds the name of the tool it configures, such as login for the *login* service, or gdm for the GDM GUI login tool. If your system uses files in */etc/pam.d*, the names of these files are typically the names that appear in this first column in a system that uses */etc/pam.conf*.

In addition to configuration lines, PAM configuration files can contain comments. These begin with a hash mark (#). Entire lines can be comments, or comments can come at the end of a line that serves some other purpose.

Module Stacks

A configuration for a single authentication tool can combine several PAM modules. This happens in two ways. First, each of the four management groups (auth, account, session, and password) requires its own configuration. Second, with each management group, multiple modules can be called. When multiple modules are called, the result is referred to as a module *stack*. For instance, a login service might have separate auth and account stacks. These stacks are likely to have some modules in common (they perform different actions depending upon the calling stack), but each may also have some unique modules.

Individual modules in a stack deliver return values that can be classified as *failures* or *successes*. In this context, these terms don't refer to program bugs or the lack thereof, but to failures or successes in authentication or other actions. For instance, if a user enters the wrong password, an authentication module will fail.

Modules in a stack are called in the order in which they're specified. This order is unimportant if all of the modules are of the required variety, but if you use other control flags—particularly requisite or sufficient—order can become important, as described shortly.

Understanding the operation of module stacks can be tricky, because the different control flags can have confusing implications. Table A-1 summarizes the consequences of successes and failures of modules called with particular control flags.

Table A-1. Consequences of control flags

Control flag	Module success result	Module failure result
requisite	Stack execution continues; stack may succeed or fail, depending on outcome of other modules	Stack execution terminates immediately; stack fails
required	Stack execution continues; stack may succeed or fail, depending on outcome of other modules	Stack execution continues, but stack fails

Table A-1. Consequences of control flags (continued)

Control flag	Module success result	Module failure result
sufficient	Stack execution terminates immediately, provided no prior required module has failed; stack succeeds (failure of a prior required module may cause stack failure, though)	Stack execution continues; stack may succeed or fail, depending on outcome of other modules
optional	Stack execution continues; stack may succeed or fail, depending on outcome of other modules, unless other modules are missing or give inconclusive results, in which case the stack succeeds	Stack execution continues; stack may succeed or fail, depending on outcome of other modules, unless other modules are missing or give inconclusive results, in which case the stack fails

These rules can become quite confusing in the event of conflicting outcomes. For instance, consider the following stack:

```
auth required    pam_unix.so try_first_pass
auth sufficient pam_krb5.so try_first_pass
auth required    pam_env.so
```

For now, you need only know that the *pam_unix.so* and *pam_krb5.so* modules authenticate users, while *pam_env.so* sets environment variables but never returns a failure code. Because this stack provides two login modules, each with two possible outcomes, you must consider four possibilities—both succeed, both fail, *pam_unix.so* succeeds while *pam_krb5.so* fails, or *pam_unix.so* fails while *pam_krb5.so* succeeds. In practice, this stack as a whole succeeds if and only if *pam_unix.so* succeeds; if it fails, its required status overrides the sufficient status of *pam_krb5.so*, and if it succeeds, that success won't be overridden by a failure of the sufficient *pam_krb5.so*. What happens if the two authentication modules' order is reversed, though?

```
auth sufficient pam_krb5.so try_first_pass
auth required    pam_unix.so try_first_pass
auth required    pam_env.so
```

In this case, because the sufficient *pam_krb5.so* module comes first, its success bypasses the later required *pam_unix.so* module, so this stack succeeds if either module succeeds. A success of *pam_krb5.so*, though, bypasses the *pam_env.so* module, which may not be desirable.

PAM Modules

Creating or modifying a PAM configuration requires at least a basic understanding of the available PAM modules. If you check your existing PAM configuration files, you're likely to see quite a range of module calls, and modifying them to get the results you expect can be tricky if you don't understand what the existing modules do.

Some PAM modules can be called for only some management groups. Others can be called as part of a stack for any management group.

Standard PAM Modules

PAM ships with quite a few different modules. Table A-2 summarizes those that you're most likely to encounter in your existing configuration files. Note that, although some modules directly relate to password handling, others don't; they're used to display information to users, set environment variables, and so on. For these modules, PAM is simply a convenient tool for accomplishing their goals. Such modules may not affect the login process at all.

Table A-2. Common standard PAM modules

Module filename	Management groups	Common arguments	Description
pam_unix.so	auth, account, session, and password	nullok, likeauth, shadow, try_first_ pass, use_first_ pass, use_authtok	Implements the traditional Unix (and Linux) authentication, based on */etc/passwd* and */etc/shadow* files.
pam_unix2.so	auth, account, session, and password	nullok, likeauth, shadow, try_first_ pass, use_first_ pass, use_authtok	A variant on *pam_unix.so* that implements additional features, such as an ability to authenticate against a Network Information Service (NIS) server.
pam_smb_auth.so	auth	use_first_pass, nolocal	This module is an alternative way to authenticate against NT domain controllers to that described in Chapter 7. It uses the */etc/pam_smb.conf* configuration file.
pam_securetty.so	auth	–	Blocks *root* access to the login service unless the environment variable PAM_TTY is set to a string listed in the */etc/securetty* file.
pam_time.so	account	–	Reads */etc/security/time.conf*, which specifies time-based access restriction rules.
pam_nologin.so	auth and account	successok	If */etc/nologin* exists, only *root* is permitted to log in, and all users are shown the contents of that file. If the file doesn't exist, the module has no effect, unless the successok parameter is used, in which case the login succeeds (as if the module were called with a sufficient control flag).
pam_homecheck.so	auth and session	abort	Prints a warning if the user's home directory or certain other files are world-writable or if they're owned by another user. If the abort option is used, the login fails under these circumstances.

Module filename	Management groups	Common arguments	Description
pam_env.so	auth	conffile=*filename*, envfile=*filename*	Sets environment variables for the login session, based on the contents of the configuration file (*/etc/security/pam_env.conf* by default).
pam_mail.so	auth and session	dir=*directory*, empty	Checks for mail in the specified directory and notifies the user if any is present. If empty is used, also informs the user when no mail is present.
pam_lastlog.so	auth	nodate, noterm, nohost, silent, never	Displays information on the user's last login. The module's options tell it what information to omit from this display. It maintains last login information in the */var/log/lastlog* file.
pam_motd.so	session	motd=*filename*	Displays the contents of the message of the day (MOTD) file, which is */etc/motd* by default, upon a successful login.
pam_deny.so	auth, account, session, and password	–	Always indicates a failure; useful at the end of certain stacks or as part of a default service to eliminate the risk of an unauthorized login due to misconfiguration.
pam_limits.so	session	conf=*filename*	Places limits, described in the */etc/security/ limits.conf* or specified configuration file, on users' resource uses (memory, CPU time, etc.). Requires kernel support for resource limits.
pam_mkhomedir.so	session	skel=*directory*, umask=*octal-umask*	Creates a home directory for users if one doesn't already exist, using the specified skeleton (skel) directory to populate the home directory with default configuration files and setting the directory's permissions based on the specified umask.
pam_access.so	account	accessfile= *filename*	Uses */etc/security/access.conf* or the specified access file to determine username/ machine name pairs that are or aren't granted access—e.g., to deny *root* the right to log in from particular machines.
pam_pwcheck.so	password	nullok, use_first_ pass, use_authtok	Performs extra checks on password changes, as defined in */etc/login.defs*, to improve security on user-selected passwords.
pam_cracklib.so	password	use_authtok and others to set specific checks	Adds checks for various features, such as passwords that have been used in the past or passwords that are too simple, to password-change interactions. Uses the *libcrack* library and a system dictionary (*/usr/lib/ cracklib_dict*).

Table A-2. Common standard PAM modules (continued)

Module filename	Management groups	Common arguments	Description
pam_stack.so	auth, account, session, and password	service=*name*	Calls a stack for the specified service. Provides easier configuration; you need to modify only one PAM configuration file to implement PAM changes across all the services that call *pam_stack.so*.

 Not all the modules mentioned in Table A-2 ship with all Linux distributions. These modules are all present and used in the default installations of at least one major distribution, though, with the exception of *pam_mkhomedir.so*. This module ships with all the major distributions but isn't used by default. It is, however, extremely useful with NT domain and LDAP add-on PAM modules.

Some modules accept parameters that are common to other modules. These common parameters include:

debug

Although it's not mentioned in Table A-2, this parameter causes most modules to dump extra debugging information to your system logfiles.

try_first_pass

Used in auth stacks, this option causes a module to try to use a password collected by a previous module for authentication. If this password fails, the module prompts the user again. Using this option on the second and subsequent password-checking modules can eliminate multiple password requests when you try to log in.

use_first_pass

This parameter works much like try_first_pass, but it causes the module that uses it to *not* request a password if the one it's given from a prior module fails.

nullok

Most modules that handle passwords refuse null passwords (that is, passwords of zero length). This option tells these modules that null passwords are acceptable. (For authentication, of course, the authentication database must contain a null password; this option doesn't bypass the password check.)

likeauth

This parameter causes the module to return the same value when called as a credential-setting module as an authentication module. This practice helps PAM navigate the module stack most efficiently.

shadow

If this option is present, the module takes extra care to maintain a system with shadow passwords. In particular, it better handles password aging, expiration, and similar information.

use_authtok
> This option causes a module in a `password` stack to use the password given to a previous module in a stack.

Linux distributions vary substantially in how they build PAM stacks from these modules. If you check two distributions' files, you'll probably find they call modules using different options, and they may call different sets of modules. Even within a distribution, different services may call different modules, even when the services are similar in function. Ultimately, though, most PAM stacks call *pam_unix.so* or *pam_unix2.so*, either directly for each service or indirectly via *pam_stack.so*. This is the most important PAM module, especially for logins.

Additional PAM Modules

Chapters 7, 8, and 9 present information on PAM modules that can be used in addition to or instead of the standard modules. In particular, these modules can replace or supplement *pam_unix.so* or *pam_unix2.so*. If you check the Internet, you can find still more PAM modules.

 As described in the relevant chapters, there's more to adding support for most network authentication modules than simply configuring PAM. These modules typically rely on external configuration files to point them to their authentication servers. Sometimes you must configure the server to accept authentication requests from your Linux system or take other special steps to get the system to work.

When you add new PAM modules for authentication, you should first decide where to add them. If your distribution uses the *pam_stack.so* module, you should modify the stack that it references—typically */etc/pam.d/system-auth*. If your distribution doesn't use this module, however, you may need to modify the configuration files for all the services that should use the new PAM module. For login services (*login*, *xdm*, *sshd*, and so on), you need to add auth and account lines:

```
auth     sufficient  /lib/security/pam_winbind.so try_first_pass
account  sufficient  /lib/security/pam_winbind.so
```

Of course, the name of the module you call depends on what you're adding. Add the auth line to the existing auth stack just after the line that references *pam_unix.so*, and add the account line just after the existing account line. This placement causes PAM to check the new service after checking the local account database. The `sufficient` control flag tells PAM that if this authentication succeeds, it doesn't need to perform additional authentication checks; however, if it fails, PAM falls back on the local account database. The `try_first_pass` option prevents PAM from prompting for a password again should this happen; it delivers the password the user entered first into the next authentication tool.

Some servers and login tools must be restarted before they'll read the new PAM configuration files, so, if you forget to restart a server, you may think your change hasn't worked, when in fact it simply hasn't yet taken effect. Try to be methodical in your tests if you run into problems. Create some test accounts and take notes on the effects.

Be sure to test the effect of *incorrect* logins—both nonexistent usernames and valid usernames with invalid passwords. Some PAM configurations result in successful logins even when invalid passwords, and sometimes even invalid usernames, are entered. If you run into this problem, try adding a required call to *pam_deny.so* and make the actual authentication modules sufficient.

For password-changing services, such as *passwd*, your concerns are a bit different from those for login services. Depending on your needs, you might consider doing any of several things:

- Adding a new entry to the password stack causes the *passwd* program to prompt for two password changes: one for the local Unix password database and again for the new service you've added.

- Adding a new entry to the password stack and using the options use_authtok or use_first_pass with the second call causes both systems to use the password you enter the first time. You may need to make both these entries sufficient rather than required.

- Replacing the existing call to *pam_unix.so* or *pam_unix2.so* causes a single prompt for a password change using the new service, leaving the local password (if it exists) untouched.

- Not changing the password stack causes only the local account to change, if it exists. Users need to use tools specific to their new authentication system, such as *smbpasswd* for an NT domain controller, to change their network passwords.

As if these concerns weren't enough, a further complication is *root*'s power to change normal users' passwords. Network authentication tools typically provide strong protections against anybody but the user or the password server's administrator from changing passwords. A local *root* account is unlikely to have this power, so chances are you'll need to use the administrative database's tools to make these changes.

Sample PAM Configurations

The preceding presentation is fairly abstract and may be hard to digest without some examples. Here, then, are some concrete examples, taken from working Linux distributions. These include a login service, a password service, and a system that uses an authentication stack.

Typical Login Services

Login services include the *login* program (used by the console and the Telnet server); the X Display Manager (XDM) and its KDE and GNOME counterparts, KDM and GDM; the SSH server; POP and IMAP mail servers; and the FTP server. Other tools that are similar, but that deviate a bit more, include the *su* and *sudo* commands and password-protected screensavers.

Example A-1 shows the */etc/pam.d/login* file from a Debian Linux system. (The original file has many comment lines, though, which Example A-1 has omitted for brevity.) Because this is a login configuration, the most important sections of this file— from the perspective of an administrator wanting to change the system to use a network password database—are the auth and account stacks. These stacks both contain calls to *pam_unix.so*, as well as a few others that can restrict access in various ways or display information.

Example A-1. Sample PAM login service configuration

```
auth       requisite   pam_securetty.so
auth       requisite   pam_nologin.so
auth       required    pam_env.so
auth       required    pam_unix.so nullok

account    requisite   pam_time.so
account    required    pam_unix.so

session    required    pam_unix.so
session    optional    pam_lastlog.so
session    optional    pam_motd.so
session    optional    pam_mail.so standard noenv

password   required    pam_unix.so nullok min=6 max=255 md5
```

To modify Example A-1 to use an LDAP server (just as an example), you would add sufficient references to the *pam_ldap.so* module to the auth and account stacks just *before* the existing *pam_unix.so* calls. You may also want to add a call to the *pam_mkhomedir.so* module to the session stack, in order to create users' home directories if they don't already exist. Example A-2 presents all of these changes, with the changed and added material shown in bold.

Example A-2. Sample PAM login service configuration with LDAP support

```
auth       requisite   pam_securetty.so
auth       requisite   pam_nologin.so
auth       required    pam_env.so
auth       sufficient  pam_ldap.so
auth       required    pam_unix.so nullok try_first_pass

account    requisite   pam_time.so
account    sufficient  pam_ldap.so
```

Example A-2. Sample PAM login service configuration with LDAP support (continued)

```
account    required    pam_unix.so

session    required    pam_unix.so
session    optional    pam_lastlog.so
session    optional    pam_motd.so
session    optional    pam_mail.so standard noenv
session    required    pam_mkhomedir.so skel=/etc/skel umask=0027

password   required    pam_unix.so nullok min=6 max=255 md5
```

Several variants on these changes are possible. For instance, instead of adding *pam_ldap.so* before *pam_unix.so*, you can add a required call to *pam_ldap.so* after *pam_unix.so*, but this requires changing the status of *pam_unix.so* from required to sufficient and also associating the try_first_pass option with *pam_ldap.so*. This order reversal can reduce network traffic if significant numbers of users have locally defined accounts. Debian's configuration doesn't call any modules in the auth or account stacks after the *pam_unix.so* call, but some distributions do make such calls. For them, the specification of which module is called as sufficient has implications for the conditions under which these subsequent modules are called.

Yet another option is to set the calls to both *pam_unix.so* and *pam_ldap.so* to sufficient and add calls to *pam_deny.so* to the ends of these stacks. This approach may be less confusing to configure because the order of modules becomes a bit less important; however, a successful login using any of the sufficient modules then bypasses all subsequent modules in the stack, which may be undesirable.

 If you want modules that must be placed after the actual password-checking modules to be called in all cases, you may want to look into using the *pam_stack.so* module. You can then place your actual password-checking calls in a substack that returns a single value, call *pam_stack.so* as a required module, and have modules that appear after this call in your individual service definitions execute no matter what tool actually authenticated your users.

Unless your system uses the *pam_stack.so* module, you should make changes similar to these on all of the PAM modules corresponding to the login and other authentication services you use. Of course, your files aren't likely to be identical to this one unless you use Debian—and even then, other Debian PAM files aren't identical to this one. You therefore need to adjust your changes to suit your own files.

One login server requires a bit of extra attention: SSH. This server sometimes doesn't work well with PAM authentication. If you can't seem to get your SSH server to use your new authentication tool, you may need to set one of two options in the */etc/ssh/sshd_config* file on the SSH server system:

```
UsePAM yes
UsePrivilegeSeparation no
```

I recommend trying UsePAM yes first. If that fails, try the second option. One of the two should get SSH to play nicely with PAM.

Password Services

The */etc/pam.d/passwd* file on most systems controls the *passwd* program's interactions with PAM. Example A-3 shows a sample file from a SuSE system. This file is a bit simpler than a typical login service definition.

Example A-3. Sample PAM password service configuration

```
auth       required   pam_unix2.so    nullok

account    required   pam_unix2.so

password   required   pam_pwcheck.so  nullok
password   required   pam_unix2.so    nullok use_first_pass use_authtok

session    required   pam_unix2.so
```

Suppose that you want to enable users to change passwords on their local accounts if they exist or on their LDAP accounts if they exist. PAM can be rather picky about such arrangements; the *passwd* command requires use of several PAM stacks to do its work, from authentication through to the actual password change. Thus, you must add references to *pam_ldap.so* to three stacks. Example A-4 shows the result, with changed or added parts highlighted in bold.

Example A-4. Sample PAM password service configuration with LDAP support

```
auth       sufficient pam_ldap.so
auth       required   pam_unix2.so    nullok use_first_pass

account    sufficient pam_ldap.so
account    required   pam_unix2.so

password   required   pam_pwcheck.so  nullok
password   optional   pam_ldap.so     use_first_pass use_authtok
password   required   pam_unix2.so    nullok use_first_pass use_authtok

session    required   pam_unix2.so
```

This configuration enables users to change their passwords much as they ordinarily do, by typing **passwd** and answering the usual password-changing prompts. Making the actual password call to *pam_ldap.so* optional changes the LDAP password if it exists but doesn't cause the operation to fail if the LDAP password doesn't exist. Thus, this configuration works for users who are defined locally, defined on the LDAP server, or both. (The required nature of the password stack call to *pam_unix2.so* would seem likely to cause a failure if the account isn't defined locally, but in practice, this isn't a problem.)

This configuration does have one drawback: the *root* user is prompted for the LDAP password of users, if they have LDAP accounts, before being allowed to change them. As a practical matter, this means that system administrators must use LDAP tools, rather than the *passwd* command, to change users' forgotten passwords or to set passwords on new accounts.

Of course, you can try variants on these changes. For instance, you can require users to have LDAP accounts; however, this might be undesirable if you want to maintain some local accounts (such as *root*) independent of the LDAP server. Alternatively, if you make the *pam_ldap.so* call in the password stack sufficient, users with both LDAP and local accounts can change only their LDAP passwords.

An Authentication Stack

Some distributions, such as Red Hat, Fedora, and Gentoo, now use the *pam_stack.so* module to place common authentication options in a single file. This approach can greatly simplify PAM configuration because you need to change only one file. Example A-5 shows the */etc/pam.d/system-auth* file from a Gentoo system. (The original includes the complete paths to the library modules; Example A-5 omits these paths to keep line lengths manageable.) In principle, this file is a combination of other PAM configuration files, defining basic features used by all of them. This file shouldn't get too specific, though; options that should apply only to a few authentication tools should go in those tools' configuration files.

Example A-5. Sample PAM stack service configuration

```
auth        required    pam_env.so
auth        sufficient  pam_unix.so likeauth nullok
auth        required    pam_deny.so

account     required    pam_unix.so

password    required    pam_cracklib.so retry=3
password    sufficient  pam_unix.so nullok md5 shadow use_authtok
password    required    pam_deny.so

session     required    pam_limits.so
session     required    pam_unix.so
```

To modify Example A-5 to use LDAP in addition to the local account database, you must add references to the *pam_ldap.so* module in the auth and account stacks. For the latter, you may also want to change the existing call to *pam_unix.so* to sufficient and add a required call to *pam_deny.so* to prevent too-easy bypassing of account-maintenance requirements, should you implement any. You may also want to add a call to the *pam_mkhomedir.so* module in the session stack; however, you might prefer putting this call in the individual server PAM modules to better control home directory creation. Once all the changes are made, the result looks like Example A-6, which shows changed or added material in bold.

Example A-6. Sample PAM stack service configuration with LDAP support

```
auth       required    pam_env.so
auth       sufficient  pam_ldap.so
auth       sufficient  pam_unix.so likeauth nullok use_first_pass
auth       required    pam_deny.so

account    sufficient  pam_ldap.so
account    sufficient  pam_unix.so
account    required    pam_deny.so

password   required    pam_cracklib.so retry=3
password   sufficient  pam_unix.so nullok md5 shadow use_authtok
password   required    pam_deny.so

session    required    pam_limits.so
session    required    pam_unix.so
session    required    pam_mkhomedir.so skel=/etc/skel/ umask=0022
```

 Fedora and Red Hat autogenerate their */etc/pam.d/system-auth* files using a tool called *authconfig* or its GUI equivalent, *system-config-authentication*. If you make changes to the raw PAM file, they may be wiped out if you run this tool. Thus, you might want to modify the file by using the configuration tool, rather than editing it directly. This tool also enables you to set configuration options for specific network authentication tools, such as locating your NT domain controller or LDAP server.

As always, many variants on this set of changes are possible. For instance, you can make changes to the password stack analogous with those described in the earlier section "Password Services"; however, I find that implementing these changes directly in the *passwd* file often produces better results.

This example configuration uses sufficient calls to several modules along with *pam_deny.so* to block accesses that fail all of these calls. This approach works well when you have no calls subsequent to the sufficient calls in a stack. In the case of a stacked configuration like this, its calling stack can then place additional module calls after the call to *pam_stack.so*, no matter how the stack module exits, if the calling stack calls *pam_stack.so* as a required or requisite module.

Changing a stack module's configuration doesn't mean you can't change individual servers' configurations. You can make general changes to */etc/pam.d/system-auth* and then add other calls to the configuration files for *login*, KDM, *su*, and other tools, as you see fit.

Summary

PAM is a powerful tool for managing authentication options in Linux. As a modular tool, PAM is easily expanded—at least, easily when compared to recompiling all of your servers and other programs that require authentication. PAM is a very flexible tool, and some of this flexibility manifests itself in a plethora of options, some of which interact in peculiar ways. Understanding at least the more common of these options will help you adapt your PAM configuration to suit your needs, including adding network authentication tools such as NT domain controllers, LDAP servers, and Kerberos realms to your system. Actually creating a working configuration is likely to take some trial and error, but the examples presented here should set you on the right path.

APPENDIX B

Linux on the Desktop

Although most of this book focuses on using Linux servers to help Windows desktop systems, Linux is beginning to find a home as a desktop OS. As a multipurpose OS, Linux can handle many desktop functions, and you may want to consider Linux in this role for many of the same reasons you'd consider Linux as a server OS—low cost, high reliability, remote administration capabilities, and so on. You might also want to use thin clients to access Linux, in which case this chapter applies to the system the thin clients access. Before deploying Linux as a desktop OS, though, you'll have to know a bit about its capabilities in this role; that's where this appendix comes in.

I begin with a look at Linux desktop applications, including a list of some common application categories and their Windows and Linux instantiations. Next is the issue of application configuration. This task is unusual in Linux because many applications, including the desktop environments that run when users log in, have both global and user configurations, so you may need to modify either type. Sometimes, you may find yourself unable to do what you want using native Linux applications, in which case Linux's ability to run Windows applications is critical, so this issue is covered. Whether or not you can use Linux applications, your ability to access data can be important. This includes both filesystem access and file compatibility across applications. Next up is a common problem area for Linux desktop systems: font handling.

Linux Desktop Applications for All Occasions

Any attempt to use Linux as a desktop OS ultimately requires Linux desktop applications that are acceptable for your intended purpose. Although tools to run Windows applications are available in Linux (as described later in the section "Running Windows Programs in Linux"), these solutions are imperfect. If all you do is run Windows programs, you might as well use Windows as your OS.

Fortunately, an array of desktop applications are available for Linux, as summarized in Table B-1. Of course, not all these components are exactly equivalent. For instance, some of the Linux applications, such as *mutt* and *cdrecord*, are command-line tools, whereas the Windows applications are overwhelmingly GUI in nature. Exact features also differ, of course, and, in some cases, the basic purpose of tools aren't equivalent. For instance, *mkisofs* and *cdrecord* work together to create a CD-R, while X-CD-Roast and Eroaster provide GUI frontends to these tools. In Windows, CD-R creation tools are usually all-in-one packages that do everything. To learn more about any of these programs, perform a web search or check your Linux installation medium to see if the program comes with your distribution.

Table B-1. Application categories and exemplars

Application category	Windows examples	Linux examples
Office Suite	Microsoft Office, WordPerfect Office, StarOffice, OpenOffice.org	OpenOffice.org, StarOffice, KOffice, GNOME Office
Bitmap Graphics Editing	Adobe Photoshop, the GIMP	The GIMP
Scanning Software	TWAIN, VueScan	SANE, Kooka, VueScan
CD-R Creation	Easy Media Creator Deluxe, Nero	*mkisofs*, *cdrecord*, X-CD-Roast, Eroaster, K3b
Multimedia Playback	Windows Media Player, Winamp, Real	XMMS, ALSA Player, *mpg123*, Real, *xine*
PDF Creation and Viewing	Acrobat and Acrobat Reader	Ghostscript, Acrobat Reader, XPDF
Web Browsing	Internet Explorer, Mozilla, Firefox, Opera	Mozilla, Firefox, Opera, Konqueror
E-Mail Client	Outlook and Outlook Express, Eudora, Netscape Mail	Evolution, Netscape Mail, Thunderbird, KMail, *pine*, *mutt*
Instant Messenging	AIM, ICQ, MSN Messenger, Jabber, X-Chat	GAIM, KAIM, *talk*, Kopete, X-Chat
Web Site Creation	FrontPage, Dreamweaver	Quanta, Nvu

If you don't see an application category that you need in Table B-1, don't panic! This table is intended to provide only a few quick pointers for some of the most common desktop tools. Try performing a web search on the category name and *Linux*. You might also check your distribution, particularly if it provides a GUI installation tool with categorized sets of software. Many Linux sites, such as *http://www.linux.org*, *http://www.sourceforge.net*, and *http://www.freshmeat.net*, also provide pointers to Linux software by category.

One critically important Linux desktop software component doesn't appear in Table B-1: the *desktop environment*. This is a collection of tools—most are fairly small by themselves—that together create the familiar set of desktop icons, program-launch tools, and so on that users see when they log in to the computer. Windows provides only one common desktop environment, which is bundled into the OS. In Linux, you have a choice between GNOME, KDE, XFce, XPde, and others. This choice is covered in more detail in the "Creating Default Desktop Configurations" section.

Configuring Applications and Environments

If you're familiar with administering Windows desktop systems, many of the issues involved in administering Linux desktop systems will be similar, but others are unique. Likewise, if you're already familiar with Linux system administration in other contexts (such as servers), desktop environments present some unique challenges. Some of the issues in Linux desktop configuration include understanding the difference between global and user configuration files, locating configuration files, creating default desktop configurations, and making desktop environments accessible as options at login time.

Global Versus User Configuration Files

Linux has long supported multiple users. Part of this support includes mechanisms to help keep users' configurations separate—enabling two users to use the same computer but set different defaults for assorted application and desktop environment options. Even if a computer has a single user, Linux uses these features, maintaining nominally separate global and user configuration files. You can take advantage of this distinction to set global defaults, which users can then modify without impacting other users' settings. On a system with a single user, you can use this distinction to easily restore a user's settings to the default if the user's settings become corrupt.

Typically, global configuration files are stored in a system area. These files can be used in one or both of two ways:

- User programs can access the global configuration files directly, using them to direct program operation in a way that's invariant from user to user. If a program supports *only* this mode of operation, users can't change their default.

- Users or user programs can copy the global configuration files to a subdirectory in the user's home directory and then access the copied files for normal operation. This approach enables users to change their personal defaults without impacting other users.

Most user programs support use of local configuration files, at least as an option. Some programs automatically copy global configuration files the first time they're run. Others use the global files directly unless users copy the global files to their home directories or create their own configuration files from scratch. Sometimes a global file serves as a template that can be modified by a local file.

Ultimately, you'll have to consult a program's documentation to learn how it treats these two types of configuration files. This knowledge can be important when setting defaults. For instance, if a program always consults a global file, you can change defaults even for users who've already begun using a program, so long as they've not explicitly changed a default; however, if a program copies global configuration files to the user's home directory the first time it's run, changing the global configuration files affects only users who begin using the program after you make changes.

The precise methods used to modify configuration files differ from one program to another. Traditionally, Unix and Linux programs have used text-mode configuration files that can be edited in a text editor. This remains true, but many of the more sophisticated GUI programs now create very complex configuration files, often using the Extensible Markup Language (XML). Such files can be difficult to modify by hand, particularly if you're not familiar with XML or the specific XML conventions used by the program in question. Thus, one approach to making changes is to create a dummy account, change the defaults using that account, and copy the dummy account's local configuration files back to the global configuration file's location.

 Don't blindly overwrite existing global configuration files. If you make a mistake, doing this can render a program unusable, at least to new users of the program. Before replacing a global configuration file, back it up someplace safe. If you don't, you may need to reinstall the program should you make a mistake in creating the new configuration file.

Locating Configuration Files

One location for global configuration files is */etc/skel*. This directory holds template configuration files that may be copied to a new user's home directory when an account is created, depending on the options to *useradd* or other account-creation tools. Once files are copied from */etc/skel*, user applications don't normally access this directory. Thus, making changes to files in */etc/skel* won't normally affect how existing users' applications work.

Typically, */etc/skel* contains a rather small set of files—perhaps just for your system's default shells, for instance. These files are normally all dot files, meaning that their filenames begin with dots (.), which means that they don't show up in file listings unless you include special options, such as the -a option to *ls*.

Other directories in */etc* hold many other application-specific global configuration files, often named after the programs they control. For instance, */etc/gimp* holds global configuration files for GIMP, */etc/xfce4* holds global configuration files for Version 4 of XFce, and */etc/xcdroast.conf* is the global configuration file for X-CD-Roast. Most configuration files in */etc*, though, belong to system utilities and servers rather than user applications.

Many desktop programs store their global configuration files somewhere in their own directory tree. One good way to locate these files is to use your package management system to list all the files that belong to a package. For many packages, though, this action produces a large list of files—documentation files in multiple languages, graphics files used to display icons in the program, and so on. You might get lucky by piping the result through *grep* to search for a string like conf, but this procedure isn't guaranteed to work.

Programs associated with the major desktop environments (particularly GNOME and KDE) often store their global configuration files in a directory along with the desktop environment. This location can vary from one distribution to another, as described shortly.

Some programs don't ship with global configuration files per se; they store their defaults in their executables and rely exclusively on user configuration files to override these defaults. If you want to change your systemwide default for such programs, you may need to generate user configuration files in a dummy account and then copy those files to */etc/skel*. This approach won't change the defaults for existing users, though.

Creating Default Desktop Configurations

Perhaps the most important type of configuration file you might want to modify is that for your desktop environment—KDE, GNOME, XFce, or what have you. Users see their desktop environments when they first log in; making frequently used programs, file shares, and so on easy to access on your network's standard desktop will go a long way to helping your users make the transition to Linux and be productive in that environment. Typically, the way you manage this task is to create a desirable template configuration in a dummy account and then to copy that template configuration to the desktop environment's global configuration file area.

Creating a template configuration

To begin the task, create a new "dummy" user—one who exists only to enable you to create a new desktop configuration. Log into this account using the desktop environment you want to modify. (If this environment isn't an option when you log in, consult the later section "Adding an Environment as a Login Option.") You can then tweak the desktop environment as you see fit. Features you might want to adjust include:

Desktop icons
> Most desktop environments, including KDE and GNOME, enable you to create desktop icons that launch programs or open file browsers on particular directories. Creating such icons for important programs and directories can help users navigate the system. Don't go overboard, though; too many icons can clutter the desktop and be confusing, particularly for users who've never used a system before.

Program launching menus
> Most desktop environments include a tool, often called the *Panel*, which houses program-launching icons. Some icons appear directly on the Panel, but more can

be referenced in menus. Most distributions attempt to provide ready access to most common programs from their Panel menus, and many will automatically add programs when you install them using the distributions' package-management tools. Nonetheless, you might want to rearrange the menus, delete programs to reduce clutter, or add programs that aren't added by default. Some desktop environments, such as KDE, maintain separate global and user program launch menus. To make global changes, the best approach is to change the global file, which for KDE is called *applnk* and is usually located in */usr/share*, */usr/kde/version/share* or a similar location.

General desktop defaults

Desktop environments all present numerous defaults that influence the overall look and feel of the system. These include default program fonts, desktop background images, keyboard repeat rate, window border decorations, and so on. Technically, these defaults may apply to dozens of different programs; however, most desktop environments provide a centralized control panel through which most or all of these options may be set. Although all major Linux distributions ship with defaults that are at least somewhat reasonable, you might want to change some, either because you think the default is not the best or to customize the system for your environment (say, using a background image with your company's logo).

You can set certain font defaults in a desktop environment; however, these defaults apply only to the desktop environment and to affiliated programs. You may need to change default fonts in many programs individually to make such a change truly universal. Actually installing new fonts that don't ship with the distribution is another matter, too; the "Font Handling" section later covers this issue in more detail.

When you're done making these changes, log out and then log back in again to be sure they're working as you intended. Some programs (particularly older ones or those that aren't officially part of a desktop environment) require you to explicitly save a configuration before its changes are saved, so it's easy to make changes and then lose them when you log out.

You may want to consult with your end users when designing a default desktop environment. Try creating two or three possible defaults and ask a few typical users to comment on them.

Copying the template to be a global configuration

Your template user's configuration is now saved in the template user's home directory. You can look for it using the -a option to *ls* (the -F option can also be helpful because it distinguishes directories from files).

```
# ls -aF /home/genie
./              .bashrc     .gnome/             .metacity/         Desktop/
../             .dmrc       .gnome2/            .nautilus/
.ICEauthority   .gconf/     .gnome2_private/    .recently-used
.bash_profile   .gconfd/    .gtkrc-1.2-gnome2   .xsession-errors
```

This example shows the files created by the desktop environment (GNOME in this case), as well as those copied from *etc/skel* during account creation and any others created during the login process. The *.ICEauthority*, *.bash_profile*, *.bashrc*, *.dmrc*, and *.xsession-errors* files aren't part of the desktop environment configuration. The *.recently-used* file, although used by GNOME, can be safely ignored because it holds information on recently accessed files; chances are you don't need or even want to copy that information into new accounts.

To copy the template you've created so that all new users can access it, you must copy the files and directories to an area in which they'll be used by new accounts. One way to do this is to copy everything into the */etc/skel* directory. When you do this, the files will be copied whenever a new account is created and its initial files set from the */etc/skel* template.

Adding an Environment as a Login Option

If you want your users to be able to log into a specific GUI environment, you must be able to tell the computer to make that environment the default, or at least to present the environment you want as a default. To do this, you must first understand how to get a GUI login tool running. Once this is done, you need to know how to change defaults and present options with your tool of choice.

Running a GUI login tool

Many Linux distributions today come configured to boot directly into GUI mode by default. Most distributions, including Fedora, Mandrake, Red Hat, and SuSE, enable you to control this feature by editing a single line in */etc/inittab*:

```
id:3:initdefault:
```

The number in the second colon-delimited field (3) in this example sets the default runlevel. Typically, runlevel 3 corresponds to a text-mode boot, whereas runlevel 5 corresponds to a full GUI boot. (Some distributions, such as older versions of SuSE, used runlevels other than 3 and 5 for these functions.) The latter is very much like the former, except that in a GUI boot, an XDMCP server is launched, as described in Chapter 11. The purpose in a default configuration isn't to provide remote access, though; the default XDMCP configuration locks down the XDMCP server so that it provides only local GUI login access.

A few distributions, such as Debian and Gentoo, do things differently: rather than use the runlevel to signal whether a GUI login should be enabled, they set a SysV startup script to do the job. You can enable or disable this startup script to change the distribution's GUI login status. Debian uses scripts called *xdm*, *gmd*, or *kdm* for

---

the X Display Manager (XDM), GNOME Display Manager (GDM), or KDE Display Manager (KDM) tools, respectively. Gentoo has a single script called *xdm* that starts whichever tool you've chosen to use.

All distributions provide some method of selecting which XDMCP server to run. Most distributions do this by setting a variable in a configuration file. Fedora, Red Hat, and Mandrake use */etc/sysconfig/desktop*; Gentoo uses */etc/rc.conf*; and SuSE uses */etc/sysconfig/displaymanager*. In all these distributions, you set the DISPLAYMANAGER variable. Most distributions accept either the name of the XDMCP server, such as KDM, or the name of an associated desktop environment, such as KDE. Debian works a bit differently; it sets the path to the default XDMCP program in the */etc/X11/default-display-manager* file.

Presenting desktop environment options

Different XDMCP servers require different configurations to present login options to users. The simplest of these tools, and the least convenient from a user's point of view, is XDM. This server presents no login-time options; instead, it relies on a configuration file to set the default desktop environment. The global version of this file is */etc/X11/xdm/Xsession*, which is often a link to */etc/X11/Xsession*. Users can override this default by providing a file called *.xsession* in their home directories. In either case, this file is a script, so you can configure it to run a particular desktop environment by providing appropriate commands, such as *gnome-session* to run GNOME, *startkde* to start KDE, or *startxfce4* to start XFce. A simple script can contain nothing but a reference to the environment startup script:

```
#!/bin/bash
/usr/bin/startxfce4
```

More complex scripts are possible, of course. The default XDM *Xsession* script typically tests for the existence of several desktop environments and, from among those that are available, starts the one that's most preferred by the distribution maintainer.

KDM and GDM are both more complex. They provide the user with a set of options, typically accessed by clicking a button in the GUI display. In most cases, when you add a new desktop environment, your KDM and GDM configurations will be modified to present the new desktop environment as an option to users. Sometimes, though, you need to take extra steps to see that this happens.

KDM and GDM both look in a directory for a list of sessions. This is often the */usr/share/xsessions* directory, although it could have another name—try typing **find /usr -name "*.desktop"** to locate the directory if you can't seem to find it. Both KDM and GDM look for files whose names end in *.desktop*. These files provide information on how to launch a desktop environment. If you need to add such a file, you should probably begin by copying an existing one and modifying it. Existing files are likely to be rather long because they often contain options to set the name in multiple languages. A short example looks like this:

```
[Desktop Entry]
Encoding=UTF-8
Name=KDE
Comment=This session logs you into KDE
Exec=startkde
TryExec=startkde
Type=Application
```

To modify the system, edit the Exec and TryExec lines to point to the desktop startup command. Modifying the Name and Comment lines will also enable your users to correctly identify the environment.

Many distributions install a large number of *.desktop* files in some other location, such as */usr/share/apps/kdm/sessions/*. These files might not be used by default, but you should be able to copy them to the appropriate directory rather than create new files. If your distribution does this, you can locate it with the *find* command mentioned earlier.

Once you've added a new environment to the configuration, you'll have to restart the XDMCP server. In most distributions, you can do this by typing **telinit 3** followed by **telinit 5** at a command prompt. This action brings the system to runlevel 3, then back to runlevel 5. In the process, it shuts down the XDMCP server and restarts it. With Debian and Gentoo, you can use the SysV startup scripts to shut down and then restart the XDMCP server.

Restarting the XDMCP server also shuts down the console's X session. Thus, you should save any unsaved work before attempting this procedure.

Running Windows Programs in Linux

Linux is a mature OS that provides programs in all common, and many uncommon, desktop software categories. Nonetheless, sometimes native Linux programs just aren't adequate. Perhaps you need a specific program to read existing data files or to exchange data with colleagues, customers, or clients off-site. Perhaps you need a program with specific features that aren't available in Linux; or perhaps you need to run an exotic program for which no Linux counterpart is available. Sometimes, you can work around the limitation by running Windows programs from Linux. This approach has advantages and disadvantages compared to running the programs on a computer that runs Windows, so understanding why you might want to run Windows programs in Linux is critical. You should also know a bit about some of the options for doing the job; several tools are available, each of which has its own advantages and disadvantages.

Why Run Windows Programs in Linux?

Ordinarily, the best way to run a program is to run it on the OS for which it was designed. Any other OS will, at best, be emulating the target OS or placing an additional layer of software or protocols between you and the program you want to run. Such procedures are inevitably imperfect and often slow down operation. However, these drawbacks can be overwhelmed by certain advantages of running Windows programs in Linux:

Reduced hardware costs
Running Linux and Windows programs on one computer can reduce hardware costs compared to running these programs on multiple computers. Related to this advantage is the fact that a single computer consumes less power and desk space than multiple computers.

Using non-x86 hardware
Some methods of running Windows programs from Linux work even with non-x86 hardware. Thus, you can run Windows programs from a Linux system running on PowerPC, Alpha, or other CPUs. This may be a big plus if you already have an office filled with such computers, and you don't want to replace them or buy more.

Easy access to Linux resources
Perhaps you want to use resources available to Linux that aren't easily accessible from Windows. For instance, you might have large numbers of data files on a Linux desktop computer's hard disk, stored on a Linux-native filesystem. Although you can often gain access to such filesystems from Windows (either through special Windows filesystem drivers or by using another Windows system and setting up a file server such as Samba on the Linux system), doing so is sometimes inconvenient.

Linux stability
Linux is a very stable OS—more stable than most versions of Windows. Thus, using Linux can mean less downtime due to system crashes. This advantage is most dramatic when comparing Linux to rather old versions of Windows—particularly Windows 9x/Me. Windows 200x has a much better reputation for reliability.

Improved productivity
Running Windows programs alongside Linux programs can improve productivity. Many methods of doing this enable you to cut-and-paste data between programs, and it's usually easier to switch between programs on a single computer than to switch between computers. If the alternative is dual booting a single computer, running Windows programs in Linux can save a great deal of time that would otherwise be wasted rebooting the computer.

These advantages all assume that you want or need to run Linux as your primary desktop OS, either site-wide or for just a few users. They tend to evaporate if you have more compelling reasons to run Windows programs than to run Linux programs.

Options for Running Windows Programs from Linux

Broadly speaking, methods of running Windows programs in Linux fall into two categories: *remote access tools* and *emulators*. Chapters 10 and 11 describe remote access tools. For accessing Windows systems from Linux, the GUI tools are almost certainly the better choice; text-mode tools are simply too limiting for most purposes.

Of course, using remote-access tools requires you to have at least one Windows system running on your network, and that system must be running an appropriate remote-access protocol server. You can then use the corresponding Linux client to log into that Windows computer remotely. One advantage of this approach is that you can use *any* Linux system, provided the appropriate software is installed; you don't need to be concerned with CPU architectures or even the speed of the computer you use for access, within broad limits. Because this approach doesn't rely on any sort of emulation, software compatibility is usually quite good. After all, the software is running on a real Windows computer, meaning that the only significant source of compatibility problems is in the protocol used to communicate between systems. Games and multimedia tools sometimes have problems running over these protocols, but most productivity tools work just fine.

Another approach is to use an emulator, which is a tool that can run one operating system's programs from another. Actually, several different types of emulators exist:

CPU emulators
> CPU emulators enable one CPU to execute instructions meant for another CPU. Using a CPU emulator, you can run x86 code on a PowerPC, SPARC, or other CPU. (Emulators for other CPUs are also available but are irrelevant for Windows emulation.) You can even run x86 code on an x86 CPU using this approach. The downside is that CPU emulators can't run software nearly as quickly as it can run on native hardware of otherwise comparable speed. The most common CPU emulator for Linux is Bochs (*http://bochs.sourceforge.net*), which is both a CPU emulator and a machine emulator (described next). The result is that you can run Windows within Bochs. In practice, this works best with older versions of Windows on new (hence fast) CPUs. Another CPU emulator is QEMU (*http://fabrice.bellard.free.fr/qemu/*), which includes a full machine emulator similar to Bochs but can also be used to launch Linux applications for one architecture on another CPU. This feature can be handy for running WINE (described shortly) on non-x86 platforms.

Machine emulators
> Another type of emulation is machine emulation, in which the non-CPU components of a computer are emulated. That is, software running in a machine

emulator "sees" a hard disk, display hardware, and so on that are emulated. The emulated disk might correspond to a file on the hard disk and an emulated display might tie in to a single window, for instance. Machine emulators typically run emulated programs directly using the host CPU, although some tools (such as Bochs) include both CPU and machine emulator components. The commercial VMware (*http://www.vmware.com*) is a popular machine emulator, which supports running several versions of Windows and other OSs from Linux. Win4Lin (*http://www.netraverse.com*) is another commercial machine emulator, but it only supports Windows 9x/Me.

OS emulators

An OS emulator makes minimal or no attempts to emulate the CPU and hardware; instead, it attempts to emulate the OS itself. In Linux, the most popular Windows OS emulator is the open source Wine Is Not an Emulator (WINE; *http://www.winehq.org*). This package duplicates the functionality of the Windows application program interface (API)—that is, the system calls used by programs. WINE can be used like a Linux GUI API to compile Windows programs as native programs, or it can be used in conjunction with a program loader to run programs compiled for Windows. Ordinarily, WINE is useful only on x86 or AMD64 systems; however, used with the QEMU CPU emulator, you can run x86 Windows programs on non-x86 CPUs. WINE runs Windows programs quickly (at least, when used on x86 hardware), but its compatibility is far from complete. Small programs and popular ones are likely to run well, but many large programs don't run or run only after extensive tweaking. Several offshoots of the WINE project exist. Most notable of these are the commercial Crossover Office (*http://www.codeweavers.com*) and the commercial Cedega (formerly known as WineX; *http://www.transgaming.com*). Crossover Office is optimized to run Microsoft Office and a few other common productivity tools, whereas Cedega is intended to run Windows games in Linux. The open source WINE can run Microsoft Office and many games; the commercial products provide easier installation and relatively minor improvements over the original.

 The expansion of WINE's name deserves elaboration, given that I'm calling it an emulator. The precise meaning of the word *emulator* varies depending on who you ask about it. This appendix uses the word fairly broadly, to apply to any of the three types of activities just described. Some people, though, including the WINE developers, prefer to confine this term to CPU emulation, hence the expansion of the WINE name.

Generally speaking, among emulators, WINE is a very good approach, particularly on x86 systems, *if* you can get the program you want to run working under it. Check *http://appdb.winehq.org* for application compatibility information before you invest a lot of time in trying to get a program working. WINE provides the best cross-OS cut-and-paste support and enables you to run an application without actually installing Windows on your computer. (Some configurations do require you to copy some Windows *.DLL* files, however.) Note that WINE's list of supported applications is much shorter than that of machine emulators. These emulators run a real copy of Windows inside their virtual environments, so they can run almost any program that doesn't require access to real low-level hardware. (Some of these programs will work but compatibility is a bit hit-or-miss.) Generally speaking, you should resort to CPU emulators only if you must run Windows programs on non-x86 hardware. Although you *can* run Windows on an x86 Linux system in a program like Bochs, the experience is likely to be painfully slow, particularly if your computer is very old or if you try to run a recent version of Windows.

File and Filesystem Compatibility

Linux desktop systems must frequently access files created by Windows computers, or store files in a way that Windows computers can handle. This task has two components. First, Linux must be able to read and write the filesystems used by Windows, at least when files are transferred on disks. Second, Linux applications must be able to process the file formats that are most commonly used on Windows. This second task can be broken down into many categories depending on the programs in question, and in this chapter I describe office file formats, PDF files, and archive files. I also provide some tips for transitioning a network from using Windows to one that uses Linux desktop systems.

Accessing Windows Disks and Filesystems

Before you can deal with file format issues, you must be able to access the files in question. In many networked environments, the easiest way to deal with this issue is to use the network. Tools like FTP and email can be a good way to transfer files, particularly over the Internet at large. The SMB/CIFS is a common file-sharing protocol among Windows systems, and using Linux as an SMB/CIFS client is described in detail in Chapter 6.

Sometimes, though, network protocols aren't the best solution. Network bandwidth may be inadequate for delivering very large files, network firewalls might prevent data exchange, or one or both of the systems might not even be on a network. Such situations are particularly common when users want to move files between home and work. Another situation in which network access may be inadequate is when moving data across time rather than space—that is, when archiving data for long-term storage or when reading files that have been so archived in the past. In all these situations, you must be able to share data on a common disk filesystem. Several filesystems are likely to be used for such data transfers:

FAT

The File Allocation Table filesystem is named after one of its key data structures. FAT is a very old filesystem, dating back to the earliest days of DOS—and earlier (FAT variants were used on DOS's predecessor OSs). FAT is actually a family of filesystems, which vary on two dimensions: the size of FAT entries, in bits (12-, 16-, or 32-bit) and filename length limits (short or *8.3* filenames, which can be no longer than eight characters with a three-character extension; VFAT long filenames; or a Linux-specific long filename extension). FAT size varies with disk size: floppies and very small hard disks generally use FAT-12; FAT-16 tops out at 2-GB partitions (4 GB for Windows NT/200x/XP); and FAT-32 is often used for disks larger than a few hundred megabytes, and *must* be used for disks larger than the FAT-16 limit. Linux auto-detects the FAT size, but you specify the nature of the filename support using one of three filesystem type codes: msdos stands for the original FAT with 8.3 filenames; vfat adds VFAT long filenames; and umsdos adds the Linux-specific long filename support to the original FAT. Note that VFAT and UMSDOS are mutually exclusive; UMSDOS and VFAT both build on the original FAT in different ways. All these drivers support both read and write access, and all are very stable and reliable. FAT (in all its variants) is most commonly found on hard disks used by Windows 9x/Me, floppy disks, Zip disks, and other removable magnetic disks.

NTFS

The New Technology File System was created for Windows NT and is the preferred filesystem for use on hard disks with all computers in the Windows NT/200x/XP family. It's seldom found on removable media, so the main reasons to access NTFS from Linux are for a dual boot configuration or if you need to recover data from an existing Windows hard disk (say, after replacing Windows with Linux). Linux provides reasonably reliable read-only support for NTFS, but read/write support is much less stable. In 2.4.x and earlier kernels, Linux's NTFS read/write support was almost certain to corrupt the NTFS partition. In the 2.6.x kernel, the NTFS read/write support is more limited in capabilities (it can modify only existing files, not create new ones), but it's less likely to damage the existing filesystem. Linux's NTFS support uses the ntfs filesystem type code.

ISO-9660 and Rock Ridge

This filesystem is the most common one of CD-ROM, CD-R, and CD-RW discs. It's also sometimes used on recordable DVD media. ISO-9660 comes in three levels. ISO-9660 Level 1 is limited to 8.3 filenames similar to those of FAT; Level 2 adds support for 32-character filenames; and Level 3 also supports 32-character filenames, but changes some internal data structures to make it easier to update an existing filesystem. Linux supports reading all three levels via its iso9660 filesystem type code. An extension to ISO-9660, known as *Rock Ridge*, supports long filenames and Unix-style ownership and permissions. Windows systems can't handle Rock Ridge extensions, but they don't interfere with Windows' ability to read the underlying ISO-9660 filesystem. Linux's iso9660 driver auto-detects Rock Ridge and uses these extensions if they're available. You can create an ISO-9660 filesystem using the Linux *mkisofs* command, which takes a wide range of options (consult its manpage for details), and burn it to a recordable disc with *cdrecord*. Windows systems have no problems reading optical discs created in this way. Various GUI frontends to these tools are also available, such as X-CD-Roast (*http://www.xcdroast.org*) and K3b (*http://www.k3b.org*).

Joliet

Microsoft created the Joliet filesystem as a way to add long filenames, Unicode filenames, and other features to CD-ROMs. Joliet typically exists side by side with an ISO-9660 filesystem, and it can be ignored by OSs that don't understand it, so, in practice, Joliet works much like the Rock Ridge ISO-9660 extensions. Linux's iso9660 driver automatically detects Joliet and will use the Joliet filesystem if it's present. When both Joliet and Rock Ridge are present, though, Linux favors the Rock Ridge extensions. The Linux *mkisofs* tool can create an image with Joliet extensions enabled.

UDF

The Universal Disk Format is a next-generation optical disc filesystem. Commercial DVDs usually employ this filesystem, and it's also used on some CD-R and CD-RW discs, particularly those created by Windows *packet writing* drivers— tools that make the CD-RW drive behave more like a conventional removable magnetic disk than a traditional write-once optical disc. Linux can mount such discs using the udf filesystem type code, but discs so mounted can't be written. The Linux *mkisofs* utility can create a UDF filesystem alongside an ISO-9660 filesystem, but this feature is considered experimental, at least as of Version 2.0.1.

Any of these filesystems may be used for data exchange between Linux and Windows systems. You can mount them just as you would Linux-native filesystems, but for most, some extra options may be helpful. In particular, most of these filesystems lack Linux ownership and permissions information, so the filesystem driver must fake this information. By default, ownership is given to the user who mounted the disk. This might or might not be appropriate. You can override the setting using various options:

uid=*value*

This option sets the UID number for all the files on the disk.

gid=*value*

This option is similar to the uid option, but it sets the GID number rather than the UID.

umask=*value*

You can set the permission bits that should be removed from all files on a FAT or UDF filesystem with this option.

dmask=*value*

> This option works much like umask, but it applies only to directories on FAT filesystems.

fmask=*value*

> This option works much like umask, but it applies only to nondirectory files on FAT filesystems.

mode=*value*

> This is the ISO-9660 and UDF equivalent to umask, but it accepts a mode to set, rather than permission bits to be removed from the mode.

norock

> This option disables use of Rock Ridge extensions on ISO-9660 filesystems.

nojoliet

> This option disables use of a Joliet filesystem, if one is found.

exec *or* noexec

> These options tell the kernel to permit (exec) or not permit (noexec) users to run programs that are marked as executable on a partition. Setting noexec can be a useful security feature to block users running unauthorized code, but it's most useful only if you take other rather extreme measures to prevent users from setting up unauthorized executable programs in other ways.

Frequently, you use these options in */etc/fstab* to specify how a filesystem should be mounted:

```
/dev/hdc   /mnt/cdrom   auto   users,noauto,gid=121,mode=0440 0 0
/dev/fd0   /mnt/floppy  auto   users,noauto,uid=567,gid=121,umask=0113 0 0
```

All these entries use the auto filesystem type code, which tells the kernel to auto-detect the filesystem type. All the entries also use the users and noauto filesystem mount options, which let ordinary users mount and unmount disks and tell the system not to attempt to mount the filesystems at boot time, respectively. The first entry uses mod=0440 to set those permissions on mounted CD-ROMs, effectively granting read access to the user who mounts the disc and to everybody in GID 121. The second line sets a specific owner and group for floppies, removes everybody's execute access, and also removes write access for users who aren't UID 567 or GID 121.

Office File Format Compatibility

Office suites are extremely popular tools. Many sites rely on them as their primary workhorse programs. Furthermore, many organizations need to exchange office files with others, in order to collaborate on projects, submit bids for new work, and so on. Thus, file compatibility of office tools is extremely important. Even if you don't need such compatibility for collaboration or other purposes outside of your site, you may need at least minimal compatibility to read old files after migrating a computer or network from Windows to Linux.

Table B-1 summarizes some of the important office suites. In some cases, you may luck out because you might only need a suite that's available across platforms. For instance, if you use StarOffice or OpenOffice.org on Windows, migrating to Linux should be relatively painless, because the Linux versions of these programs use the same file formats. (In fact, OpenOffice.org is the open source variant of the commercial StarOffice, and both use the same file formats.)

One obstacle to Linux migration is the fact that the most ubiquitous office suite today is Microsoft Office, and it's not available for Linux (although it can be run in WINE, Crossover Office, and other emulators). Fortunately, most Linux office suites offer the ability to read Microsoft Office files, although that ability is never perfect. Of these file types, Microsoft Word files are the most difficult to handle. OpenOffice.org and StarOffice provide the best Microsoft Word import ability, although AbiWord is also reasonably good. Others tend to drop a lot of the more advanced formatting features. File exports from native Linux formats to Microsoft Word formats suffer from similar problems. For any of these file types, you should definitely test the import and export abilities. For simple documents, most any program's import/export filters should work adequately. For very complex documents that rely on advanced features, even OpenOffice.org or StarOffice might be inadequate.

Creating and Reading PDF Files

PDF files are extremely important today. Many web sites provide white papers, specification sheets, and other data in PDF form. If you expect to be able to read such files, you must have a PDF-reading program. Likewise, if you want to place such documents on your own web site, you must be able to create these files. Fortunately, Linux has good PDF support, for both creating and reading.

Many Linux PDF-creation tools revolve around Ghostscript (*http://www.cs.wisc.edu/ ~ghost/*). This program accepts PostScript input and creates outputs in any of several formats. Most of these formats are bitmap graphics files, but Ghostscript can also create PDF files. Because most Linux programs that can print do so by creating Post-Script files and sending them to a print queue, you can usually create a PDF file from a Linux program that can print. One way to do this is to start from a PostScript file on disk (presumably created using an application's "print to disk" feature). The *ps2pdf* script can pass a PostScript file through Ghostscript with all the correct options to generate a PDF file as output:

```
$ ps2pdf sample.ps
```

The result of typing this command is an output file called *sample.pdf*; *ps2pdf* generates the output filename based on the input filename. If you like, you can use *ps2pdf12*, *ps2pdf13*, or *ps2pdf14* instead of *ps2pdf*. These variants generate output using the Version 1.2, 1.3, or 1.4 PDF specifications, respectively. Most modern readers can handle any of these formats, but if you know the reader used to access the file handles one format or another better, you can force the issue. As of Ghostscript 7.07, the default output of *ps2pdf* is equivalent to *ps2pdf12*, but this might change in later versions.

Some programs include explicit PDF-generation support, usually in whatever area handles printing. For instance, Figure B-1 shows KWord's Print dialog box. Rather than select a printer in the Name area, you can select Print to File (PDF), which generates a PDF file. (You must also enter an output filename in a field that's hidden in Figure B-1. Most programs that provide such support rely on Ghostscript; these features merely pass PostScript output through Ghostscript to generate the file you specify.

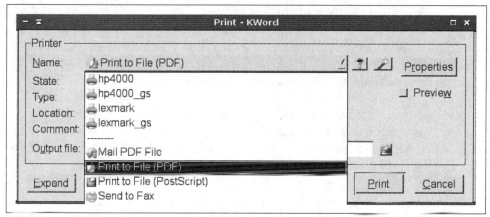

Figure B-1. Many programs provide a way to directly generate PDF files

Another approach to generating PDF files is to link the feature to a printer share. Chapter 4 described this approach with respect to Samba printer shares; you can set up a Samba printer share to pass its input through a custom print command to generate PDF output. You can then call this share from any Samba client, including a Linux system configured to print through the Samba server.

As for reading PDF files, Ghostscript can handle PDF inputs as well as PostScript inputs, so Ghostscript can do the job. Ghostscript by itself isn't exactly a convenient viewer, though. Typically, you'll use a GUI frontend, such as *gv* (*http://wwwthep. physik.uni-mainz.de/~plass/gv/*) or KGhostview (a part of KDE). Another alternative is to use Xpdf (*http://www.foolabs.com/xpdf/*), which is a dedicated PDF viewer that's independent of Ghostview. Another such tool is Adobe's own Acrobat Reader (*http:// www.adobe.com/products/acrobat/*). This program is not open source, but it is freely available. Because Adobe originated the PDF format, Acrobat Reader may be considered the "official" PDF viewer, and it occasionally does a better job with some PDF files, particularly if the creator used was very recent. Unfortunately, Adobe's Linux version is available in binary form only, so you might not be able to run it if you're using an unusual CPU platform.

Managing Cross-Platform Archive Files

Sometimes you must bundle files together, or unbundle files that others have bundled into a carrier archive file. Several classes of files are commonly used for this purpose:

Tarballs

These files are archives with *tar* and compressed using *compress*, *gzip*, or *bzip2*. These files most commonly have *.tar.Z*, *.tar.gz*, *.tar.bz2*, *.tgz*, or *.tbz* filename extensions. They're most frequently created on Linux or Unix systems, and Linux can handle them just fine. Common Windows archiving programs can usually uncompress these files, but if you know a file will be going to a Windows user, a Zip archive is usually better.

Zip files

Zip files are denoted by *.zip* filename extensions. This file format is most popular on Windows systems, which use tools such as PKZIP (*http://www.pkware.com*) or InfoZip (*http://www.info-zip.org/pub/infozip/*) to create them. Both utilities are available in Linux, although only InfoZip is open source. It's usually in a package called *zip*. This package includes programs called *zip* and *unzip* to compress and uncompress files, respectively. Zip files are usually the safest format when sending archive files to Windows users, and they're the format you're most likely to encounter from Windows users.

CAB files

Microsoft uses its Cabinet (CAB) file format to distribute software. Chances are you won't need to create a CAB file in Linux, but if you run across a CAB file you want to extract, you can do the job with *cabextract* (*http://www.kyz.uklinux.net/cabextract.php*). This might be helpful if you run across some fonts or want to view the instructions that come with a CAB file holding a Windows program before extracting it on a Windows system.

StuffIt files

The StuffIt format originated on the Mac OS platform and is usually denoted by a *.sit* filename extension. You're unlikely to run into StuffIt archives from Windows users, but you might run into such files from Macintosh users. The best way to handle these files in Linux is to use the commercial Stuffit Expander (*http://www.stuffit.com*). A demo version that can extract files is available for free, but the full version requires payment.

In addition to these major formats, quite a few minor ones exist. Most are supported by Linux programs, so try doing a web search on the filename extension of an unknown archive file and the keyword *Linux* to locate information on the Linux program. You might also check your Linux distribution's package management system; some have a readily viewed category for archiving utilities.

Some Windows archives are distributed as *self-extracting archives*. These files have *.EXE* or *.COM* extensions, but they really consist of another file format along with a short program to extract the data, all in a single file. These formats are often used for program installers. Self-extracting archives can usually be extracted in Linux using an appropriate Linux program, such as *unzip* for a self-extracting Zip file archive. The trick is finding the right archiving tool. In theory, the *identify* might help, but in practice it often fails to be helpful. You may need to simply try one format after another. Most Windows self-extracting archives are either Zip or CAB files, but other formats do crop up from time to time.

Tips for a Smooth Migration

Migrating desktop users from Windows to Linux can be a trying experience. Users are likely to have large numbers of datafiles they rely on. Ensuring that these files aren't lost or damaged can be a tricky proposition. Users must also be trained in the new OS and its applications, and of course the transition period is likely to be chaotic simply because of the number of ongoing changes.

How can you make matters run more smoothly? You can employ several tricks to help minimize the risk of disaster and smooth the transition from Windows to Linux:

Use backups
> Before doing anything destructive to users' desktop systems, back them up—or at least back up critical user datafiles. (Locating such files may be very challenging; if you can possibly afford it, perform a full backup.) The network backup procedures described in Chapter 14 can be very helpful in performing this backup. When something else goes wrong (and in a big transition, it will), a backup can be a life-saver.

Use file servers
> You can set up a Samba file server (or a Windows file server) and instruct your users to copy or move all their important files to this server. (You may need to keep an eye on the server to be sure they don't copy their Windows system files and program files, though!) When users are transitioned over to Linux, you can configure the new desktop systems to access the same files, thus minimizing your need to copy user files during the transition process. This can be a useful strategy even if you don't want to use the file server on a long-term basis; create a transition schedule and cycle users' files on and off the temporary file server.

Use IMAP servers
> Ahead of the transition, you can set up an IMAP server, as described in Chapter 13, to handle mail. Instruct your users to store their mail on the IMAP server, using their Windows mail clients. When users transition to Linux, they'll find all their email files present on the IMAP server, thus minimizing email

disruption and obviating the need to copy mailbox files or convert their format. The risk, of course, is that if users don't move their mail files to the IMAP server, those files might be lost.

Consider personal files and conversions

Some types of files may need to be converted, copied to new locations, or abandoned. For instance, web browser bookmark files and email address books are likely to require conversion. (You can use Mozilla or Firefox on Windows to convert Internet Explorer bookmarks, then move the *bookmarks.html* file to Linux.) If you can find command-line utilities to handle such files, you may be able to write a script to handle the most important of these files, or at least create a checklist to help you convert them manually.

Rotate upgrades

Rather than try to upgrade the system at a user's desk, install Linux on a computer, swap it with a user's existing machine, install Linux on that machine, and then repeat the process. You should be able to perform the physical machine swap in just a few minutes, minimizing the user's downtime. Of course, you'll have to carefully plan this operation so that users don't receive machines with radically different capabilities than their existing ones—unless of course you want to provide upgrades (or downgrades) to some users. Another problem is in managing users' local datafiles, which may change until the last minute. Using a file server to store such files, as just described, can help with this problem.

Use Linux emergency systems

If you plan to migrate existing hardware, use an emergency or demo Linux system, such as Knoppix (*http://www.knoppix.org*), to test the hardware before wiping the hard disk and installing Linux. Such tools are likely to turn up problems with unsupported video cards or other hardware problems before you get too far into the installation process. If a potential problem looks too tough, you can delay the upgrade on that computer rather than spend time on it in a time-critical period.

Provide adequate training

You can't expect the average user to pick up Linux with no trouble. Training is therefore imperative and should be done before users are faced with their new OS.

Perform test conversions

Try converting a small number of users in a nondestructive way—say, by setting them up with new computers while leaving their old Windows computers in place, at least temporarily. This practice will enable you to locate potential trouble spots in the conversion, and if this goes badly enough, you can back out.

New-hire conversions

You can introduce Linux initially for new users and keep their systems upgraded, but upgrade existing Windows systems less frequently. This practice tends to create a user-driven demand for conversion, particularly among users of older Windows systems. Having users asking to be switched to Linux can be very helpful because you won't be fighting your users on this point.

Generally speaking, you should think through the upgrade process. What tasks are likely to require a lot of time, either on your part or on the part of the users? Can anything be done to minimize this time investment? A little thought and experimentation before you begin can prevent a lot of chaos down the road.

Font Handling

A perennial thorn in the side of Linux desktop use is font handling. In the past, X programs relied exclusively on X's font features (the *X core fonts*, as they're now known), which were primitive compared to those of Windows or Mac OS. Since 2000, new font tools have appeared (namely, *Xft fonts*), and they are now used by many of the most popular X-based Linux programs. Although the new systems are easier to use and present fonts that most users find more visually appealing, they add complexity to the overall Linux font-handling system. Thus, you must understand both these font systems. Many programs also provide their own font-handling tools, although most are converging on Xft. Of those that have not yet adopted Xft, OpenOffice.org (and its commercial twin, StarOffice) is the most important.

Linux Font-Handling Systems

Linux provides two major GUI font-handling systems: X core fonts and Xft fonts. In addition, individual X-based programs sometimes employ their own font-handling systems. This profusion of font-rendering tools can lead to some confusion if you're not aware of the differences between these systems, each of which has its own unique quirks.

The oldest X font-handling system is the X core fonts system. X core fonts are *server-side fonts*, meaning that the X server (the system at which the user sits, in most cases) handles the fonts. X clients (that is, X programs) tell the X server what font to display and at what size, and the X server does the rest.

X core fonts were originally designed with *bitmap fonts* in mind, meaning that individual characters were designed for display at a specific size in pixels. To support scaleable fonts, which can be resized, multiple bitmap font files are required, one for each size. X servers, including the XFree86 and Xorg-X11 X servers for Linux, ship with several bitmap fonts in a variety of sizes, designed for both 72 dots per inch (dpi) and 100-dpi displays. Most modern fonts, though, use *scaleable font* (a.k.a. *outline font*) technologies, in which the font is described in terms of mathematical descriptions of lines and curves. These descriptions provide an outline of a character, which the font renderer can scale to any desired resolution and fill in. The two most common scaleable font formats today are PostScript Type 1 (a.k.a. Adobe Type Manager or ATM) fonts and TrueType fonts. XFree86 has supported both formats since Version 4.0 (before that, it didn't support TrueType fonts), and Xorg-X11 also supports both formats.

Because X core fonts are server-side, relatively little data needs to be transferred between the client and server to display text. This feature can be helpful for remote logins but isn't very important for typical desktop operations.

Some Linux distributions implement X core fonts via a *font server*, which is a server designed to deliver bitmap font data to X servers. X ships with a font server, *xfs*, which can deliver bitmap font data from bitmap font files or generated from Type 1 or TrueType fonts. This topic is described in more detail shortly, in the section "Configuring a font server."

The X core font system was designed years ago, and in the intervening years, font technology has progressed. X core fonts were readily adapted to some new technologies, such as scaleable fonts, but basic limitations in X core fonts have presented more of a challenge. One of these problems has been the fact that X core fonts can't readily handle more than two colors per font (such as black for the foreground and white for the background). This limitation means that a new font technology known as *font smoothing* or *anti-aliasing* was slow to come to Linux. Font smoothing uses shades of gray to deliberately blur fonts. Counter-intuitively, this has the subjective effect of improving the appearance of fonts, because it tends to hide the jagged edges along diagonal lines and curves. Not everybody cares for this effect, but many people do, and font smoothing is a standard part of Windows and Mac OS. Another problem with the X core fonts system has been that installing fonts can be tricky, as described in the next section. Finally, X core fonts were not designed with printing in mind, and coordinating the display and print fonts can be a challenge when using these fonts.

The solution to these problems with X core fonts is the Xft font system. Unlike the X core fonts, Xft fonts are *client-side*, meaning that they're installed on the same computer as the programs that call them. This fact means that more data may need to be transferred over the network when they're used, but if a program relies on particular fonts, it's easier to guarantee that they'll be available because the user's server configuration is irrelevant. Xft was designed around the FreeType library, which was originally a tool for rendering TrueType fonts. Today, though, Xft supports both TrueType and Type 1 fonts. Xft fonts also support font smoothing, although this feature can be shut off. Xft fonts provide a few more hooks to help with printing, although screen/printer font coordination in Linux has improved more because of extra libraries than because of Xft. Installing Xft fonts is easier than installing X core fonts, as well. However, configuring these fonts requires changing yet another system. In the short term, this has caused increased problems because administrators must manage both X core fonts and Xft fonts. In the long term, Xft fonts are likely to increase in importance, and X core fonts may become so unimportant that their configuration will be trivial. In fact, this may have already happened for some environments. The GNOME and KDE projects have both embraced Xft fonts, as have many other programs, so it's possible you'll see very few or no X core fonts in use on some systems.

In addition to X core fonts and Xft fonts, some individual programs handle their own fonts. Traditionally, word processing programs have done this; however, many Linux word processors have now switched to Xft. A few, though, such as OpenOffice.org and its commercial twin StarOffice, continue to require their own font configuration.

Installing X Core Fonts

Installing X core fonts requires placing font files in directories of your choosing, creating or modifying files in that directory to describe the fonts, and pointing the X server to the fonts. These tasks must be done on the X server computer, so if you use X terminals (as described in Chapter 12), you may need to make these changes on many systems. One way to simplify this task, particularly for a large network, is to use a font server, which places most of the administrative burden on one computer. Some Linux distributions, such as Fedora, Mandrake, and Red Hat, use font servers locally, so you may need to deal with font server configuration even for standalone desktop systems.

Preparing font directories

The first task in X core font configuration is to install the fonts. Part of this task is fairly obvious: you copy font files from some source, such as a commercial font CD-ROM or an Internet font download site, to a directory of your choice. For locally installed fonts, */usr/local/fonts* or a subdirectory of that directory is a logical choice. Linux systems usually install their default fonts in */usr/share/fonts*, although older distributions used */usr/X11R6/lib/X11/fonts* or other locations.

Once the font files are installed, you must create a configuration file that describes the fonts. This file is called *fonts.dir* and resides in the same directory as the fonts themselves. Its first line contains nothing but a number that denotes the number of fonts described in the configuration file. Subsequent lines have a format that looks deceptively simple:

```
filename.ext  XLFD
```

The *filename.ext* is the font filename. For TrueType fonts, this ends in *.ttf*; for Type 1 fonts, it's either *.pfa* or *.pfb*. Various bitmap font formats exist, each with its own extension.

The tricky part of the *fonts.dir* file is the XLFD field, which describes an X Logical Font Descriptor (XLFD). The XLFD consists of multiple fields of its own, separated by dashes (-). These fields contain the name of the font creator, the name of the font, the weight of the font, a code for its slant, numbers relating to its size, and so on. Even if you understand every field, XLFDs can be difficult to read because the fields tend to blur together in the eye. An example of a complete *fonts.dir* entry looks like this:

```
couri.pfa -ibm-courier-medium-i-normal--0-0-0-0-m-0-iso8859-1
```

As a practical matter, it's usually best to create the *fonts.dir* file with a helper program. Several such programs exist, each with its own unique qualities:

type1inst

> This program may not be installed in your distribution, although most distributions do provide it under the package name *type1inst* or *font-tools*. Once it's installed, type **type1inst** in the directory that holds Type 1 fonts. You should see a *fonts.dir* file appear, along with *fonts.scale* (which is similar to *fonts.dir*, but describes only scaleable fonts). This program isn't useful for handling TrueType fonts.

ttmkfdir

> This program is essentially a TrueType counterpart to *type1inst*. It's usually delivered in a package called *ttmkfdir* or *freetype-tools*. It sends its output to *stdout* by default, so you must redirect it, as in **ttmkfdir > fonts.dir**.

mkfontscale

> This program ships with Xorg-X11 and XFree86 4.3 and later. It creates a *fonts.scale* file that describes both TrueType and Type 1 fonts. To create a *fonts.dir* file, you must type **mkfontscale** and then either copy this file to *fonts.dir* or type **mkfontdir**. This program creates a *fonts.dir* file from the contents of *fonts.scale* and information on any bitmap fonts in the directory.

As a general rule, I recommend creating separate directories for each font type you use—Type 1, TrueType, and bitmap or more exotic font formats you install. This practice gives you greater flexibility in the use of programs that generate *fonts.dir* files.

Setting the X font path

Once you've installed font files, you can move on to editing the X server's configuration file: */etc/X11/XF86Config* or */etc/X11/xorg.conf*. (This file sometimes appears in */etc* rather than */etc/X11*.) The *XF86Config* file controls the XFree86 server, which most distributions abandoned in 2004 because of a licensing change with Version 4.4.0. The *xorg.conf* file controls Xorg-X11, which is based on the last version of XFree86 prior to the license change, so the two servers are nearly identical, at least as of XFree86 4.4.0 and Xorg-X11 6.7.0 (the first formal release version). Likewise, their configuration files are virtually identical. One important difference, though, is that their default font directories are different.

X looks for fonts in directories in the Files section of *XF86Config* or *xorg.conf*. Specifically, the configuration file holds a series of lines that begin with the keyword FontPath, and each line contains a path or other reference in quotes:

```
FontPath "/usr/share/fonts/75dpi/:unscaled"
FontPath "/usr/share/fonts/misc/"
FontPath "/usr/share/fonts/Type1/"
FontPath "/usr/share/fonts/TTF/"
FontPath "/usr/share/fonts/75dpi/"
FontPath "tcp/gutenberg:7100"
FontPath "unix/:-1"
```

Most of the entries in this example point to subdirectories of */usr/share/fonts*, which is the default location for fonts in Xorg-X11. In an *XF86Config* file, this location is more likely */usr/X11R6/lib/X11/fonts*. In any event, two broad classes of entries may be present:

Local font directories

Entries that look like font directory names are just that. X looks in these directories for font configuration files (described shortly) and displays the fonts they contain when programs ask for them. The first entry in the preceding example deserves elaboration, though: the :unscaled code tells X to deliver bitmap fonts from this directory only if they can be delivered at precisely the requested size. For instance, if a program asks for Times at 10 points, and if the directory holds Times at 9 points and 12 points but not at 10 points, X doesn't display Times from this directory. The idea is that a subsequent directory is likely to hold the font at the precisely requested size or in a scaleable form. Later in this list, the same directory appears without the :unscaled qualifier, so if all the other possibilities don't match the font, X delivers a font bitmap that's been scaled from another bitmap. The result is likely to look quite ugly, but it's better than not delivering a font at all.

Font servers

The last two examples from the preceding example are font servers. The first of these specifications (tcp/gutenberg:7100) tells X to use a remote computer (*gutenberg*) via TCP/IP on port 7100. The second entry (unix/:-1) tells the system to use Unix domain sockets to connect to a local font server on port -1. Distributions that use local fonts servers are likely to have *XF86Config* or *xorg.conf* files that refer exclusively to such a local font server; they may not refer directly to any font directories.

If your X configuration file refers only to a local font server, you can either add your new font directories directly to the X configuration file or modify your X font server configuration. The latter is likely to be less confusing in the long run because your true font path will be accessible from a single location.

Configuring a font server

If your distribution uses a font server, you might want to modify its configuration rather than the main X configuration file. The standard location for an *xfs* configuration file is */etc/X11/fs/config*. This file contains several lines that set various options, such as whether to bind to TCP ports (which is required for access by other computers). The lines that adjust the font path, though, begin with the keyword catalogue:

```
catalogue = /usr/share/fonts/75dpi/:unscaled,
            /usr/share/fonts/misc/,
            /usr/share/fonts/Type1/,
            /usr/share/fonts/TTF/,
            /usr/share/fonts/75dpi/
```

This example sets the font path identically to the one described earlier, except that it refers to no other font servers. (You should point X servers directly at font servers; don't try to point font servers at other font servers.) The rules for :unscaled references are identical, but the format of the font path is different. In the */etc/X11/fs/ config* file, the font path is a comma-delimited list that may span multiple lines; the last entry does not end in a comma. Although the entries are often split across lines, they need not be; you can present a single very long font path on one line. Quotes are *not* placed around individual entries.

Both the main X server and font servers require the same configuration in the font directories—namely a *fonts.dir* file that describes the font files.

Once you change this configuration, you must restart your X font server. Typically, you can do this by using a SysV startup script:

```
# /etc/init.d/xfs restart
```

The system should shut down and restart the font server, but the fonts won't yet be accessible. To use them, you must tell X to reexamine its font path.

Using the fonts

After you change your X font configuration (either via the X server's main configuration file or a font server), you must tell X to use the new fonts. If you've edited your X configuration file, the safest way to do this and to be sure you've made no errors is to shut down X and restart it. On most distributions, logging out of a GUI login will do this job. If you don't want to completely restart X, though, you can type the following commands:

```
$ xset fp+ /new/font/path
$ xset fp rehash
```

The first of these commands adds a directory to your font path. Be sure to type this directory *exactly* as you entered it on the FontPath line in your X configuration file. One problem with this approach is that it adds the new font directory to the *end* of the font path, which may not be where you added it. Thus, results might not exactly match what you'll get when you restart X, particularly if there's overlap in font names.

The second line tells X to reexamine the fonts in its font path, effectively adding the new fonts to the list of available fonts. You should type this command *without* the previous one if you've modified your X font server configuration and want to use the new fonts that it's now offering.

 Modifying the font path while X is running is potentially risky. If you make a mistake, critical fonts might disappear. This can cause programs to hang. In extreme cases, X might crash. Save your work before making such changes and be prepared to log in using some other means (a text-mode console login, SSH from another system, or what have you) to correct any problems that might develop.

Installing Xft Fonts

Compared to installing X core fonts, installing Xft fonts is relatively straightforward. Xft 2.0 and later use a configuration file called */etc/fonts/fonts.conf* to control themselves. You shouldn't directly edit this file, however; it can be overwritten in a package upgrade. Instead, Xft sets aside */etc/fonts/local.conf* for local changes. To add a font directory to the Xft font path, place this line just above the </fontconfig> line:

```
<dir>/usr/local/fonts</dir>
```

 Versions of Xft prior to 2.0 used another configuration file, */etc/X11/ XftConfig*, to control their overall operation. This configuration file is very different from the Xft 2.0 configuration file described here.

This line tells Xft to look in the */usr/local/fonts* directory and all its subdirectories for font files. In fact, because Xft looks in subdirectories of the specified font directories means that you may not even need to modify the Xft configuration file at all: simply place your font files in a subdirectory of a directory that's specified in */etc/fonts/fonts. conf*. Most Xft configurations list */usr/share/fonts* as a directory, so placing new fonts in a subdirectory of that directory should work. Furthermore, most Xft configurations list *~/.fonts* as a font directory, meaning that individual users can install fonts themselves by placing them in this directory.

Once the font directories are set, and fonts are placed in them, users can begin using fonts immediately; there's no need to restart X or issue any special commands. There is a modest benefit to using one command, though: *fc-cache*. If you've installed new fonts in a particular directory, type this command:

```
# fc-cache /path/to/fonts
```

The *fc-cache* command is the main interface to FontConfig, which is responsible for configuring Xft fonts. This command creates a font index file (*fonts.cache-1*) that's conceptually similar to the X core fonts' *fonts.dir*. Unlike X core fonts, though, Xft enables users to maintain their own font index files, and if Xft detects that directories on the font path have been updated more recently than their matching index files, FontConfig runs *fc-cache* in a way that updates users' individual font configuration files (*~/.fonts.cache-1*). Thus, if you fail to perform this step, users can still access new fonts; however, they may experience slight delays when starting new applications soon after you add fonts, as *fc-cache* does its job.

Installing Fonts in OpenOffice.org

OpenOffice.org supports its own font-rendering system. As a result, fonts you install as X core fonts or Xft fonts won't appear as options in the OpenOffice.org menus, at least as of OpenOffice.org 1.1.2. (Future versions might switch to supporting Xft.)

 OpenOffice.org is the open source twin of StarOffice. These two programs are virtually identical, and both work the same way in terms of font configuration.

OpenOffice.org provides a printer and font administration tool in which you can adjust the program's printer list and install or remove fonts. To do the latter, follow these steps:

1. In a command-prompt window, type **oopadmin** to launch the program. A window entitled Printer Administration should appear.

2. Click the Fonts button. A Fonts dialog box should appear, as shown in Figure B-2.

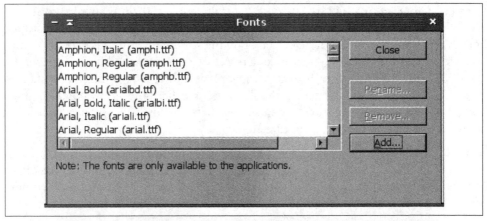

Figure B-2. OpenOffice.org provides a GUI tool that adds or deletes fonts

3. Click Add in the Fonts dialog box to add new fonts. A dialog box entitled Add Fonts should appear, as shown in Figure B-3.

4. Type a path to your fonts in the "Source directory" field or click the "..." button to select a directory using a file selector. If you type the path, wait a few seconds after you finish the path. The system should then populate the top field in the Add Fonts dialog box with font names and filenames.

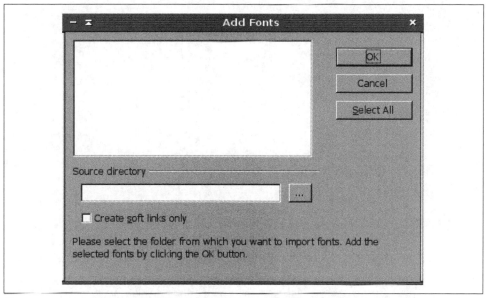

Figure B-3. OpenOffice.org's Add Fonts dialog box lets you locate and select fonts

5. Select any and all fonts you want to add by clicking their names in the Add Fonts dialog box.

6. Click Add in the Add Fonts dialog box. The system should respond with a report on the number of fonts it added.

7. Click Close in the Fonts dialog box, followed by Close in the Printer Administration dialog box.

You can perform these steps as either *root* or as an ordinary user. If the former, the fonts are installed in the main OpenOffice.org directory; if the latter, they're installed in the user's home directory.

Summary

Linux's credentials as a desktop OS are growing. Traditionally deployed as a server, Linux's GUI tools and application programs are improving rapidly, to the point that increasing numbers of organizations are deploying the OS on the desktop as well as in the server room. Doing this requires that you know a bit about Linux desktop applications, starting with the desktop environments available for Linux. Sometimes Linux's ability to run Windows programs (either by itself or with the help of a remote server) is important for Linux desktop deployment. Accessing data from Windows desktop systems and managing fonts are a couple more areas that are important for Linux desktop use.

Index

We'd like to hear your suggestions for improving our indexes. Send email to *index@oreilly.com*.

About the Author

Roderick W. Smith is a longtime Linux user and administrator, having begun with Linux in 1994. He is the author or coauthor of over a dozen books on Linux, networking, and related technologies, including *Linux Power Tools* (Sybex) and *The Definitive Guide to Samba 3* (Apress).

Colophon

Our look is the result of reader comments, our own experimentation, and feedback from distribution channels. Distinctive covers complement our distinctive approach to technical topics, breathing personality and life into potentially dry subjects.

The image on the cover of *Linux in a Windows World* depicts members of the Native American Nez Percé tribe playing cards. In the mid-1850s, a treaty with the U.S. government made most of the Nez Percé lands (parts of Idaho, Washington, and Oregon) into a reservation. However, with the discovery of gold on the reservation, the government tried to push through a new treaty reducing the land to a quarter of its size. The tribe refused to accept it, and war broke out. After a long campaign, with his warriors facing starvation, Chief Joseph surrendered. The captured warriors were housed in a temporary village near Fort Leavenworth, Kansas, before being assigned to a reservation (not, however, with their people in the Northwest, as had been promised).

Mary Anne Weeks Mayo was the production editor and copyeditor, and Marlowe Shaeffer was the proofreader for *Linux in a Windows World*. Sarah Sherman and Claire Cloutier provided quality control. Keith Fahlgren and Lydia Onofrei provided production assistance. John Bickelhaupt wrote the index.

Emma Colby designed the cover of this book, based on a series design by Hanna Dyer and Edie Freedman. The cover image is a 19th-century engraving from the Dover Pictorial Archive. Emma Colby produced the cover layout with Adobe InDesign CS using Adobe's ITC Garamond font.

David Futato designed the interior layout. The chapter opening images are from the Dover Pictorial Archive; *Marvels of the New West: A Vivid Portrayal of the Stupendous Marvels in the Vast Wonderland West of the Missouri River*, by William Thayer (The Henry Bill Publishing Co., 1888); and *The Pioneer History of America: A Popular Account of the Heroes and Adventures*, by Augustus Lynch Mason, A.M. (The Jones Brothers Publishing Company, 1884).

This book was converted by Julie Hawks to FrameMaker 5.5.6 with a format conversion tool created by Erik Ray, Jason McIntosh, Neil Walls, and Mike Sierra that uses Perl and XML technologies. The text font is Linotype Birka; the heading font is

Adobe Myriad Condensed; and the code font is LucasFont's TheSans Mono Condensed. The illustrations that appear in the book were produced by Robert Romano, Jessamyn Read, and Leslie Borash using Macromedia FreeHand 9 and Adobe Photoshop 6. The tip and warning icons were drawn by Christopher Bing. This colophon was written by Mary Anne Weeks Mayo.